BUSINESS/SCIENCE/TECHNOLOGY DIVISION
STREET
CHICAGO ILLINOIS 60605

REF
QA
76.9
.D3
K7344
1999

HWLCTC

D1309443

Oracle Database Administration

The Essential Reference

Oracle Database Administration

The Essential Reference

David C. Kreines and Brian Laskey

O'REILLY®

Beijing · Cambridge · Farnham · Köln · Paris · Sebastopol · Taipei · Tokyo

Oracle Database Administration: The Essential Reference
by David C. Kreines and Brian Laskey

Copyright © 1999 O'Reilly & Associates, Inc. All rights reserved.
Printed in the United States of America.

Published by O'Reilly & Associates, Inc., 101 Morris Street, Sebastopol, CA 95472.

Editor: Deborah Russell

Production Editor: Madeleine Newell

Printing History:

April 1999:   First Edition.

Advanced Networking Option, ORACLE, Oracle, Oracle Application Server, Oracle Developer/2000, Oracle Enterprise Manager, Oracle Forms, Oracle Network Manager, Oracle Reports, Oracle Security Server, Oracle Server, Oracle Server Manager, Oracle7, Oracle8, Oracle 8*i*, Net8, SQLDBA, SQL*Loader, SQL*Net, SQL*Plus, and Trusted Oracle are trademarks of Oracle Corporation.

Certain portions of copyrighted Oracle Corporation user documentation have been reproduced herein with the permission of Oracle Corporation.

Nutshell Handbook, the Nutshell Handbook logo, and the O'Reilly logo are registered trademarks of O'Reilly & Associates, Inc. The association between the image of a group of ladybugs and the topic of Oracle database administration is a trademark of O'Reilly & Associates, Inc. Many of the designations used by manufacturers and sellers to distinguish their products are claimed as trademarks. Where those designations appear in this book, and O'Reilly & Associates, Inc. was aware of the trademark claim, the designations have been printed in caps or initial caps.

While every precaution has been taken in the preparation of this book, the publisher and authors assume no responsibility for errors or omissions, or for damages resulting from the use of the information contained herein.

ISBN: 1-56592-516-5   [1/01]
[M]

BUSINESS/SCIENCE/TECHNOLOGY DIVISION
CHICAGO PUBLIC LIBRARY
400 SOUTH STATE STREET
CHICAGO, ILLINOIS 60605

R0174696557

For my wife, Suzanne, of course!
—David C. Kreines

To Sherry, my wife and friend.
—Brian Laskey

Table of Contents

Preface

The Oracle database is the most popular database in the world, by far eclipsing its closest competitors. Oracle Corporation has achieved this enviable position by providing a product that, to borrow from one of Oracle's old marketing themes, is compatible, scalable, and portable. In addition, it is capable of performing incredibly fast. The advantages Oracle holds over its competition come with a price, however—the Oracle database is a very complex product, and is becoming more so with every release. As a result, database administration has become critical, and the database administrator (DBA) has become key to the successful implementation of Oracle.

Oracle Database Administration: The Essential Reference was written *by* Oracle database administrators *for* Oracle database administrators. If you are an Oracle DBA, or are thinking about becoming one, this book is definitely for you. This book is designed for reference; it is intentionally presented in a terse, to-the-point format. Since we assume that most of the information presented is already somewhat familiar to the working DBA, we provide this information in a location and format that allows you to access it quickly, as required. If you want clear, concise information about Oracle database administration, and plenty of summary tables and quick references to syntax and usage, you have come to the right place. However, if you are just learning database administration, and you want a tutorial that will teach you about the topic from start to finish, you will probably need to begin with an introductory text. Similarly, if you are a programmer, developer, webmaster, or manager, you will find much useful information in this book, but if you don't know anything about database administration, you might want to begin with something more introductory.

We don't mean to deter you from buying or reading this book! We simply want you to know up front that our approach here is to cram as much concise and fast-moving material as possible into these pages.

Why We Wrote This Book

Database administration is a set of tasks, and a database administrator is a highly skilled individual who is responsible for performing those tasks under a variety of conditions. The DBA needs access to a large amount of information about Oracle in order to perform those tasks efficiently and correctly.

Years ago, when Oracle was a somewhat less complex product, those of us who worked as DBAs were able to read manuals, take training courses, and attend user conferences, and thereby learn everything we needed to know about Oracle. Back in those days, if you needed to look at a manual, you couldn't be a "real" DBA. Obviously, things have changed. It is no longer possible for any individual to learn all there is to know about Oracle. Even if it *were* possible, the product is advancing so fast that all that accumulated knowledge would soon be out of date anyway!

Today, it's necessary for the DBA to have a high degree of understanding about the Oracle database, and to have a huge amount of information available when it is needed. Unfortunately, most of this information is available only in the Oracle manuals, and there are at least two impediments to accessing that information in a timely and efficient manner:

- Oracle manuals are organized strictly by topic structure. As a result, you usually need two or three different manuals to get all the information you need about a specific DBA task. It is very difficult to find the right sections of the right manuals—especially when you are under pressure.

- Unless you (or your employer) are willing to spend a lot of extra money, Oracle manuals are now available only electronically (on CD-ROM, or they may be viewed or downloaded from Metalink, Oracle's online support service, at *www.oracle.com/support*). This makes them difficult to use, especially when you need to access multiple manuals simultaneously. If you are like us, you want your information in front of you on old-fashioned paper.

We decided to write this book because we saw a real need for having all the important day-to-day information a DBA needs in a clear, concise form, logically organized in a single volume. Our goal is not to replace the Oracle manuals. In fact, there is a tremendous amount of information in the Oracle manual set that cannot be duplicated here. There will probably be many occasions where the basic information you need is found in our book, but you will still want to refer to the appropriate Oracle manual for some more detailed information.

As we worked on the book, it became clear to both of us that this was a much larger task then we had ever suspected; in fact, there were times when we doubted it could be done at all. The original plan for this book called for about three hundred pages, and as you can see, we've gone on a bit longer than that! A lot of time and effort was expended researching the information provided, and attempting to distill a huge amount of information into a volume of manageable size that, in the end, would be useful to you, the working Oracle DBA. We've drawn on our combined twenty-five-plus years of DBA experience in this attempt to save you time, make your job easier, and maybe even avert a potential disaster. We've tried to provide you with the details, while keeping the big picture in focus. We hope we have succeeded in this task. Let us know what you think!

Versions of Oracle

This book covers both Oracle7 and Oracle8. Where necessary, we point out differences between the two. Although many organizations have begun to use Oracle8 (and to look forward to Oracle8*i*), many others are still using Oracle7. Since we want this book to help DBAs do their day-to-day work, we've elected to cover the earlier Oracle7 platform as well. In the next edition, we'll also cover Oracle 8*i*, and we'll probably phase out the Oracle7 material if most of the industry has adopted the later releases.

How This Book Is Organized

This book is divided into two parts.

Part I, *DBA Tasks*

Part I provides essential information on a variety of critical DBA functions and examples of how to perform these functions. To aid you in planning and implementing new Oracle installations, this part is presented in roughly the same sequence in which these functions would be performed in real life. Part I consists of the following chapters:

Chapter 1, *Introduction*, introduces database administration and the typical tasks performed by a DBA, and presents a basic introduction to the Oracle architecture and options. It also provides an overview of configuration planning.

Chapter 2, *Installation*, summarizes the operations you will need to perform to install the Oracle product and start up the database.

Chapter 3, *Maximizing Oracle Performance*, presents basic information about operating system and Oracle configuration, object sizing, and tuning.

Chapter 4, *Preventing Data Loss*, describes your options for backing up and recovering an Oracle database.

Chapter 5, *Oracle Networking*, discusses the Oracle network architecture, summarizes the characteristics of the major networking products, and provides configuration and troubleshooting information for the SQL*Net (Net8 for Oracle8) product.

Chapter 6, *Security and Monitoring*, provides a brief discussion of two particularly important aspects of Oracle database administration: security and monitoring.

Chapter 7, *Auditing*, describes how auditing works in the Oracle database and presents the statements and options you can use to enforce your organization's auditing policy.

Chapter 8, *Query Optimization*, describes the two Oracle optimizers (cost-based optimizer and rule-based optimizer), how they work on queries, and how you can affect their operation by specifying optimizer hints.

Chapter 9, *Oracle Tools*, describes the basic Oracle tools that a DBA will use most frequently: SQL*Plus, Oracle Server Manager, SQLDBA, Oracle Network Manager, SQL*Loader, and Oracle Enterprise Manager.

Part II, *DBA Reference*

Part II provides the detailed reference information you'll need to perform DBA functions, including extensive statement syntax and parameter settings. Part II consists of the following chapters:

Chapter 10, *The Oracle Instance*, describes the elements of the Oracle instance—in particular, the various Oracle processes and memory structures.

Chapter 11, *The Oracle Database*, describes the elements of the database—physical files and tablespaces—and describes storage allocation.

Chapter 12, *Initialization Parameters*, provides a quick reference to the Oracle initialization parameters (those stored in the *INIT.ORA* file).

Chapter 13, *SQL Statements for the DBA*, provides a quick reference to the SQL statements used by the DBA.

Chapter 14, *The Oracle Data Dictionary*, provides a quick reference to the data dictionary views used by the DBA.

Chapter 15, *System Privileges and Initial Roles*, provides a quick reference to the system privileges implemented by Oracle and to the initial, or default, roles created by Oracle.

Chapter 16, *Tools and Utilities*, provides a quick reference to the commands and parameters used with the tools (SQL*Plus, Export, Import, and SQL*Loader) most often used by the DBA.

Appendix: Resources for the DBA summarizes the books, magazines, organizations, web sites, discussion groups, and list servers that DBAs should find to be helpful sources of additional information.

Conventions Used in This Book

The following conventions are used in this book:

Italic
> Used for script, file, and directory names.

`Constant width`
> Used for code examples.

`Constant width italic`
> In code examples, indicates an element (e.g., a parameter) that you supply.

UPPERCASE
> In code examples, generally indicates Oracle keywords.

lowercase
> In code examples, generally indicates user-defined items such as variables.

[ ] In syntax examples, square brackets enclose optional items.

{ } In syntax examples, curly brackets enclose a list of items; you must select one item from the list.

| In syntax examples, a vertical line separates the items in a bracketed list.

Indicates a tip, suggestion, or general note. For example, we'll tell you if you need to use a particular Oracle version or if an operation requires certain privileges.

Indicates a warning or caution. For example, we'll tell you if Oracle does not behave as you'd expect or if a particular operation has a negative impact on performance.

Comments and Questions

Please address comments and questions concerning this book to the publisher:

O'Reilly & Associates, Inc.
101 Morris Street
Sebastopol, CA 95472
800-998-9938 (in the U.S. or Canada)
707-829-0515 (international or local)
707-829-0104 (fax)

There is a web page for this book, where we list any errata, examples, and additional information. You can access this page at:

http://www.oreilly.com/catalog/oradba/

To ask technical questions or comment on the book, send email to:

bookquestions@oreilly.com

For more information about our books, conferences, software, Resource Centers, and the O'Reilly Network, see our web site at:

http://www.oreilly.com

Acknowledgments

We are indebted to a great number of people who have contributed to the creation of this book.

From Dave Kreines: I would like to thank my family for allowing me the time in my "basement cave" to work relatively undisturbed on this project, which has been time-consuming and stressful for all concerned. My thanks to my coauthor, Brian Laskey, whom I have considered for many years to be one of the outstanding DBAs. I am proud to work with Brian and call him a friend. I would also like to thank my coworkers at Rhodia, who have (albeit unintentionally) provided both opportunity and substance for this book.

From Brian Laskey: I would like to thank my wife, Sherry, and my two daughters, Tiffany and Chandra, for putting up with this project. The time and effort that it took were far beyond my initial estimates. I would also like to thank Dave Kreines for agreeing to work on this project with me. Thanks to John King for his ongoing technical comments and to Lois Huff for her comments on how to make the book easier to read. It is also very important that I acknowledge my coworkers at the University of Michigan Hospital, Cheryl Fox and Kathie McFry. We authored a paper for the IOUG-A Live! 98 Conference on Oracle Parallel Server implementation on an IBM SP/2 system. Much of the Parallel Server information in this book is derived from that paper. Finally, I would like to thank Steve Lavender, who, during the darkest days of this project, gave me the kick I needed to get it finished.

From both of us: Much of our knowledge and expertise is a result of our interactions with the large and incredibly talented group of fellow DBAs with whom we've had the privilege to be associated. In particular, many of the members of the International Oracle Users Group–Americas (IOUG-A), the European Oracle

Users Group (EOUG), and many other Oracle users around the world have contributed to the collective knowledge of the Oracle community. The staff of Oracle Corporation in general, and of Oracle Support in particular, also deserve our thanks for the wealth of information shared.

Special thanks go to our technical reviewers: John Beresniewicz, Steve Hazeldine, John King, Matt Reagan, and especially Jonathan Gennick, who went beyond the call of duty by not only performing a careful and thoughtful technical review of his own, but by then reviewing the reviews! We would also like to thank Marlene Theriault, who reviewed some of the early draft chapters. Finally, we owe a debt of thanks to Michael Hartstein, Director of Oracle 8*i* Product Management, Server Technologies Product Management at Oracle Corporation, for his technical review, and for his quick response to a number of requests to verify particular facts and concepts. Ken Jacobs, Vice President, Data Server Product Management at Oracle Corporation, also quickly responded to several requests for help. These Oracle experts gave freely of their time to help make certain that the information presented would be clear and technically accurate. We appreciate their help, and sincerely thank them.

This book certainly would not have been possible without a tremendous amount of hard work and support from the staff of O'Reilly & Associates. In particular, we would like to express our thanks to Debby Russell, our editor, who recognized the value of this book and encouraged, nurtured, and prodded us during the year-plus that we have worked on this project. Many thanks as well to Madeleine Newell, the production editor of this book, and to Steve Abrams and Michael Blanding, who helped edit the book under enormous pressure. And special thanks to Edie Freedman (the Bug Czar) who designed the cover—and gave us a beautiful group of insects.

I

DBA Tasks

This part of the book describes the typical, day-to-day functions that a database administrator will perform; the chapters are arranged in roughly the same sequence in which these functions will be performed in real life:

- Chapter 1, *Introduction*, introduces database administration and the typical tasks performed by a DBA, and presents a basic introduction to the Oracle architecture and options. It also provides an overview of configuration planning.

- Chapter 2, *Installation*, summarizes the operations you will need to perform to install the Oracle product and start up the database.

- Chapter 3, *Maximizing Oracle Performance*, presents basic information about operating system and Oracle configuration, object sizing, and tuning.

- Chapter 4, *Preventing Data Loss*, describes your options for backing up and recovering an Oracle database.

- Chapter 5, *Oracle Networking*, discusses the Oracle network architecture, summarizes the characteristics of the major networking products, and provides configuration and troubleshooting information for the SQL*Net (Net8 for Oracle8) product.

- Chapter 6, *Security and Monitoring*, provides a brief discussion of two particularly important aspects of Oracle database administration: security and monitoring.

- Chapter 7, *Auditing*, describes how auditing works in the Oracle database and presents the statements and options you can use to enforce your organization's auditing policy.

- Chapter 8, *Query Optimization*, describes the two Oracle optimizers (cost-based optimizer and rule-based optimizer), how they work on queries, and how you can affect their operation by specifying optimizer hints.

- Chapter 9, *Oracle Tools*, describes the basic Oracle tools that a DBA will use most frequently: SQL*Plus, Oracle Server Manager, SQLDBA, Oracle Network Manager, SQL*Loader, and Oracle Enterprise Manager.

1

Introduction

Welcome to the world of Oracle database administration! This chapter provides an overview of Oracle database administration, and supplies some basic information required to understand the structure and characteristics of the Oracle database.

Oracle Database Administration

If one hundred Oracle database administrators were asked to define what a DBA does, the exercise would probably result in one hundred different descriptions. Nonetheless, there would be a high degree of commonality among these descriptions, and taken as a whole they would probably yield a fairly accurate job description for an Oracle DBA.

When Educational Testing Service (ETS) set out to develop a certification examination for Oracle DBAs a few years ago, the company's first step was to perform a *job analysis*, which is a formal way of evaluating and describing a job. The process ETS followed included these steps:

1. A group of experts was asked to assemble a laundry list of the tasks, skills, and abilities required of a DBA. A survey instrument was developed that listed these items along with a rating scale for the importance of each item.

2. The survey was administered to a large number of Oracle DBAs around the world.

3. The survey results were tabulated, yielding an average importance rating for each task, skill, and ability. Those falling below a predetermined cutoff level were eliminated.

The result was a detailed description of the tasks performed by a DBA, and of the specific knowledge and abilities required to perform those tasks. This DBA job analysis then became the blueprint for the Certified Oracle Database Administrator examination.

A DBA Job Description

Here is a summary of the DBA job description that resulted from the ETS study. Prefix each of the following elements with "An Oracle DBA must be able to...."

Oracle architecture and options

- Demonstrate an understanding of the memory structures and processes that make up an Oracle instance

- Demonstrate an understanding of the logical and physical structures associated with an Oracle database

- Demonstrate an understanding of PL/SQL constructs (triggers, functions, packages, procedures) and their processing

- Demonstrate an understanding of distributed architecture and client server

- Demonstrate an understanding of locking mechanisms

Security

- Create, alter, and drop database users

- Monitor and audit database access

- Develop and implement a strategy for managing security (roles, privileges, authentication)

- Demonstrate an understanding of the implications of distributed processing on the security model

Data administration

- Manage integrity constraints

- Implement the physical database from the logical design

- Evaluate the implications of using stored procedures and constraints to implement business rules

Backup and recovery

- Understand backup options

- Develop backup and recovery strategies

- Manage the implementation of backup procedures

- Recover a database

Software maintenance and operation

- Install and upgrade Oracle and supporting products
- Configure the Oracle instance using the initialization parameters
- Configure and manage SQL*Net
- Distinguish among startup and shutdown options
- Create a database
- Demonstrate an understanding of the capabilities of underlying operating systems as they relate to the Oracle database

Resource management

- Create and manage indexes
- Evaluate the use of clusters and hash clusters
- Allocate and manage physical storage structures (e.g., datafiles, redo logs, control files)
- Allocate and manage logical storage structures (e.g., tablespaces, schemas, extents)
- Control system resource usage by defining proper profiles
- Perform capacity planning

Tuning and troubleshooting

- Diagnose and resolve locking conflicts
- Use data dictionary tables and views
- Monitor the instance
- Collect and analyze relevant database performance information
- Identify and implement appropriate solutions for database performance problems
- Use vendor support services when necessary
- Solve SQL*Net problems

In short, the DBA is responsible for installing the Oracle database, keeping it running at peak performance, and attending to the day-to-day administrative needs of a large, complex database.

The DBA and This Book

The authors of this book were members of the expert panel assembled by ETS, and we relied heavily on the DBA job analysis when we developed our content outline.

The tasks DBAs do

We recognized that the job of a DBA is composed of a number of major tasks: database installation, configuration, backup and recovery, networking, and much more. Part I of this book is organized around these tasks. In fact, the chapters in Part I are presented in an order which is similar to the order in which a DBA will be likely to perform each task; thus, installation (Chapter 2, *Installation*) comes before configuration (Chapter 3, *Maximizing Oracle Performance*), which comes before backup and recovery (Chapter 4, *Preventing Data Loss*). In each chapter, we try to present the basic information that a working DBA will need to perform the tasks associated with that chapter.

The information DBAs need

No matter how experienced an Oracle DBA is, there is a huge amount of information that simply cannot be committed to memory, but must be looked up. Examples include details of Oracle architecture, configuration parameters, the syntax of a particular SQL statement, and perhaps the options for an Oracle utility. Part II of this book organizes this vast array of information into relevant chapters that are designed to make it easy for the DBA to quickly find accurate information for the task he or she is working on.

An experienced DBA knows that a well-managed Oracle database doesn't just happen. It takes planning—lots of planning. In the remainder of this chapter, we'll provide you with a high-level look at Oracle. We will introduce the Oracle architecture and discuss some options for licensing the Oracle software. Finally, we'll provide you with many questions, and show you how to implement your database based on your answers.

Oracle Architecture

This section gives a brief overview of the Oracle architecture. More detailed information is provided in Part II of the book, especially in Chapter 10, *The Oracle Instance*, and Chapter 11, *The Oracle Database*.

Database Versus Instance

For most Oracle users, the terms *database* and *instance* are used synonymously. However, there are differences that become especially important if you are using the Oracle Parallel Server (OPS) Option. The *database* is the data on disk, stored in operating system files (or possibly, under Unix, in raw files). The *instance* is composed of the System Global Area (SGA) memory and the background processes. The instance is STARTed using Oracle Server Manager or Oracle Enterprise Manager (OEM). The database is then MOUNTed on the instance and is finally

OPENed. The users CONNECT to the instance in order to access the data in the database. Figure 1-1 shows the basic components of the Oracle database and instance.

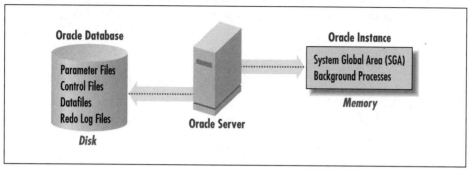

Figure 1-1. The Oracle database and the Oracle instance

Except in an OPS environment, there is a one-to-one correspondence between instance and database. In the OPS world, the database can be MOUNTed on multiple instances.

Background Processes

The background processes take care of the database. Depending on the options configured and the values specified in the Oracle initialization file, usually known as the *INIT.ORA* file, there can be from 6 to 50 or more background processes. Each background process has a specific responsibility to perform. See Chapter 10, *The Oracle Instance*, for more details on their functions. Oracle created the background processes as separate entities to allow them to run independently of each other, performing their functions as needed and, if possible, simultaneously.

The *INIT.ORA* parameter SINGLE_PROCESS forces the background processes to run as one process. This is primarily used for system debugging with Windows NT. All of the *INIT.ORA* parameters are described in Chapter 12, *Initialization Parameters*.

System Global Area (SGA)

The System Global Area (SGA) is the shared memory area used by the instance to store information that must be shared between the database and user processes. The main components of the SGA include the database buffer cache, shared pool, and redo log buffers. The *database buffer cache* contains actual copies of data blocks from the database. When you update a table, the information is first modified in the data buffer and is later written to disk. The *shared pool* contains the SQL and PL/SQL statements being executed; every SQL statement executed is stored in the shared pool, which allows Oracle to reuse all the information it has generated about the statement. This reuse produces significant improvements in processing speeds for users in an online transaction processing (OLTP) environment who are executing the same SQL statements. The *redo log buffer* collects the redo entries for the online redo logs prior to their being flushed to disk.

Files

Four types of files are used by the Oracle instance, and comprise the database:

Parameter files
> These files (usually called the *INIT.ORA* files) specify how the instance is configured and point to the control files.

Control files
> These files contain the names of all the datafiles and the online and archived log files.

Datafiles
> These files contain the actual information in the database.

Redo log files
> These files contain a record of all changes made to the database.

When you START the instance, the parameter file is read. When you MOUNT the database, the control files are read. When you OPEN the database, the datafiles are referenced. When a database is being updated, changes are recorded in the online log files, which provide a mechanism for recovery in case of a failure.

Logical Database Structures

In addition to the physical files used by the database, Oracle maintains many types of logical structures. Some of the most important are summarized here:

Tablespaces
> The basic storage allocation in an Oracle database is a tablespace. Each tablespace is composed of one or more physical (operating system) files. Every database is created with the SYSTEM tablespace. Other tablespaces are created by the DBA. Note, however, that if you allow the Oracle Installer to create a database automatically, it will create additional tablespaces (see Chapter 2, *Installation*).

Schemas
> In Oracle, a schema is essentially the same as an account or a username. Each object in the database is owned by a schema. Every Oracle database is created with two initial schemas: SYS, which is used to store the data dictionary, and SYSTEM, which often stores some data dictionary extensions as well as

critical tables for other tools. Other schemas are created by the DBA. Each schema can be granted quotas in any tablespace. There is no necessary relationship between a schema and a tablespace.

Segments

Each object that takes up space is created as one or more segments. Each segment can be in one and only one tablespace.

Extents

Each segment is composed of one or more extents. An extent is a contiguous allocation of space within a datafile of a tablespace. At the time a segment is created, you can specify the size of the initial and next extents, as well as the minimum and maximum number of extents.

Rollback segments

Every time you update a table, Oracle writes the old value into the rollback segment, which allows other users to maintain a consistent read on the table. It also allows Oracle to restore the contents of the table in the event that you do not commit the change.

Temporary segments

Temporary segments are used by Oracle during table and index creation and for sorting, as well as for temporary storage required for other operations, such as hash joins.

Tables

All data in a database is stored in a table. Data includes not only the user data, but also the contents of the data dictionary.

Indexes

Indexes are used both to facilitate the quick retrieval of data from the table and to enforce the uniqueness of column values. Indexes are stored in separate segments from the table data, except for Oracle8 index-organized tables, which are actually indexes that contain all the data.

Software Options

The Oracle relational database management system (RDBMS) is sold as a base product with options. Typically, new functionality is first introduced as an extra-cost option, and later bundled into the base product. The information provided here is current at the time of publication. Please contact your Oracle sales representative or the Oracle web site (*www.oracle.com*) for additional information.

Base Product

The base product is available in two versions: Enterprise Server and Server. Originally, these two versions were referred to as the Server and the Workgroup Server.

The Enterprise Server is the full-function version of the RDBMS. It contains all of the base features mentioned in Table 1-1, and it can support all of the Oracle options and data cartridges. The Server version is less feature-rich; it is designed to compete at the low end. The Server version does not support all the functionality of the Enterprise Server, it cannot be configured with all of the options and data cartridges, and, in some cases, it may be limited by the number of users or the size of the machine on which it can run. However, the Server version carries a lower price per user than the Enterprise Server, and may be attractive for that reason.

Table 1-1. Oracle Base Product Features

Feature	Oracle8 Server	Enterprise Server
Oracle Enterprise Manager (OEM)	Y	Y
Manageability Packs	N	Y
Fail safe for Oracle8 on NT	Y	Y
Client failover	N	Y
Server-managed backup and recovery	Y	Y
Recovery Manager (RMAN)	Y	Y
Online backup and recovery	Y	Y
Incremental backup	N	Y
Parallel backup and recovery	N	Y
Legato Storage Manager	Y	Y
Point-in-time tablespace recovery	N	Y
Bitmap indexes	N	Y
Star query optimization	Y	Y
Parallel Query	N	Y
Parallel DML	N	Y
Parallel index scans	N	Y
Parallel bitmap star query joins	N	Y
Parallel load	N	Y
Parallel index build	N	Y
Parallel analyze	N	Y
Distributed queries	Y	Y
Distributed transactions, two-phase commit, XA support	Y	Y
Heterogeneous services	Y	Y
Basic replication	Y	Y
Advanced replication	N	Y
Net8	Y	Y
Oracle Security Server (OSS)	Y	Y
Oracle Names	Y	Y

Table 1-1. Oracle Base Product Features (continued)

Feature	Oracle8 Server	Enterprise Server
Oracle Connection Manager	N	Y
Connection pooling	Y	Y
Connection multiplexing	Y	Y
Multi-protocol connectivity	N	Y
Pro*C	Y	Y
Oracle Call Interface (OCI)	Y	y
Objects for OLE	Y	Y
ODBC driver	Y	Y
Advanced queuing	N	Y
Reverse key indexes	Y	Y
Password management	Y	Y
Index-organized tables	Y	Y
PL/SQL stored procedures, triggers	Y	Y
Large object (LOB) support	Y	Y
ConText Cartridge	Y	Y
Video Cartridge	Y	Y
Image Cartridge	N	Y
Visual Information Retrieval Cartridge	N	Y
Time Series Cartridge	N	Y
Spatial Data Cartridge	N	Y
Objects Option	N	Y
Partitioning Option	N	Y
Advanced Networking Option	N	Y
Enterprise Manager Tuning Pack	N	Y
Parallel Server Option	N	Y

Options

The Oracle options summarized in this section are currently available.

Advanced Networking Option (ANO)
> Implements additional network security and encryption. Also provides support for third-party authentication services.

Oracle Enterprise Manager Tuning Pack
> Extra-cost add-on to Enterprise Manager.

Objects Option

Allows the creation of object classes such as object data types and methods. Implementation of the Objects Option begins the process of converting Oracle from a relational database to an object-relational database. Many of the new data types and SQL statements are available only with this option.

Parallel Server Option

Allows loosely coupled nodes in a cluster (shared disk) or a massively parallel processor (MPP) configuration to share a common database. This allows for scalability to larger databases than could be supported on a single computer system. Each computer node has a separate instance. In an MPP configuration, the database is distributed across multiple (up to 1024) computer systems. When Parallel Query is also built into the system, Oracle is able to distribute the workload for large-scale queries across the multiple nodes.

Partitioning Option

Allows large tables to be split into multiple segments based upon value ranges for one or more columns, called the *partition key*. At the time the table is created, you specify the number of partitions and the largest value for the partition key in each partition. Since each partition is a separate segment, you can also specify different tablespaces for each partition. Indexes can be created as local (for the partition) or global (for the entire table).

You can make large-scale queries run more efficiently by using *partition elimination*. In this process, Oracle is able to determine, through the WHERE clause of a SELECT statement, that a particular row cannot be in a given partition, and in this way is able to eliminate that partition during the SELECT. Massive data warehouse loads can also be made more efficient when local indexes are used. By keeping new data in a few partitions, no work is necessary to maintain the indexes for the partitions not updated.

Splitting the table into partitions also provides enhanced functionality for the database administrator. Individual partitions can be exported separately, taken offline, or even dropped without impacting the rest of the table. Such splitting can be used to facilitate the aging of information, or can help to reduce downtime because only a portion of a table may be impacted by disk failures.

Data Cartridges

The Oracle data cartridges described in this section are currently available.

ConText Cartridge

Provides support for full text retrieval and linguistic services on structured textual information. Provides additional capabilities for storing textual information beyond the traditional VARCHAR2 datatype, and removes the 4000-character limit.

Image Cartridge

> Provides support for two-dimensional data stored in most popular image formats and the ability to convert data between common formats.

Spatial Cartridge

> Provides support for geographic information. Allows you to add location data to your application, making it possible to easily display or aggregate data points by geographic location.

Time Series Cartridge

> Provides enhanced support of temporal data. Also provides additional time series, time scaling, and calendaring functions to query and manipulate time-based information.

Video Cartridge

> Provides support for the storage and delivery of full-motion, full-screen video and digital audio on demand.

Visual Information Retrieval Cartridge

> Provides the ability to characterize, sort, and compare images based upon color, structure, and texture. Licensed from Virage, Inc., this cartridge allows you to search for images that are like another.

Development Tools

In addition to the RDBMS software and options, Oracle also manufactures and sells a complete line of application development tools. These tools provide support for the development of complex applications using character mode terminals, two-tier client/server, and N-tier client/server utilizing web browser technology. These tools, which are designed to facilitate exploiting the features of the Oracle RDBMS environment, are beyond the scope of this book.

Applications

Oracle also manufactures and sells a complete line of applications for the enterprise resource planning (ERP) marketplace, as well as for vertically integrated industry-specific applications. These applications, which are designed to take advantage of the features of the Oracle RDBMS environment, are also beyond the scope of this book.

Licensing by the User

The Oracle RDBMS, options, data cartridges, tools, and applications are bundled in a variety of packages. Originally, the software was licensed only at the server level—that is, once you licensed the server, as many users as could access the server would be entitled to use the Oracle software. Over time, server-level licensing has given way to per-user licensing.

The most popular form of licensing currently in use is the *concurrent user license*, with which you specify a maximum number of concurrent users who can access the database at a given time. The other common mechanism is the *named user license*, with which you are limited to a total number of prespecified users who can be allowed to use the system. Typically, the per-user cost for a named license is less than that of a concurrent user license. The final license type is the *site license*, which is typically only available for large organizations that are licensing multiple hundreds of concurrent users.

Oracle is constantly looking to improve its range of licensing options to remain competitive in the marketplace. Therefore, it is important for you to contact your Oracle sales representative directly to get information about the current licensing policy.

Version Numbers

Oracle version numbers can be confusing at first. The RDBMS uses a four-number version number—for example, 8.0.4.2. In this number:

- The first digit refers to the major release of the RDBMS.

- The second digit refers to a minor release of the RDBMS. The first two digits together define a release level whose functionality has been defined and documented by Oracle Corporation.

- The third digit refers to a code release by the base engineering group for the release level.

- The fourth digit defines a patch set of specific cumulative patches to the code release.

The version number referenced above, 8.0.4.2, is the second patch set to the fourth code release of the 8.0 functionality (see Figure 1-2).

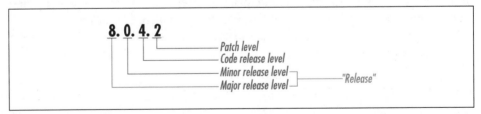

Figure 1-2. Oracle product version numbers

Some Oracle releases (most notably those for Unix platforms) use a five-digit numbering system, but the fifth digit is almost always 0 or 1.

Configuration Planning

Once your organization has decided which Oracle options to acquire, you need to start planning the implementation. Here are some of the areas you will have to consider.

Availability

One of the most important functions of the DBA is to provide for the continued availability of the information in the database. Prior to implementing the database, you need to specify how long you can afford to be down in the event of an emergency, as well as how long you can be down for normal maintenance. How you answer these questions determines what sort of redundancy you need to build into your configuration, and dictates how you will perform backups and standard system maintenance.

We recommend that the availability issue be discussed with the owners of the system and, if necessary, that their agreement be received in writing.

A number of Oracle facilities can help guarantee availability; we recommend that you consider the use of the replication, hot standby database, and Oracle Parallel Server facilities, described briefly in the following sections.

Replication

Replication allows you to maintain separate databases, where the updates that are performed to one database are automatically propagated to the others. These redundant databases can be used both to maintain local copies of data (eliminating long network propagation delays) and to provide a second copy (which can continue in the event of failure of one of the databases). Once the failed database is brought back online, all updates that have occurred since the failure will be automatically applied to the database.

Replication does require that you completely duplicate the entire physical implementation, including multiple computer systems and storage. You will also have to implement a reasonably fast network communication link between the multiple computer systems. However, replication can be used to survive not only hardware or software problems, but also sitewide emergencies (assuming, of course, that the replicated database is running offsite).

Hot standby database

With the hot standby database, you actually use only one database at a time. The second database is constantly in recovery mode. As an archived redo log file is generated, it is copied over to the remote site and applied to the database. In the event of a failure of the primary database, you complete the recovery process and bring up the standby database.

With this facility, you will have to maintain redundant computer and storage systems, and in the case of a recovery, you will have lost any committed transactions that have not been moved to an archived log file. However, you will not need to maintain a high-speed communication line between the databases as you must with replication. In fact, the connection does not even have to be continuous.

Oracle Parallel Server

The Oracle Parallel Server (OPS) allows multiple computer systems in a loosely coupled configuration or massively parallel processor configuration to share a common database (shown in Figure 1-3). With this option, you will be able to survive the failure of a single computer system as long as your shared disk storage remains available. With OPS, you will still need to maintain redundant computer systems, and you will want to use a redundant disk technology. However, you might be able to use the additional computer systems during normal operation.

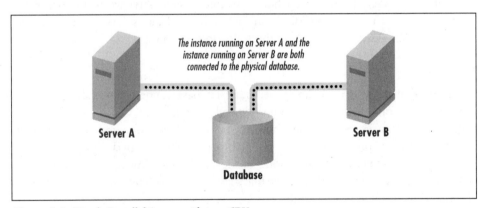

Figure 1-3. Oracle Parallel Server with two CPUs

Backup and Recovery

Even with redundant hardware, you will still need to back up your database. You can do this through a logical backup (export) or a physical backup at the datafile level. As you'd expect, there are tradeoffs with each mechanism in terms of how long it takes to recover, how long the database might be unavailable, and how consistent the backup is. Chapter 4, *Preventing Data Loss*, covers this subject in some detail.

Export/import

The Export utility, known as EXP, takes a logical backup of the database. EXP writes, in a proprietary format, all the SQL commands necessary to recreate the database objects as well as insert all the data. The companion Import utility, IMP, reads this file and executes all the statements. You can export at the database level, schema level, or table level, and you can import all or a portion of the export file.

Export is the only backup utility that allows you to recreate a single table. In addition, Export is the only backup technique that will allow you to recover your database to a different hardware platform running a different operating system—and perhaps even a different version of Oracle. This utility can be used to recover from both user and processing errors. For information on the use of IMP and EXP, see Chapter 4, *Preventing Data Loss*, and Chapter 16, *Tools and Utilities*.

 In a relational database, it may not be possible (or make sense) to recover only one table. Multiple tables may need to be recovered in order to maintain referential integrity. Also, recovery can only be performed to the time of the export. Any changes made to the database after the export will be lost.

Archivelog mode

When you run the database in archivelog mode, Oracle saves a copy of the redo logs into separate files called *offline redo logs,* or *archive log files*. Just as it uses the redo logs to perform the roll-forward process when restarting the database, Oracle can use the archive log files to replay transactions taken after a backup. Archive log files can be applied to either a hot or a cold backup (described in the following sections).

Cold backup

A cold backup is a physical backup of all datafiles and control files taken while the database is down and while all of its files are closed (cold). A complete cold backup of all database and control files can be used to recreate the database as of the time of the cold backup. If redo logs and archive log files exist, they may be used with a cold backup to bring the database back up to the time of the last committed transaction.

Hot backup

When you are running the database in archivelog mode, you can back up the database while it is still running, or hot. By placing each tablespace in backup mode,

Oracle can continue to run the database while allowing an operating-system-level backup of the corresponding physical files. Using the information stored in the log files, Oracle is able to access the physical backups of database files taken while the database is running and can roll transactions forward to a consistent point in time.

Recovery Manager (RMAN)

The Recovery Manager, or RMAN, is a facility provided by Oracle8 to manage hot and cold backups and the associated archive files. RMAN maintains a recovery database (in a different database) of all files necessary to recreate the database to a particular point in time, along with the location of the files. RMAN also allows you to perform incremental hot backups. It is able to look at each data block and determine whether it has changed since the time of the last backup, and write out only those blocks that have changed. This feature can significantly reduce the amount of time and storage required to back up a large database.

The Recovery Manager is a new feature as of Oracle8, and while it helps automate the recovery process, it is not necessary. DBAs have been successfully backing up and restoring databases without RMAN for years. There are also several third-party tools available that provide support for backing up databases.

The Recovery Manager provides support only for cold and hot backups. It does not support exports.

Performance

Performance is a somewhat nebulous term; everyone has a different idea about what it means. Performance can be measured by how fast one person can get a long query done, or by how many people can perform concurrent OLTP transactions, or by how fast a given batch job runs. Good performance for one user may mean poor performance for another, so it is important to define your expectations before pursuing performance improvements. Performance can, however, be measured objectively, and, therefore, changes to the system can be observed and quantified.

Performance is impacted by how queries are written, how disks are laid out, the amount of memory, and the CPU, disk, and bus speeds. You will probably need to work with your system administrator and/or hardware vendor to determine whether your system has sufficient capacity to provide good performance.

Memory

The more memory you can acquire for your computer system, the better. In fact, adding memory is typically the best way to improve performance. In addition to Oracle's using memory for the System Global Area, the operating system will use memory to track each process and handle disk I/O. For detailed information about how Oracle uses memory, see Chapter 10, *The Oracle Instance*. You want sufficient memory to allow the entire SGA to remain in memory without causing swapping and paging. A rule of thumb is that your system memory should be at least three times the size of the SGA.

Of course, adding memory is only the first step; Oracle must be configured to utilize the additional memory—for example, by adding additional database buffers or shared pool. See Chapter 3, *Maximizing Oracle Performance*, for more information.

Disk layout

Oracle, like all relational databases, will probably be I/O bound. The second most important way to improve performance (after adding more memory) is to improve the overall performance of the I/O system. The more disks you can provide to Oracle, the better your I/O performance will be. Remember, for each table update you perform, Oracle will perform the following disk I/Os:

- The write to the table
- Updates to any indexes
- Rollback information for the table and indexes
- Redo log buffer writes to disk for the table and indexes
- Updates to the data dictionary if new extents are needed

For the best performance, follow these guidelines when you are laying out the disk subsystem:

- Allocate separate disks for data, redo logs, and archive files.
- Use multiple controllers when available.
- Use disk striping (either by the operating system or by Oracle).
- Keep data and index segments on separate disks for a given table.
- Use a separate disk for rollback segments.
- Keep the system tablespace on a separate disk or a lightly used disk.
- Avoid the use of RAID-5 disks (RAID stands for redundant arrays of inexpensive disks) for high-write files. Such files include rollback segments, temporary tablespaces, redo logs, and tables with high amounts of inserts, updates, and deletes. RAID-5 maintains data and parity information on multiple disks. The time spent reading, calculating, and writing to multiple disks will impact your total performance.

For more information about how Oracle uses disks and files, see Chapter 11, *The Oracle Database*.

2

In this chapter:
- *Media Selection*
- *The Oracle Installer*
- *Installable Components*
- *Dependencies*
- *Pre-Installation Checklist*
- *Critical Decisions*
- *Post-Installation Tasks*

Installation

It probably goes without saying, but Oracle installation is a prerequisite to most of the administration topics mentioned in this book. Installation is probably one of the most important tasks a DBA will perform.

Oracle runs on a wide variety of hardware platforms, from personal computers to large mainframes, and there is a corresponding variety of installation methodologies. This chapter gives an overview of the Oracle installation process and the tools provided by Oracle to help with installation. We'll give you the critical information you need to complete an installation that will both function now and be maintainable in the future. However, this chapter cannot replace the appropriate *Oracle Installation and User's Guide* for your platform. Although we are experienced DBAs, we begin every installation with a careful review of the appropriate Oracle documentation, and we urge you to do the same.

To successfully complete an Oracle installation, you must perform the following tasks:

- Make pre-installation decisions.
- Obtain appropriate media.
- Install the Oracle software.
- Create a database.
- Configure the database.

We'll discuss each of these tasks in this chapter. See Figure 2-1 for an outline of the installation process.

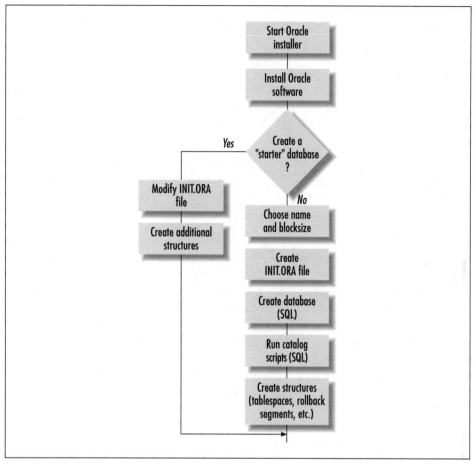

Figure 2-1. The Oracle installation process

Media Selection

One of the first decisions you'll need to make before beginning an Oracle installation is the selection of an appropriate installation medium. For each platform on which Oracle runs, one or more types of installation media are available. These media include:

- CD-ROM
- DAT tape
- Cartridge tape (various types)

On some platforms, there may be no choice of media. For example, Oracle for Windows 98 is available only on CD-ROM. On other platforms, there may be a variety of media available. Oracle for Unix, for example, is available on CD-ROM,

DAT tape, and cartridge tape. When ordering installation media, be certain that the media offered:

- Is supported by the hardware on your system
- Is the correct physical size
- Is the correct format
- Is intended for the operating system running on your hardware

 To obtain installation media or to arrange for replacement of faulty or incorrect media, contact Oracle Customer Relations by calling Oracle Support.

The Oracle Installer

No matter what hardware platform Oracle is to be installed on, installer software is provided as part of the installation media. Normally, this installer software is called *orainst*; it may be called *orainst, orainst.exe, orainst.com,* and so on, depending on the operating system naming standards for executable files. Although the Oracle installer may look different or operate differently on different hardware platforms, its basic function is essentially the same. The Oracle installer will:

- Install Oracle software components
- Optionally create a starter database
- Perform operating system functions required to run Oracle

Depending on your operating system and hardware, the installer may be offered in one or more of the following modes:

Character mode
This variation of the installer is the most common and is intended to run on plain, character-based terminals like a VT-100. The character mode installer uses few graphics (other than line characters) and requires only a keyboard to operate.

Windows mode
On Windows-based machines (e.g., Intel machines running Windows 95, Windows 98, or Windows NT), a native Windows installation program is provided, which takes full advantage of Windows functionality, including a graphical user interface (GUI), which generally requires a keyboard and a mouse.

Motif mode

This type of installer is common on Unix implementations, and is also called X Windows. It is similar to a Windows implementation, and takes advantage of the Motif GUI. The Motif mode installer requires an X terminal (or X terminal emulation) with a keyboard and a mouse.

 Strictly speaking, a mouse is not necessary to run the installer under Windows or Motif. The keyboard can be used to position the cursor, but this is very cumbersome and is not often done.

When multiple installers are available, the *Oracle Installation and User's Guide* for your platform will explain how to run each installer. In general, the mode chosen affects the look and feel of the installer, but the installer functionality is the same regardless of the mode you select.

Installable Components

When you begin your installation, you will need to indicate to the installer exactly which Oracle software components you wish to install. Typically, Oracle installation media include all components available for the platform. However, some of these components may require separate licensing, and some may either be unnecessary or inappropriate for your particular installation. For example, SQL*Net will be included on the installation media, including all available SQL*Net protocol adapters. In most cases, you will only be using one or two SQL*Net protocols, so it would not make sense to install any others.

 The Oracle installer may be able to detect network protocols running on your machine and may attempt to install protocol adapters to support those found. Be sure that you want to install all the adapters that the installer selects. For example, the IPX protocol may be running on your machine, but you may not want SQL*Net to utilize that protocol, so in this case you would choose not to install the SPX protocol adapter.

There will be many database options and tools presented to you in the "available" list, and you should carefully choose those you wish installed. For example, in most Oracle installers, you must choose not only "Oracle Server (RDBMS)" but also "PL/SQL" if you want to use PL/SQL (and who doesn't need that?).

Dependencies

Many Oracle components have dependencies—that is, one component requires one or more other components. The Oracle installer handles these dependencies automatically, so you can be assured that all required components will be installed. For example, if you choose to install the Oracle Server, the appropriate Required Support Files (RSF) will be recognized as a dependency and will be included automatically in your installation. At the end of the installation, you will see a list of installed components. Don't be surprised to see components listed there that you did not explicitly request—they are the result of dependency checking.

Pre-Installation Checklist

Before beginning an Oracle installation session, make sure that:

- The *Installation and User's Guide* (IUG) has been read and is available.
- Any included *Release Notes* have been carefully reviewed. Don't forget the *README* file usually found on the installation media—this file often contains critical information.
- Appropriate installation media are available.
- Required operating system changes have been made (e.g., kernel parameters and patches).
- Sufficient disk space is available.
- Sufficient system memory is available.
- Desired Oracle components are identified.
- Root, system manager, or other appropriate passwords are available.
- The directory structure for Oracle files has been carefully planned.

Critical Decisions

While most decisions made during installation can be changed at a later time, some decisions are either very difficult or impossible to change, so it is important that you make these decisions correctly at the time of installation. They include:

- Creation of a starter database
- Location of Oracle software (*ORACLE_HOME*)
- Directory structure for Oracle datafiles
- Language to be used
- Database blocksize

- Number, size, and location of online log files

- Maximum number of datafiles to be allowed

We describe each of these decisions in the following sections.

The Starter Database

On most Oracle platforms, when you install the Oracle software you are given an option to create an initial or *starter* database, which normally consists of:

- Default database name (usually ORCL)

- Default database blocksize (usually 2048)

- A SYSTEM tablespace

- A USERS tablespace

- Users SYS, SYSTEM, and SCOTT

- Three online redo log files

- A single control file

- A single non-SYSTEM rollback segment

- A standard initialization file (generally referred to as *INIT.ORA* in this book)

The sizes and locations of the files associated with this initial database vary from platform to platform. For all but the most simplistic database application, we strongly recommend that the starter database not be installed. Rather, you should carefully plan the database installation and create the database according to that plan. We recommend against using the starter database for the following reasons:

- The database should be meaningfully named.

- The default blocksize is usually too small.

- The operating system file locations do not follow the Optimal Flexible Architecture (OFA), described in the next section.

- The initial file sizes are usually inadequate.

- Users are created with inappropriate DEFAULT and TEMP tablespace assignments.

- The redo log files have not been sized and are not located properly.

- Multiple (mirrored) control files should always be used to protect against damage or loss.

- Multiple rollback segments should be defined in a non-SYSTEM tablespace.

- Initialization parameters should be planned and tuned for the database.

While it is certainly possible for the DBA to allow Oracle to create an initial database and then make appropriate modifications, it is far more efficient and less complex and time-consuming to create the appropriate database from scratch.

> Some implementations of Oracle may not give you a choice regarding the installation of the starter database. In this case, you can either modify it after creation to meet your needs, or delete it after installation and create your own database.

A sample script for creating a database is included at the end of this chapter. Note that this script is for example purposes only and, as such, is probably more simplistic than the script you'd use to create an actual production database.

Oracle Directory Structure

Oracle has published a standard called the Optimal Flexible Architecture (OFA), which describes an ideal directory structure for Oracle software and database files. While the OFA was defined primarily for Unix environments (as it has many specific advantages for the Unix environment), the principles of OFA can be applied to most operating system environments.

OFA provides a very precisely defined structure, including directory names. In many installations it may be necessary and even desirable to make modifications to the OFA standard, and we do so in this book. However, even when modified, the key to OFA is a standard directory structure. On a Unix machine with five disk drives, hosting two databases (DB1 and DB2) running two versions of Oracle (7.3.4 and 8.0.5), the structure might look like this:

```
/disk00/oracle/product/7.3.4/...
/disk00/oracle/product/8.0.5/...
/disk01/oracle/oradata/DB1/...
/disk02/oracle/oradata/DB1/...
/disk03/oracle/oradata/DB2/...
/disk04/oracle/oradata/DB2/...
```

The key elements of this structure are:

- Each mount point (disk) has the same name and is numbered sequentially (*disk00* is the first disk, *disk01* is the second, etc.).

- Below each mount point is a directory called *oracle*. All Oracle files will be created below this point. On the disk that contains the Oracle software, the directory to this point (*/disk00/oracle*, in our example) is called *ORACLE_BASE*.

- The next level can contain the software directory (named the *product* directory according to the OFA standard), which in turn contains a directory for each Oracle version installed. This directory normally exists only on a single disk, and the directory to this level (*/disk00/oracle/product/7.3.4* or */disk00/oracle/product/8.0.5* in our example) is called *ORACLE_HOME*. All Oracle software is organized in predefined directories below *ORACLE_HOME*, and on most platforms, *ORACLE_HOME* must be defined at the operating system level. Only the account that actually runs Oracle should have permission to access these directories.

- At the same level as the *product* directory, each disk or mount point will have an *oradata* directory. A separate directory for each database (usually given the same name as the database) is then created below *oradata*. All Oracle datafiles are created here. The OFA standard requires that a given disk drive must contain only files for a single database (i.e., datafiles for DB2 cannot reside on the same disk as datafiles for DB1), but in practice, this is probably not reasonable, and you may want to relax this part of the OFA standard at your site. Files in these directories should be protected so that only the account that actually runs Oracle has permission to alter them.

Before beginning the installation of Oracle software, you should create at least the directory structure for *ORACLE_HOME*. The remainder of the structure should be created prior to attempting to create a database.

 The Oracle White Paper "Optimal Flexible Architecture," by Cary Millsap, provides a complete definition of the OFA standard and is available on Oracle's web site (*www.oracle.com*).

Post-Installation Tasks

Once the Oracle software has been installed on the machine, there are a number of tasks you need to perform to create a functioning Oracle database. For example, on Unix systems, the root user must run a script called *root.sh* after installation.

We also recommend that you run the installer to check the list of components actually installed. In some cases, the Oracle Installer will install components that you did not request and that are not necessary. For example, the Oracle Web Server is automatically installed on some platforms, even though it was not requested and requires separate licensing. If you find an unnecessary component, it can be removed with the installer.

Creating a Database

The first task you must perform after ensuring that the Oracle software has been correctly installed is creation of the database. This task consists, in turn, of several discrete subtasks, described in the following sections.

Choosing a blocksize

While Oracle has defined a default blocksize for every operating system environment (often 2048), this blocksize is often not correct for the database being created. Few characteristics of the database are as important to overall performance as the database blocksize. The blocksize is specified in the *INIT.ORA* file with the DB_BLOCK_SIZE parameter, and once a database is created with a particular blocksize, it cannot be changed. It is, therefore, important to consider the options for database blocksize and define one that will provide good performance for your site. A few factors to consider are the following:

- The blocksize must be at least as big as a single block or disk sector on the host hardware.

- The blocksize should be a multiple of the host operating system and/or hardware blocksize. For example, many systems write 512-byte blocks to disk, so the blocksize should be a multiple of 512.

- The blocksize should not be bigger than the largest amount of data that the host operating system and/or hardware can read or write in one operation. For example, an operating system may be able to transfer 8192 bytes in a single operation to disk.

- Small blocksizes require less data to be transferred to and from disk, and may result in better I/O operation.

- Small blocksizes hold fewer rows of data and require more overhead (see Chapter 11, *The Oracle Database*, for detailed information on block structures).

- Small blocksizes may require more blocks to be read in order to return all data for a query.

- Small blocksizes use less redo log space for the update of a single row when the tablespace is in backup mode.

- Large blocksizes require that larger amounts of data be transferred to and from disk, and may be less I/O efficient as a result. However, modern controllers with disk caching can often negate this fact.

- Large blocksizes hold more rows of data per block, and as a result, less overhead is required.

- Large blocksizes require fewer blocks to be read in order to return all data for a query.

- Large blocksizes require more redo log space for the update of a single row when the tablespace is in backup mode.

While every database and application environment is different, we can make the following general recommendations for choosing a database blocksize:

- Choose a small blocksize (2048 or 4096) for transaction systems where there are frequent queries, inserts, and updates that involve a single row.

- Choose a large blocksize (8192 or larger) for data warehouses and other large database applications where most data is bulk loaded, there are few updates, and most queries return multiple rows or involve full table scans.

Choosing the name

Before you create an Oracle database, you must choose a name for it as well as for the Oracle instance which will mount and open it. We recommend that the database name and the instance name be the same, unless you are running Oracle Parallel Server. In that case, we recommend choosing a database name and appending the instance number to it to form a unique name for each instance. For more information about the database and the instance, see Chapter 10, *The Oracle Instance*, and Chapter 11, *The Oracle Database*.

While the names can be somewhat arbitrary, it is usually best to choose meaningful names—this will pay dividends later. The instance name must be unique on the host machine (that is, if you run more than one Oracle instance on a single machine, each must have a different name) for the following reasons:

- Oracle appends the instance name to a standard prefix in order to create known filenames that are used by default. For example, the default name for the initialization file is created by adding the instance name to the prefix INIT. So, if the instance name is TEST, then Oracle will expect an initialization file called *initTEST.ora* (unless the pfile parameter is explicitly specified when starting the instance). The alert log filename is generated in a similar manner: the alert file for the TEST instance will be *alert_TEST.log*.

- On most platforms, the internal process names used for the background processes are created by appending the instance name to a standard process name. For example, the PMON process for the TEST instance will be *ora_pmon_TEST* on a Unix system.

While it is not required, we recommend that database and corresponding instance names be unique across your entire enterprise in order to eliminate later confusion. We also recommend that names be four characters long, because Oracle appends the instance name to a standard prefix to create known filenames, and some operating systems have an eight-character filename limit.

 The database and instance names are case sensitive on most platforms, so *TEST* is not the same as *test* or *Test.*

The database name is specified in the CREATE DATABASE command and in the DB_NAME parameter in the *INIT.ORA* file. These names must match. The instance name is specified in an operating system specific manner, usually using an environment variable. Table 2-1 shows where the instance name is defined for some popular systems.

Table 2-1. Sources of Oracle Instance Names for Popular Operating Systems

Operating System	Instance Name Comes From
Windows (pre-95)	ORACLE_SID environment variable
Windows 95/98	ORACLE_SID entry in the registry
Windows NT	ORACLE_SID entry in the registry
Unix	ORACLE_SID environment variable
VMS	ORASID logical name

Creating the parameter file

Every database must have an associated initialization parameter file (usually known as *INIT.ORA*), which provides information on the configuration of the database (see Chapter 3, *Maximizing Oracle Performance*, and Chapter 12, *Initialization Parameters*, for more information). When first creating a database, the *INIT. ORA* file only needs to contain parameter assignments, which should include:

DB_NAME
> This parameter specifies the name of the database, and must correspond to the name used in the CREATE DATABASE statement.

DB_BLOCK_SIZE
> As discussed earlier, this parameter specifies the blocksize to be used for this database.

DB_FILES
> This parameter sets the maximum number of datafiles that can be opened for this database. This parameter should be set no higher than the value of the MAXDATAFILES parameter specified during database creation.

CONTROL_FILES

This parameter specifies the names and locations of all control files. We recommend that at least two (and, if possible, more than two) control files be created on different disk devices (and, if possible, on different controllers). Oracle automatically mirrors control file information to each file specified (see Chapter 11, *The Oracle Database*, for more information on control files). By creating multiple, mirrored control files, you reduce the risk of being unable to start your database if a single control file is lost or damaged.

Once you have decided on the parameters and values to be placed in the initial *INIT.ORA* file, the file can be created using any standard text editor. The file is expected to be in the *dbs* directory of *ORACLE_HOME* (on Unix systems, this would be *$ORACLE_HOME/dbs*). For some systems, the *INIT.ORA* file is found in the *database* directory of *ORACLE_HOME* (on Windows NT, it is found in *orant\ database*). See Chapter 12, *Initialization Parameters*, for other variants.

Be careful to use a plain text editor to create the *INIT.ORA* file. Do not use a word processing program, since these programs often embed control codes and other characters that may cause errors in the *INIT.ORA* file. If you must use a word processing program, be sure to save the file as plain text, or the equivalent, to ensure a usable file.

Building Database Creation Scripts

Although you may enter the commands to create a database directly from the keyboard using Oracle Server Manager, we advise you to create a script containing the SQL statements required to create the database. By creating a script and saving it on disk, you will:

- Have an opportunity to review your creation statements for accuracy before executing them

- Automate the actual database creation process

- Be able to create a log file with a record of the statements executed

- Document the exact method used to create the database

- Be able to recreate the database in the future, if required

It is possible to generate a script containing all the database creation statements from an existing database. *Oracle Scripts*, by Brian Lomasky and David C. Kreines (O'Reilly Associates, 1998), describes a utility that performs this function.

The script may be created using any plain text editor, and should be saved to disk in a known, standard location. The OFA standard specifies a directory called *create* below *ORACLE_HOME* for this purpose.

The database creation script must do the following:

- Create the database, specifying the filename and size for the SYSTEM tablespace. The SYSTEM tablespace does not usually need to be very big—50 to 80 megabytes will usually do—and it should be on a different disk from other datafiles, if possible. You will need to define the names, locations, and sizes of the redo log files. You should define at least three redo log files, and they should be sized properly. See Chapter 11, *The Oracle Database*, for more information on redo log files.

- Create the data dictionary views using the Oracle-supplied script *catalog.sql*. This script is normally found in the *rdbms/admin* directory below *ORACLE_HOME*.

- Create the objects required by Oracle's procedural components (i.e., PL/SQL) using the Oracle-supplied script *catproc.sql*. This script is normally found in the *rdbms/admin* directory below *ORACLE_HOME*.

- Create a rollback segment in the SYSTEM tablespace, and place it online. A rollback segment is required in order to create any additional tablespaces. This rollback segment can be taken offline and removed later, if desired.

- Create a rollback tablespace. Rollback segments should be created in a tablespace created for this purpose. Make the tablespace large enough to hold all of your rollback segments (allow space for growth). Ideally, the file for the rollback tablespace will reside on a disk separate from other database files, in order to avoid I/O contention. We recommend that this tablespace be called ROLLBACK and that the default storage be defined with equal-size INITIAL and NEXT extents (remember that rollback segments must have at least two extents).

- Create one or more rollback segments. Specify a size that will accommodate your expected transaction load, and consider using the OPTIMAL parameter to allow rollback segments to shrink back to a predetermined size. Be sure to add the names of the rollback segments to the *INIT.ORA* file before the next database startup; otherwise, they will not be used.

- Create a TEMPORARY tablespace. By default, Oracle will use the SYSTEM tablespace as the temporary tablespace for each user. This should be avoided, since performance will be negatively impacted. Create a separate tablespace for temporary segments. We recommend that this tablespace be called TEMP.

- Create any additional tablespaces required. You will probably want to create one or more tablespaces for tables and one or more for indexes. Ideally, the data and index tablespaces should be on different disks in order to avoid I/O contention.

- Run any other required Oracle-supplied scripts. These scripts will be located in the same directory as the *catalog.sql* script and will be used to create data and objects to support the particular set of Oracle features installed.

- Modify the SYSTEM account to set default and temporary tablespaces. By default, both the DEFAULT tablespace and TEMPORARY tablespace are set to SYSTEM for this account, and you will not want to create any new objects there. You should also change the TEMPORARY tablespace for the SYS account, since it will be set to SYSTEM by default.

A sample script

The following SQL script will create a database called DB1 using the OFA architecture. You will find a copy of this script at the O'Reilly web site (see the *Preface* for details).

```
REM * **************************************************************
REM * Script to create DB1 instance with db_block_size = 8192
REM *
REM *   Created:   Dave Kreines - 10/18/98
REM *
REM *
REM * **************************************************************
spool /disk00/oracle/software/7.3.4/dbs/crdbDB1.log

REM * Start the instance (ORACLE_SID must be set to <DB1>).
REM *
connect internal
startup nomount pfile=/disk00/oracle/software/7.3.4/dbs/initDB1.ora

REM * Create the <DB1> database.
REM *
create database "DB1"
    maxinstances 2
    maxlogfiles  32
    maxdatafiles 1000
    character set "US7ASCII"
datafile '/disk00/oracle/oradata/DB1/system01.dbf' size 50M
logfile   '/disk01/oracle/oradata/DB1/log01.log' size 512K,
          '/disk01/oracle/oradata/DB1/log02.log' size 512K,
          '/disk01/oracle/oradata/DB1/log03.log' size 512K,
          '/disk01/oracle/oradata/DB1/log04.log' size 512K;

REM * Now perform all commands necessary to create
REM * the final database after the CREATE DATABASE command has
REM * succeeded.

REM * install data dictionary:
@/disk00/oracle/software/7.3.4/rdbms/admin/catalog.sql
```

```
REM * install procedural components:
@/disk00/oracle/software/7.3.4/rdbms/admin/catproc.sql

REM * Create additional rollback segment in SYSTEM since
REM * at least one non-system rollback segment is required
REM * before creating a tablespace.
REM *
create rollback segment SYSROLL tablespace system
storage (initial 25K next 25K minextents 2 maxextents 99);

REM * Put SYSROLL online without shutting
REM * down and restarting the database.
REM *
alter rollback segment SYSROLL online;

REM * Create a tablespace for rollback segments.
REM *
create tablespace ROLLBACK
 datafile '/disk01/oracle/oradata/DB1/rbs01.dbf' size 25M
 default storage (
  initial      500K
  next         500K
  pctincrease  0
  minextents   2
);

REM * Create the "real" rollback segments.
REM *
create rollback segment RBS01 tablespace ROLLBACK
storage (initial 500K next 500K minextents 2 optimal 1M);
create rollback segment RBS02 tablespace ROLLBACK
storage (initial 500K next 500K minextents 2 optimal 1M);
create rollback segment RBS03 tablespace ROLLBACK
storage (initial 500K next 500K minextents 2 optimal 1M);
create rollback segment RBS04 tablespace ROLLBACK
storage (initial 500K next 500K minextents 2 optimal 1M);

REM * Use ALTER ROLLBACK SEGMENT ONLINE to put rollback segments online
REM * without shutting down and restarting the database.
REM *
alter rollback segment RBS01 online;
alter rollback segment RBS02 online;
alter rollback segment RBS03 online;
alter rollback segment RBS04 online;

REM * Since we've created and brought online 4 more rollback segments,
REM * we no longer need the rollback segment in the SYSTEM tablespace.
REM * We could delete it, but we will leave it here in case we need it
REM * in the future.
alter rollback segment SYSROLL offline;

REM * Create a tablespace for temporary segments.
create tablespace TEMP
 datafile '/disk02/oracle/oradata/DB1/temp01.dbf' size 25M
```

```
default storage (
initial     100K
next        100K
maxextents  UNLIMITED
pctincrease 0
);

REM * Create a tablespace for database tools.
REM *
create tablespace TOOLS
 datafile '/disk03/oracle/oradata/DB1/tools01.dbf' size 25M
 default storage (
initial     50K
next        50K
maxextents  UNLIMITED
pctincrease 0
);

REM * Create tablespaces for user activity.
REM *
create tablespace DATA
 datafile '/disk04/oracle/oradata/DB1/data01.dbf' size 100M
 default storage (
   initial     250K
   next        250K
   maxextents  UNLIMITED
   pctincrease 0
);

REM * Create tablespaces for indexes.
REM *
create tablespace INDEXES
 datafile '/disk05/oracle/oradata/DB1/index01.dbf' size 100M
 default storage (
   initial     250K
   next        250K
   maxextents  UNLIMITED
   pctincrease 0
);

REM * Alter SYS and SYSTEM users, because Oracle will make SYSTEM
REM * the default and temporary tablespace by default, and we don't
REM * want that.
REM *
alter user sys temporary tablespace TEMP;
alter user system default tablespace TOOLS temporary tablespace TEMP;

REM * Now run the Oracle-supplied scripts we need for this DB.
REM *
@/disk00/oracle/software/7.3.4/rdbms/admin/catexp.sql
@/disk00/oracle/software/7.3.4/rdbms/admin/dbmspool.sql
@/disk00/oracle/software/7.3.4/rdbms/admin/prvtpool.plb

REM * Now run the Oracle-supplied script to create the DBA views
REM * for the SYSTEM account.  Change to SYSTEM first.
```

```
REM *
connect system/manager
@/disk00/oracle/software/7.3.4/rdbms/admin/catdbsyn.sql

REM * All done, so close the log file and exit.
REM *
spool off
exit
```

3

Maximizing Oracle Performance

If you ask a room full of Oracle database administrators, "What is the single biggest part of your job?", chances are that the almost universal response will be "Configuration and tuning of the database." Oracle is a very complex and powerful product, and part of its power lies in its ability to get the best possible performance out of each individual database configuration. This chapter presents our approach to the configuration and tuning of an Oracle database and provides guidelines for implementing a high-performance database at your site.

The ongoing, day-to-day responsibility of most Oracle DBAs is to get the best possible performance from the Oracle database. A number of definitions may be offered for "performance," but we define performance as the objective, measurable amount of time required to perform a typical operation in the database in question. Yes, this is a simplistic definition that ignores other metrics like resource utilization, but let's face it: the database is expected to be as *fast* as possible, so this is a reasonable definition for this purpose.

Entire books have been written on the subject of Oracle performance (see the appendix, *Resources for the DBA*, for some we consider worthy of your attention*), so we cannot hope to address all the intricacies of Oracle performance tuning in a single chapter. Rather, we hope to document a straightforward approach to performance tuning and to provide some practical guidelines that can be applied to a variety of installations.

It is important to realize that every Oracle installation is different in terms of its physical and logical database implementation, the types of transactions processed,

---

* We particularly recommend Mark Gurry and Peter Corrigan's *Oracle Performance Tuning*, Second Edition (O'Reilly & Associates, 1997).

and the performance requirements for those transactions. As a result, there cannot be an automatic tuning methodology, although several vendors, including Oracle, have attempted to provide one. Nor can a single set of rules provide a method for maximizing database performance. What can be provided, however, is a methodology that, when properly applied and combined with the knowledge and experience of a working DBA, will result in good performance for any given database.

Configuration and Tuning—What's the Difference?

Getting maximum performance from an Oracle database requires careful attention to both configuration and tuning of the database. These terms are often used interchangeably, but in reality, they are two different tasks—admittedly, with a bit of grey area between them.

Configuration is the process of setting up the physical and logical components of the database and its host systems, while *tuning* is the process of modifying the internal behavior of the database so that operations are performed in a particular manner. The entire process can become somewhat circular, since proper tuning often includes modifying the configuration, which then requires another look at tuning. Figure 3-1 shows the basic steps in the configuration and tuning process.

What Can Be Configured?

Some items that can be configured in an Oracle database are the following:

- Components of the database that affect the allocation of system processes, such as:

  SQL*Net
  Multi-Threaded Server (MTS)
  Parallel Query
  Parallel Server

- The layout and sizes of physical storage

- The sizing of database objects, such as:

  Tables
  Indexes
  Rollback segments
  Sort areas
  Temporary tablespaces
  Redo logs
  Partition tables
  Index-only tables

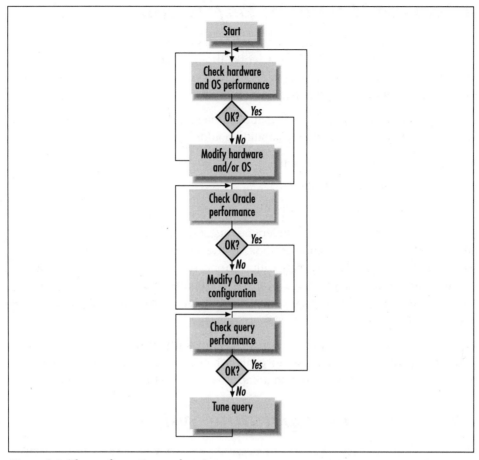

Figure 3-1. The configuration and tuning process

- The amount and allocation of memory, such as:

   Database buffers
   Redo log buffers
   Shared pool

What Can Be Tuned?

Aspects of the Oracle database that can be tuned include the following:

- Memory utilization

- Disk utilization

- SQL statement execution

Achieving Maximum Performance

Achieving maximum performance for your Oracle database doesn't just happen—it is usually the result of a lot of hard work, thought, and planning. The rewards, however, are well worth the effort expended: your database runs at peak efficiency, your users are happy, and *you* look good!

Our approach to maximizing performance is hierarchical in nature. Three distinct areas must be addressed, and they should be addressed in order. These areas are:

- Operating system configuration
- Oracle resource configuration
- Object creation and SQL execution

These areas are not necessarily independent; in fact, significant changes in one area are likely to require another look at the other areas. They are, however, sequence dependent. That is, you cannot hope to get good performance out of Oracle unless and until you have properly configured and tuned your operating system. Likewise, good query execution depends on a properly configured Oracle environment.

Every Oracle database is different, so we cannot tell you exactly how to accomplish your configuration and tuning goals, or even what those goals should be. What we can do is provide you with an approach we've found to be successful.

Configuring the Operating System

This one is usually easy, since (in most cases) it's not your job! In most installations, there is a system administrator or manager who is responsible for addressing operating system and hardware issues. This system administrator is usually an expert on the hardware and operating system software, and most DBAs are not in a position to second-guess him or her. While deferring to the system administrator's expertise, here are a few points you might want to make sure are addressed:

- Physical memory should be fully utilized, but swapping (in environments that swap memory) should not occur. Swapping memory to disk is a very slow process, so if your system needs more memory, buy more memory! In particular, make certain that you do not create a System Global Area (SGA) that is too big for physical memory, since swapping of the SGA will severely degrade Oracle performance.
- The CPU should approach 100% utilization at peaks, but processes should not have to wait for the CPU.

- Disks and controllers should be running at or near their optimal capacities (usually 60 to 90% of maximum) with minimal I/O waits. As the DBA, you do have some control over this area as well, as we'll describe later in this chapter.

- Network throughput should not be a bottleneck. Consider backbone networks to link servers to each other, and separate client/server traffic from server/server traffic where possible.

- Try to keep your Oracle server machine a pure server, and move users to another machine.

- Be sure any operating system components (including patches) that may affect Oracle are installed.

Because Oracle is a major vendor in the database marketplace, most major hardware vendors have Oracle "experts" on staff who can provide advice on hardware and operating system issues that may affect Oracle's execution on their hardware. Take advantage of this expertise!

Configuring Oracle

Oracle's overall performance is affected by the components that are installed, as well as by how those components are configured. A high-performance Oracle database is essential to obtaining maximum performance from transactions run against that database. This section provides general configuration guidelines and some specific recommendations for configuring SQL*Net/Net8, MTS, Parallel Query, and Parallel Server.

Configuration Guidelines

While every installation is different, there are some general configuration guidelines that can be applied to most databases, regardless of the components installed or the use of the particular database. These general guidelines are described in the following sections.

Check the documentation

This one may seem obvious, but it needs to be said: read the documentation. Even experienced DBAs will benefit from a quick read of the pertinent documentation before beginning an Oracle installation. We recommend that you look at the following (at least):

- Hardware-specific *Installation and User's Guide (IUG)*
- *Server Administrator's Guide*

- *Release Notes* (usually packed with the media)

- The *README* file, which is usually found on the installation media and contains last-minute information that may not be in the printed documentation.

Check resource requirements

Before beginning an installation, be certain that sufficient system resources are available. The *IUG* for your platform contains comprehensive information about disk storage and memory requirements. Remember that these requirements are minimums, and that the resources required may actually be higher, depending on other configuration decisions you make. For example, more memory will be required if you specify a larger SGA.

In particular, make sure there is enough disk space available on the device where you place the Oracle software (typically called *ORACLE_HOME*) to load all software and ancillary files.

Check system privileges

Most operating systems require the account that is performing the Oracle installation to have certain privileges. Be sure to check the *IUG* for these, and make sure the system administrator has set them properly. Note that these privileges may include the right to create directories and files on specific devices.

Determine control file locations

Oracle requires at least one control file. You should require at least two, and usually more, control files. This is critical because if all copies of the control file are lost, you will be unable to mount your database. Plan to place control files on different disk devices and, where possible, on different disk controllers.

SQL*Net Configuration

SQL*Net (Oracle7) and Net8 (Oracle8) must be configured, usually using Oracle Network Manager or the Net8 Assistant. This is typically done after the database software is installed and after at least one Oracle instance is up and running, but the configuration should be planned in advance. Before beginning a SQL*Net/Net8 configuration, you must know:

- The types of network protocols that will be used to access Oracle in your environment

- The naming scheme you will use to identify Oracle network nodes

- The names and network locations of all servers, gateways, and MultiProtocol Interchanges in your environment

Once SQL*Net/Net8 is configured, the following files (at least) must be placed on each server:

listener.ora
>   Controls the operation of the SQL*Net listener process

tnsnames.ora
>   Maintains the relationship between logical node names (aliases) and physical locations in the network when the Oracle Names software is not used

sqlnet.ora
>   Controls logging of Oracle network operations (not required but highly desirable)

If you are using the Multi-Threaded Server, this fact must also be configured in the *INIT.ORA* file, as shown in the next section.

Multi-Threaded Server Configuration

The Multi-Threaded Server (MTS) is configured in the *INIT.ORA* file, as shown in the following sample *INIT.ORA* parameter settings:

```
mts_dispatchers="ipc,1"
mts_dispatchers="tcp,1"
mts_max_dispatchers=10
mts_servers=1
mts_max_servers=10
mts_service=TEST
mts_listener_address="(ADDRESS=(PROTOCOL=ipc)(KEY=TEST))"
mts_listener_address="(ADDRESS=(PROTOCOL=tcp)(HOST=10.74.72.42)(PORT=1526))"
```

This example will configure a Multi-Threaded Server that will handle TCP/IP connections to the TEST database. A maximum of 10 dispatchers will be started, and up to 10 server processes will be created.

Remember that each MTS process counts against the total count specified in the *INIT.ORA* parameter PROCESSES, as well as against the maximum processes allowed for the Oracle user at the operating system level.

Parallel Query Configuration

Parallel Query Option (PQO) is a powerful feature of Oracle, but in order to use it properly, the database must be configured properly. Parallel Query allows multiple CPU systems to divide certain database tasks (usually full table scans) into several pieces that can be executed at the same time (in parallel). In order to perform this task, the following are required:

- Multiple parallel processes must be permitted by setting the *INIT.ORA* parameter PARALLEL_MAX_SERVERS to a value greater than 0.

- Tablespaces must be created using multiple datafiles, which should be allocated to separate devices. Ideally, there will be as many devices allocated to each tablespace as there are CPUs in the system.

- Tables taking advantage of Parallel Query should have their degree of parallelism set (using the PARALLEL clause in the CREATE TABLE statement) to the number of datafiles comprising the tablespace in which the table is created.

Parallel Server Configuration

In order to utilize Oracle Parallel Server (OPS), which allows a single Oracle database to be shared by multiple Oracle instances, you must carefully specify the Parallel Server characteristics using *INIT.ORA* parameters on each participating instance, including:

PARALLEL_SERVER
Must be set to TRUE to enable the Oracle Parallel Server (Oracle8 only).

INSTANCE_NUMBER
Identifies the instance to the database.

ROLLBACK_SEGMENTS
Specifies the private rollback segments to be used by each instance. Public rollback segments can also be specified, but this is not necessary.

THREAD
Identifies the redo log thread to be associated with the instance.

GC_DB_LOCKS
The total number of instance locks (Oracle7 only).

GC_FILES_TO_LOCKS
The number of database file locks.

GC_LCK_PROCS
The total number of distributed locks.

GC_ROLLBACK_LOCKS
The total number of rollback locks.

GC_SAVE_ROLLBACK_LOCKS
The number of rollback save locks (Oracle7 only).

GC_SEGMENTS

The maximum number of segments that may have activities impacting space management performed on them simultaneously (Oracle7 only).

INSTANCE_GROUPS

Assigns the instance to one or more specified groups (Oracle8 only).

LM_LOCKS

The number of locks that will be configured for the lock manager (Oracle8 only).

LM_PROCS

The number of processes for the lock manager (Oracle8 only).

LM_RESS

The number of resources that can be locked by each lock manager instance (Oracle8 only).

OPS_ADMIN_GROUP

Assigns the instance to a group for monitoring (Oracle8 only).

PARALLEL_INSTANCE_GROUP

Identifies the parallel instance group to be used for spawning parallel query slaves (Oracle8 only).

ROW_LOCKING

Should be set to ALWAYS.

SERIALIZABLE

Should be set to FALSE (Oracle7 only).

SINGLE_PROCESS

Should be set to FALSE (Oracle7 only).

Additional information on these parameters can be found in Chapter 12, *Initialization Parameters*. Because Oracle Parallel Server is a very complex product, you should consult the *Oracle Parallel Server Concepts and Administration Guide* before attempting to configure a Parallel Server environment. Here are a few points to keep in mind when doing this configuration:

* On Unix platforms, all datafiles must be created in raw partitions.

* When creating a database, only redo thread 1 is created automatically; additional threads must be explicitly created, and you must specify which thread a redo log belongs to.

* Although not required, ensuring that the instance number and thread number are the same will avoid confusion.

The terms "Parallel Query" and "Parallel Server" are often confused. Parallel Query refers to the ability of a single Oracle instance to divide an operation (for example, a full table scan) across multiple CPUs on the same host computer and merge the completed results. Parallel Server, on the other hand, is a feature whereby multiple Oracle instances on different host machines share a single physical database. In this case, work is divided across Oracle instances either by distributing users across multiple instances, or by spawning parallel query processes across instances.

Sizing and Configuring Database Objects

Proper sizing and configuration of database objects are critical to achieving maximum database performance. Proper object sizing is an ongoing task; as objects are created and modified, you must continue to examine their characteristics and make changes when necessary. Some sizing-related problems that negatively impact performance are:

Tablespace fragmentation

This problem, which leaves many unusable small extents scattered about a tablespace, can result when objects are created with inappropriate INITIAL or NEXT extent sizes.

Row chaining

This problem, which causes the data from a single row to reside in multiple Oracle blocks, typically occurs when an insufficient PCTFREE setting is specified and updates subsequently occur to the table.

Multiple extents

Multiple extents, which may cause data for a particular object to be spread across one or more datafiles, result when objects are created with improper INITIAL or NEXT extent sizes. This problem may become critical when the MAXEXTENTS parameter is permitted to assume the default value, since an attempt to allocate an extent beyond that number will result in a failure.

Log waits

Log waits, which cause a process to wait while log buffer records are written to a log file or while a log file switch is occurring, can add significant processing time. These are usually caused by a combination of an insufficient number of log files and log files that are too small.

Failure to extend a rollback segment
> Such failures, which can cause a transaction to roll back, are caused when not enough rollback segments are allocated, or when the rollback segments allocated are not large enough.

The following sections contain specific guidelines and suggestions that may help prevent some of these performance problems.

Tables

Tables are the basic units of data storage in an Oracle database, so their configuration and resulting performance will have a large impact on overall database performance. Some guidelines for table configuration are as follows:

- Try to estimate how big a table will be and allocate a sufficiently large INITIAL extent to hold the entire table. However, if you are using Parallel Query, allocate the total space across as many extents in different datafiles as the degree of parallelism for the table.

- Consider using multiple tablespaces for tables, each for a different size or type of table. For example, you might have three tablespaces: LARGE_DATA, MEDIUM_DATA, and SMALL_DATA, each of which would be used to hold tables of a particular size. If you are using multiple tablespaces for tables, be sure to allocate each table in the appropriate tablespace.

- Be sure to assign a DEFAULT TABLESPACE to each user. If one is not assigned, Oracle will use the SYSTEM tablespace by default.

- If possible, always allocate INITIAL and NEXT extents in multiples of the same size units; for example, allocate in multiples of 512K. This way, extents will be of uniform size and it will be easier to allocate additional extents without fragmenting the tablespace. Where possible, consider making all extents in a tablespace the same size.

- Set the PCTINCREASE parameter to 0, in order to prevent runaway extent allocation and to preserve uniform extent sizes.

- Set MAXEXTENTS to UNLIMITED. This will prevent running out of extents, since multiple extents have little performance impact in and of themselves (although widely scattered extents can negatively affect performance). Do this to prevent errors, but do not use it as a substitute for proper INITIAL sizing.

- Set PCTFREE to 0 if no updates will be performed on the table. If updates will be performed, try to estimate the degree to which columns of a row will grow, and allocate a PCTFREE that will prevent block chaining without excessive unused space in the block.

- Set INITRANS to a value greater than 1 (the default) if multiple transactions will access the table simultaneously.

- Set MAXTRANS to the maximum number of simultaneous accesses expected on the table. A lower value will result in one or more transactions waiting for a prior transaction to complete.

Indexes

Perhaps no other single feature of Oracle can provide as much performance improvement as the proper use of indexes. While many performance gains will result from tuning SQL statements (see Chapter 8, *Query Optimization*), there are also several configuration guidelines we suggest you follow:

- Create a separate tablespace for indexes, and make certain that the datafiles for this index tablespace are not on the same disk device as any datafiles for tablespaces that contain indexed tables.

- Try to estimate the size of an index and allocate a sufficient INITIAL extent to hold the entire index, unless you are using Parallel Query, in which case you should allocate the total space across as many datafiles as the degree of parallelism for the index.

- If possible, always allocate INITIAL and NEXT extents in multiples of the same size units; for example, allocate in multiples of 512K. This way, extents will be of uniform size and it will be easier to allocate additional extents without fragmenting the tablespace.

- Set PCTINCREASE to 0 in order to prevent runaway extent allocation and to preserve uniform extent sizes.

- Set MAXEXTENTS to UNLIMITED. This guideline will prevent your running out of extents, since multiple extents have little performance impact in and of themselves (although widely scattered extents can negatively affect performance). Do this to prevent errors, but do not use it as a substitute for proper INITIAL sizing.

Rollback Segments

Rollback segments are used by Oracle to maintain data consistency and to allow transactions to be cancelled or rolled back. The use of rollback segments is fairly I/O intensive, and the following guidelines apply to their configuration:

- Create a separate tablespace for rollback segments and, if possible, place the datafiles for this tablespace on a different disk device from other Oracle datafiles.

- Never create rollback segments in the SYSTEM tablespace (except for the temporary rollback segment required during database creation; see Chapter 2, *Installation*).

- Be sure that there is enough space allocated to your rollback tablespace to allow rollback segments to grow as large as necessary to accommodate large update transactions. Remember that batch transactions tend to be large.

- Always use the same value for the INITIAL and NEXT extents for rollback segments (define them in the DEFAULT STORAGE clause of the CREATE TABLESPACE statement). This guideline will prevent space fragmentation by allocating rollback segment space in equal-size chunks.

- Remember that each rollback segment must have at least two extents, so the initial size of a segment will actually be the sum of INITIAL + NEXT.

- Define an OPTIMAL value so that rollback segments that are required to grow in size to accommodate a large transaction can be shrunk to a more reasonable size. Don't make this size too small, however, or time will be wasted allocating additional extents to your rollback segments.

Sort Areas

Oracle uses the *INIT.ORA* parameter SORT_AREA_SIZE to allocate memory for use in sorting data. When a sort cannot be completed in memory, Oracle uses temporary segments in the database, which is considerably slower. A careful balance is required for SORT_AREA_SIZE, since large sizes can dramatically increase performance by decreasing I/O, but will also use up memory and can result in paging.

Remember that this parameter applies to each user process. Each user process performing a sort will have SORT_AREA_SIZE memory allocated. So, if SORT_AREA_SIZE is set to 1 megabyte, and 100 user processes are performing sorts, a total of 100 megabytes of memory may be allocated.

Temporary Tablespaces

When insufficient sort memory is allocated to the user process to perform a required sort, Oracle performs the sort on disk by creating temporary segments in the tablespace specified by the TEMPORARY TABLESPACE parameter for the user. In addition, temporary segments are used to perform complex queries like joins,

UNIONs, and MINUSes, and for index creation. Guidelines for temporary areas include the following:

- Create a separate tablespace (usually called TEMP) for temporary segments, and place the datafile(s) for this tablespace on a separate disk device, if possible.

- Specify INITIAL and NEXT parameters in the DEFAULT STORAGE clause of the CREATE TABLESPACE command. Use the same value for both in order to eliminate space fragmentation, which is particularly likely in the TEMP tablespace, where objects are constantly being created and dropped.

- Be certain to specify a TEMPORARY TABLESPACE for each user. If one is not specified, Oracle defaults to SYSTEM, which is almost guaranteed to have a negative impact on performance.

Redo Logs

Redo logs, also called *online redo log files*, are critical to Oracle's ability to recover from a failure. Proper configuration of redo logs is critical not only to overall database performance, but also to your ability to recover the database (see Chapter 4, *Preventing Data Loss*). Guidelines include the following:

- Use Oracle's built-in mirroring capability and put multiple sets of redo log files on different disk devices.

- Allocate enough redo log files so that Oracle does not have to wait for a file to complete archiving before it is reused. Oracle requires at least two redo log files, but four or more may be necessary.

- Allocate redo log files that are large enough to prevent too many log switches, but small enough to support good recovery if the current online log file is lost in a failure. With smaller files, you will probably be able to recover all transactions that have been archived, whereas a large log file size exposes the database to the potential for more lost transactions.

- Set the *INIT.ORA* parameter LOG_CHECKPOINT_INTERVAL to a value larger than the size of your redo log files. This will prevent checkpoints until the log file is full (which forces a checkpoint). This parameter is expressed in database blocks.

 Remember that a log switch causes dirty (i.e., updated) buffers to be written to disk from the SGA.

- If you are running Oracle7, consider setting the *INIT.ORA* parameter CHECKPOINT_PROCESS to TRUE. Doing so creates a separate process that performs the checkpoint, rather than the LGWR (Log Writer) process. See Chapter 10, *The Oracle Instance*, for more information.

Archive Log Destination

An often overlooked aspect of configuration is making certain there is enough space available in the archive log destination. If the database is running in archivelog mode when an online redo log file fills, Oracle's ARCH process copies the contents of that file to the directory specified in the *INIT.ORA* parameter ARCHIVE_LOG_DEST. If this destination is too small, ARCH is unable to copy the log file, and once all online log files are full, the entire database stops until the situation is resolved. Experienced DBAs will immediately recognize that this condition is most likely to occur in the middle of the night, just as REM sleep has begun!

Tuning Oracle

Perhaps no single aspect of the DBA's job consumes as much time as tuning. Successful Oracle tuning requires a blend of knowledge and experience, and can be both challenging and frustrating—often at the same time! Entire volumes have been written on Oracle tuning (see the appendix, *Resources for the DBA*), and we cannot hope to cover all aspects of tuning in a single section. Instead, as we mentioned earlier, we will outline for you an approach to tuning that can be applied to a variety of situations.

A Structured Tuning Approach

Successful tuning of an Oracle database requires a careful, disciplined approach. Like overall system configuration, tuning must address the following:

- Hardware and operating system performance
- Oracle instance performance
- Individual transaction (SQL) performance

These should be addressed in sequence, since database performance tuning is not possible until the operating system and hardware have been well tuned, and an individual SQL statement cannot be properly tuned if Oracle is not running efficiently. When tuning any of these areas, there are three distinct steps in the process:

1. Measure current performance.
2. Make appropriate changes.
3. Assess the result.

Some changes to the Oracle instance may result in the need for changes to the operating system environment. For example, allocating additional database buffers may cause the operating system to start paging, which may require additional operating system tuning to eliminate.

The tuning process is almost always an iterative one. That is, after completing the three steps outlined above, the DBA must return to step 1 and repeat the process. This continues until no additional performance gains are possible.

Oracle Instance Tuning

Most performance improvement at the Oracle instance level will be achieved by tuning two areas: memory utilization and disk I/O.

Memory utilization

It should come as no surprise that memory-based operations are much faster (sometimes by thousands of times) than disk operations. As a result, tremendous performance improvements may be achieved by replacing disk I/O with memory access of data. The three primary ways in which this can be done are described in the following list:

Allocate additional DB_BLOCK_BUFFERS

This is probably the single most effective method of improving overall performance, particularly on queries. Additional database buffers allow more data blocks to remain in memory, so the data contained in these blocks can be accessed at memory speed with no need for disk I/O. Buffers are allocated using the *INIT.ORA* parameter DB_BLOCK_BUFFERS, and the value is the number of database block buffers to be allocated. So, if the database block size is 8192, each DB_BLOCK_BUFFER will be 8192 bytes. Note that changes to DB_BLOCK_BUFFERS do not take effect until the next time the database is started.

Be careful not to allocate so many DB_BLOCK_BUFFERS that the operating system begins to page; paging will eliminate any performance gain you may have achieved and will probably have an overall negative effect on performance.

Allocate additional shared pool

The shared pool size is controlled by the *INIT.ORA* parameter SHARED_ POOL_SIZE, which specifies a shared pool size in bytes. The primary contents of the shared pool are the dictionary cache and the shared SQL area. Since the various components of the dictionary cache are automatically allocated by Oracle, any increase in the size of the shared pool results in additional memory for both the dictionary cache and the shared SQL area.

The shared SQL area contains copies of the most recently executed SQL statements, along with associated information like their execution plans. With a larger shared pool, it is more likely that a particular SQL statement has already been parsed and is resident in the shared SQL area, thereby saving the time required to reprocess the statement. This can be of particular value in a transaction processing system, where the same SQL statements are executed multiple times and where speed is a requirement.

Allocate additional log buffer space

The log buffer is used to hold data to be written to the online redo log file. The size of the log buffer is controlled by the *INIT.ORA* parameter LOG_ BUFFER, and the value is expressed in bytes. By allocating additional memory to the log buffer, disk I/O will be reduced, especially when transactions are long or numerous.

Disk I/O

Disk access is the slowest operation on any computer system. As a database system, Oracle relies heavily on disk access for storage of and access to data. Consider a typical SQL statement that updates a row of a table. The following operations take place:

1. The data dictionary is read to get information about the table and row being manipulated.

2. The appropriate index is read to locate the row to be updated.

3. The data block containing the row is read.

4. Rollback information is written to a rollback segment.

5. Update information is written to the online log file.

6. The data block is rewritten.

7. The index block is rewritten.

All these operations potentially require disk I/O, although some may be eliminated by efficient use of memory, as we described in the previous section. By making disk I/O as efficient as possible, overall performance will be enhanced. The basic guidelines for maximizing disk I/O are the following:

- Segregate I/O operations to separate disks wherever possible. In this way, there is no need to wait for one disk operation to finish before another is performed. For example, if both the rollback segment and the log file were on the same disk, the rollback record would be written; then the disk head would need to be moved to another part of the disk where the log file record would be written. This would be very time-consuming.

- Place high-I/O-volume disks on different controllers. Most modern controllers can handle a limited number of concurrent operations, but using as many controllers as possible will eliminate any controller waits and will speed performance.

- Place busy files and tablespaces (e.g., log files, rollback segments, some indexes) on the fastest available disks.

A note about RAID

Recent developments in disk technology have made RAID (Redundant Arrays of Inexpensive Disks) a popular option on many systems. Often, when the term RAID is used, hardware administrators immediately think of RAID level 5 (or RAID-5), which allows multiple disk devices to be combined to form one large device. By allocating one device for the storage of redundant data, a RAID-5 disk array is protected from the failure of any single disk in the array, and is often *hot swappable*, which means that a failing disk can be replaced even as the other drives continue to function, with no need to shut down the system.

RAID-5 is, in fact, very powerful and inexpensive. It is also a technology to be avoided in most cases when configuring your Oracle database! This may seem a harsh statement, but the reality is that although RAID-5 provides good levels of data protection at a low monetary cost, this comes at a very high cost for disk I/O. In particular, write operations on RAID-5 arrays can be orders of magnitude slower than the same operations on a single disk.

A good alternative to the RAID-5 array is the use of RAID level 1, commonly known as disk mirroring. Although more expensive than RAID-5 (one-half of the disks are used for storing redundant data), RAID-1 provides complete data protection with no sacrifice in I/O efficiency.

 RAID-1 requires sufficient hardware resources. In particular, since each write operation actually results in two writes to disk, the load on the controller is doubled compared to non-RAID.

The best RAID performance available today is called RAID-0+1, sometimes called RAID-10. This level of RAID combines mirrored disks (as in RAID-1) with *striping* (RAID-0) of data across multiple drives, which can eliminate any delay while waiting for disk head positioning. While not available from all RAID controllers, RAID-0+1 is well worth considering.

Operating system striping

Many operating systems offer automatic striping of disk sectors across multiple devices. This striping permits disk I/O to continue sequentially without a delay for head positioning. While this technique provides better performance than that achieved on a single disk, it has a disadvantage: combining disks into a single striped unit means that the DBA is no longer able to control the location of individual files on separate devices. If you can only have a few large disk devices on your system, you should consider operating system striping, but multiple devices or multiple RAID-0+1 arrays will usually yield better performance from Oracle.

Oracle striping

As the DBA, you can achieve results similar to operating system striping by carefully allocating datafiles to individual devices or RAID-0+1 arrays. For example, to set up Oracle striping across four disks, do the following:

*   Create a tablespace with four datafiles, each located on a different device.

*   Create objects in the tablespace, specifying MINEXTENTS 4. Oracle will allocate the four extents on the four datafiles, thereby implementing striping. This action is not automatic; it can be accomplished by using the ALTER TABLE ... ALOCATE EXTENT command.

The Oracle striping technique is very powerful, especially when combined with Parallel Query, which will allow query processing by multiple CPUs.

SQL Tuning

Suppose that the host server and operating system are running smoothly at your site, and you have configured and tuned Oracle to run at the peak of perfection, but performance on your critical application is still poor. Unfortunately, this is not an uncommon occurrence. The solution is to tune the application by examining and tuning the SQL statements being executed.

SQL tuning is a subject that deserves a book of its own. In fact, there are several good books on the market that address tuning in much more detail than is available here. We urge you to check the sources listed in the appendix, *Resources for the DBA*. In this section, we'll offer some brief advice and guidelines for tuning your SQL statements.

Query processing

Chapter 8, *Query Optimization*, describes how Oracle creates a plan for a particular SQL statement. Oracle currently uses one of two methods for determining how to execute a SQL statement:

Rule-based method
> Applies a standard, inflexible (but often efficient) set of rules to the statement

Cost-based method
> Considers the available statistical information about the objects referenced by a SQL statement (along with available indexes) and creates a plan based on those statistics

The keys to tuning a SQL statement are understanding how the Oracle query optimizers work and knowing how to change Oracle's behavior so it will process the statement more efficiently.

Of course, before you can tune a SQL statement, you must know what it is doing and how. There are many tools on the market today that will help with this task, and one of the most useful (if not the flashiest) is the EXPLAIN PLAN command available in SQL*Plus. By creating a plan table (usually known as PLAN_TABLE) and examining the result of an EXPLAIN PLAN statement, you'll easily see how Oracle executes a particular statement. For example, the SQL statement:

```
SELECT ename,loc,sal,hiredate
FROM    scott.emp, scott.dept
WHERE   emp.deptno=dept.deptno;
```

can be explained with the following command:

```
EXPLAIN PLAN SET STATEMENT_ID='DEMO' FOR
SELECT ename,loc,sal,hiredate
FROM    scott.emp, scott.dept
WHERE   emp.deptno=dept.deptno;
```

The results stored in PLAN_TABLE can be selected using a simple query:

```
SELECT LPAD(' ',2*level) || operation || '' || options || ' '||
       object_name EXPLAIN_PLAN
FROM plan_table
CONNECT BY PRIOR id = parent_id
START WITH id=1
```

and will look like this:

```
EXPLAIN_PLAN
-------------------------------
NESTED LOOPS
  TABLE ACCESSFULL DEPT
  TABLE ACCESSFULL EMP
```

This plan shows that both the DEPT and EMP tables will be accessed using a full table scan. This is fine for two small tables like EMP and DEPT; in fact, we want them to be full table scans, because the tables will be cached in memory and no disk I/O will be required (after the first execution, at least). However, if the tables were large, this query could run for a long time, and so we would want to change the way this query is performed.

There are three basic ways to modify the behavior of Oracle's query optimizer:

- Provide one or more indexes to be used in executing the query.
- Rewrite the SQL to use a more efficient method.
- Provide direction to the query optimizer in the form of hints.

If we try the first option and add an index on EMP(deptno), the plan will change as follows:

```
EXPLAIN_PLAN
---------------------------------------------
  NESTED LOOPS
    TABLE ACCESSFULL DEPT
    TABLE ACCESSBY ROWID EMP
      INDEXRANGE SCAN EMPDEPT_IX
```

You can now see that Oracle will use the index to retrieve rows from EMP via the ROWID, which was obtained from the newly created index, and a full table scan is no longer necessary.

There is often more than one way to perform a particular function using SQL, and it is good programming practice to try several methods (with appropriate benchmarking) before settling on the correct SQL statement to use. Chapter 8, *Query Optimization*, provides more detailed information on SQL tuning.

Other Useful Tuning Features

Oracle has continued to improve its database product by adding new features that help boost performance. It is important to check the *Release Notes* on even minor upgrades to Oracle, since new performance features are often included. Some of the features and facilities you might find useful are listed in this section.

Partitioned tables

Partitioned tables, which are available beginning with Oracle8, allow a table to be created across multiple subtables, each of which holds a particular subset of the table data. For example, a table could be partitioned by year, with all data from 1998 in one partition, all 1999 data in another, and so on. Partitioning is particularly useful for large tables, since queries involving only an identifiable subset of data can operate on the data in the appropriate partitions without accessing other partitions. For example, updating 1999 records would only require Oracle to perform I/O operations on the 1999 partition of the table. Partitioning is specified in the CREATE TABLE statement. In order to use this feature, you must:

- Identify the data field that will define the partition (for example, sales_year).

- Specify the ranges of values in the CREATE TABLE ... PARTITION BY RANGE clause.

- Specify a different tablespace (for best performance, place each on a separate disk) for each partition of the table. Note that separate tablespaces are not required, but this practice allows a partition of the table to be taken offline while maintaining access to the balance of the table.

Partitioned tables should usually be accompanied by a corresponding partitioned index, as follows:

- Use the LOCAL keyword in the CREATE INDEX command to tell Oracle to create a separate index for each partition of the indexed table.

- Use the GLOBAL keyword in the CREATE INDEX command to tell Oracle to create a single index using values that may not correspond to the partitioning of the indexed tables. GLOBAL indexes may also be partitioned.

Index-only tables

In some cases, all the data that would normally be stored in a table can be stored in an index, and the table is not necessary. An index-only table, available starting with Oracle8, keeps the data sorted according to the primary key column. There are some limitations to this type of object:

- Since the data is not stored in a table, there are no ROWIDs available.

- A primary key must be defined for the table.

- No additional indexes can be created; only the primary key may be indexed.

An index-only table is created by using the ORGANIZATION INDEX clause of the CREATE TABLE command.

Bitmap indexes

Bitmap indexes can yield greatly improved performance when the data being indexed has low cardinality—that is, if there are relatively few distinct values for the indexed column. An example of a good candidate for a bitmap index would be GENDER, which would have values of "M" or "F". A poor candidate for a bitmap index would be SALES_AMOUNT, which is likely to have a different value for almost every row.

Creating a bitmap index is similar to creating a standard index; you include the keyword BITMAP in the CREATE INDEX statement. For example, to create a bitmap index on the GENDER column of an EMPLOYEE_MASTER table, you'd specify the following statement:

```
CREATE BITMAP INDEX empmast_ix ON employee_master(gender);
```

Temporary tablespaces

Oracle7 introduced the concept of temporary tablespaces, which are used exclusively for Oracle's sort segments. By eliminating serialization of space management operations involved in the allocation and deallocation of sort space, all operations that use sorts can benefit from improved performance when sorts are too large to fit in memory. These performance gains are particularly significant when running Oracle Parallel Server.

A temporary tablespace can be used only for sort segments; no permanent objects may be created in a temporary tablespace.

To create a temporary tablespace, use the keyword TEMPORARY in the CREATE TABLESPACE statement. For example, the following statement will create a temporary tablespace called TEMP:

```
CREATE TABLESPACE TEMP
DATAFILE '/disk99/oracle/oradata/TEST/temp01.dbf' SIZE 50M
DEFAULT STORAGE (INITIAL 64K NEXT 64K MAXEXTENTS UNLIMITED)
TEMPORARY;
```

An existing non-temporary tablespace may be converted to a temporary tablespace by using the SQL statement if it contains no permanent objects:

```
ALTER TABLESPACE tablespace TEMPORARY;
```

Unrecoverable operations

Beginning with Oracle 7.2, it has been possible to create a table or index without writing redo log records. This option provides better performance, since significantly less I/O is required. To take advantage of this feature, specify either UNRECOVERABLE (Oracle7 syntax) or NOLOGGING (Oracle8 syntax) in the object creation statement. For example, suppose that you are moving data from another database using a database link and that you use the statement:

```
INSERT INTO newtable
SELECT * from oldtable@oldlink;
```

This method would certainly work, but redo log records would be created for each insert, which could be costly. The same task could be accomplished with the following statement:

```
CREATE TABLE newtable AS
SELECT * from oldtable@oldlink
NOLOGGING;
```

The NOLOGGING option is particularly useful when rebuilding indexes. The inclusion of the NOLOGGING keyword can cut substantial time from index creation. The SQL statement would look similar to this:

```
CREATE INDEX indexname ON table(column)
NOLOGGING;
```

Note, however, that if you experience a system failure at some point after an unrecoverable statement has completed, you will be unable to recover the transactions using the roll forward mechanism. You must recognize that a system failure has occurred and rerun the statement.

4

Preventing Data Loss

Once the database is operational, your most important responsibility is to ensure the availability of the data in that database. You need to develop a backup and recovery plan in advance. This chapter describes the various situations you may encounter and introduces the basic tools you can use to recover your data. Chapter 16, *Tools and Utilities*, gives the detailed syntax for using the tools described in this section.

Types of Backups

The time to plan for a recovery is before you need to recover data. There are several ways in which your data can be backed up, and each way has its limitations. No two installations will have the same requirements, nor will they necessarily back up data in the same way. In Table 4-1, we list the most common scenarios and show the appropriate backup strategies.

Table 4-1. Common Backup and Recovery Scenarios

If You Need to...	Use This Mechanism
Recover up to the point of failure	Hot backups Cold backups with archivelog mode
Recover individual tables	Exports Tablespace point-in-time recovery
Recover on a different operating system	Exports
Create a point-in-time view of the data for historical records	Exports Cold backups

Table 4-1. Common Backup and Recovery Scenarios (continued)

If You Need to...	Use This Mechanism
Recover the database to a point prior to a failure	Hot backups Cold backups with or without archivelog mode Exports
Not have downtime for backups	Hot backups Exports

Physical Backups

A physical backup of the database is one in which the datafiles are backed up. Most installations copy the datafiles to tape, but copies can be made to disk or to another computer system. Unless otherwise noted, we'll assume in our discussion that the datafiles have been copied to tape.

Benefits

With physical backups, the recovery process is usually faster than with logical backups, since you only need to restore files from the tape backup.

Limitations

You can usually only restore to a computer system that's running the same operating system as the one from which the backups were made. There may also be limitations on operating system and Oracle release levels.

The backup process doesn't take into account the database objects that are stored within the database. The granularity of the recovery in this case is the entire database.

 Some techniques allow individual objects to be recovered from a physical backup (these are discussed in later sections). However, these techniques are time consuming, require additional disk space, and need to be practiced before they are put into operation.

Logical Backups

A logical backup is one in which individual database objects are backed up. The information is stored in a way that allows objects to be created and data inserted into tables.

Benefits

With logical backups, individual objects can be recovered separately. You can usually restore to different computer systems, operating systems, and release levels.

Limitations

With logical backups, as objects are being created and rows inserted through the SQL buffer, indexes have to be rebuilt as well. Since individual tables can be recreated through these backups, you need to be careful to ensure that referential integrity rules are maintained.

Archivelog Mode

Archivelog is an optional mode for the database. You can set it with the *INIT.ORA* parameter ARCHIVELOG or in the ALTER DATABASE statement. In this mode, the ARCH background process copies the contents of each redo log to an archive file at the time of a log switch. Be sure to allocate enough redo logs so that ARCH has sufficient time to copy the redo log to the archive file before the redo log is reused. Archivelog mode comes at a cost of increased overhead. The ARCH process reads from the most recently used redo log at the same time that the LGWR process is writing to the current redo log.

Some Oracle manuals use the term *media recovery enabled* as a synonym for archivelog mode.

Benefits

The contents of the archive files are used in conjunction with a physical backup to roll the database forward during recovery.

Limitations

If the database is in archivelog mode and the ARCH process cannot copy the redo logs to the archive files, the database will hang until ARCH is successful.

Many installations use a user-written daemon process to track the generation of archive files. As they are created, they are moved off the computer to secondary storage. This helps ensure availability of the archive files if they are needed for database recovery after a hardware failure.

Incremental Backups

An incremental backup makes a copy only of what has changed since the last backup. With physical backups, this means either the datafiles or the individual data blocks that have changed. With logical backups, this means the objects that have been changed.

Benefits

With incremental backups, the amount of tape or disk storage is less than that needed for a full backup.

Limitations

There are several limitations on performing incremental backups:

- If you have performed a full backup followed by one or more incremental backups, you will have to restore using all of the backups.

- Depending upon the specific backup utility you use, there may be restrictions on the order in which backups are restored.

- If you are missing a backup, you may have holes or inconsistencies in your data.

Database Backup

This section describes the available backup techniques you can use to back up your database.

Cold Backup

A *cold backup* (also known as an *offline backup*) is a physical backup that is taken when the database is not operational—it is "cold." A complete cold backup of the database, including the control files and redo logs, can be used to recreate the database to the time of the cold backup.

Benefits

There are two major benefits of performing cold backups:

- A cold backup is the easiest mechanism for performing backups. Any mechanism for creating a copy of the datafiles will work.

- A cold backup can be used with the database in either archivelog or noarchivelog mode.

Limitations

For cold backups, the database must be down for the time it takes to back up the entire database. For sites that have an availability requirement, this may not be viable. Unless you are in archivelog mode, the entire database must be backed up at the same time and restored as a whole. Oracle refers to this operation as a *full backup*.

In our discussion, the assumption is generally that you want to recover the entire database. However, it is possible to recover a subset of the tablespaces. A procedure for doing this is provided in the following sections.

Hot Backup

A *hot backup* (also known as an *online backup*) is a physical backup that is taken when the database is operational—that is, "hot." Oracle provides specific support for hot backups through archivelog mode and the ALTER TABLESPACE BEGIN/ END BACKUP commands. Tablespaces are placed into backup mode, backed up, then taken out of backup mode. Oracle performs a checkpoint of all datafiles in a tablespace when a tablespace is placed into backup mode, and records the checkpoint number in the header of all datafiles.

Before you back up a datafile, its tablespace must be placed in backup mode with the command:

```
ALTER TABLESPACE BEGIN BACKUP
```

At this point, the database marks the datafile(s) as being in backup mode and starts writing information to the redo log at the block level, rather than at the byte level. You may then back up the datafile using any mechanism you choose. Once the datafile has been backed up, you issue the command:

```
ALTER TABLESPACE END BACKUP
```

This tells the database to resume normal operation.

When performing hot backups, it is imperative that you follow the procedure we describe here. Standard operating system backups of the database files while the tablespace is not in backup mode will *not* work.

Benefits

Hot backups are the most flexible of the backup facilities. The database does not have to be down during the backup, and you do not have to back up all the datafiles at one time. Individual datafiles can even be backed up on different days. Oracle refers to this type of backup as a *partial backup*.

Limitations

You must be in archivelog mode to perform a hot backup.

EXPort/IMPort

EXP (Export) is an Oracle utility that creates a logical backup of the database. IMP (Import) is the corresponding utility that reads the logical backup and inserts the data into the database. The powerful Export/Import facility is the most mature of the various mechanisms supported by Oracle for performing backups, and it supplies unique benefits. However, some DBAs see it as an obsolete mechanism for performing backups because of its various limitations.

Benefits

The Export/Import facility was designed to move table data in and out of Oracle in various ways. You may export or import at the table, user, or database level.

Limitations

Largely because Export/Import is the most mature of the backup facilities, it also has the most serious restrictions:

- The size of the export file may be limited by operating system restrictions (the limit is typically 2GB in many Unix systems).

- You cannot explicitly export or import objects other than tables. However, these objects are processed automatically when doing user or full database exports or imports.

- After a table is imported, its indexes must be rebuilt. (Import can do this automatically.)

- Each table exported is a separate transaction. In order to get a consistent backup, you need to specify the CONSISTENT=Y parameter in the control file. However, for large or active databases, you then run the risk of getting a "snapshot too old" error message.

Using incremental exports

Export has the ability to perform three levels of exports: full, cumulative, and incremental. This is similar to the approach used by operating system backup utilities. You specify which level you are selecting via the INCTYPE parameter. See Chapter 16, *Tools and Utilities*, for more information on how to specify export parameters.

Oracle has announced that it is dropping support for incremental and cumulative exports effective December 31, 1999.

To select the type of export, specify one of the following keywords as the value of INCTYPE:

FULL
    Processes all objects in the database.

CUMULATIVE
    Processes all objects modified since the last cumulative or full export.

INCREMENTAL
    Processes all objects modified since the last export.

In cumulative and incremental exports, the entire table is exported even if only one row has changed. In Oracle8, individual partitions in a partitioned table can be separately exported.

Direct path versus conventional path

The *conventional path export* method, which is the Export default, uses the standard SQL buffer to fetch rows. It simply issues a SELECT * FROM TABLE to retrieve all the rows. The *direct path export* method, on the other hand, bypasses the normal processing and retrieves the data blocks directly into its own buffer. In most cases, the direct path export is noticeably faster than the conventional path export. Other than a notation in the export file, there are no differences in the file generated by these two methods.

Since the direct path export bypasses the SQL buffer, character set translation is not performed. The user process performing the export must have the same character set specified as the database. This limitation does not apply to the import.

In Oracle8 Release 8.0, tables with large objects (LOBs) cannot be processed using the direct path export method.

Using the EXP tables

The following data dictionary views can be used to identify which export file is required to restore a given table. The information is stored if the Export RECORD parameter is set to Y. See Chapter 16, *Tools and Utilities*, for more details on specifying export parameters.

DBA_EXP_FILES
> This view has one row for each successful export since (and including) the last full export.

DBA_EXP_OBJECTS
> This view has one row for each exported object in the database. It specifies the last export version that contained that object.

DBA_EXP_VERSION
> This view has one row and one column, EXP_VERSION, which contains the last successful export.

By joining DBA_EXP_OBJECTS and DBA_EXP_FILES, you can locate the export file necessary to restore a given table. These data dictionary views are updated every time an export occurs. If you need historical information beyond the last time an object was exported, copy these data dictionary views into a permanent table.

Other uses for Export

Because the Export utility provides a logical backup of the database, it can be used to move data in and out of the database. As a DBA, you can use Export/ Import as follows:

- To move data between operating systems or versions of Oracle. If you do move data between computer systems, use a binary mode file copy rather than a record-based copy (see Chapter 16 for details).

- To assist in changing some of the storage attributes of a table. Once you have exported a table, you can drop it, recreate it with different storage parameters, or even place it in a new tablespace and then reimport the table. If you are doing this, make sure that you specify IGNORE=Y in the Import control file.

- To change the owner of the table. Any export file written by a non-DBA user can be imported by any other user. The userid specified when invoking Import will become the owner of the objects. If the export was performed by a DBA, then the import can only be performed by a DBA, but the FROM-OWNER and TOOWNER clauses can be used to change the owner of the objects.

The Export/Import facility is not the only way to accomplish these tasks; you can use a series of SQL statements and SQL*Net to perform all of these actions. However, in many cases, using Export/Import is easiest, and requires less storage within the database.

Database Recovery

The whole purpose of backups is to be able to recover the database. This section discusses the various reasons why you may need to perform a recovery and provides an overview of the new tablespace point-in-time recovery process.

Recovery Scenarios

The following sections briefly describe how you can recover from different types of failure.

System failure

A system failure means that the entire system is unavailable. A failure of this kind may be the result of either a site outage (caused by fire or natural disaster) or a total failure of the server.

 It is standard practice to have at least two copies of your backup tapes, with one copy stored at a different location. This way, you not only do not have a single point of failure if the tape containing your archive file breaks, but you also are able to get at your tapes in the event of a disaster. Even storing a single copy of your tapes in a fireproof vault will not work if you cannot cross a police line after an explosion.

In the case of a system failure, you have three options:

- Recover the entire database from a cold backup.
- Recover the entire database from hot or cold backups and apply as many archive files as you have available.
- Recover the entire database from exports using full, cumulative, and incremental exports.

Disk failure

A disk failure is the most common form of database failure. With the cost of RAID solutions (including mirroring and parity solutions such as RAID-1 and RAID-5) coming down, most sites have moved to a hardware solution to prevent a single disk failure from impacting the database. If your site does not use these solutions, then at some point in your career you will have to perform a recovery from a disk failure.

We recommend multiple control files, separate disks for archive files, and mirroring redo logs either with redo log groups or operating system mirroring. With mirrored redo logs and multiple control files on separate disks, no single disk failure will cause a loss of the database. If you have only one control file or only one redo member per group, then losing the disk containing the control file or the active redo log would be catastrophic to the database. Placing archive files on a separate disk from the redo logs (if mirroring is not used) at least ensures that you can recover the database up to the point of the last archive file.

In the case of a disk failure, you have the following options:

- Restore the datafile to a new disk, rename it using the ALTER DATABASE RENAME DATAFILE command, and recover the file using archive files and online redo logs.

- If you are not running in archivelog mode, you can still use the tablespace point-in-time recovery procedure from a cold backup.

- Recover the entire database using a cold backup.

- Place the tablespace containing the missing datafiles offline using the ALTER TABLESPACE OFFLINE TEMPORARY command; then drop the tablespace. Recreate the tablespace and restore the contents from previous exports.

- Recover the entire database from exports using full, cumulative, and incremental exports.

Database corruption

With data corruption, the internal structure of the database is inconsistent. Data corruption is usually caused by a hardware failure or an anomaly in the Oracle software. This will manifest itself in any number of Oracle error messages. Most likely you will be able to identify the actual database block that is corrupt. Your options for recovery depend on the kind of information stored in that location:

Table data
> You should be able to salvage rows from blocks that are not corrupt by copying them over to another table and then dropping the table. It may be necessary to exclude rows using unique keys or ROWIDs. Alternately, you may have to perform datafile or database recovery.

Index
> You can drop and recreate the index.

Data dictionary

You will have to either recover the SYSTEM tablespace using media recovery or recreate the database and recover using full, cumulative, and incremental exports.

Rollback segments

If there are uncommitted transactions, you will have to perform datafile or tablespace recovery.

Data corruption

Data corruption occurs when the structure of the database is intact but the data is not. This situation is caused by incorrect or accidental SQL statements being executed and committed. In this case, you have the following options:

- Restore the incorrect table or tables from the most recent export. Take care to ensure that referential integrity is maintained.

- Restore the tablespace (in Oracle8), using the tablespace point-in-time recovery process, to just prior to the data corruption. Of course, changes to any other tables in that tablespace made after the recovery point will be lost.

- Recover the entire database to a time prior to the data corruption, using either hot or cold backups.

Tablespace Point-in-Time Recovery

Tablespace point-in-time recovery is a new feature implemented with Oracle8. With tablespace point-in-time recovery, you are able to recover one or more tablespaces to a point in the past, independent of the other tablespaces. The tablespaces to be restored are referred to as the *recovery set*. However, note that the SYSTEM tablespace cannot be recovered using tablespace point-in-time recovery.

Overview of the process

To perform tablespace point-in-time recovery, follow these steps. Please refer to the *Oracle8 Backup and Recovery Guide* for a more detailed set of directions.

1. Identify any objects in the original database that may be impacted by the tablespace point-in-time recovery. This will include any dependent objects, tables with referential integrity, and indexes and objects created after the point-in-time recovery time. The various constraints will have to be removed prior to tablespace point-in-time recovery.

2. Create a second, or clone, database. Using hot or cold backups, restore the datafiles to the clone database. Normally, you will only need the datafiles corresponding to the SYSTEM tablespace, the rollback segments, any temporary

tablespaces, and the tablespace containing the tables to be recovered. If necessary, use archive files to roll forward the tablespaces to the desired point.

3. Mount the clone database using the ALTER DATABASE MOUNT CLONE DATABASE command.

4. Use the Export utility to export metadata about the objects in the tablespaces to be recovered.

5. Alter the original database to rename the datafiles to the recovered tablespace datafiles.

6. Input this special export. All objects in the tablespaces are effectively dropped and recreated.

7. Delete the remaining datafiles in the clone database.

Benefits

With tablespace point-in-time recovery, you have the ability to recover specific tables to a previous point without having to roll back the entire database. This form of recovery is likely to take less time than recovering the entire database to the specific point or recovering a large table from exports.

Limitations

As implied by the name tablespace point-in-time recovery, all tables in the tablespace will be recovered—you cannot recover just one table. Therefore, you have to have sufficient disk space and memory to run the original and clone databases. Any objects in the recovered tablespaces created after the point-in-time recovery time will be dropped.

Data dictionary views

The following data dictionary views are used by the tablespace point-in-time recovery facility:

TS_PITR_CHECK

Identifies objects that will be impacted by the tablespace point-in-time recovery. As long as any items are included in this view, tablespace point-in-time recovery will fail. To query the view, use the following:

```
SELECT * FROM SYS.TS_PITR_CHECK
WHERE (ts1_name IN recovery_set AND ts2_name NOT IN recovery_set) OR
      (ts1_name NOT IN recovery_set AND ts2_name IN recovery_set);
```

TS_PITR_OBJECTS_TO_BE_DROPPED

Lists objects created after the tablespace point-in-time recovery time. These objects will be dropped as part of the recovery process. You must make a copy of these objects prior to completing tablespace point-in-time recovery. If you don't, the information in them will be lost.

Automated Utilities

This section introduces the various automated backup and recovery utilities available to Oracle DBAs.

Oracle Recovery Manager

The Oracle Recovery Manager (RMAN) is provided by Oracle for use with an Oracle8 database. Using a catalog located in a different database, RMAN automates the processes of performing hot and cold backups and moving archive files to secondary storage. RMAN also supports the creation of incremental hot backups. RMAN works with many of the commercial media management systems; contact Oracle Corporation for a complete list of third-party vendors that are supported.

Oracle Enterprise Backup Utility

The Oracle Enterprise Backup Utility (EBU) is provided by Oracle for use with an Oracle7 database. Using a catalog located in a different database, EBU automates the processes of performing hot and cold backups and moving archive files to secondary storage. EBU works with many of the commercial media management systems; contact Oracle Corporation for a complete list of third-party vendors that are supported.

Third-Party Utilities

In addition to RMAN and EBU, there are a number of third-party operating system backup vendors that provide automated utilities for performing Oracle database backup and recovery. Contact your backup vendor to see if they have an Oracle backup module.

 Some third-party vendors support incremental hot backups. However, Oracle Corporation does not support incremental hot backups outside the RMAN environment.

Practice Scenarios

This section provides complete scenarios for testing recovery using exports and hot and cold backups. It is important that you use these, or other scenarios you develop, to test your backup strategy. Such scenarios not only fully exercise your backup media and hardware, but also give you practice performing the recovery. And don't worry if you fail the first time; most people do.

Export/Import

The following scenarios are designed to allow you to gain experience and comfort with the Export and Import utilities. They are presented in order of increasing complexity.

1. Take a full export of your database.

2. Drop a table and then import it.

3. Drop a user and then import the user.

4. Perform a full import of the database.

5. Drop a table and then use the data dictionary to determine whether to import using the full or incremental export.

6. Perform a full import of the database using the full and incremental exports.

Hot or Cold Backups

The following scenarios are designed to allow you to gain experience and comfort recreating the database from backups. They are presented in order of increasing complexity.

1. Recover the database from a full cold backup:

   a. Recover a single datafile.

   b. Recover the entire database.

2. Put the database in archivelog mode and then perform a hot backup:

   a. Create a table in a tablespace with only one datafile. Then insert one or more rows.

   b. Perform enough ALTER SYSTEM SWITCH LOGFILE commands to cycle through all redo logs.

   c. Shut down the instance (optional).

   d. Delete the datafile containing the created table.

   e. Restore the datafile from the hot backup.

   f. Perform media recovery on the datafile. Then verify that the database requested at least one archive file.

   g. Verify that the table was recreated and has all the information required.

3. If you have a backup tool that performs incremental hot backups (e.g., some third-party tools and Oracle8 Recovery Manager), do the following:

    a. Take a hot backup.

    b. Create a table; then insert one or more rows. Place the table in a tablespace with only one datafile.

    c. Perform an incremental backup. Then verify that portions of the datafile were backed up.

    d. Perform enough ALTER SYSTEM SWITCH LOGFILE commands to cycle through all redo logs.

    e. Stop the database (optional).

    f. Delete the datafile containing the created table.

    g. Use your restore utility to restore the table. Then verify not only that the original hot backup was restored, but also that the incremental backup was restored.

    h. Perform media recovery. Then verify that at least one archive file is required.

    i. Verify that the table was recreated and has all the information required.

4. Test tablespace point-in-time recovery by doing the following:

    a. Take a hot backup.

    b. Create a table; then insert one or more rows. Place the table in a tablespace with only one datafile.

    c. Create an index on the table in another tablespace that will not be recovered.

    d. Take note of the time for tablespace point-in-time recovery.

    e. Create another table. Then insert more rows in the first table.

    f. Use the tablespace point-in-time recovery process to create a clone database as of the time noted in step d.

    g. Note that the second table is listed in the TS_PITR_OBJECTS_TO_BE DROPPED data dictionary view.

    h. Note that the index created in step c is listed in the TS_PITR_CHECK data dictionary view.

    i. Complete the tablespace point-in-time recovery.

    j. Verify that the second table and the rows added in step e are no longer in the database.

Other Techniques

There are many ways to verify that your table has been correctly restored. If the table is small enough, simple visual inspection may be sufficient. Other techniques may include the following:

- Compute the sum or average of a numeric column.
- Generate a report before and after and use operating system tools to compare the results.
- Create a copy of the table before the recovery test.
- Compare the two tables using the MINUS operator.

5

Oracle Networking

Few, if any, concepts are as important to the proper administration of an Oracle database as the concept of networking. *Connectivity*—the ability to make connections between clients and databases, as well as between databases—has been a key component of Oracle for over a decade. While some of the terminology and technology has changed, the need for a clear understanding of networking and how it functions with the Oracle framework is at least as critical today as it was when *client/server* was a brand new buzzword.

This chapter discusses networking and how it relates to Oracle. It also shows you the tools Oracle provides for managing its networking components and lays out the networking capabilities of the modern Oracle database.

Oracle Network Architecture

The complexity of Oracle networking arises to some extent from its basic simplicity. Although that statement appears to contradict itself, it points out a basic characteristic of the Oracle networking architecture: it is a simple structure that can be used to implement complex solutions. Oracle's networking architecture is simple because it is designed to allow any Oracle product, running on any supported platform, to "talk" to any other Oracle product without regard for network topologies or protocols. Figure 5-1 shows several Oracle databases and clients connected via a "cloud" with no network identification.

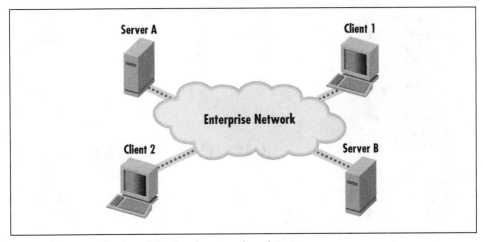

Figure 5-1. A simple view of the Oracle network architecture

Because Oracle is designed to run on almost any network, using almost any accepted protocol, the configuration of the Oracle components that interface with the network can be very complex, which often leads to frustration when the DBA is not sure where to turn in order to solve a problem. This is because Oracle often hides its underlying complexity. For example, the simple connection shown in Figure 5-1 could, in reality, look more like the more complex connection shown in Figure 5-2, where the physical and logical components of the network can be seen. That figure shows a client and server connected using TCP/IP, 10BaseT, and token ring with routers.

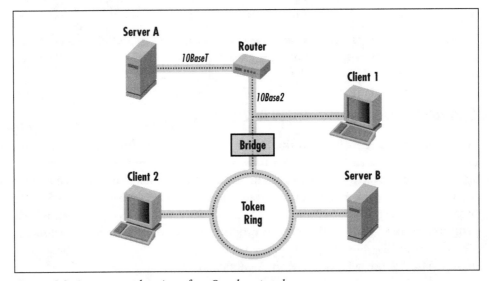

Figure 5-2. A more complex view of an Oracle network

SQL*Net and Net8

Oracle achieves its goal of transparent connectivity between and among its products through the use of a product called SQL*Net.

 With the introduction of Oracle8, SQL*Net has been renamed Net8. However, except for some added functionality, Net8 and SQL*Net are the same product; thus, when we refer to SQL*Net, we will mean both SQL*Net and Net8 unless otherwise noted.

SQL*Net functionality

Simply put, SQL*Net provides all the facilities required for an Oracle client (that is, a network machine running a tool that will connect to the Oracle database) to connect to an Oracle database, to maintain that connection, and to process transactions on the database. This is done without regard for location (*location transparency*), network protocol (*network transparency*), host operating system, or any other factor. SQL*Net also supports the complexities of distributed transactions, and so is able to:

- Determine the location of each server involved in a transaction

- Resolve any issues arising from character set differences on the participating nodes

- Create and maintain connections to each required node, regardless of network attributes

- Handle any network disconnects or other errors

How SQL*Net works

SQL*Net is designed to run on top of an existing network protocol, and is therefore independent of the particular hardware and software being used to implement a network. As long as SQL*Net on both sides of the connection is using the same basic protocol (e.g., TCP/IP, LU6.2 or IPX), it won't matter to Oracle how the underlying network transports the information. Figure 5-3 shows the relationship between SQL*Net and the underlying network; it illustrates Oracle, SQL*Net, TCP/IP, and physical transport on both sides.

The key here is that connectivity to and from the Oracle database and tools is achieved by using SQL*Net, which presents a consistent interface to Oracle. By utilizing an appropriate protocol adapter (in this case, TCP/IP) on each side, SQL*Net is able to conform to the network protocol in use. SQL*Net creates data packets using the native network protocol, and it does not matter how the network is

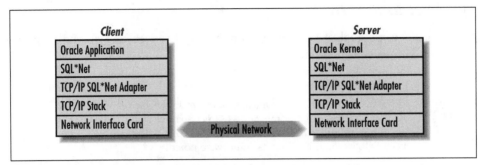

Figure 5-3. Relationship between SQL*Net and the underlying network

implemented to actually carry the SQL*Net packets. In fact, SQL*Net does not even know if a network exists, and it is possible to use SQL*Net without any network at all by making an internal connection between a client process and a server running on the same machine.

SQL*Net protocol adapters are available to support a variety of network protocols, including:

TCP/IP

Probably the most common universal protocol, TCP/IP originated on Unix systems but is now widely supported by a variety of operating systems and network hardware.

SPX/IPX

This protocol was developed by Novell for use in Netware and is available on a variety of operating systems.

LU6.2

This protocol was developed by IBM and is widely used in its SNA (System Network Architecture) strategy.

Named pipes

This protocol is used by Microsoft for Windows networking.

When Oracle is installed, both SQL*Net and one or more supported protocol adapters must be installed. Note that not all protocols are supported on every host operating system. For example, Oracle for Windows NT does not provide a protocol adapter for LU6.2, since this is not a protocol normally supported in a Windows environment.

Oracle services

SQL*Net connections to Oracle databases are made through *services*, which are actually processes running on the Oracle Server host machine. Each Oracle server maintains one or more listener processes, which are used to monitor the network for incoming connection requests. When such a request is received, the listener process is responsible for determining which Oracle instance the incoming request is seeking a connection with, and establishing an appropriate server process for that connection. The server process may be established as a dedicated process, or may use the Multi-Threaded Server, depending on how the Oracle instance is configured. For more information, see Chapter 10, *The Oracle Instance*.

In order to identify the Oracle instance to connect with, the SQL*Net connection request specifies the name of a service (sometimes called a *database alias*), which in turn corresponds to a particular Oracle instance on a specific host machine. The relationships between service names and specific instances and hosts are typically maintained in the file *tnsnames.ora* (discussed in more detail later in this chapter). For example, the service name "test" might actually refer to an Oracle database instance with an SID of TST23, which is accessible via TCP/IP at address 123. 234.210.001 using port 1526. It is certainly simpler to refer to "test"!

Advanced Networking Option

In addition to the standard functionality provided by SQL*Net and Net8, Oracle now offers the Advanced Networking Option (ANO) as an extra-cost option. This option provides additional security-related functionality to Oracle connectivity. Among the capabilities of the Advanced Networking Option are:

- Network security
- Single sign-on
- DCE integration

Network security

Improved network security is provided through the following security features:

Encryption

The transformation of data so that it is unreadable by anyone without a (secret) decryption key. Encryption ensures the confidentiality of information by keeping its content hidden from anyone for whom it is not intended, even those who can see the encrypted data. The Advanced Networking Option also utilizes public key encryption. In this scheme, each person receives a pair of keys: a public key and a private key.

Each person's public key is published, while the private key is confidential. Messages encrypted with a public key can only be decrypted with the corresponding private key. Messages encrypted with a private key can only be decrypted with the corresponding public key. Keys may not be deduced from each other. The sender and receiver of an encrypted message do not share confidential information, since all communications involve only public keys. Private keys are neither transmitted nor shared.

Digital signature

A non-forgeable way of authenticating the sender of a message that supports non-repudiation of messages. Use of a digital signature ensures that only the purported sender of a message could actually have sent the message. The sender cannot later claim that someone impersonated her or him.

Digital certificate

A mechanism used to establish confidence in the identity associated with a public key by incorporating public keys. A digital certificate is a binding of a public key to a user by a trusted third party known as a Certificate Authority (CA). The public key and user identity, together with other information such as the certificate expiration date, are digitally signed by the CA. CAs serve as electronic notaries, attesting to the identity of users and the validity of their public keys.

Single sign-on

The single sign-on feature allows users to access multiple accounts and applications with a single password. This feature eliminates the need for multiple passwords for users and simplifies management of user accounts and passwords for system administrators. Authentication adapters provide centralized, secure authentication services that confirm the identity of users, clients, and servers in distributed environments. Network authentication services also can provide the benefit of single sign-on for users. The following authentication adapters are supported:

- Kerberos
- CyberSAFE
- SecurID
- Biometric (Identix)

DCE integration

Distributed Computing Environment (DCE) integration enables users to transparently use Oracle tools and applications to access Oracle servers in a DCE environment. The Oracle DCE integration product consists of two major components:

- DCE communications/security adapter
- DCE CDS (cell directory service) naming adapter

The DCE communications/security adapter provides:

Authenticated remote procedure call (RPC)

RPC is the transport mechanism that enables multivendor interoperability for DCE integration. RPC also uses additional DCE services, including directory and security services, to provide location transparency and secure distributed computing.

Integrated security

> DCE integration works with the DCE security service to provide security within DCE cells. It enables a user logged onto DCE to securely access any Oracle application without specifying a username or password. This function is referred to as *external authentication* to the database. In addition, clients and servers not running DCE authentication services can interoperate with systems that have DCE security by specifying an Oracle password.

Data privacy and integrity

> DCE integration uses multiple levels of security to ensure data authenticity, privacy, and integrity. Users are provided with a range of choices, from no protection to full encryption for each connection, with a guarantee that no data has been modified in transit.

DCE naming adapter

The DCE CDS naming adapter offers a distributed, replicated repository service for the names, addresses, and attributes of objects across the network. Because servers register their name and address information in the DCE CDS naming adapter, Oracle clients can make location-independent connections to Oracle servers. An Oracle utility is provided to load the Oracle service names with corresponding connect descriptors into the DCE CDS naming adapter. After the names are loaded, Oracle connect descriptors can be viewed from a central location with standard DCE tools, and services can be relocated without any changes to the client configuration.

Oracle Names

The process of resolving a service name (or database alias or global name) into a server's physical address is known as *name resolution.* While the information needed to perform name resolution between service names and specific Oracle instances and hosts is normally maintained in the *tnsnames.ora* file, that approach requires propagation of modifications to *tnsnames.ora* across the enterprise whenever there is a change to any component. This may be inconvenient or even impossible in installations where changes occur often or where coordination of *tnsnames. ora* files is difficult. To solve this problem, Oracle developed a product called Oracle Names, which provides dynamic resolution of service names through the use of an Oracle Names server. By using Oracle Names, a network node only needs to know how to connect to the Oracle Names server, which then resolves any service names without a need for *tnsnames.ora.* In addition, Oracle Names is able to integrate with many native naming services, such as Network Information Services (NIS), Novell NetWare Directory Services (NDS), and Banyan Vines StreetTalk.

The Oracle Names method for name resolution has a number of positive attributes. This method:

- Resolves service names quickly

- Allows central control of service names and corresponding physical attributes (e.g., hosts and instance names)

- Provides dynamic access to modified locations

- Provides fault tolerance by supporting multiple name servers

In order to use Oracle Names, one or more Names servers must be configured and implemented using the Oracle Network Manager, described later in this chapter. Once installed, Names servers are server-based services and must be controlled using the program *namesctl*. This control program, which is similar to the *lsnrctl* control program for the SQL*Net listener, performs routine tasks such as starting and stopping the Names server, obtaining status information, and maintaining the name cache.

MultiProtocol Interchange

Modern networks can be extremely complex, supporting multiple network protocols in a large, geographically dispersed network. In order to truly support network independence, SQL*Net must be able to communicate using more than one protocol. For example, a truly independent and open system would allow a workstation running IPX/SPX in a Novell environment to access an Oracle server running TCP/IP in a Unix environment. To provide this capability, Oracle developed the MultiProtocol Interchange (MPI).

The MultiProtocol Interchange performs protocol conversions to allow SQL*Net data originating on a network utilizing one protocol to flow to a network utilizing a different protocol. Figure 5-4 shows a node on a network running IPX with the MPI in the center connecting to a network and server running TCP.

As can be seen from this figure, the MultiProtocol Interchange requires:

- A host machine (which may be a PC)

- The MPI software

- Two or more network interface cards (NICs), one for each supported protocol

- Appropriate software to implement the supported network protocols

Because the MPI utilizes multiple NICs, it is able to convert data not only from one protocol to another, but also from one physical network implementation to another. For example, a MultiProtocol Interchange may convert SQL*Net data from token ring to 10BaseT.

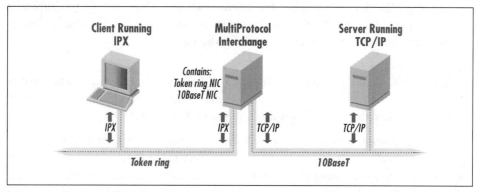

Figure 5-4. Using MultiProtocol Interchange

The MPI runs as a process on a host machine, which may be as simple as a PC workstation. The MPI is configured using the Oracle Network Manager, which specifies the location in the network of any MultiProtocol Interchanges in use, as well as routing information (including cost data) and the protocols supported.

The MPI consists of a *listener* and a *data pump*. These components function in a manner similar to the SQL*Net Multi-Threaded Server, which provides a *listener* and a *server process*. When the MPI listener detects a connection request, it allocates a data pump to handle the connection. One or more data pumps may be available, and each data pump is able to handle a single protocol.

The MPI is controlled using the program *intctl*. This program is similar to the SQL*Net *lsnrctl* and Oracle Names *namesctl* programs, and provides the ability to start, stop, and obtain status information on the MultiProtocol Interchange.

Connecting to Non-Oracle Databases

Oracle provides several methods for connecting to databases provided by other vendors. These databases range from small, single-user databases like Microsoft Access to large, multi-user databases like Sybase or Microsoft SQL Server.

Open DataBase Connectivity

The Open DataBase Connectivity (ODBC) is actually an Application Programming Interface (API) specification developed by Microsoft. Because ODBC provides a standard interface to both the application program and the backend server, it allows any ODBC-compliant application to connect to any ODBC-compliant database. ODBC has been implemented for Oracle in two ways:

Native mode ODBC

    The ODBC driver duplicates the functionality of SQL*Net, so a client running an ODBC driver can connect to a server running SQL*Net without actually running SQL*Net software on the client machine. Thus, the ODBC driver is able to emulate SQL*Net. This capability is not provided by Oracle, but is implemented by other vendors of ODBC drivers.

*SQL*Net integrated*

The ODBC driver provides an interface to SQL*Net that, in turn, actually carries the data to the target node. This is the more common implementation of ODBC, where the ODBC layer actually sits on top of SQL*Net.

Because many applications have been built to interface with ODBC, this technology allows a wide range of applications to connect to an Oracle database without the need to provide a native SQL*Net interface. However, because ODBC relies on SQL*Net for its underlying transport, communications using ODBC are typically less efficient than native SQL*Net. In addition, some Oracle functionality is not fully supported by ODBC drivers. This lack of functionality is easily mistaken for an application problem, and may be difficult to detect and correct. If full Oracle functionality is required, use the Oracle Call Interface (OCI), rather than ODBC.

Gateways

Oracle has responded to the need for access to non-Oracle databases such as IBM's DB2 by developing gateway products. These gateways run as processes on the non-Oracle host machine, and essentially operate by emulating SQL*Net and an Oracle database on the non-Oracle host. For example, IBM provides a native SQL database on its AS/400 computers, which are very popular small office machines. Oracle does not have a database product that runs on AS/400, but it does provide an AS/400 gateway. This gateway has a listener process that functions just like the listener on any Oracle server, and is used to establish connections to Oracle servers. Once a connection is established, gateway software translates Oracle SQL queries into native AS/400 queries, and then returns the data to the Oracle server, essentially making the data stream look as if it had come from another Oracle server.

One restriction on the use of an Oracle gateway is that it can only be accessed from an Oracle server using a database link; an Oracle client is not able to directly connect to a gateway.

 Not all gateways support Oracle's two-phase commit mechanism for distributed transactions. If you require this functionality, consult the appropriate Oracle documentation for the gateway.

Oracle Network Manager

The Oracle Network Manager is a poorly named tool; it does not perform network management at all. Rather, it is a tool provided by Oracle to configure the various components of Oracle's networking software.

Oracle networks can be very complex, often with servers running on various operating systems, and with multiple network topologies running different protocols and frequently utilizing WAN technologies to implement geographically dispersed networks. In such complex networks, change is often the norm, and since detailed information about the composition of most components of the network must be made available to Oracle products in various parameter files, it would be difficult indeed to keep all network parameter files up to date.

Network Manager was developed and bundled with Oracle7 to help handle this network complexity and to simplify the DBA's job of configuring and maintaining an Oracle network. Network Manager is a GUI tool that you can use to create, change, and distribute the required Oracle parameter files.

It is important to know that Network Manager was originally developed to run under Windows 3.1, and while it runs on Windows 95, Windows 98, and Windows NT clients, it is not installed with the normal Oracle installer on those platforms. Rather, you must navigate to the \WINDOWS\INSTALL directory on the Oracle client installation CD-ROM, then run ORAINST to install Network Manager. The resulting executable will be found in the \ORAWIN\BIN directory on the client, rather than in the expected \ORAWIN95 directory.

Although Network Manager can be used to configure a network running Oracle8 and Net8, Oracle is now shipping a new configuration product called the Net8 Assistant that replaces Network Manager for Oracle8 installations.

Network Manager is a GUI tool that runs only on the Windows 95/ 98 and Windows NT platforms. The files that are created are used on other host machines, but must be created in the Windows environment.

Network Manager Data Storage

A major advantage of Network Manager is that data about the network is entered only once, then stored in a repository that may be either a flat file (operating-system-level) structure or an Oracle database. When a change is required, only the affected component is changed, and all parameter files can be quickly and easily regenerated and distributed as required.

If the Network Manager data is being stored in the database, several scripts must be run by the SYSTEM account to create the required database objects. These scripts, which are normally found in the \ORAWIN\DBS directory on a Windows client machine, are shown in Table 5-1.

Table 5-1. Network Manager Scripts Required to Run

Script Name	Function
rosbild.sql	Builds the Resource Object Store database objects
rosgrnt.sql	Grants access to the Resource Object Store objects
rosrvke.sql	Revokes access to the Resource Object Store objects
rosdrop.sql	Drops Resource Object Store objects from the database
nmcbild.sql	Builds database objects required by Network Manager
nmcgrnt.sql	Grants access to Network Manager database objects
nmcrvke.sql	Revokes access to Network Manager database objects
nmcdrop.sql	Drops Network Manager objects from the database

Using Network Manager

Before beginning to define an Oracle network using Network Manager, you'll need to collect the answers to some basic questions, including the following:

- What protocols will be supported?

- Will the MultiProtocol Interchange be used?

- How will you name your Oracle services?

- Will you use Oracle Names?

- What are the physical or logical addresses of the servers in your Oracle network?

- What are the SIDs (instance names) of the databases on each server?

Once this information is available, you can begin defining your network. Network Manager easily walks you through the configuration process. After starting Network Manager, choose the "new" option from the "File" menu, and answer "yes" to the prompt that asks "Would you like to walk through configuration of a network definition?" From this point on, you can simply answer questions on the screen and provide the necessary information to complete your configuration.

Files Created by Network Manager

When the network is specified to Network Manager (or a change is made to an existing network definition), a set of SQL*Net configuration files is created on the Windows workstation. Individual directories are created for each client and server node defined in the network. In each of these directories, you'll find the files shown in Table 5-2.

Table 5-2. Files Generated by Network Manager

File	Distributed to	Description
tnsnames.ora	Client (and server when using database links or distributed processing)	Contains all service names for all databases and interchanges on the network.
sqlnet.ora	Client	Contains parameters to control SQL*Net diagnostics (logging and tracing).
tnsnav.ora	Client	Contains a list of local communities in the client profile or node. This file also contains information to identify the location of interchanges for connections across communities.
listener.ora	Server	Contains information unique to each server specifying how SQL*Net should configure and operate the TNS (Transparent Network Substrate) listener on the server.
intchg.ora (Oracle7)	MultiProtocol Interchange	Contains parameters to control the operation of a particular MultiProtocol Interchange.
tnsnet.ora	MultiProtocol Interchange	Contains information to describe the relationships of all the communities and interchanges in the network.
cman.ora (Oracle8)	Connection Manager	Contains parameters to control the operation of the Oracle Connection Manager.
names.ora	Names Server	Contains parameters to control the operation of a single Oracle Names server.

Once these files are created, the DBA must copy the files, using a technique such as FTP or Windows copy, to the appropriate node (identified by the directory name).

Oracle Net8 Assistant

Beginning with Oracle8, Oracle introduced the Oracle Net8 Assistant, a tool that eases the burden of configuring and administering a distributed network. This tool is implemented in Java and is available on any platform where Net8 is installed. The Oracle Net8 Assistant replaces most of the functionality previously provided by Oracle Network Manager and the Easy Configuration Tool, which were supported only on Windows platforms.

Manual Network Configuration

While Network Manager provides a relatively easy way to create and modify Oracle network parameter files, many DBAs find it useful to occasionally (and some more than occasionally) make manual modifications to one or more of these files. Such a practice, while not approved by Oracle, is acceptable as long as:

- The DBA is knowledgeable about the parameters being modified.

- The structure of the file is maintained.

- The change is made with an appropriate editor that saves plain text (ASCII in most cases). Avoid word processors, which usually store other control characters with the text.

- Backup copies are made of the files being changed—just in case!

 Oracle Corporation states in their documentation that they will not support any Oracle network that has not been configured using Network Manager or Net8 Assistant. To our knowledge, Oracle has never withheld support. However, be cautious when making manual changes, and be aware that Oracle Support may take exception to the practice.

Sample SQL*Net Files

The following sections contain listings of sample SQL*Net configuration files. For complete information on the contents of these files, please refer to the *Oracle Network Manager Administrator's Guide* or the *Net8 Administrator's Guide*. These files may be obtained from the O'Reilly & Associates web site; see the *Preface* for details.

listener.ora

The following file will configure a listener for a single database instance (ORAC) using the TCP/IP protocol:

```
SQLNET.AUTHENTICATION_SERVICES = (NONE)
USE_PLUG_AND_PLAY_LISTENER = OFF
USE_CKPFILE_LISTENER = OFF
LISTENER =
  (ADDRESS_LIST =
        (ADDRESS=
        (PROTOCOL=IPC)
        (KEY= ORAC.world)
        )
```

```
                    (ADDRESS=
                    (PROTOCOL=IPC)
                    (KEY= ORAC)
                )
                    (ADDRESS =
                    (COMMUNITY = TCP.world)
                    (PROTOCOL = TCP)
                    (Host = 10.10.1.2)
                    (Port = 1526)
                )
            )
    STARTUP_WAIT_TIME_LISTENER = 0
    CONNECT_TIMEOUT_LISTENER = 10
    TRACE_LEVEL_LISTENER = OFF
    SID_LIST_LISTENER =
        (SID_LIST =
            (SID_DESC =
                (GLOBAL_DBNAME = ORAC.world)
                (SID_NAME = ORAC)
                (ORACLE_HOME = /disk01/oracle/product/7.3.4)
                (PRESPAWN_MAX = 10)
                (PRESPAWN_LIST =
                    (PRESPAWN_DESC = (PROTOCOL = TCP) (POOL_SIZE = 10) (TIMEOUT = 0))
                )
            )
        )
```

tnsnames.ora

The following file will allow Oracle client machines to access three databases on the network: DB1 is accessed using TCP/IP, DB2 is accessed using SPX/IPX, and DB3 is accessed using the named pipes protocol:

```
    DB1.world =
        (DESCRIPTION =
            (ADDRESS_LIST =
                (ADDRESS =
                    (COMMUNITY = tcp.world)
                    (PROTOCOL = TCP)
                    (HOST = Production1)
                    (PORT = 1526)
                )
            )
            (CONNECT_DATA = (SID = DB1)
            )
        )
    DB2.world =
        (DESCRIPTION =
            (ADDRESS_LIST =
                (ADDRESS =
                    (COMMUNITY = spx.world)
                    (PROTOCOL = SPX)
                    (SERVICE = Server_lsnr)
                )
```

```
       )
       (CONNECT_DATA = (SID = DB2)
       )
     )
DB3.world =
  (DESCRIPTION =
    (ADDRESS_LIST =
       (ADDRESS =
         (COMMUNITY = nmp.world)
         (PROTOCOL = NMP)
         (SERVER = FinanceServer1)
         (PIPE = ORAPIPE)
       )
     )
     (CONNECT_DATA = (SID = DB3)
     )
   )
```

sqlnet.ora

The following file will configure a client for no logging of SQL*Net events, and
provide default values for domain and zone:

```
AUTOMATIC_IPC = OFF
TRACE_LEVEL_CLIENT = OFF
NAMES.DEFAULT_DOMAIN = world
NAME.DEFAULT_ZONE = world
```

SQL*Net Troubleshooting

Even in the best planned network, problems can and do occur. There are few
things more frustrating than to have what appear to be a properly configured client and server that refuse to connect. Even in the simplest network, there could be
several potential causes of this failure, including:

- A problem with a SQL*Net configuration parameter
- A non-functioning network protocol
- A failure in a logical network component, like a router
- A failure in the physical network, like a broken wire or unplugged connection

The key to diagnosing network connectivity problems is to logically analyze the
problem and confirm the proper operation of each component. You must determine if the failure is due to a problem in:

- The Oracle software
- The network protocol layers
- The physical network

In diagnosing the problem, you may be able to take advantage of tools and techniques provided by the host operating system as well as by Oracle.

One easy way to determine whether SQL*Net is properly installed, configured, and running on a particular server is to perform a loopback test on the server host. This technique uses SQL*Net to connect to the database, even though it is local on that machine. To perform a loopback test using SQL*Plus:

1. Verify that the database is up and running by connecting locally using SQL*Plus. For example, issue the command line:

   ```
   sqlplus scott/tiger
   ```

   to establish a connection to the database.

2. Connect to the database using a SQL*Net loopback connection by specifying a SQL*Net connect string. If you are still logged into SQL*Plus, just enter:

   ```
   connect scott/tiger@host
   ```

   where *host* is the SQL*Net connect string for the local database, as defined in *tnsnames.ora*. Note that the loopback test has the following requirements:

   — The SQL*Net listener must be configured and running on the host.

   — The *tnsnames.ora* file must exist and must contain an entry for the database running on this host.

   — If *tnsnames.ora* requires TCP/IP name resolution, the appropriate entry must exist either in an accessible DNS or in the local hosts file.

Most modern operating systems provide diagnostic tools to verify proper operation of network components. In many cases, simply running another non-Oracle application that connects across the network can confirm whether a network connection is functioning. Consider the following situation:

- A simple TCP/IP network running on a 10BaseT topology
- One Oracle server running on a Unix host with the SQL*Net TCP/IP protocol
- One Oracle client workstation running on Windows 98 with the Microsoft TCP/IP protocol stack

The Unix operating system provides a simple utility called *ping*, which will determine whether TCP/IP packets are being properly transmitted between two nodes on a network. Typically, *ping* is invoked as:

```
ping nodename
```

where *nodename* is the name or IP address of the machine with which communication is desired. *ping* will either respond with the length of time it takes for each test packet to make a round trip, or fail with an error message indicating that communication has failed. No matter what the result, this simple test provides valuable information, since it confirms whether or not basic communication between machines is possible. Other operating systems and other network protocols provide their own diagnostic tools similar to Unix's *ping* utility.

Oracle also provides a utility called *tnsping*, which can help diagnose network problems. The *tnsping* utility was originally distributed with some versions of Oracle 7.0, but was missing from some platforms and disappeared altogether from Oracle 7.3. It has been included, however, in Oracle8, where it is now called *tnsping80. tnsping* functions much like the Unix *ping* utility and is invoked as:

```
tnsping service_name count
```

where *service_name* is the service name defined in *tnsnames.ora* or Oracle Names, and *count* is the number of times the *tnsping* program will attempt to reach the server (the default is 1).

 tnsping is of limited use, since it does not actually establish a connection but merely verifies the existence of a listener process on the server side. On the other hand, knowing whether SQL*Net can communicate with the host computer is often valuable.

The Net8 Easy Configuration utility also provides a mechanism to determine whether or not a workstation can reach a network listener process. To perform this test, start the Net8 Easy Configuration program, then select "Test" and enter an existing service name. A "Connection Test" window then appears, which will request a username and password. Once these are entered, you can click the "Test" button, and the test result will be displayed.

Some Common ORA Errors, Causes, and Corrective Actions

Table 5-3 summarizes the most common ORA errors, why they occur, and how you can correct them.

Table 5-3. Common ORA Errors

Error	Description	Corrective Action
ORA-12154	The service name could not be found in *tnsnames.ora*.	Check the service name.
ORA-12162	The connection description has an error.	Check *tnanames.ora* for syntax, especially mismatched parentheses.
ORA-12163	The connection description is too long.	Correct the problem by shortening the connection description.
ORA-12197	The connection description has an error.	Check *tnsnames.ora* for syntax errors.

Table 5-3. Common ORA Errors (continued)

Error	Description	Corrective Action
ORA-12198	A path could not be found via interchanges.	Check *tnsnav.ora* for errors.
ORA-12203	Unable to connect to destination.	Check the underlying network problems, including physical problems or non-functioning routers.
ORA-12208	*tnsnav.ora* could not be found.	Make sure *tnsnav.ora* is in the correct directory.
ORA-12210	Improper configuration of *tnsnav.ora*.	Check *tnsnav.ora* syntax.
ORA-12500	Could not start a dedicated server process.	Check process count in the operating system and *listener.ora* parameters.
ORA-12504	SID could not be resolved.	Check CONNECT_DATA in *tnsnames.ora* and verify that SID is specified correctly.
ORA-12505	SID could not be resolved.	Check *listener.ora* on the server or run *lsnrctl status* to make sure a listener is running for the specified SID.
ORA-12510	No dispatcher available to accept a connection using the multithreaded server.	Increase the number of dispatchers available.
ORA-12511	Dispatchers are too busy using the multithreaded server.	Try again or increase the number of dispatchers available.

SQL*Net Troubleshooting Procedures

If, after eliminating any possible network or operating system problems, you still cannot connect an Oracle client to an Oracle server on your network, then you need to follow basic troubleshooting procedures. The steps listed in the following sections are intended as a guide, but we cannot anticipate every possible problem, so you may ultimately need to rely on the most basic diagnostic tool of all—your own intellect and experience.

Determine basic server operation

Ask these questions:

- Can any workstation or server connect to the server? If so, then the server is operating properly and you should diagnose the client.

- Is the database running? If not, start the database and retest the connection.

- Is the listener running? If not, start the listener and retest the connection.

- Can a loopback test be performed on the server? If so, you should diagnose the client. If not, the problem lies either in the SQL*Net configuration or in the network protocol stack on the server host.

- If you are using Oracle Names, is the Names server running and reachable? If not, start the Names server or correct any connectivity problem.

Determine basic client connectivity

Verify TCP/IP connectivity if you are using TCP/IP:

- Can the server be reached using the *ping* utility?

- If the *tnsnames.ora* file uses logical service names resolved by a DNS server, verify that the DNS server is properly resolving the name by using the logical name in the *ping*.

- If the logical name is not resolved by a DNS server, verify that the logical name is in the *hosts* file on the client.

- If the logical name cannot be resolved, try using the server's IP address in *tnsnames.ora*.

Verify IPX/SPX connectivity if you are using IPX/SPX or Novell networking:

- Can you perform a NetWare login to a Novell server on the network?

Verify named pipes connectivity if you are using named pipes in a Windows 95/ 98/NT environment:

- Using the Network Neighborhood icon, can you see other nodes on the local network?

Verify SQL*Net operation on the client:

- Is SQL*Net or Net8 installed on the client?

- Is the correct protocol adapter installed on the client?

- Is the correct *tnsnames.ora* file installed on the client, in the correct directory?

- Is the correct *sqlnet.ora* file installed on the client, in the correct directory?

6

Security and Monitoring

Up to this point, this book has primarily focused on getting the database installed and operational. This chapter takes you into the day-to-day business of being an Oracle database administrator. We focus on two important areas of administration here: security and monitoring.

Security

One of your most important responsibilities as a database administrator is the security of the data in your database. You are responsible for ensuring that there is no unauthorized access to the data. Oracle has provided you with many basic features that, when applied properly and in combination, make the process of managing security relatively painless. This section covers the basic security functions of the DBA and the Oracle features that you will use.

Security Policy

Before you can implement specific features, you must develop a security policy. You, your management, the application support team, and your users have to decide on how open the database and its data will be. This decision depends upon the specifics of the application and the requirements of your organization. Security policies vary widely. We have seen read-only databases where everyone in the company has access to query all data, and we have seen databases so sensitive that all access is through restricted terminals.

The following summaries provide lists of questions you will have to answer when establishing your own site's security policy. Later sections contain basic information on how to implement your decisions.

User access to the database

Every user must connect to the database using an authorized userid and password. Questions you'll have to address include the following:

- Will users share one or more common userids (this is common with many vendor applications) or will each user have a unique userid?
- Should passwords expire after a period of time?
- Do you need to implement a minimum length for passwords or impose other content restrictions?
- Do you want to limit the number of concurrent sessions for a given user?
- Will users be able to create their own objects?
- Will you be able to restrict access to DBA or other privileged accounts?
- Will the database be accessible for remote connections using SQL*Net or Net8?
- Will the database be accessible for distributed queries?

Read sensitivity of the data

By default, data in a table is only accessible to:

- The userid that owns the table
- Anyone with the SELECT ANY TABLE system privilege

Questions you'll have to address include the following:

- Will the application data be accessible to all users of the database?
- Will different levels of access to the data be granted to different users?
- Will object grants be given to each user, or will they be grouped using roles?

Write sensitivity of the data

By default, tables can only be modified by:

- The owner of the table
- Anyone with INSERT ANY TABLE, UPDATE ANY TABLE, or DELETE ANY TABLE system privileges for inserts, updates, or deletes

In addition to the questions listed above for select access, questions you'll have to address include the following:

- Will some tables contain data that can be updated?
- Should some tables be used as logs, with insert-only access granted to users?

- Will some data need to be reconstructed so that rows can't ever be deleted, only marked as being logically deleted?

- Will some data need to be reconstructed so that rows can't ever be deleted, only marked as being replaced with new rows inserted?

Audit policy

Once you determine who should have access to the data, you'll need to decide if you want to know who has accessed the data. Decisions you'll need to make include the following:

- Do you need to know who has selected from, inserted into, updated, or deleted from the table?

- Do you simply need to know that they did it during their session, or do you need to pinpoint the exact time of every access?

- Do you need to know only that someone accessed the table, or do you need to know the specific row that was accessed?

See Chapter 7, *Auditing*, for more information about creating and implementing an audit policy.

Creating Users

Each person accessing the database must have an Oracle userid. While userids are normally created by a DBA, they can be created by anyone who has the CREATE ANY USER system privilege. The usual syntax to create a user is as follows:

```
CREATE USER username IDENTIFIED BY password
    DEFAULT TABLESPACE default_tablespace_name
    TEMPORARY TABLESPACE temporary_tablespace_name
    QUOTA 10M ON default_tablespace_name
    PROFILE profile_name;
```

If you do not specify a default tablespace or a temporary tablespace, Oracle will automatically assign the SYSTEM tablespace. However, you must specify a quota for the default tablespace, or the user will still not be able to create any tables or indexes in the default tablespace. You do not need to specify a quota for the temporary tablespace. See Chapter 13, *SQL Statements for the DBA*, for the complete CREATE USER syntax.

All options that can be specified in the CREATE USER command can also be changed for existing users with the ALTER USER command.

Profiles

User profiles were introduced in Oracle7 as a way that the DBA could limit the amount of system resources that could be consumed by any particular user. In Oracle8, user profiles have been expanded to support password control. There are two flavors of profiles, resource control and password control, discussed in the following sections.

Profiles are created using the CREATE PROFILE command and can be altered with the ALTER PROFILE command. At database creation time, a single profile, named DEFAULT, is created. You can use the DBA_PROFILES data dictionary view to determine which profiles have been created, and the values of each of the limits contained in the profiles.

If a profile is not specified for a user in the CREATE USER command, the DEFAULT profile is used. A user's profile can be changed with the ALTER USER command. You can use the DBA_USERS data dictionary view to see which profile has been assigned to a given user.

Resource control

Each user profile has eight individual resource limits and one composite limit that can be specified. For each limit, the possible values are an integer or the keywords UNLIMITED or DEFAULT. When DEFAULT is used, the value is replaced by the corresponding value in the DEFAULT profile.

The limits are summarized here:

COMPOSITE_LIMIT

Weighed sum of CPU_PER_SESSION, CONNECT_TIME, LOGICAL_READS_PER_SESSION, and PRIVATE_SGA. The weights applied to each parameter are specified using the ALTER RESOURCE COST command. Parameters that are not specified take a weighted value of 0. Initially, each parameter has a weighted value of 0. If this value is exceeded, the current operation is aborted, an error message is returned, and the user is only able to commit or roll back and then exit.

The data dictionary view RESOURCE_COST shows the assigned values for each parameter.

CPU_PER_SESSION

Total amount of CPU that can be used by the session. Value is in hundredths of a second. If this value is exceeded, the current operation is aborted, an error message is returned, and the user is only able to commit or roll back and then exit.

CPU_PER_CALL

Total amount of CPU that can be used by any one parse, execute, or fetch call. Value is in hundredths of a second. This can be used to terminate runaway queries. If this value is exceeded, the current operation is aborted, an error message is returned, and the user is only able to commit or roll back and then exit.

CONNECT_TIME

Total amount of elapsed time for which a given connection can be maintained. Value is in minutes. This can be used to ensure that a given session does not remain connected to the database indefinitely. If this value is exceeded, the current transaction is rolled back and the user receives an error on the next SQL statement.

IDLE_TIME

Total amount of elapsed time allowed between any two SQL statements. Value is in minutes. This is used to time out inactive sessions, either to free up session slots or to limit exposure when someone leaves an active session on their workstation. If this value is exceeded, the current transaction is rolled back and the user receives an error on the next SQL statement.

LOGICAL_READS_PER_SESSION

Total number of disk blocks (either from memory or disk) that can be read by the session. Value is in blocks. This is used to place a total limit on the amount of I/O that can be done by a session. If this value is exceeded, the current operation is aborted, an error message is returned, and the user is only able to commit or roll back and then exit.

LOGICAL_READS_PER_CALL

Total number of disk blocks (either from memory or disk) that can be read by a parse, execute, or fetch call. Value is in blocks. This is used to place a limit on the amount of I/O that can be performed by a given call in an attempt to identify and stop runaway queries. If this value is exceeded, the current operation is aborted, an error message is returned, and the user is only able to commit or roll back and then exit.

PRIVATE_SGA

Total amount of private space that can be allocated to the session out of the shared pool area for private SQL and PL/SQL areas. This does not apply to the shared SQL or PL/SQL areas. Value is in bytes, but the K and M suffixes are accepted to specify kilobytes or megabytes. This parameter is only used in a Multi-Threaded Server (MTS) system.

SESSIONS_PER_USER

Total number of concurrent sessions the user can have active at a given time. Value is in sessions. This value is normally used to limit a user to a specified maximum number of concurrent sessions. The SESSIONS_PER_USER parameter not only limits the number of concurrent sessions, but also limits the number of Parallel Query sessions that can be used. If the value of SESSIONS_PER_ USER is less than the degree of parallelism used by the query, an ORA-2391 error will be generated.

Password control

Effective with Oracle8, the DBA can establish a password policy through the use of profiles. The user profile has been extended to include parameters that control a password's lifetime, ability to be reused, and even its length and format. There are also parameters that allow you to lock out an account if unsuccessful attempts are made to connect to it.

The password control parameters include the following:

FAILED_LOGIN_ATTEMPTS

The number of failed login attempts before the account is locked. Value is in failed attempts. This parameter is primarily used to lock an account in the event of an apparent break-in attempt. Once an account is locked, it remains locked for the time specified in PASSWORD_LOCK_TIME.

PASSWORD_GRACE_TIME

The number of days after the password has expired during which you are allowed to continue to connect to the database. During the grace period, an error message is returned upon login that warns you to change your password. The grace period begins the first time a user connects after the password has expired. Value is in days.

PASSWORD_LIFE_TIME

The number of days that a password, once set, is valid. This allows you to establish a password policy that requires passwords to be changed on a regular interval. Value is in days.

PASWORD_LOCK_TIME

The length of time an account is locked after the FAILED_LOGIN_ATTEMPTS maximum is exceeded. Once an account is locked, it can be unlocked either by waiting for the number of days specified in the PASSWORD_LOCK_TIME parameter, or with this SQL command:

```
ALTER USER username ACCOUNT UNLOCK;
```

PASSWORD_REUSE_MAX

> The number of different passwords that must be used before a user is allowed to reuse the same password. If this parameter is set to an integer value, then PASSWORD_REUSE_TIME must be set to UNLIMITED.

PASSWORD_REUSE_TIME

> The number of days that must elapse before a user can reuse the same password. If this parameter is set to a non-zero value, then the PASSWORD_REUSE_MAX parameter must be set to UNLIMITED.

PASSWORD_VERIFY_FUNCTION

> Specifies a PL/SQL procedure that is invoked to validate the password. You can use this PL/SQL procedure to enforce any restrictions that can be implemented with PL/SQL. Oracle provides an example PL/SQL procedure in the file *$ORACLE_HOME/rdbms/admin/utlpwdmg.sql*. The PL/SQL procedure must be owned by SYS.

Default profile

At the time the database is created, an initial profile named DEFAULT is established. This is the default profile, and has two functions:

- To act as the default profile for a user where no profile is specified
- To act as a definition of default values for other profiles

Any of the parameters documented above can have a specified value DEFAULT. Oracle uses the value specified in the DEFAULT profile for that parameter. This process is repeated each time a user connects, so a change to the DEFAULT profile will automatically take effect with the next connection.

Implementing profiles

Enforcing profile limits is a three-step process:

1. Profiles must be defined with the CREATE PROFILE command.
2. Profiles must be assigned to users with the CREATE USER or ALTER USER command.
3. Limit checking must be enabled globally at the database level. This can be done either through the *INIT.ORA* parameter RESOURCE_LIMITS or through the ALTER SYSTEM commands. See Chapter 12, *Initialization Parameters*, and Chapter 13, *SQL Statements for the DBA*, for the complete syntax.

System Privileges

System privileges allow a user of the database to perform specific actions within the database. In Oracle8 Release 8.0, there are 90 system privileges that can be assigned to a user or role. In Oracle7 Release 7.3 there are 78 system privileges that can be assigned to a user or role. See Chapter 15, *System Privileges and Initial Roles*, for a complete list of system privileges that can be assigned.

Object Privileges

Object privileges allow you to access or manipulate objects in the database. Depending upon the type of object, different object privileges apply. Table 6-1 shows the mapping of object privileges to object types.

Table 6-1. Object Privileges Allowed by Object Type

Object Option	Object Type Applicable
ALTER	Table, sequence
DELETE	Table, view, snapshot
EXECUTE	Package, procedure, function, library
INDEX	Table, snapshot
INSERT	Table, view, snapshot
READ (Oracle8 only)	Directory
REFERENCES	Table
SELECT	Table, view, sequence, snapshot
UPDATE	Table, view, snapshot

By default, only the owner of any object automatically has all object privileges for an object. The owner must grant access to the object to other users or roles in order for other users to access the object. The exception to this rule is that someone with the DBA role or with one of the system privileges that allow you to manipulate objects in any schema (they are listed in Table 15-4 in Chapter 15, *System Privileges and Initial Roles*, which describes privileges in some detail) will be able to access the schema object directly.

The WITH GRANT OPTION clause

The owner of an object can grant it to another user by specifying the WITH GRANT OPTION clause in the GRANT statement. In this case, the new grantee can then grant the same level of access to other users or roles. Here are three points to keep in mind about the WITH GRANT OPTION clause:

- You cannot grant WITH GRANT OPTION to a role.

- If you revoke access to a user who had been granted access to an object WITH GRANT OPTION, and that user had granted access to another user, both sets of grants will be revoked.

- The WITH GRANT OPTION does not come automatically with the system privileges listed in Table 15-4 that allow you to manipulate objects in any schema. Thus, although a DBA can create a table in someone else's schema through the CREATE ANY TABLE system privilege, and you can SELECT, INSERT, UPDATE, or DELETE from it through the SELECT ANY TABLE, INSERT ANY TABLE, UPDATE ANY TABLE, and DELETE ANY TABLE system privileges, you cannot grant access to the table to any other user or role.

Roles

Roles are the mechanism used by Oracle to facilitate the granting of system and object privileges to users. The granting of roles is a three-step process:

1. The role is created by someone with the CREATE ROLE system privilege.

2. System or object privileges are granted to the role by anyone with the proper authorization.

3. The role is granted to a user by anyone who has the GRANT ANY ROLE system privilege, or by anyone who has been granted the role via the WITH ADMIN OPTION.

Default roles

Normally, when a role is granted to a user, it becomes a default role—that is, the role is automatically active at the time the user connects to the database. However, one of the options available with the CREATE USER and ALTER USER commands is the ability to specify a subset of the roles that are granted to the user by default. You can use this approach if you want a user to be granted a role with the condition that explicit actions must be taken to enable it.

The most common use of non-default roles is to ensure that specific system or object privileges are available only from within an application. In this case, the application would enable the role through the SET ROLE command.

The SET ROLE command specifically enables only those roles listed. Any default roles that are not listed will be disabled. Make sure that any non-default role that is to be enabled at runtime contains all system and object privileges necessary to continue normal processing.

Maximum number of enabled roles

The *INIT.ORA* parameter MAX_ENABLED_ROLES specifies the maximum number of enabled roles a user can have. This number includes the unlisted PUBLIC role.

You can determine which roles are currently active by querying the data dictionary view SESSION_ROLES. Oracle counts all roles that have been granted either directly or indirectly through other roles against this limit. Thus, for example, enabling the DBA role actually uses seven of the allocated slots:

```
DBA
SELECT_CATALOG_ROLE
HS_ADMIN_ROLE
EXECUTE_CATALOG_ROLE
DELETE_CATALOG_ROLE
EXP_FULL_DATABASE
IMP_FULL_DATABASE
```

A slot is also used for the PUBLIC role.

Since roles are established at connect time or when the SET ROLE command is executed, the most common effect of the MAX_ENABLED_ROLES parameter is for a connection to fail with an ORA-1925 error, which indicates that too many roles have been granted to the user.

Password-enabled roles

Roles can have associated passwords, which are established using the IDENTI-FIED BY clause in the CREATE ROLE or ALTER ROLE commands. When a role has an associated password, the user must provide the password at the time the role is enabled with the SET ROLE command. The two most common scenarios for this are as follows:

- A role is needed to allow an application to have the object privileges necessary to function properly. The role is granted as a non-default role to the user. The application has the password available to it and provides the password independently of the user. This ensures that the user is not able to use ad hoc query and update tools like SQL*Plus to access the objects directly outside the application environment.

- The user occasionally requires elevated privileges, but does not normally want to run with the privileges enabled. In this case, the role can be established as a non-default role with a password, requiring the user to explicitly enable the role and provide a password through the SET ROLE command. A user does not have to know the password for any default roles, unless the role needs to be reenabled after a SET ROLE command.

The WITH ADMIN OPTION clause

Special attributes of roles can be granted to a user by including the WITH ADMIN OPTION clause in the GRANT statement. In this case, the user is allowed to grant the role to other users or roles. If you are able to grant a role to someone because you have the role WITH ADMIN OPTION, and then the role is revoked from you, the cascaded grants remain. The situation is different in cases where you simply have object privileges.

 A user who has been granted a role WITH ADMIN OPTION also has the ability to change the role's password and to drop the role.

Normally, when a role is granted to a user, it is granted as a default role. The exception is when the DEFAULT ROLE clause has previously been used in the CREATE USER or ALTER USER commands. In this case, the role may be granted as a non-default role. In order for the person granting the role to ensure that the role is a default role, he or she must also have been granted the ALTER ANY USER system privilege.

Common Security Holes

This section discusses some of the most common security holes in an Oracle environment.

Not changing privileged user passwords

All standard users created by Oracle have associated passwords. The two primary DBA accounts, SYS and SYSTEM, have (unfortunately) well-documented passwords. Most break-ins into Oracle databases are through one of these accounts, where the initial passwords provided with the installed systems have never been changed.

Using the same password in all databases

Most users have a strong tendency to keep passwords simple. One of the easiest ways to do this is to have the same password for all of your accounts—either all DBA accounts in the database or all accounts in all databases. The problem with specifying passwords in this way is that if your password is stolen, it opens up multiple accounts for improper usage.

The SCOTT/TIGER account

Most DBAs automatically create the SCOTT account with the well-known password TIGER. This account has been used in demos for years by Oracle and by Oracle Education (utilizing the EMP and DEPT tables). However, if this account exists, any grants made to PUBLIC are also available to the SCOTT account. If an

unauthorized person accesses the database using the SCOTT account, you may
have a security breach.

Shared UTL_FILE access to directories

The UTL_FILE built-in package allows a user to read from and write to an operating system file from within PL/SQL. The *INIT.ORA* parameter UTL_FILE_DIR specifies a list of operating system directories you can use with UTL_FILE. Any PL/SQL
procedure executed by any user of the database can read from or write to any file
in the directory.

Auditing

After implementing a security policy, you need to audit actions within the database. Chapter 7, *Auditing*, provides specific information on implementing an
auditing policy.

Monitoring

Monitoring is the process of watching what is happening at a physical level within
the database. As a database administrator, you monitor the utilization of scarce
resources within the database and instance to ensure that sufficient reserves are
available. For most systems, the resources most people are concerned about
include memory, storage, disk I/O, and network activity. A number of proprietary
Oracle and third-party monitoring utilities will automatically watch activity in the
database, record information, and alert you to potential problems.

This section concentrates primarily on memory and storage. These are the areas
over which the DBA has the most control. This is not to minimize the importance
of disk I/O and network traffic. After all, the whole process of query optimization
(described in Chapter 8, *Query Optimization*) involves reducing the amount of disk
I/O required to retrieve the rows in the result set. And normally mild-mannered
applications can become beasts when they are converted from running on the same
machine to running in a distributed environment. However, there are very good
tools that allow you to look at disk and network traffic from outside the database
environment.

What to Monitor

What should you monitor? As we mentioned, the two areas we've found that
return the most information for the amount of effort involved are memory and
storage, described in the following sections.

Memory utilization

Memory is probably the key to good database performance. Disk I/O is very slow compared to memory access, so the more you can place into memory, the better. The System Global Area (SGA) is the primary area of memory you need to monitor. Since the SGA is the shared memory area used by the instance, the larger you can configure the SGA, the better your performance will be. However, you will have to make tradeoffs between a larger SGA and total available memory. You don't want to make the SGA so large that you start incurring excessive swapping or paging. Ideally, you want the SGA to remain in memory, and in some operating systems you can pin the SGA into memory. However, you may gain little if the SGA remains in memory and all user processes end up being paged out.

Later in this chapter, we provide SQL scripts you can run over time to watch your system's memory utilization.

Storage utilization

While the instance maintains all of its information about the database in memory in the SGA, the database itself is stored on disk. The tablespaces are composed of datafiles, which are operating system files or raw partitions. Each segment is stored in a tablespace. You have some flexibility in that datafiles can be configured to AUTOEXTEND if the tablespace runs out of room, and segments can be set to have an UNLIMITED number of extents. However, there is always a practical limit in that a datafile cannot AUTOEXTEND if there is no more space left in the filesystem, and a segment cannot grow past the available free space in a tablespace.

In the next section, we provide a set of SQL queries that track storage utilization in the database over time.

How to Monitor

This section provides specific details of how to set up and perform monitoring of your database.

Getting a baseline

When you set up a monitoring system, the first thing you need to do is establish a baseline. This will give you initial statistics you can use to measure both the effectiveness of your tuning processes and the impact of growth in the database over time.

The SQL scripts in the following section include the capability to store results of queries in tables. This historical record can be used at your discretion.

SQL queries to monitor SGA utilization

When monitoring SGA size and utilization, you need to think about the data buffers (controlled by the *INIT.ORA* parameter DB_BLOCK_BUFFERS) and the rest of the SGA. In Chapter 3, *Maximizing Oracle Performance*, we presented mechanisms for tracking the usage of the data buffers. This section focuses on the rest of the SGA. There are two dynamic performance views that provide information about how the SGA is being utilized (see Chapter 14, *The Oracle Data Dictionary*, for more information on these views). These are the V$RESOURCE_LIMIT and V$SGASTAT views.

The scripts presented here do two things: first, they create a separate table in which to store current values from these tables; second, they store the values. The first set of scripts should be run only once. The second set should be run on a periodic basis, depending upon your circumstances.

The following script creates the storage tables. Note that you may want to modify this script to specify tablespace and storage parameters.

```
CREATE TABLE dba$resource_limit
            (timestamp           DATE,
             resource_name       VARCHAR2(30),
             current_utilization NUMBER,
             max_utilization     NUMBER,
             initial_allocation  VARCHAR2(10),
             limit_value         VARCHAR2(10));

CREATE TABLE dba$sgastat
            (timestamp           DATE,
             pool                VARCHAR2(30),
             name                VARCHAR2(30),
             bytes               NUMBER);
```

The next script copies current values into the storage table for future reference:

```
INSERT INTO dba$resource_limit
            (timestamp,
             resource_name,
             current_utilization,
             max_utilization,
             initial_allocation,
             limit_value
             )
SELECT TRUNC(SYSDATE),
       resource_name,
       current_utilization,
       max_utilization,
       initial_allocation,
       limit_value
FROM v$resource_limit;
```

```
INSERT INTO dba$sgastat
                (timestamp,
                 pool,
                 name,
                 bytes
                )
SELECT TRUNC(SYSDATE),
       pool,
       name,
       bytes
FROM v$sgastat;
COMMIT;
```

SQL queries to monitor storage utilization

When monitoring storage, you need to pay attention to two separate areas: objects that are going to run out of room or extents in the near future, and total growth over time. You worry about objects in the short term so that you can avoid having your applications fail. You worry about growth in space over time so that you can project when you will need to acquire more disk space.

The following script identifies segments that are getting close to running out of contiguous free space for a NEXT extent:

```
SELECT owner,
s.tablespace_name,
segment_name,
s.bytes,
next_extent,
MAX(f.bytes) largest
FROM dba_segments s,dba_free_space f
WHERE s.tablespace_name = f.tablespace_name(+)
GROUP BY owner,s.tablespace_name,segment_name,s.bytes,next_extent
HAVING next_extent*2>max(f.bytes)
/
```

The following script identifies segments that are getting close to their MAX-EXTENTS value:

```
SELECT owner,tablespace_name,segment_name,bytes,extents,max_extents
FROM dba_segments
WHERE extents*2 > max_extents
/
```

The following scripts store information about the size and number of extents of objects in the database. The scripts create historical tables to store information about tablespaces and segments:

```
CREATE TABLE dba_tablespace_history
(
    timestamp              DATE,
    tablespace_name        VARCHAR2(30),
    num_of_files           NUMBER,
    num_of_blocks          NUMBER,
```

```
        num_of_bytes              NUMBER
)
PCTFREE 0
TABLESPACE tools
STORAGE (INITIAL 393216
NEXT 196608
PCTINCREASE 0);

CREATE TABLE dba_segments_history
(
        timestamp                 DATE,
        owner                     VARCHAR2(30),
        segment_name              VARCHAR2(30),
        partition_name            VARCHAR2(30),
        segment_type              VARCHAR2(17),
        tablespace_name           VARCHAR2(30),
        bytes                     NUMBER,
        blocks                    NUMBER,
        extents                   NUMBER
)
PCTFREE 0
TABLESPACE tools
STORAGE (INITIAL 1966080
NEXT 983040
PCTINCREASE 0);
```

The following script collects current information about tablespaces and segments:

```
INSERT INTO dba_tablespace_history
SELECT TRUNC(sysdate),
       tablespace_name,
       count(*),
       sum(blocks),
       sum(bytes)
FROM dba_data_files
GROUP BY TRUNC(sysdate),tablespace_name;

INSERT INTO dba_segments_history
SELECT TRUNC(sysdate),
       owner,
       segment_name,
       partition_name,
       segment_type,
       tablespace_name,
       bytes,
       blocks,
       extents
FROM dba_segments;
```

 The column PARTITION_NAME in the DBA_SEGMENTS
data dictionary view is only available in Oracle8.

The following script creates a history table to store information about Oracle tables. Note that some of the columns are only populated after a table has been analyzed. We feel that this information is invaluable. The blocks column allows you to track the highwater mark for used space; this will give you a more accurate picture of table growth than the bytes column from the DBA_SEGMENTS view.

```
CREATE TABLE dba_tables_history
(
      timestamp              DATE,
      owner                  VARCHAR2(30),
      table_name             VARCHAR2(30),
      num_of_rows            NUMBER,
      num_of_blocks_u        NUMBER,
      num_of_blocks_f        NUMBER
)
PCTFREE 0
TABLESPACE tools
STORAGE (INITIAL 786432
NEXT 393216
PCTINCREASE 0);
```

The following script populates dba_tables_history:

```
INSERT INTO dba_tables_history
SELECT TRUNC(sysdate),owner,table_name,num_rows,blocks,empty_blocks
FROM dba_tables;
```

This last set of scripts creates a history table for indexes. Note that we grab the information from the INDEX_STATS view. This table is populated one index at a time after an index has been analyzed with the VALIDATE STRUCTURE option. This is because the information available in INDEX_STATS is more complete than that found in DBA_INDEXES, even after the index has been analyzed using the normal strategy.

```
CREATE TABLE dba_index_history
(
      timestamp              DATE,
      owner                  VARCHAR2(30),
      height                 NUMBER,
      blocks                 NUMBER,
      name                   VARCHAR2(30),
      lf_rows                NUMBER,
      lf_blks                NUMBER,
      lf_rows_len            NUMBER,
      lf_blk_len             NUMBER,
      br_rows                NUMBER,
      br_blks                NUMBER,
      br_rows_len            NUMBER,
      br_blk_len             NUMBER,
      del_lf_rows            NUMBER,
      del_lf_rows_len        NUMBER,
```

```
        distinct_keys              NUMBER,
        most_repeated_key          NUMBER,
        btree_space                NUMBER,
        used_space                 NUMBER,
        pct_used                   NUMBER,
        rows_per_key               NUMBER,
        blks_gets_per_access       NUMBER
)
PCTFREE 0
TABLESPACE tools
STORAGE (INITIAL 1966080
NEXT 983040
PCTINCREASE 0);
```

The following script analyzes the index and populates the history table. It is passed two parameters, owner and index_name. You must run this script for every index for which you want to analyze and store information.

```
ANALYZE INDEX &owner..&index_name VALIDATE STRUCTURE;
INSERT INTO dba_index_history
SELECT TRUNC(sysdate),
       '&owner',
       height,
       blocks,
       name,
       lf_rows,
       lf_blks,
       lf_rows_len,
       lf_blk_len,
       br_rows,
       br_blks,
       br_rows_len,
       br_blk_len,
       del_lf_rows,
       del_lf_rows_len,
       distinct_keys,
       most_repeated_key,
       btree_space,
       used_space,
       pct_used,
       rows_per_key,
       blks_gets_per_access
FROM index_stats;
```

UTLBSTAT and UTLESTAT are a paired set of scripts provided by Oracle to collect statistics about the activity of the database over time. You typically use these scripts to monitor how the instance reacts to a given stimulus, perhaps a benchmark or a periodic monitoring. The scripts work as follows:

1. Begin the process by running the script *$ORACLE_HOME/rdbms/admin/ utlbstat.sql.*

2. Select the event you want to monitor or the length of time you want the monitor to run.

3. End the process by running the script *$ORACLE_HOME/rdbms/admin/utlestat. sql*.

UTLBSTAT creates a set of tables that store current copies of many of the dynamic performance data dictionary views. When UTLESTAT is run, it compares the stored values with the then current copies and generates a report. The report is stored as *$ORACLE_HOME/rdbms/admin/report.txt*.

7

Auditing

Once the database is operational, you will want to track various types of activity within the database. This tracking is called *auditing*. Using the AUDIT SQL statement, you can track access to individual objects, use of specific SQL statements, or the exercise of any of the system privileges.

Don't confuse auditing with *monitoring* the database. While auditing lets you see what is happening at a logical level, monitoring lets you see what is going on physically within the instance. Monitoring, described briefly in Chapter 6, *Security and Monitoring*, is primarily designed to support tuning.

About Auditing

Oracle's auditing facility is action oriented. When it processes a SQL statement that meets specific requirements, it writes a record to the audit trail. It records the time, user, action taken (SQL statement used), and database object against which the action was performed. Normally, the audit trail is stored as the table SYS.AUD$, but you can override this default on some operating systems by having Oracle write to the operating system audit trail.

Types of Auditing Supported

Oracle provides specific support for three types of auditing:

Schema object auditing
    Allows you to specify schema objects to be audited. Oracle will write an audit record based upon the schema object being accessed.

SQL statement auditing
> Allows you to specify SQL statements to be audited. Oracle will write an audit record based upon the fact that a user executed a specific SQL statement.

System privilege auditing
> Allows you to specify particular system privileges to be audited. Oracle will write an audit record based upon the fact that a user exercised a specific system privilege.

You'll find more details on how to implement each of these three audit options, along with examples, later in this chapter.

Scope of Auditing

The audit facility allows you to specify the scope of the audit action as follows:

BY USER
> The SQL statement and system privilege auditing options allow you to specify a specific user to audit (with the BY USER clause of the AUDIT statement). If you do not specify a user, all users are audited by default.

WHENEVER SUCCESSFUL/WHENEVER NOT SUCCESSFUL
> All three forms of auditing allow you to specify whether you want auditing to occur at all times, or only whenever the specific action was successful or unsuccessful. The WHENEVER SUCCESSFUL clause allows you to audit who is actually performing a specific action, while WHENEVER NOT SUCCESSFUL allows you to better check on unsuccessful access. Unsuccessful accesses are usually due to insufficient privileges, allowing you to monitor for break-in attempts or for people making unauthorized searches.

BY SESSION/BY ACCESS
> All three forms of auditing allow you to specify how often audit records are to be generated. The BY SESSION clause specifies that Oracle is to write a single audit record for every database session, while the BY ACCESS clause tells Oracle to write a record for every action that qualifies. The tradeoff for knowing exactly when every audited action occurs is that BY ACCESS generates many records.

Limitations of Auditing

Oracle's auditing facility only works at the statement level. It is able to capture that a particular user executed a SELECT statement against a specific table, but it is not able to tell you which rows were retrieved. Likewise, Oracle can record that an UPDATE statement was executed by a specific user against a table, but it cannot tell you which rows were updated.

Row-level auditing is possible, however, and can be implemented through a series of user-created triggers applied to individual tables. We include an example of a trigger to implement row-level auditing in the section "Row-Level Auditing," later in this chapter.

Implementing Auditing

By default, auditing is disabled when the database is started up. You have to activate it by following these steps:

1. Enable auditing at the database level with the *INIT.ORA* parameter AUDIT_TRAIL.

2. Enable the level of auditing through the AUDIT SQL statement.

The AUDIT_TRAIL parameter must be enabled for auditing to work. The valid values for this parameter are DB, NONE, and OS:

DB
> Enables auditing to the internal data dictionary

NONE
> Disables all auditing

OS
> Enables auditing to the operating system audit trail

This parameter is highly platform dependent. Consult your platform's installation guide to determine if it is enabled for your configuration. Please refer to Chapter 12, *Initialization Parameters*, for more information about setting *INIT.ORA* parameters.

Disabling Auditing

Auditing can be disabled by using the reverse of the mechanisms listed previously. Any auditing option enabled using the AUDIT command can be disabled with the corresponding NOAUDIT command. Auditing can be completely turned off by setting the *INIT.ORA* parameter AUDIT_TRAIL to NONE.

Forms of the AUDIT Statement

This section provides detailed information on how to implement each of the three forms of auditing.

Schema Object Auditing

Schema object auditing lets you track access to an object. The object can be any Oracle table, view, sequence, package, function, procedure, snapshot, library, or directory.

 Oracle will audit embedded objects. That is, if you have turned on auditing for a table, and that table is referenced in a view, then accessing the view will generate an audit record for the table.

The specific syntax for schema object auditing is:

```
AUDIT object_privilege[,object_privilege ...] ON [schema.]objectname |
DEFAULT
    [BY SESSION [WHENEVER [NOT] SUCCESSFUL]
    [BY ACCESS [WHENEVER [NOT] SUCCESSFUL]
```

Table 7-1 lists the various object privileges and the schema object types to which they can apply. Detailed syntax is provided in Chapter 13, *SQL Statements for the DBA.*

Table 7-1. Schema Object Audit Privileges Allowed by Object Type

Object Privilege	Object Type Applicable
ALTER	Table, sequence, snapshot
AUDIT	Table, view, sequence, package, procedure, function, snapshot, directory
COMMENT	Table, view, snapshot
CREATE	Table, view, snapshot
DELETE	Table, view, snapshot
EXECUTE	Package, procedure, function, library
GRANT	Table, view, sequence, package, procedure, function, snapshot, library, directory
INDEX	Table, snapshot
INSERT	Table, view, snapshot
LOCK	Table, view, snapshot
READ	Directory
REFERENCES	Table
RENAME	Table, view, package, procedure, function, snapshot
SELECT	Table, view, sequence, snapshot
UPDATE	Table, view, snapshot
WRITE	Directory

You can specify a default level for schema object auditing by using the keyword DEFAULT instead of a schema object name. From that point on, all schema objects created will have that level of auditing turned on. You must have the AUDIT ANY system privilege to specify this level.

Examples of schema object auditing

The following examples show how to use the schema object auditing facility. The first example generates an audit record for every session that successfully executes a SELECT on the scott.emp object:

```
AUDIT SELECT ON scott.emp WHENEVER SUCCESSFUL
```

The next example generates an audit record for every unsuccessful UPDATE statement on scott.dept. Since most of these failures occur because the user does not have UPDATE access on scott.dept, this can be used to track attempts to update the table inappropriately.

```
AUDIT UPDATE ON scott.dept BY ACCESS WHENEVER NOT SUCCESSFUL
```

Statement Auditing

Statement auditing allows you to track who is issuing specific types of statements. The AUDIT statement form of the AUDIT command allows you to specify any SQL statement to be audited. You are also able to audit the use of a SQL statement by all users or a specific user.

```
AUDIT sql_statement[, sql_statement ...]
    [BY user[,user ...]]
    [BY SESSION [WHENEVER [NOT] SUCCESSFUL]
    [BY ACCESS [WHENEVER [NOT] SUCCESSFUL]
```

In this case, the *sql_statement* can be either a SQL statement or shortcut provided by Oracle. When you use one of the shortcuts, you are able to specify a group of SQL statements to be audited.

> There is a certain level of overlap between statement auditing and privilege auditing. For example, the AUDIT CREATE TABLE statement is regarded as both a statement audit command (CREATE TABLE SQL statement) and a privilege audit command (CREATE TABLE system privilege). See Chapter 13, *SQL Statements for the DBA*, for a list of SQL statements relevant to the DBA, and Chapter 15, *System Privileges and Initial Roles*, for a list of all system privileges.

Table 7-2 provides a list of shortcuts for DDL statements; Table 7-3 provides a list of shortcuts for DML statements.

Table 7-2. DML Statement Auditing Shortcuts

SQL Statement Shortcut	SQL Statements Represented
CLUSTER	CREATE CLUSTER AUDIT CLUSTER DROP CLUSTER TRUNCATE CLUSTER
DATABASE LINK	CREATE DATABASE LINK DROP DATABASE LINK
DIRECTORY	CREATE DIRECTORY DROP DIRECTORY
INDEX	CREATE INDEX ALTER INDEX DROP INDEX
NOT EXISTS	All SQL statements that fail because a specified object does not exist
PROCEDURE	CREATE FUNCTION CREATE LIBRARY CREATE PACKAGE CREATE PACKAGE BODY CREATE PROCEDURE DROP FUNCTION DROP LIBRARY DROP PACKAGE DROP PROCEDURE
PROFILE	CREATE PROFILE ALTER PROFILE DROP PROFILE
PUBLIC DATABASE LINK	CREATE PUBLIC DATABASE LINK DROP PUBLIC DATABASE LINK
PUBLIC SYNONYM	CREATE PUBLIC SYNONYM DROP PUBLIC SYNONYM
ROLE	CREATE ROLE ALTER ROLE DROP ROLE SET ROLE
ROLLBACK SEGMENT	CREATE ROLLBACK SEGMENT ALTER ROLLBACK SEGMENT DROP ROLLBACK SEGMENT
SEQUENCE	CREATE SEQUENCE CROP SEQUENCE
SESSION	Logins
SYNONYM	CREATE SYNONYM DROP SYNONYM
SYSTEM AUDIT	AUDIT {SQL statements | system privileges} NOAUDIT {SQL statements | system privileges}
SYSTEM GRANT	GRANT {system privileges and roles} REVOKE {system privileges and roles}

Table 7-2. DML Statement Auditing Shortcuts (continued)

SQL Statement Shortcut	SQL Statements Represented
TABLE	CREATE TABLE DROP TABLE TRUNCATE TABLE
TABLESPACE	CREATE TABLESPACE DROP TABLESPACE ALTER TABLESPACE
TRIGGER	CREATE TRIGGER ALTER TRIGGER DROP TRIGGER ALTER TABLE schema.table ENABLE ALL TRIGGERS ALTER TABLE schema.table DISABLE ALL TRIGGERS
TYPE	CREATE TYPE CREATE TYPE BODY ALTER TYPE DROP TYPE DROP TYPE BODY
USER	CREATE USER ALTER USER DROP USER
VIEW	CREATE VIEW DROP VIEW
ALL	All shortcuts listed in Table 7-2

Table 7-3. DDL Statement Auditing Shortcuts

SQL Statement Shortcut	SQL Statements Represented
COMMENT TABLE	COMMENT ON TABLE COMMENT ON COLUMNS
DELETE TABLE	DELETE FROM {table or view}
EXECUTE PROCEDURE	Execution of any procedure or function, or access to any variable, library, or cursor inside a package
GRANT DIRECTORY	GRANT privilege ON directory REVOKE privilege ON directory
GRANT PROCEDURE	GRANT privilege ON procedure, function, or package REVOKE privilege ON procedure, function, or package
GRANT SEQUENCE	GRANT privilege ON sequence REVOKE privilege ON sequence
GRANT TABLE	GRANT privilege ON table, view, or snapshot REVOKE privilege ON table, view, or snapshot
GRANT TYPE	GRANT privilege ON TYPE REVOKE privilege ON TYPE
INSERT TABLE	INSERT INTO {table or view}
LOCK TABLE	LOCK TABLE {table or view}

Table 7-3. DDL Statement Auditing Shortcuts (continued)

SQL Statement Shortcut	SQL Statements Represented
SELECT SEQUENCE	Any statement containing sequence.CURRVAL or sequence. NEXTVAL
SELECT TABLE	SELECT FROM {table, view, or snapshot}
UPDATE TABLE	UPDATE {table or view}

Examples of statement auditing

The following examples show how to use the SQL statement auditing facility. The first example causes Oracle to audit every CREATE TABLE SQL statement issued by user scott:

```
AUDIT CREATE TABLE BY scott;
```

The next example causes Oracle to audit every CREATE USER, ALTER USER, or DROP USER SQL statement issued by anyone in the database:

```
AUDIT USER;
```

System Privilege Auditing

System privilege auditing lets you track the use of system privileges. In the AUDIT command, you can specify any system privilege. An audit record will be generated any time you exercise the specified system privilege. You are also able to audit the exercise of a system privilege by all users or a specific user.

```
AUDIT system_privilege [,system_privilege ...]
    [BY user[,user ...]]
    [BY SESSION [WHENEVER [NOT] SUCCESSFUL]
    [BY ACCESS [WHENEVER [NOT] SUCCESSFUL]
```

In this case, *system_privilege* can be any system privilege or one of the system privilege shortcuts. Table 7-4 lists all the system privilege shortcuts that have been defined.

Table 7-4. System Privilege Auditing Shortcuts

System Privilege Shortcut	System Privileges Represented
CONNECT	CREATE SESSION
RESOURCE	ALTER SESSION CREATE CLUSTER CREATE DATABASE LINK CREATE PROCEDURE CREATE ROLLBACK SEGMENT CREATE SEQUENCE CREATE SYNONYM CREATE TABLE CREATE TABLESPACE CREATE VIEW

Table 7-4. System Privilege Auditing Shortcuts (continued)

System Privilege Shortcut	System Privileges Represented
DBA	SYSTEM GRANT statement option AUDIT SYSTEM CREATE PUBLIC DATABASE LINK CREATE PUBLIC SYNONYM CREATE ROLE CREATE USER
ALL	Equivalent to all SQL statement options in Table 7-2
ALL PRIVILEGES	Equivalent to all system privileges

Audit Trail Views and Lookup Tables

All Oracle-generated audit trail information is stored in the SYS.AUD$ base table and is made available to the DBA through the various audit trail data dictionary views.

Data Dictionary Views

All of the audit trail data dictionary views are created by the *cataudit.sql* script. The following sections summarize these views.

Views containing audit trail information

DBA_AUDIT_EXISTS

A subset of DBA_AUDIT_TRAIL containing information about actions referencing objects that do not exist

DBA_AUDIT_OBJECT

A subset of DBA_AUDIT_TRAIL containing audit trail information specific to objects being audited

DBA_AUDIT_SESSION

A subset of DBA_AUDIT_TRAIL containing auditing information about individual connections to the database

DBA_AUDIT_STATEMENT

A subset of DBA_AUDIT_TRAIL containing auditing information about the use of specific audited SQL statements

DBA_AUDIT_TRAIL

The full audit trail; contains all information included in all other audit trail views

USER_AUDIT_OBJECT

A subset of USER_AUDIT_TRAIL containing audit trail information for the current user's objects

USER_AUDIT_SESSION

> A subset of USER_AUDIT_TRAIL containing audit trail information about the current user's connections to the database

USER_AUDIT_STATEMENT

> A subset of USER_AUDIT_TRAIL containing audit trail information about the current user's use of audited SQL statements

USER_AUDIT_TRAIL

> A subset of DBA_AUDIT_TRAIL containing audit trail information for the current user

Views containing auditing specifications

ALL_DEF_AUDIT_OPTS

> Lists the current default schema object auditing levels for schema objects that may be created in the future

DBA_OBJ_AUDIT_OPTS

> Lists the current object auditing levels for every object in the database

DBA_PRIV_AUDIT_OPTS

> Lists the current system privileges being audited; if auditing is turned on for a particular user, that information is also included in this view

DBA_STMT_AUDIT_OPTS

> Lists the current SQL statements being audited; if auditing is turned on for a particular user, that information is also included in this view

USER_OBJ_AUDIT_OPTS

> A subset of DBA_OBJ_AUDIT_OPTS that shows object auditing levels for objects owned by the current user

Lookup Tables

The following lookup tables map internal audit codes to keywords that are basically understandable to humans. The first three tables are created as part of the database creation process from the *sql.bsq* file; AUDIT_ACTIONS is created by the *cataudit.sql* script.

TABLE_PRIVILEGE_MAP

> Lists the valid object audit options that can be specified for schema object auditing

SYSTEM_PRIVILEGE_MAP

> Lists the valid system privileges that can be specified for system privilege auditing

STMT_AUDIT_OPTION_MAP

Lists the valid SQL statements that can be specified for statement auditing

AUDIT_ACTIONS

Lists the internal audit codes and descriptions

Establishing an Audit Policy

Auditing consumes system resources. The audit trail table contains a row for every audit item saved. Auditing also uses additional session slots. Therefore, we recommend that you keep the amount of auditing to a minimum, and that you turn on more detailed auditing only as required.

Depending upon your requirements, the audit trail information will have varying life spans. You may need to keep a record of every access to a table to satisfy legal requirements, or you may only want to know the distribution of access to the database by department over a month's time. You may not care how often a table is queried, but you may need to keep track of which rows have been modified, who did it, when it was done, why, what column was changed, the old and new values, and which program was used. In other words, the old journalist mantra: who, what, where, when, why, and how?

It is our experience that the following policy works well:

- Use AUDIT CONNECT to keep track of who is using the database, how often they access the database, and how much I/O is generated by that user. This information will be useful later on to augment any monitoring you are doing for capacity planning. It will also allow you to answer questions from management about who is using the database.

- Use AUDIT DBA to record the use of any activity that requires DBA privileges. This will be invaluable to you at some point when you are trying to figure out which DBA dropped a user and when it was done.

- Use row-level triggers to audit table activity only where there is a legal or financial requirement to maintain that information.

- On a periodic basis, usually weekly or monthly, clean out the audit trail table. Summarize connection information into a different table, copy historical access information with a retention period to a separate table, and delete the rows from the audit trail table. The next section describes audit trail maintenance.

When there is a need to know more about access to specific tables, turn on auditing for that table. The two most common scenarios for this are:

- You need to find out if a table is still being accessed, since you are planning the migration of the database.

- You suspect inappropriate access to a table, and need to track who is accessing the table.

Maintaining the Audit Trail

The audit trail table needs to be cleaned out on a periodic basis. You should periodically move the audit trail information out of the audit trail and into your own set of tables. There are several reasons why you need to maintain the audit trail in this way:

1. The audit trail base table, SYS.AUD$, is created in the SYSTEM tablespace as part of the database creation process. If you have any level of auditing turned on, the audit trail will usually grow to become the single largest table in the SYSTEM tablespace. You cannot afford to allow this single table and its index to use up all free space in the SYSTEM tablespace.

2. The audit trail is a view with a join; thus, if the table becomes large, queries to it will be slow. If you copy the information to a separate table and index it, your query performance may improve.

3. If you have auditing enabled BY ACCESS, or if you have many small transactions connecting to the database, you may have more information in the audit trail than you expect.

4. Because the audit trail base table, SYS.AUD$, is owned by SYS, it is not exported when a full or incremental export operation is performed. In the event of a database disaster that forces you to rebuild the database from an export, all existing audit trail information will be lost.

We recommend that you maintain the audit trail by following these steps:

1. Determine what information you need to keep over time. In addition, ask whether you need to keep this information as it is recorded in the database (BY ACCESS or BY SESSION), or whether you can aggregate it further by time period.

2. For information you need to keep, create a table that matches the data dictionary view you are interested in. Periodically insert into this new table rows selected from the data dictionary.

3. Connect to the database as SYS and delete the rows from the data dictionary table.

4. You will sometimes be auditing specific actions, allowing you to reconstruct what happened when there are irregularities in the database. This type of auditing is usually enabled with the AUDIT DBA statement. Unless you have a retention policy, delete these rows from the audit trail base table after a certain period of time, usually a week or month.

Example Script to Copy and Summarize Session Information

The following script is used in a production database to summarize connection information on a daily basis. We include the SQL statements to create the summary table. However, the CREATE TABLE and CREATE INDEX statements obviously do not need to be executed each day.

```
CREATE TABLE system.dba_audit_session_daily
(os_username varchar2(255),
username varchar2(30),
userhost varchar2(255),
terminal varchar2(255),
timestamp date,
sessions number,
elapse_time number,
logoff_lread number,
logoff_pread number,
logoff_lwrite number)
TABLESPACE tools
STORAGE (INITIAL 10M NEXT 10M PCTINCREASE 0);

CREATE INDEX system.dba_audit_session_daily_i
ON dbsa.dba_audit_session_daily (timestamp)
TABLESPACE tools
STORAGE (INITIAL 10M NEXT 10M PCTINCREASE 0)
/
INSERT INTO system.dba_audit_session_daily
(os_username,username,userhost,terminal,timestamp,sessions,elapse_time,
logoff_lread,logoff_pread,logoff_lwrite)
SELECT os_username,username,userhost,terminal,TRUNC(timestamp),COUNT(*),
SUM(logoff_time-timestamp),SUM(logoff_lread),SUM(logoff_pread),
SUM(logoff_lwrite)
FROM dba_audit_session
WHERE action_name IN ('LOGOFF','LOGOFF BY CLEANUP')
AND logoff_time < trunc(sysdate)
GROUP BY os_username,username,userhost,terminal,TRUNC(timestamp);
```

You can change the roll-up period by changing the TRUNC operation. Note that we are only copying rows corresponding to sessions that have been terminated. Any session that was started on the previous day but is still active will not be included. The information for that session will be included when the session finally terminates. In this case, there may be multiple records for that user for a given day.

Example Script to Clean Out the Audit Trail

The following script is used in conjunction with the previous script. In this example, you must be connected to the instance as SYS.

```
DELETE FROM aud$ a
WHERE logoff$time < trunc(sysdate)
AND action BETWEEN 101 AND 102
AND EXISTS
(SELECT 'x' FROM system.dba_audit_session_daily d
    WHERE trunc(a.timestamp)   = d.timestamp);
```

In this example, we are using audit actions 101 and 102. These correspond to the 'LOGOFF' and 'LOGOFF BY CLEANUP' actions used in the previous example. The AUDIT_ACTIONS table provides the mapping between the ACTION_NAME used in DBA_AUDIT_SESSIONS and the ACTION stored in AUD$.

Row-Level Auditing

Oracle's built-in audit capability stops at the table level. That is, you can audit who has accessed a table, but not which row was accessed. However, Oracle has provided a mechanism that lets you build your own row-level audit facility. Through the use of after-insert, after-update, or after-delete triggers, you can capture this information yourself and write it out to a separate table. The following trigger is an example of an update trigger.

If you need to audit SELECT access to an individual row, you will have to do this from within your application. Here is an example trigger used to audit row-level inserts, updates, and deletes:

```
CREATE OR REPLACE TRIGGER log_actions
AFTER INSERT OR UPDATE OR DELETE
ON generic_table
FOR EACH ROW
DECLARE
    action_id char(1);
    event_id int;
    table_key varchar(80);
    timestamp date;
    table_name varchar(30);
    username varchar(30);
BEGIN
    SELECT event_seq.nextval INTO event_id FROM dual;
    SELECT sysdate INTO timestamp FROM dual;
    SELECT user INTO username FROM dual;
    table_name := 'generic_table;
    IF DELETING THEN
        action_id := 'D';
        table_key := to_char(generic_table.primary_key);
    END IF;
    IF UPDATING THEN
        action_id := 'U';
        table_key := to_char(generic_table.primary_key);
    END IF;
    IF INSERTING THEN
        action_id := 'I';
        table_key := TO_CHAR(generic_table.primary_key);
```

```
      END IF;

rem
rem    The debugging lines can be left in. They will not have an effect
rem    unless serveroutput is turned on in SQL*Plus
rem
        dbms_output.enable(10000);
        dbms_output.put_line('tablename '||table_name);
        dbms_output.put_line('actionid  '|| action_id);
        dbms_output.put_line('username  '|| username);
        dbms_output.put_line('tablekey  '|| table_key);
        dbms_output.put_line('eventid   '|| event_cdr_id);
        dbms_output.put_line('timestamp '|| timestamp);

    INSERT INTO event_table_audit_t (event_id,
                                     timestamp,
                                     table_name,
                                     table_key,
                                     action)
                           VALUES (event_id,
                                     timestamp,
                                     table_name,
                                     table_key,
                                     action_id);
END;
/
```

This example is based upon a production row-level auditing trigger. In this case, an audit trail record is written for every insert, update, and delete. If you use this example, please remember to replace the placeholders *generic_table* and *primary_ key* with your actual table name and the columns in your primary key. We are also assuming that the primary key itself will never be updated.

A useful variant of this trigger would be to grab the old and new values for the columns being updated and to write those out to a table. This would allow you to know not only which row was changed, but also which columns and values were changed.

8

Query Optimization

In most environments, the database administrator is expected to help tune poorly performing queries. After all, the DBA is the expert and is responsible for overall database performance. Indeed, tuning a query to eliminate excessive disk I/O or CPU processing will generally buy more in performance than you can normally get by tuning the System Global Area (SGA) or by optimizing the placement of datafiles on disk.

This chapter is designed to help you optimize queries or, more accurately, to help you help the Oracle optimizers. The optimizer is that portion of the kernel that evaluates the SQL statement and determines the optimal way to retrieve the desired result set. We'll begin by reviewing the various types of queries, then look at the various ways in which Oracle can perform a join. Next, we'll discuss the cost-based optimizer and the rule-based optimizer. We present the information in this order so that when we get to the optimizers, we can better discuss how they handle the different types of queries and joins. Finally, we'll discuss what you have to do to make the cost-based optimizer work, and how to provide it with query optimization hints, which override the normal processing of the cost-based optimizer. Hints are necessary because, after all is said and done, you still know more about your data and the application than the optimizer will ever be able to figure out.

Types of Queries

Our emphasis in this section is on optimizing queries. We focus on queries here because all DML (Data Manipulation Language) statements can have a query as part of their processing. Even INSERT statements can have subqueries in them.

Simple Queries

The simplest of the queries is the *simple query*, or a query against one table. An example is:

```
SELECT ename,deptno FROM emp;
```

Minimal effort is required to determine how to process this query. In this case, Oracle performs what is called a *full table scan*; that is, Oracle reads every row in the table from disk.

Joins

A *join* is the relational operator that combines information from two or more tables. The WHERE clause specifies how the tables are to be combined. In a database with referential constraints enabled, this is usually accomplished by matching foreign keys to primary keys. An example of a join is:

```
SELECT emp.ename, emp.empno, emp.job, dept.dname
FROM emp, dept
WHERE emp.deptno = dept.deptno;
```

Subqueries

A *subquery* is a query inside another query. Normally, subqueries are used in INSERT, UPDATE, and DELETE statements. An example of a statement with a subquery is the following, in which we change King's department to Sales:

```
UPDATE emp
SET  deptno = (SELECT deptno FROM dept WHERE dname = 'SALES')
WHERE ename = 'KING';
```

In another example, everyone in the SALES department is given a 10% raise:

```
UPDATE emp
SET sal = sal * 1.1
WHERE deptno = (SELECT deptno FROM dept WHERE dname = 'SALES');
```

A final example shows how a query can be written as a join or as a subquery; specify either:

```
SELECT ename
FROM emp
WHERE deptno = (SELECT deptno FROM dept where dname = 'SALES');
```

or:

```
SELECT ename
FROM emp, dept
WHERE emp.deptno = dept.deptno
AND dept.dname = 'SALES';
```

Correlated Subqueries

A *correlated subquery* is a subquery that is executed for each row of the base table. An example of a correlated subquery in a WHERE clause is shown here:

```
UPDATE emp e
SET e.deptno = (SELECT deptno FROM dept WHERE dname = 'SALES')
WHERE NOT EXISTS
(SELECT 'X' FROM dept d
WHERE  e.deptno = d.deptno);
```

In this example, all employees that do not have a department are assigned to the Sales department. The key characteristic of a correlated subquery is that it is called for each row retrieved.

Cartesian Product

A *Cartesian product* is the result of joining every row in one table with every row in another table. This occurs when there is no WHERE clause to restrict rows. While this is legitimate in some cases, most occurrences of a Cartesian product are mistakes. The Cartesian product is somewhat analogous to a correlated sub-query—that is, it performs a full table scan on the second table for every row in the first table. An example of a Cartesian product is:

```
SELECT ename,empno,dname
FROM emp,dept;
```

In this example, the result would have a row for each employee listed as being in every department. In the standard emp and dept tables, there are 14 employees and 4 departments. This leads to a result set of 56 rows. If you have a larger case, where you are joining two tables with 10,000 rows each, you end up with 100,000,000 rows. It is important to understand when the Oracle optimizer will attempt to perform a Cartesian product and, if so, what the impact will be.

Types of Join Access Paths

The various joins described in the previous sections demonstrate some of the different ways in which a SQL statement can be written. We even provided an example showing how the same query could be written using two different formats. The job of the optimizer is to take the SQL statement and determine the most efficient (we hope) manner in which to process the query.

This section continues the background discussion by presenting some of the more common ways in which Oracle processes a query. The term *access path* is used for the manner in which Oracle identifies the rows to be retrieved and retrieves them.

Nested Loops

The *nested loop* is the original join access path. In this case, Oracle designates one of the tables as the driving table. Unless there is an index on the driving table that can be used to reduce the number of rows chosen, Oracle performs a full table scan on the driving table. It then uses an index to retrieve rows based upon the WHERE clause from the second table.

Merge Joins

A *merge join* is performed when there is no viable index to use in a nested loop. In this case, Oracle retrieves all rows from each of the two tables, and sorts them prior to performing the join.

Hash Joins

A *hash join* is a modified version of the merge join. Oracle uses a hash function on the join criteria to eliminate the need to sort each table. The overhead of the hash function is normally less than the time required to sort the tables.

Determining the Access Plan

How can you find out how the Oracle optimizer is processing your query? This section discusses some of the ways to determine what the optimizer is doing.

The PLAN_TABLE Table

All of the methods listed in this section rely upon the PLAN_TABLE table. This table is created by the *$ORACLE_HOME/rdbms/admin/utlxplan.sql* script. Table 8-1 shows the structure of the PLAN_TABLE table.

Table 8-1. Structure of PLAN_TABLE

Column	Format
STATEMENT_ID	VARCHAR2(30)
TIMESTAMP	DATE
REMARKS	VARCHAR2(80)
OPERATION	VARCHAR2(30)
OPTIONS	VARCHAR2(30)
OBJECT_NODE	VARCHAR2(128)
OBJECT_OWNER	VARCHAR2(30)
OBJECT_NAME	VARCHAR2(30)
OBJECT_INSTANCE	NUMBER(38)

Table 8-1. Structure of PLAN_TABLE (continued)

Column	Format
OBJECT_TYPE	VARCHAR2(30)
OPTIMIZER	VARCHAR2(255)
SEARCH_COLUMNS	NUMBER
ID	NUMBER(38)
PARENT_ID	NUMBER(38)
POSITION	NUMBER(38)
COST	NUMBER(38)
CARDINALITY	NUMBER(38)
BYTES	NUMBER(38)
OTHER_TAG	VARCHAR2(255)
PARTITION_START	VARCHAR2(255)
PARTITION_STOP	VARCHAR2(255)
PARTITION_ID	NUMBER(38)
OTHER	LONG
DISTRIBUTION	VARCHAR2(30)

The EXPLAIN PLAN Statement

Oracle provides the EXPLAIN PLAN SQL statement as a way to query the optimizer. By preceding the SQL statement you want to examine with the EXPLAIN PLAN statement, you direct Oracle to populate the PLAN_TABLE table with information about the access plan for that SQL statement. The EXPLAIN PLAN statement contains options for specifying a statement identifier so that multiple statements can be stored in the PLAN_TABLE. You can also provide an override for the PLAN_TABLE by specifying any other table by name that has the same structure. For details of the EXPLAIN PLAN statement, see Chapter 11, *The Oracle Database*.

The following example shows how to use EXPLAIN PLAN and retrieve information from PLAN_TABLE. Note that this is the same structure used by AUTOTRACE, TKPROF, and the Oracle Enterprise Manager (OEM) Top Sessions display, as we'll describe in later sections.

```
SQL> EXPLAIN PLAN
  2   SET STATEMENT_ID = 'Sample Query'
  3   FOR
  4   SELECT emp.ename,emp.empno,emp.job,dept.dname
  5   FROM emp,dept
  6   WHERE emp.deptno = dept.deptno
  7   /

Explained.
```

```
SQL> SELECT LPAD(' ',2*(LEVEL-1))||OPERATION Operation,
  2         OPTIONS Options,
  3         OBJECT_NAME "Object Name",
  4         POSITION Position
  5  FROM PLAN_TABLE
  6  START WITH ID = 0 and STATEMENT_ID = 'Sample Query'
  7  CONNECT BY PRIOR id = parent_id
  8      and STATEMENT_ID = 'Sample Query';


OPERATION               OPTIONS     Object Nam  POSITION
--------------------    ----------  ----------  ---------
SELECT STATEMENT
  NESTED LOOPS    1
    TABLE ACCESS      FULL        EMP              1
    TABLE ACCESS      BY ROWID    DEPT             2
      INDEX           RANGE SCAN  DEPTI            1

5 rows selected.
```

SQL*Plus AUTOTRACE

The SQL*Plus AUTOTRACE facility was implemented effective with SQL*Plus 3.3 (shipped with Oracle7 Release 7.3). It provides an easier interface to get EXPLAIN PLAN information. AUTOTRACE still requires you to have a PLAN_TABLE, and it requires you to have the PLUSTRACE role. The PLUSTRACE role and its grants are defined in the file *$ORACLE_HOME/sqlplus/admin/plustrce.sql*, which must be run from SYS.

The full syntax for enabling AUTOTRACE is:

```
SET AUTOTRACE {OFF | ON | TRACEONLY} [EXP[LAIN]] [STAT[ISTICS]]
```

OFF

Turns off AUTOTRACE

ON

Turns on AUTOTRACE

TRACEONLY

Forces AUTOTRACE to not display the query output

EXPLAIN

Forces AUTOTRACE to only show the execution plan

STATISTICS

Forces AUTOTRACE to only show the statistics

An example of running AUTOTRACE follows:

```
SQL> set AUTOTRACE TRACEONLY
SQL> SELECT emp.ename,emp.empno,emp.job,dept.dname
```

```
  2  FROM emp,dept
  3  WHERE emp.deptno = dept.deptno;
```

14 rows selected.

Execution Plan

```
  0       SELECT STATEMENT Optimizer=CHOOSE
  1   0   NESTED LOOPS
  2   1     TABLE ACCESS (FULL) OF 'EMP'
  3   1     TABLE ACCESS (BY ROWID) OF 'DEPT'
  4   3       INDEX (RANGE SCAN) OF 'DEPTI' (NON-UNIQUE)
```

Statistics

```
    0  recursive calls
    2  db block gets
   46  consistent gets
    4  physical reads
    0  redo size
  872  bytes sent via SQL*Net to client
  615  bytes received via SQL*Net from client
   11  SQL*Net roundtrips to/from client
    1  sorts (memory)
    0  sorts (disk)
   14  rows processed
```

SQL Trace and TKPROF

The SQL Trace facility is built into the Oracle kernel. Once enabled, it writes information about every SQL statement executed to a trace file in the user dump directory. This trace file can then be processed by TKPROF, an Oracle-supplied utility that reads SQL Trace dump files and produces a human-readable report.

Initialization parameters

The following *INIT.ORA* parameters have an impact on the trace file produced by the SQL Trace facility:

MAX_DUMP_FILE_SIZE
   Establishes the maximum size of the generated trace file. The values are in operating system blocks. The default value for Oracle7 is 500; the default for Oracle8 is 10000.

SQL_TRACE
   When set to TRUE, turns the SQL Trace facility on for all sessions. The effect is to generate a separate trace file for each session. The output will be large, so set SQL_TRACE to TRUE only in extreme conditions. A value of FALSE still allows you to turn on SQL Trace for specific sessions, as shown in the next section.

TIMED_STATISTICS

When set to TRUE, tells Oracle to collect information about how long the parse, execute, and fetch calls take. This output is in addition to the automatically generated execution plan. Enabling this parameter forces Oracle to make several additional internal calls when processing each statement; thus, it will have some minor impact on performance.

USER_DUMP_DEST

Specifies the directory in which the trace files are generated.

Enabling SQL Trace for a specific session

There are two ways to enable SQL Trace for your own session, and there is also a way to turn on SQL Trace for any current session.

You can enable SQL Trace for your own session with the following SQL statement:

```
ALTER SESSION SET SQL_TRACE = TRUE;
```

Alternately, from PL/SQL, you can make the following procedure call:

```
DBMS_SESSION.SET_SQL_TRACE (TRUE);
```

Finally, you can turn on SQL Trace for any connected session by issuing the following command:

```
EXECUTE DBMS_SYSTEM.SET_SQL_TRACE_IN_SESSION(sid,serial#,TRUE);
```

You can obtain the values of sid and serial# from the V$SESSION dynamic view by issuing the following query:

```
SELECT sid,serial# FROM v$session WHERE username = 'CDSTEST';
```

In all three cases, once SQL Trace is turned on, it can be disabled by using the same call, replacing the keyword TRUE with FALSE. For example:

```
ALTER SESSION SET SQL_TRACE = FALSE;
```

Postprocessing with TKPROF

After the trace file has been created, you can process it using TKPROF, which takes the trace file as input and generates multiple output files. These include:

- A log file containing the formatted information from the PLAN_TABLE, and statistics about the processing of each SQL statement.

- A SQL script containing the processed SQL statements. This file can be used to replay the statements after making changes to the database.

- A SQL script that inserts into a table information about each statement. This table can then be used to generate your own statistics and reports.

Actually, by default, TKPROF uses a plan table, with the name PROF$PLAN_ TABLE. You can override this default by specifying any table with the same structure as the PLAN_TABLE. Full syntax for running TKPROF can be found in Oracle Corporation's guide, *Oracle8 Server Tuning*.

Oracle Enterprise Manager Top Sessions

The Top Sessions monitor included in the Oracle Enterprise Manager (OEM) Diagnostic Pack also allows you to see the EXPLAIN PLAN information. Click on the session you wish to view, go to the Cursors tab, and choose the EXPLAIN PLAN button.

The Top Sessions monitor has two limitations, but both can be easily handled. The first is that Top Sessions explicitly looks for SYS.PLAN_TABLE. You must execute the *utlxplan.sql* script while connected as SYS or INTERNAL. The other limitation is that Top Sessions can only process true DML statements. For example, it cannot process a CREATE TABLE … AS SELECT statement because it is a DDL (Data Definition Language) statement. You must first create the table, then populate it with an INSERT statement.

For example, the following will not be processed:

```
CREATE TABLE emp AS SELECT * FROM scott.emp;
```

But it can be replaced with:

```
CREATE TABLE emp AS SELECT * FROM scott.emp WHERE 1 = 2;
INSERT INTO emp SELECT * FROM scott.emp;
```

In this example, note that the WHERE 1 = 2 clause is recognized by the optimizer as ensuring that no rows will match. Thus, it automatically creates the table with no rows and does not perform the query. An alternative to this clause might be WHERE ROWNUM < 0.

Cost-Based Optimizer

The cost-based optimizer (CBO) is Oracle's preferred optimizer. All new functionality added to the kernel will only be supported from within the cost-based optimizer. Likewise, all research being done to find ways to improve performance of existing features will only be reflected in enhancements to the cost-based optimizer.

The cost-based optimizer uses information about the objects in the query to determine the most cost-efficient access path. It uses information about the number of rows in the tables and the distribution of values in indexed columns to calculate the relative costs of the various ways in which the query can be optimized. It then chooses the access path with the lowest computed cost.

Unlike the rule-based optimizer (described in the "Rule-Based Optimizer" section, later in this chapter), the cost-based optimizer is very configurable. There are multiple *INIT.ORA* parameters that need to be set properly in order for the cost-based optimizer to work efficiently. Once you've assigned the appropriate parameter values, you'll need to collect information about the size of the tables and the distribution of data within columns in order for the cost-based optimizer to make the proper decisions. Finally, because you know your data better than Oracle does, you can provide hints to the optimizer to improve its ability to choose wisely.

Initialization Parameters

These *INIT.ORA* parameters determine how the cost-based optimizer will perform; see Chapter 12, *Initialization Parameters*, for valid values and defaults.

ALWAYS_ANTI_JOIN
> Sets the type of antijoin that the Oracle Server uses. The system checks to verify that it is legal to perform an antijoin; if it is, the system processes the subquery depending on the value of this parameter. When set to the value NESTED_LOOPS, the Oracle Server uses a nested loop antijoin algorithm. When set to the value MERGE, the Oracle Server uses the sort merge antijoin algorithm. When set to the value HASH, the Oracle Server uses the hash antijoin algorithm to evaluate the subquery.

B_TREE_BITMAP_PLANS
> Allows the optimizer to use bitmap index plans even though a table only has B-Tree indexes.

BITMAP_MERGE_AREA_SIZE
> Specifies the amount of memory used to merge bitmaps retrieved from a range scan of the index. A larger value should improve performance because the bitmap segments must be sorted before being merged into a single bitmap.

COMPLEX_VIEW_MERGING
> Determines whether complex views and subqueries are evaluated on their own or are merged into the entire query for evaluation.

DB_FILE_MULTIBLOCK_READ_COUNT
> Specifies the maximum number of blocks read in one I/O operation during a sequential scan. The total number of I/Os needed to perform a full table scan depends on factors such as the size of the table, the value of MULTI_BLOCK_READ_COUNT, and whether Parallel Query is being utilized for the operation. Batch environments typically have values for this parameter in the range of 4 to 16. Decision Support System (DSS) and data warehouse database environments tend to benefit from maximizing the value for this parameter. The actual maximum varies by operating system and is always less than the operat-

ing system's maximum I/O size expressed as Oracle blocks (maximum I/O size divided by DB_BLOCK_SIZE). Attempts to set this parameter to a value greater than the maximum will cause the maximum to be used.

FAST_FULL_SCAN_ENABLED

Allows the optimizer to perform a full index scan rather than a full table scan if all the necessary columns are in the index.

HASH_AREA_SIZE

Specifies the maximum amount of memory, in bytes, to be used for hash joins.

HASH_JOIN_ENABLED

Determines whether or not hash joins are allowed to be used by the optimizer.

HASH_MULTIBLOCK_IO_COUNT

Specifies how many sequential blocks a hash join reads and writes in one I/O. When operating in Multi-Threaded Server mode, however, this parameter is ignored (a value of 1 is used even if you set the parameter to another value). The maximum value is always less than the operating system's maximum I/O size expressed as Oracle blocks.

OPTIMIZER_FEATURES_ENABLED

This parameter collectively enables or disables B_TREE_BITMAP_PLANS, COMPLEX_VIEW_MERGING, FAST_FULL_SCAN_ENABLED, and PUSH_JOIN_PREDICATE.

OPTIMIZER_MODE

Specifies the behavior of the optimizer. When set to RULE, this parameter causes rule-based optimization to be used unless hints are specified in the query. When set to CHOOSE, the optimizer uses the cost-based approach for a SQL statement if there are statistics in the dictionary for at least one table accessed in the statement; otherwise, the rule-based approach is used. FIRST_ROWS causes the cost-based optimizer to choose execution plans that minimize response time. ALL_ROWS causes the cost-based optimizer to choose execution plans that minimize total execution time.

OPTIMIZER_PERCENT_PARALLEL

Specifies the amount of parallelism that the optimizer uses in its cost functions. The default of 0 means that the optimizer chooses the best serial plan. A value of 100 means that the optimizer uses each object's degree of parallelism in computing the cost of a full table scan operation. Low values favor indexes; high values favor table scans.

OPTIMIZER_SEARCH_LIMIT

Specifies the search limit for the optimizer.

PUSH_JOIN_PREDICATE

Allows the optimizer to push certain predicates into a view on the right side of an outer join. This can result in a more efficient access path being generated.

SORT_AREA_SIZE

Specifies the maximum amount, in bytes, of Program Global Area (PGA) memory to use for a sort. If MTS is enabled, the sort area is allocated from the SGA. After the sort is complete, when all that remains to be done is to fetch the rows, the memory is released down to the size specified by SORT_AREA_ RETAINED_SIZE. After the last row is fetched, all memory is freed. The memory is released back to the PGA or SGA, not to the operating system. Increasing SORT_AREA_SIZE size improves the efficiency of large sorts. Multiple allocations never exist; there is only one memory area of SORT_AREA_SIZE for each user process at any time. The default is usually adequate for most OLTP (online transaction processing) operations, but it may be desirable to adjust this parameter for decision support systems, batch jobs, or large CREATE INDEX operations.

SORT_DIRECT_WRITES

SORT_DIRECT_WRITES can improve sort performance if memory and temporary space are abundant on your system. This parameter controls whether sort data will bypass the buffer cache to write intermediate sort results to disk. When it is set to the default of AUTO, and when the sort area size is greater than ten times the block size, memory is allocated from the sort area to write intermediate results. When SORT_DIRECT_WRITES is TRUE, additional buffers are allocated from memory during each sort, and additional temporary segment space may be required. When SORT_DIRECT_WRITES is set to FALSE, the sorts that write to disk write through the buffer cache.

Data Dictionary Requirements

In order for the cost-based optimizer to function properly, it needs to know the sizes of your database tables and the distribution of data within the columns of those tables. Oracle, unlike some other relational database management systems, does not automatically keep this information. In Oracle, you have to generate the information using the ANALYZE command, which can be used to analyze tables, indexes, and columns, as shown in the following sections. See Chapter 13, *SQL Statements for the DBA*, for complete syntax.

ANALYZE TABLE

The first way the ANALYZE command is used is to analyze a table. ANALYZE TABLE causes Oracle to determine how many rows are in the table and how storage is allocated. It also calculates the number of chained rows.

The most important pieces of information the optimizer gets from this process are the number of rows and the number of blocks. When joining two or more tables, the optimizer will attempt to use the table with the fewest number of rows or blocks as the driving table. This should reduce the total amount of disk I/O necessary, and thus improve performance.

You should analyze all tables that will ever be used in a join, which probably means that you must analyze every table in your application.

Oracle specifically advises us not to ANALYZE tables belonging to SYS. The internal access paths used to query the data dictionary have already been optimized in the kernel code. Furthermore, in some releases of Oracle7, analyzing tables owned by SYS can cause an ORA-600 error.

An example of the ANALYZE TABLE command is shown here:

```
ANALYZE TABLE scott.emp COMPUTE STATISTICS FOR TABLE;
```

When you analyze a table, Oracle populates the following columns in the DBA_TABLES, ALL_TABLES, and USER_TABLES data dictionary views:

NUM_ROWS
The number of rows in the table.

BLOCKS
The number of data blocks in use.

EMPTY_BLOCKS
The number of data blocks above the highwater mark. Note that BLOCKS + EMPTY_BLOCKS + 1 equals the total number of blocks allocated to the table. The highwater mark is represented by the BLOCKS value. Remember that the first extent of every table must be equal to at least two blocks, with the first block being used for the segment header.

AVG_SPACE
The average number of free bytes in each block.

CHAIN_CNT
The number of chained rows in the table. You can use the optional parameter LIST_CHAINED_ROWS to populate a table with the ROWID of every chained row. The table is of a specific format, and can be created using the SQL script *$ORACLE_HOME/rdbms/admin/utlchain.sql*.

AVG_ROW_LEN
The average length of all the rows in the table.

AVG_SPACE_FREELIST_BLOCKS (Oracle8 only)

The average free space in all blocks in the freelist.

NUM_FREELIST_BLOCKS (Oracle8 only)

The number of blocks in the freelist.

SAMPLE_SIZE (Oracle8 only)

The number of rows used in determining the statistics. A value of 0 indicates that all rows were used.

LAST_ANALYZED (Oracle8 only)

Timestamp of the last ANALYZE command.

ANALYZE INDEX

The next way the ANALYZE command is used is to analyze an index. There are actually two versions of this command, ANALYZE INDEX and ANALYZE TABLE ... FOR ALL INDEXES. When you use this command, Oracle calculates information about the B-tree depth and the distribution of leaf and branch blocks. Perhaps most importantly, it calculates the number of distinct rows in the index; the more distinct rows there are, the more likely that a given index lookup will result in very few rows. Fewer rows means fewer disk I/Os.

You should ANALYZE any index that could be a candidate for a join. Since your indexes have been created either in support of a unique or primary key or to facilitate a WHERE clause, this basically means that you must analyze all indexes.

Examples of using the ANALYZE command to analyze an index are shown here:

```
ANALYZE TABLE scott.emp COMPUTE STATISTICS FOR ALL INDEXES;
ANALYZE INDEX scott.emp_I COMPUTE STATISTICS;
```

When you analyze an index, Oracle populates the following columns in the DBA_INDEXES, ALL_INDEXES, and USER_INDEXES data dictionary views:

BLEVEL

The depth of the B-tree.

LEAF_BLOCKS

The number of leaf blocks in the index.

DISTINCT_KEYS

The number of distinct keys in the index. For a unique index, this will equal the value of NUM_ROWS.

AVG_LEAF_BLOCKS_PER_KEY

The average number of leaf blocks per key; that is, on average, the number of index leaf blocks that contain a given distinct key.

AVG_DATA_BLOCKS_PER_KEY

The average number of data blocks per key. That is, on average, the number of table data blocks that must be retrieved for every distinct key value.

CLUSTERING_FACTOR

The measurement of the likelihood that given key values are located close to each other in the table. The higher the value, the more likely that when you retrieve a data block to get the first row from the index, other rows will be in the same block or close to it.

NUM_ROWS (New in Oracle8)

The total number of rows in the table.

SAMPLE_SIZE (New in Oracle8)

The number of rows actually used to determine the values. A value of 0 indicates that all rows were used.

LAST_ANALYZED (New in Oracle8)

Timestamp of the last ANALYZE INDEX command.

ANALYZE TABLE . . . STATISTICS FOR COLUMNS

Sometimes the distribution of data in a column is not uniform. For example, a column may have three distinct values, A, B, and C, with relative distributions of 1%, 49%, and 50%, respectively. In this case, using an index to find all rows with a value of A would make sense, but it would not work for the values B and C. The results of the ANALYZE INDEX command would indicate that there are three distinct values, but would give no indication of the relative distribution of the data.

This is where histograms come into play. By grouping the values into *buckets*, Oracle can determine the distribution of data. With a histogram in place, Oracle would know that if it were looking for rows with a value of A (in the example above), an index would work just fine, but if it were looking for rows with either a B or C value, a full table scan would be more efficient.

Oracle uses a height-balanced histogram. That is, once it determines the number of buckets to use, it divides the total number of rows by the number of buckets. Each bucket then represents that many rows in sorted order. Oracle keeps track of the distribution of keys by storing the highest key value for each bucket. This is different from a width-balanced histogram, where the same number of distinct keys are stored in each bucket with a separate indication of the number of rows represented by each bucket.

The operation of the ANALYZE TABLE command changed slightly in Oracle7 Release 7.2. Since that time, if you do not include a FOR TABLE or a FOR COLUMNS clause, Oracle computes two bucket histograms for all columns in the table. This takes significantly more time to complete, and provides the optimizer with extraneous, often confusing information.

The EXP (Export) utility saves information about whether a table has been analyzed so the IMP (Import) can reanalyze the table after all rows are inserted. However, EXP has not been updated to reflect this new syntax, so it does not include the FOR TABLE clause. Thus, when you import a table that has been analyzed, IMP forces the creation of two bucket histograms for every column. For this reason, we recommend that you include the STATISTICS=NONE clause in the EXP parameter file, and that you separately generate statements to reanalyze the tables. See Chapter 16, *Tools and Utilities*, for a discussion of syntax.

Although we recommend that you analyze all tables and indexes, you should choose carefully the columns that you analyze. You should only analyze columns that are indexed, that are used in a WHERE clause, and that have a skewed distribution. You do not need to analyze unique columns or columns with a relatively high number of distinct keys, as those columns are analyzed when an ANALYZE INDEX operation is performed. You want to analyze columns where the distribution of data is such that Oracle uses the index only for specific key values.

An example of using the ANALYZE command to generate histograms is shown here:

```
ANALYZE TABLE scott.emp COMPUTE STATISTICS FOR COLUMNS empno, deptno;
```

When you analyze a table to generate column information, Oracle7 populates columns in the following views:

> DBA_TAB_COLUMNS
> USER_TAB_COLUMNS
> ALL_TAB_COLUMNS

In Oracle8, the columns are updated in the views:

> DBA_TAB_COL_STATISTICS
> DBA_PART_COL_STATISTICS

These are the view columns that Oracle populates:

NUM_DISTINCT
　　The number of distinct key values.

LOW_VALUE
　　The lowest keyed value for the column.

HIGH_VALUE
　　The highest keyed value for the column.

DENSITY
　　A representation of the distribution of key values within the column.

NUM_NULLS

> The number of NULL values.

NUM_BUCKETS

> The number of histogram buckets used.

LAST_ANALYZED

> The date the column was last analyzed.

SAMPLE_SIZE

> The sample size used to calculate the histogram. A value of 0 indicates that the values were computed.

ESTIMATE versus COMPUTE

The ANALYZE command allows you to specify how many rows are to be sampled when creating the statistics used by the cost-based optimizer.

You can tell Oracle to compute the statistics by looking at all rows:

```
ANALYZE TABLE scott.emp COMPUTE STATISTICS FOR TABLE;
```

You can tell Oracle to use a sample of 1064 rows:

```
ANALYZE TABLE scott.emp ESTIMATE STATISTICS FOR TABLE;
```

You can specify the number of rows to be used in the sample:

```
ANALYZE TABLE scott.emp ESTIMATE STATISTICS FOR TABLE SAMPLE 10000 ROWS;
```

You can specify a percentage of the rows to be used in the sample:

```
ANALYZE TABLE scott.emp ESTIMATE STATISTICS FOR TABLE SAMPLE 10 PERCENT;
```

Oracle claims that for sufficiently large tables, a 5 percent sampling is sufficient. This is consistent with current statistical modeling theory. The problem is determining that your table is sufficiently large.

Even when you estimate statistics, some information stored in the data dictionary is computed exactly. For tables, this is the number of blocks below and above the high water mark. For indexes, this is the depth of the B-tree.

Our recommendations are as follows:

1. If you have sufficient time and computer resources, use COMPUTE STATISTICS to get the best analysis.

2. If not, step down to ESTIMATE ... SAMPLE 40 PERCENT.

3. If this is still too much, step down to ESTIMATE ... SAMPLE 20 PERCENT.

4. Finally, if this is still too much, step down to ESTIMATE ... SAMPLE 5 PERCENT for tables with at least one million rows.

How often to ANALYZE

The information created and stored by the ANALYZE command is static. That is, once generated and stored, the same values will be used until you generate new information. You need to reanalyze after there is a significant change to the data. Of course, what constitutes a significant change to the data is a purely subjective decision. Some purists will claim that you need to reanalyze every night; however, this is probably not cost-effective. Our recommendations are as follows:

1. Analyze the tables, indexes, and histograms after the first load of the data.

2. If the tables are updated only on a known periodic basis, say, monthly, in a data warehouse environment, analyze them after the periodic update.

3. If the tables are updated on an ongoing basis, and the number of rows in the table is changing by more than 5% per week, analyze daily.

4. If the tables are updated on an ongoing basis, and the number of rows in the table is changing by less than 5% per week, analyze weekly.

This schedule ensures that tables are automatically analyzed.

Script to automate the ANALYZE process

The last few pages have been designed to convince you that if you are using the cost-based optimizer, you have to analyze your tables, indexes, and some of your columns. However, you don't want to generate and maintain a script that goes out and analyzes every table, index, and column. The following SQL*Plus script takes as a parameter a username. It then generates another SQL script that will:

- Analyze all tables owned by the passed username

- Analyze all indexes owned by the passed username

- Analyze all previously analyzed columns owned by the passed username

```
SET HEAD OFF
SET VERI OFF
SET FEED OFF
SET ECHO OFF
SPOOL &1..sql
SELECT 'ANALYZE TABLE '||owner||'.'||table_name||'
COMPUTE STATISTICS FOR TABLE;'
FROM dba_tables WHERE owner = '&1';

SELECT 'ANALYZE TABLE '||owner||'.'||table_name||'
COMPUTE STATISTICS FOR ALL INDEXES;'
FROM dba_tables WHERE owner = '&1';

Select 'ANALYZE TABLE '||owner||'.'||table_name||'
COMPUTE STATISTICS FOR COLUMNS '||column_name||' size 254;'
FROM dba_histograms
WHERE owner = '&1'
```

```
GROUP BY owner,table_name,column_name;

SPOOL OFF
SET HEAD ON
SET VERI ON
SET FEED ON
SET ECHO ON
@&1..sql
```

Specifying Hints

Here's the rub: for all its advances, the cost-based optimizer still may not find the best access path. For years, developers and DBAs were used to rewriting queries to ensure that the rule-based optimizer would use the most efficient path. You cannot do this with the cost-based optimizer. However, you can provide hints to the cost-based optimizer, giving additional information and guidelines on how to do the best optimization.

How to specify a hint

A hint is provided to the cost-based optimizer in the form of a comment within the SQL statement. Specifically, after you begin the comment (with either the "--" or "/* " comment syntax), start the hint with a "+" followed by the specific hint. If the hint is not properly formatted, it will not be honored.

The cost-based optimizer is unable to distinguish between an incorrectly specified hint and a comment. If you do not use correct syntax to provide the hint, not only will the hint not be taken, no error message will be generated.

Following are two ways you can specify the same hint:

```
SELECT /*+ RULE */  emp, ename, job, dname
FROM emp,dept
WHERE emp.deptno = dept.deptno;

SELECT --+ RULE
emp, ename, job, dname
FROM emp,dept
WHERE emp.deptno = dept.deptno;
```

Scope of a hint

The scope of a hint is at the statement block level. This would be either for the entire statement in a simple query or for the parent statement or subquery level in a complex query.

The following is a hint that applies only to a subquery:

```
SELECT ename, empno, job FROM emp
WHERE deptno IN
    (SELECT /*+ RULE */ deptno FROM dept WHERE dname = 'SALES');
```

Goal hints

Hints in this category allow you to specify a goal for the query. These are the values that can be specified at the database level with the *INIT.ORA* parameter OPTIMIZER_MODE or at the session level with the ALTER SESSION SET OPTIMIZER_MODE command. The following list describes each hint in this category and provides an example of its use:

ALL_ROWS

Tells the optimizer to choose the access path that provides the best throughput by minimizing total system resources.

```
SELECT /*+ ALL_ROWS */  ename,dname
FROM emp, dept
WHERE emp.deptno = dept.deptno;
```

FIRST_ROWS

Tells the optimizer to choose the access path that minimizes initial response time.

```
SELECT /*+ FIRST_ROWS */  ename,dname
FROM emp, dept
WHERE emp.deptno = dept.deptno;
```

CHOOSE

Tells the optimizer to use cost-based optimization if at least one of the tables in the join has been analyzed. Otherwise, revert to RULE.

```
SELECT /*+ CHOOSE */  ename,dname
FROM emp, dept
WHERE emp.deptno = dept.deptno;
```

RULE

Tells the optimizer to revert to using the rule-based optimizer rules.

```
SELECT /*+ RULE */  ename,dname
FROM emp, dept
WHERE emp.deptno = dept.deptno;
```

If the optimizer uses cost-based optimization and one or more of the tables have not been analyzed, Oracle will automatically perform an ANALYZE TABLE ... ESTIMATE STATISTICS with the default 1064 rows, use the results, and then not store them. If this table is used often, Oracle will constantly reanalyze the table.

Access method hints

Hints in this category allow you to specify which access path to use. The following list describes each hint in this category and provides an example of its use:

FULL

Forces the optimizer to perform a full table scan on the specified table.

```
SELECT /*+ FULL(emp) */   ename,dname
FROM emp, dept
WHERE emp.deptno = dept.deptno;
```

ROWID

Forces a table scan using the ROWID for the specified table.

```
SELECT /*+ ROWID(emp) */   ename,dname
FROM emp, dept
WHERE emp.deptno = dept.deptno;
```

CLUSTER

Forces the optimizer to use a cluster scan for the specified table. Obviously, this can only apply to clustered tables.

```
SELECT /*+ CLUSTER(emp) */   ename,dname
FROM emp, dept
WHERE emp.deptno = dept.deptno;
```

HASH

Forces the optimizer to use a cluster hash scan to access the specified table. Obviously, this can only apply to clustered tables.

```
SELECT /*+ HASH(emp) */   ename,dname
FROM emp, dept
WHERE emp.deptno = dept.deptno;
```

HASH_AJ

Tells the optimizer to transform a NOT IN subquery into a hash anti-join.

```
SELECT /*+ HASH_AJ */ ename
FROM emp
WHERE deptno NOT IN  (10,20);
```

HASH_SJ

Forces the optimizer to convert a correlated EXISTS subquery into a hash semi-join.

```
SELECT /*+ HASH_SJ */ ename
FROM emp
WHERE EXISTS
    (SELECT 'x' FROM dept
    WHERE emp.deptno = dept.deptno);
```

INDEX

Forces the optimizer to use an index scan on the specified index.

```
SELECT /*+ INDEX(emp emp_pk) */ *
FROM emp
WHERE empno =  7900;
```

INDEX_ASC

Forces the optimizer to use an index scan on the specified index. It further specifies that the index range scan be performed in ascending order. In Oracle7 and Oracle8, this is the current practice, so this hint works exactly like the INDEX hint.

```
SELECT /*+ INDEX_ASC(emp emp_pk) */ *
FROM emp
WHERE empno =  7900;
```

INDEX_COMBINE

There are two forms of this hint. The first form specifies only a table. In this case, the optimizer will use whatever Boolean combination of bitmap indexes it determines is best for the query.

```
SELECT /*+ INDEX_COMBINE (dept) */ *
FROM dept
WHERE dname = 'SALES' AND loc = 'CHICAGO';
```

The second form specifies one or more bitmap indexes that should be included in the Boolean combination.

```
SELECT /*+ INDEX_COMBINE (dept dept_loc_i) */ *
FROM dept
WHERE dname = 'SALES' AND loc = 'CHICAGO';
```

INDEX_DESC

Forces the optimizer to perform an index scan on the specified index. It further specifies that the index range scan be performed in descending order. This hint can only be used with SQL statements that access one table.

```
SELECT /*+ INDEX_DESC(emp emp_pk) */ *
FROM emp
WHERE empno =  7900;
```

INDEX_FFS

Causes a fast full index scan rather than a full table scan.

```
SELECT /*+ INDEX_FFS(emp emp_pk) */ *
FROM emp
WHERE empno =  7900;
```

MERGE_AJ

Transforms a NOT IN subquery into a merge anti-join.

```
SELECT /*+ HASH_AJ */ ename
FROM emp
WHERE deptno NOT IN  (10,20);
```

MERGE_SJ

Transforms a correlated EXISTS subquery into a merge semi-join.

```
SELECT /*+ HASH_SJ */ ename
FROM emp
WHERE EXISTS
    (SELECT 'x' FROM dept
     WHERE emp.deptno = dept.deptno);
```

AND_EQUAL

Explicitly causes the optimizer to choose an access plan that merges scans on several single-column indexes. You must specify at least two, and no more than five, indexes.

```
SELECT /*+ AND_EQUAL (emp  emp_deptno emp_sal) */ *
FROM emp
WHERE deptno = 20 and sal = 3000;
```

USE_CONCAT

Forces the optimizer to convert a query with an OR statement into a UNION ALL.

```
SELECT /*+ USE_CONCAT /* *
FROM emp
WHERE deptno = 20 OR sal = 3000;
```

In this case, the optimizer would convert this query into:

```
SELECT *
FROM emp
WHERE deptno = 20
UNION ALL
SELECT *
FROM emp
WHERE sal = 3000;
```

Join order hints

Hints in this category allow you to specify the order of the join operation. The following list describes each hint in this category and provides an example of its use:

ORDERED

Forces the optimizer to drive the join order based upon the order in which the tables are listed in the WHERE clause.

```
SELECT /*+ ORDERED */  emp,dname
FROM emp, dept
WHERE emp.deptno = dept.deptno;
```

In this case, the optimizer would perform a full table scan on the EMP table and perform a nested loop to query the DEPT table. This is the opposite order from that in which the rule-based optimizer would drive the tables.

STAR

Forces the optimizer to perform a star query. In order for this to work, you must have at least three tables in the query, and the largest table should have a concatenated index with at least three columns.

```
SELECT /*+ STAR */ fact.a, fact.b, dim1.c, dim2.d, dim3.e
FROM fact, dim1, dim2, dim3
WHERE fact.i1 = dim1.i1
AND fact.i2 = dim2.i2
AND fact.i3 = dim3.i3;
```

Join operation hints

Hints in this category allow you to specify how to perform the join operation. The following list describes each hint in this category and provides an example of its use:

USE_NL

> Forces the optimizer to perform a nested loop join, with the listed table as the inner table.

```
SELECT /*+ USE_NL(emp) */  ename,dname
FROM emp,dept
WHERE emp.deptno = dept.deptno;
```

USE_MERGE

> Forces the optimizer to perform a cascading merge join. The first two tables in the hint are joined using a merge join, and succeeding tables are joined, one by one, to the result set, using a merge join.

```
SELECT /*+ USE_MERGE(emp,dept) */  ename,dname
FROM emp,dept
WHERE emp.deptno = dept.deptno;
```

USE_HASH

> Forces the optimizer to perform a cascading hash join. The first two tables in the hint are joined using a hash join, and succeeding tables are joined, one by one, to the result set, using a hash join.

```
SELECT /*+ USE_HASH(emp,dept) */  ename,dname
FROM emp,dept
WHERE emp.deptno = dept.deptno;
```

DRIVING_SITE

> Forces the optimizer to use a specific site for driving distributed queries.

```
SELECT /*+ DRIVING_SITE(dept) */ *
FROM emp,dept@drsite
WHERE emp.deptno = dept.deptno;
```

Parallel operation hints

Hints in this category allow you to specify the degree of parallelism used in the query. These hints would override any PARALLEL values in the *INIT.ORA* file or specified at the table level. The following list describes each hint in this category and provides an example of its use:

PARALLEL

> Overrides the default parallelism values that would normally be used for a table. This hint has three parameters: the table name, the degree of parallelism, and an optional third parameter that specifies the number of instances in a parallel server that can be used.

```
SELECT /*+ FULL(emp) PARALLEL(emp,4,4) */ ename
FROM emp;
```

NOPARALLEL

Overrides the default parallelism value for a table to preclude the use of a parallel query.

```
SELECT /*+ NOPARALLEL(emp) */  ename
FROM emp;
```

Note that this is the same as:

```
SELECT /*+ PARALLEL(emp,1,1) */ ename
FROM emp;
```

APPEND

This hint is used for INSERTs. With the hint, data is appended to the end of the table, and unused free space in data blocks is ignored. This is the default mode for parallel INSERTs in Oracle8.

```
INSERT /*+ APPEND */
INTO emp
SELECT * from scott.emp;
```

NOAPPEND

This hint is used for INSERTs to override APPEND mode. In this case, all available free space in the data blocks is used first before appending to the end of the table.

```
INSERT /*+ NOAPPEND */
INTO emp
SELECT * FROM scott.emp;
```

PARALLEL_INDEX

This hint is similar to the PARALLEL hint. It allows you to override the normal parallelism values for parallel index scans for partitioned indexes. There are four parameters: the table name, the index name, the degree of parallelism, and the number of instances to use in a Parallel Server environment.

```
SELECT /*+ PARALLEL_INDEX (emp, emp_deptno, 4,4) */ ename
FROM emp
WHERE deptno = 10;
```

NOPARALLEL_INDEX

This hint is similar to the NOPARALLEL hint. It overrides the default parallelism values for a parallel index scan by forcing the optimizer not to use parallelism.

```
SELECT /*+ NO_PARALLEL_INDEX (emp, emp_deptno) */ ename
FROM emp
WHERE deptno = 10;
```

This is the same as specifying:

```
SELECT /*+ PARALLEL_INDEX (emp, emp_deptno, 1,1) */ ename
FROM emp
WHERE deptno = 10;
```

Additional hints

These miscellaneous hints can also be used to force the optimizer to function in certain ways. The following list describes each hint in this category and provides an example of its use:

CACHE

Forces blocks that are retrieved as part of a full table scan to be placed at the front of the least recently used (LRU) queue, thus helping ensure they stay in memory. Normally, data blocks that are read as part of a full table scan are not moved to the front of the queue.

```
SELECT /*+ FULL(emp) CACHE (emp) */  ename
FROM scott.emp;
```

NOCACHE

Forces blocks that are retrieved as part of a full table scan not to be placed at the front of the LRU queue. This is the normal process for full table scans.

```
SELECT /*+ FULL(emp) NOCACHE(emp) */ ename
FROM scott.emp;
```

MERGE

Forces the *INIT.ORA* parameter COMPLEX_VIEW_MERGING to be evaluated to TRUE for this query. This allows the optimizer to decompose a view or sub-query and evaluate it with all other WHERE conditions. In the following example, emp_view is a view.

```
SELECT /*+ MERGE(v) */  v.ename, d.dname
FROM emp_view v, dept d
WHERE v.deptno = d.deptno;
```

NOMERGE

Forces the *INIT.ORA* parameter COMPLEX_VIEW_MERGING to be evaluated to FALSE for this query. This forces the optimizer to evaluate the view prior to joining the results with the WHERE conditions. In the following example, emp_view is a view.

```
SELECT /*+ NOMERGE(v) */  v.ename, d.dname
FROM emp_view v, dept d
WHERE v.deptno = d.deptno;
```

PUSH_JOIN_PRED

Forces the *INIT.ORA* parameter PUSH_JOIN_PREDICATE to be evaluated to TRUE for this query. This allows the optimizer to push join predicates into views within the query for potentially better performance. In the following example, emp_view is a view.

```
SELECT /*+ PUSH_JOIN_PRED(v) */  v.ename, d.dname
FROM emp_view v, dept d
WHERE v.deptno = d.deptno;
```

NO_PUSH_JOIN_PRED

Forces the *INIT.ORA* parameter PUSH_JOIN_PREDICATE to be evaluated to FALSE for this query. This forces the optimizer to evaluate the specified view without pushing join predicates into the view. In the following example, emp_ view is a view.

```
SELECT /*+ NO_PUSH_JOIN_PRED(v) */  v.ename, d.dname
FROM emp_view v, dept d
WHERE v.deptno = d.deptno;
```

PUSH_SUBQ

Allows the optimizer to consider evaluating views that have not been merged early in the execution plan. Normally, nonmerged views are evaluated at the end. If the nonmerged view will generate a significant reduction in rows, it may be beneficial to use this hint. In the following example, emp_view is a view.

```
SELECT /*+ PUSH_SUBQ */  v.ename, d.dname
FROM emp_view v, dept d
WHERE v.deptno = d.deptno;
```

STAR_TRANSFORMATION

Forces the optimizer to choose the best transformation access path of those generated, even if a nontransformation access path has a lower cost. Normally, the optimizer will choose the lowest cost access path. Note that if the optimizer is unable to generate the required subqueries in order to create a star transformation, it will ignore this hint.

```
SELECT /*+ STAR_TRANSFORMATION */  id, customer_name
FROM order_view
WHERE settle_currency='UK Pounds'
AND quoted_currency='US Dollars'
AND sales_office_id='North America'
```

Rule-Based Optimizer

The rule-based optimizer (RBO) was the original optimizer delivered with Oracle. It was very simplistic in its approach, but that was actually its biggest strength. You were always able to predict how it would handle a particular situation. If you did not like the access plan it developed, you could change how the query was written.

The rule-based optimizer has been augmented with the separate cost-based optimizer (CBO), and Oracle has announced that as new features are added to the product, only the cost-based optimizer will be enhanced to support them. For example, the rule-based optimizer is unable to use a bitmap index.

Since Oracle considers the rule-based optimizer obsolete, we wondered if it would still be appropriate to include information about the rule-based optimizer in this chapter. As we talked to people in the Oracle community, however, we found that the rule-based optimizer is still very much alive and kicking. Many experienced DBAs feel that there is too much overhead required to maintain the statistics used by the cost-based optimizer. And, in our own experience, when all else fails, you can often get the best performance from a query by using the RULE hint and letting the old rule-based optimizer do its work.

Rules of Precedence

The rule-based optimizer has 15 rules that it uses to determine how to parse a query. Each rule has a rank. The optimizer looks at all the combinations it can find, then chooses the access path with the lowest rank. Table 8-2 lists the 15 rules in order.

Table 8-2. Rule-Based Optimizer Rules of Precedence

Rank	Access Path
1	Single row by ROWID
2	Single row by cluster join
3	Single row by hash cluster key with unique or primary key
4	Single row by unique or primary key
5	Cluster join
6	Hash cluster key
7	Indexed cluster key
8	Composite key
9	Single-column indexes
10	Bounded range search on indexed columns
11	Unbounded range search on indexed columns
12	Sort-merge join
13	Maximum or minimum of indexed column
14	Order by an indexed column
15	Full table scan

If the rule-based optimizer finds a situation where it can apply a rule with a ranking of 11 or less, it will perform a nested loop join. For example, assume that you are joining two tables, one without an index and the other with a unique index. The unique index has a rank of 4. Therefore, the rule-based optimizer will perform a full table scan on the table without an index, using a nested loop join to query the rows out of the second table.

Outside In

When the rule-based optimizer is processing a SQL statement, it looks for one of the 15 rules above to apply. If it finds that it can apply the same level rule for the same two tables, it falls back to the order in which the SQL statement is written. The table listed last in the FROM clause will be used to drive the nested loop join.

Most Recently Created Index

When Oracle has a choice of more than one index to use to select rows from the driving table, it will use the most recently created index.

Examples

The following examples using the SCOTT.EMP and SCOTT.DEPT tables show how the rule-based optimizer will process a query based upon the 15 rules listed in Table 8-2:

```
SQL>
SQL> rem
SQL> rem  use the standard emp and dept tables
SQL> rem  create new copies without indexes.
SQL> rem
SQL>
SQL> create table emp as select * from scott.emp;

Table created.

SQL> create table dept as select * from scott.dept;

Table created.

SQL>
SQL> rem
SQL> rem force rule based optimization and turn on
SQL> rem autotrace
SQL> rem
SQL>
SQL>
SQL> alter session set optimizer_mode = rule;

Session altered.

SQL> set autotrace traceonly explain
SQL>
SQL>
SQL> rem
SQL> rem  show that with no indexes, there are no real differences
SQL> rem  but the order of the driving tables is based on the last
SQL> rem  table in the from clause
SQL> rem
```

```
SQL>
SQL> select empno,ename,job,dname
  2  from emp, dept
  3  where emp.deptno = dept.deptno
  4  /

Execution Plan
----------------------------------------------------------
   0        SELECT STATEMENT Optimizer=RULE
   1    0     MERGE JOIN
   2    1       SORT (JOIN)
   3    2         TABLE ACCESS (FULL) OF 'DEPT'
   4    1       SORT (JOIN)
   5    4         TABLE ACCESS (FULL) OF 'EMP'

SQL>
SQL> select empno, ename, job, dname
  2  from dept,emp
  3  where emp.deptno = dept.deptno
  4  /

Execution Plan
----------------------------------------------------------
   0        SELECT STATEMENT Optimizer=RULE
   1    0     MERGE JOIN
   2    1       SORT (JOIN)
   3    2         TABLE ACCESS (FULL) OF 'EMP'
   4    1       SORT (JOIN)
   5    4         TABLE ACCESS (FULL) OF 'DEPT'

SQL>
SQL> rem
SQL> rem create an index on emp
SQL> rem in this case, since there is an index,
SQL> rem the nested loop will use the index, no matter
SQL> rem the order of the tables in the from clause
SQL> rem
SQL>
SQL> create index empi on emp(deptno);

Index created.

SQL>
SQL> select empno,ename,job,dname
  2  from emp, dept
  3  where emp.deptno = dept.deptno
  4  /

Execution Plan
----------------------------------------------------------
   0        SELECT STATEMENT Optimizer=RULE
   1    0     NESTED LOOPS
   2    1       TABLE ACCESS (FULL) OF 'DEPT'
   3    1       TABLE ACCESS (BY INDEX ROWID) OF 'EMP'
   4    3         INDEX (RANGE SCAN) OF 'EMPI' (NON-UNIQUE)
```

```
SQL>
SQL> select empno, ename, job, dname
  2  from dept,emp
  3  where emp.deptno = dept.deptno
  4  /

Execution Plan
-----------------------------------------------------------
   0      SELECT STATEMENT Optimizer=RULE
   1    0   NESTED LOOPS
   2    1     TABLE ACCESS (FULL) OF 'DEPT'
   3    1     TABLE ACCESS (BY INDEX ROWID) OF 'EMP'
   4    3       INDEX (RANGE SCAN) OF 'EMPI' (NON-UNIQUE)

SQL>
SQL> rem
SQL> rem  now create an index on dept.
SQL> rem  with an index on both tables,
SQL> rem  the rule-based optimizer will now
SQL> rem  perform nested loops using the
SQL> rem  last table in the from clause as the
SQL> rem  driving table
SQL> rem
SQL>
SQL>
SQL>
SQL> create index depti on dept(deptno);

Index created.

SQL>
SQL> select empno,ename,job,dname
  2  from emp, dept
  3  where emp.deptno = dept.deptno
  4  /

Execution Plan
-----------------------------------------------------------
   0      SELECT STATEMENT Optimizer=RULE
   1    0   NESTED LOOPS
   2    1     TABLE ACCESS (FULL) OF 'DEPT'
   3    1     TABLE ACCESS (BY INDEX ROWID) OF 'EMP'
   4    3       INDEX (RANGE SCAN) OF 'EMPI' (NON-UNIQUE)

SQL>
SQL> select empno, ename, job, dname
  2  from dept,emp
  3  where emp.deptno = dept.deptno
  4  /

Execution Plan
-----------------------------------------------------------
   0      SELECT STATEMENT Optimizer=RULE
   1    0   NESTED LOOPS
```

```
     2    1       TABLE ACCESS (FULL) OF 'EMP'
     3    1       TABLE ACCESS (BY INDEX ROWID) OF 'DEPT'
     4    3          INDEX (RANGE SCAN) OF 'DEPTI' (NON-UNIQUE)


SQL>
SQL>
SQL> rem
SQL> rem  now drop the index on emp.  with only an
SQL> rem  index on dept, the optimizer will always
SQL> rem  perform a nested loop using emp as the
SQL> rem  driving table.
SQL> rem
SQL> rem
SQL>
SQL>
SQL> drop index empi;

Index dropped.

SQL>
SQL> select empno,ename,job,dname
  2  from emp, dept
  3  where emp.deptno = dept.deptno
  4  /

Execution Plan
----------------------------------------------------------
     0       SELECT STATEMENT Optimizer=RULE
     1    0    NESTED LOOPS
     2    1       TABLE ACCESS (FULL) OF 'EMP'
     3    1       TABLE ACCESS (BY INDEX ROWID) OF 'DEPT'
     4    3          INDEX (RANGE SCAN) OF 'DEPTI' (NON-UNIQUE)

SQL>
SQL> select empno, ename, job, dname
  2  from dept,emp
  3  where emp.deptno = dept.deptno
  4  /

Execution Plan
----------------------------------------------------------
     0       SELECT STATEMENT Optimizer=RULE
     1    0    NESTED LOOPS
     2    1       TABLE ACCESS (FULL) OF 'EMP'
     3    1       TABLE ACCESS (BY INDEX ROWID) OF 'DEPT'
     4    3          INDEX (RANGE SCAN) OF 'DEPTI' (NON-UNIQUE)
```

9

Oracle Tools

Oracle database administration is like most other professional endeavors: the quality of job performance is often related to the tools available. Oracle database administrators are fortunate to have a variety of tools available to aid them in the day-to-day administration of the Oracle database. This chapter provides an overview of the most popular and useful Oracle tools, and shows how each tool can make the DBA's job a bit easier.

Tools provided run in either GUI (Graphical User Interface) mode, usually on Windows or Motif platforms, or in the more traditional character mode. Since GUI tools are designed to operate intuitively and have complete online help files, we only briefly describe their capabilities. Character mode tools, on the other hand, typically rely on command-line parameters or parameter files and have little or no online help. For these tools, we give information on usage here, and we supply more detailed information on specific character mode syntax in Chapter 16, *Tools and Utilities*.

About the Tools

Oracle has long recognized that without appropriate tools, a database is just a collection of bits and bytes, of little use to anyone. While some vendors assume that tools will be built by the user or purchased from another vendor, Oracle provides a powerful set of tools with the base distribution of the database that are useful for administration and configuration of the database as well as for application development. In fact, it is entirely possible to design and build a functioning database application using just this set of included tools. Table 9-1 provides a quick guide to selecting appropriate Oracle-supplied tools. Note that Import and Export are described in Chapter 4, *Preventing Data Loss*.

Table 9-1. Oracle-Supplied Tools

If You Want to	Use This Tool
Administer one or more Oracle databases	Oracle Enterprise Manager
Configure Net8 (Oracle8)	Net8 Assistant
Configure SQL*Net (Oracle7)	Oracle Network Manager
Create a database object	SQL*Plus
Create a formatted report of data from the database	SQL*Plus
Create or modify physical database structures	SQL*Plus, Server Manager, or Oracle Enterprise Manager
Export a copy of all or part of the database	Export
Generate SQL statements using SQL	SQL*Plus
Insert, update, or delete data in the database	SQL*Plus
Load data into a database	SQL*Loader
Modify a database object	SQL*Plus, Server Manager, or Enterprise Manager
Monitor the database	Oracle Enterprise Manager or Server Manager (GUI mode)
Perform DBA tasks in a GUI environment	Oracle Enterprise Manager or Server Manager (GUI mode)
Perform DBA tasks in line mode	Server Manager
Reload all or part of the database from a previous export	Import

SQL*Plus

SQL*Plus is almost certain to be the first Oracle tool that comes to mind, and for good reason. SQL*Plus has been available since the earliest versions of Oracle, when it was called the User Friendly Interface (UFI). SQL*Plus is primarily an interface to the database that allows the execution of SQL statements, but it is also much more than that. SQL*Plus can execute the following types of statements:

SQL
> Corresponds to the ANSI SQL standard and Oracle extensions

PL/SQL
> A proprietary SQL language extension from Oracle

*SQL*Plus*
> A proprietary formatting and operational tool from Oracle

SQL*Plus can't be easily categorized. Its behavior is probably closest to that of an interpreter, which means that it works with source statements directly without the need for separate compilation. SQL and PL/SQL statements are sent to the Oracle kernel, either locally or via SQL*Net, where they are parsed (a process similar to compilation) and executed. SQL*Plus statements are operated on and executed directly by the running copy of SQL*Plus.

SQL from SQL

One of the most powerful features of SQL*Plus is its ability to use SQL statements to create a new set of SQL statements, which in turn yield an interesting or useful result. For example, as the DBA, you might want to drop a set of tables from a particular user's schema. You could, of course, list all the tables and then issue a DROP TABLE command for each, but it would be much easier to write a SQL script (a collection of SQL*Plus, SQL, and/or PL/SQL statements) to do it. Here is a simple script that will, in turn, generate and run a script to drop all of SCOTT's tables:

```
set verify off
set pagesize 0
set termout off
set feedback off
set sqlprompt ''
spool dropem.sql
SELECT 'DROP TABLE',owner||'.'||table_name,';'
FROM dba.tables
WHERE owner='SCOTT'
/
spool off
set verify on
set feedback on
start dropem.sql
exit
```

When the script listed above is run, it will create an output file called *dropem.sql*. That file will contain the following:

```
DROP TABLE SCOTT.BONUS;
DROP TABLE SCOTT.DEPT;
DROP TABLE SCOTT.EMP;
DROP TABLE SCOTT.SALGRADE;
```

 This technique of generating SQL from SQL only works when the script is placed in a file and run using the START or @ command. The script will not work properly if it is executed interactively from the terminal.

As you can see, the first script generated a set of SQL statements that dropped all of SCOTT's tables. This script may be made more general, so that all tables belonging to any owner can be dropped by using a SQL*Plus substitution variable, as follows:

```
set verify off
set pagesize 0
set termout off
set feedback off
spool dropem.sql
SELECT 'DROP TABLE',owner||'.'||table_name,';'
FROM dba.tables
WHERE owner=UPPER(&Owner)
/
spool off
set verify on
set feedback on
start dropem.sql
exit
```

The substitution variable &Owner will cause SQL*Plus to prompt for the name of a schema owner, and will then substitute the value entered into the SQL statement as though it had been entered directly. This technique is extremely powerful, and allows the DBA to perform many functions with relative ease.[*]

Producing Reports

SQL*Plus also contains a powerful set of commands for formatting output and producing reports. While not as powerful or flexible as a full commercial report writing system, reports generated by SQL*Plus are attractive and easy to program, and may satisfy a variety of reporting needs.

Consider the following SQL statement, which lists all employees in the scott.emp table and prints a projected new salary based on a 10% increase:

```
SELECT empno,ename,sal,sal*1.10,comm
FROM scott.emp
/
```

When this statement is executed, the following output is produced:

```
    EMPNO ENAME           SAL   SAL*1.10      COMM
--------- --------- --------- --------- ---------
     7369 SMITH           800       880
     7499 ALLEN          1600      1760       300
     7521 WARD           1250      1375       500
     7566 JONES          2975    3272.5
     7654 MARTIN         1250      1375      1400
     7698 BLAKE          2850      3135
```

---

[*] For a collection of ready-made scripts, see *Oracle Scripts*, by Brian Lomasky and David C. Kreines (O'Reilly & Associates, 1998). For a complete discussion of SQL*Plus, see *Oracle SQL*Plus: The Definitive Guide*, by Jonathan Gennick (O'Reilly & Associates, 1999).

```
7782  CLARK          2450    2695
7788  SCOTT          3000    3300
7839  KING           5000    5500
7844  TURNER         1500    1650         0
7876  ADAMS          1100    1210
7900  JAMES           950    1045
7902  FORD           3000    3300
7934  MILLER         1300    1430

14 rows selected
```

While this output is readable and contains the requested information, it is probably not a report you would want to present to senior management. Try adding a few SQL*Plus formatting commands:

```
set space 2
set feedback off
set linesize 54
set pagesize 30
COLUMN empno heading "Employee|Number" format 9999
COLUMN ename heading "Employee|Name" format a10
COLUMN sal heading "Current|Salary" format $9999.99
COLUMN newsal heading "New|Salary" format $9999.99
COLUMN comm heading "Commission" format $9999.99
TTITLE LEFT 'The Totally Bogus Company' -
       RIGHT 'Page: ' FORMAT 99 SQL.PNO SKIP 2
BTITLE CENTER 'Company Confidential'
SELECT empno,ename,sal,sal*1.10 newsal,comm
FROM scott.emp
/
```

Now the following report will be produced:

```
The Totally Bogus Company                       Page:  1


Employee  Employee      Current      New
Number    Name           Salary     Salary   Commission
--------  ----------   ---------   ---------   ----------
    7369  SMITH          $800.00    $880.00
    7499  ALLEN         $1600.00   $1760.00     $300.00
    7521  WARD          $1250.00   $1375.00     $500.00
    7566  JONES         $2975.00   $3272.50
    7654  MARTIN        $1250.00   $1375.00    $1400.00
    7698  BLAKE         $2850.00   $3135.00
    7782  CLARK         $2450.00   $2695.00
    7788  SCOTT         $3000.00   $3300.00
    7839  KING          $5000.00   $5500.00
    7844  TURNER        $1500.00   $1650.00       $.00
    7876  ADAMS         $1100.00   $1210.00
    7900  JAMES          $950.00   $1045.00
    7902  FORD          $3000.00   $3300.00
    7934  MILLER        $1300.00   $1430.00


              Company Confidential
```

Oracle Server Manager

Oracle Server Manager is a tool included with each database for use in database administration. There are actually two versions of Server Manager: the graphical (GUI) version and the line-mode version. The line-mode version is available on every platform, while the GUI version is available on all platforms that support a GUI environment.

Server Manager can be used to administer any database running Oracle Version 7. 0 or later. In order to use Server Manager, the Oracle-supplied script *catsvrmg.sql* must be run as SYS on the database being administered. Normally, this script is automatically executed by *catproc.sql*.

Graphical Version

The graphical version of Server Manager is divided into three components:

Administration Manager
> Provides the DBA with a graphical interface to perform a variety of functions:

- Manage storage in the database

- Manage database security

- Start and stop database instances

- Manage database sessions

- Back up and restore a database

- Examine database schema objects

- Manage replication

SQL Worksheet
> Similar in function to SQL*Plus; allows you to dynamically enter and execute SQL and PL/SQL statements, run SQL scripts, and view the results.

System Monitor
> Allows the DBA to access a variety of performance statistics, including:

- Rollback segments

- File I/O

- System I/O

- Session activity

- Locks

- Latches

- Process

- Table access

All aspects of the operation of the graphical version of Server Manager are controlled by windows and pull-down menus.

Server Manager adapts itself to the particular platform on which it is running. For example, on a Unix server running Motif, Server Manager runs as a Motif application, while on a Windows platform, Server Manager runs as a Windows application.

Line-Mode Version

The line-mode version of Server Manager is provided on all Oracle platforms. It may be used on platforms that do not support a GUI environment, or when a command-line interface is desired or required. In this mode, commands are entered and executed one at a time. Line mode is especially useful for remote (dial-in) access to the database, as well as for automated operations, such as shell scripts run from *cron* on Unix systems.

Server Manager in line mode has limited functionality when compared to the GUI version. A limited number of commands may be executed, and SQL or PL/SQL statements may be entered and run. There is no monitoring capability in line mode.

Statements entered in line mode may extend to multiple lines, and each line may be terminated by a backslash (\) character. The semicolon (;) is used as the execute command.

SQL scripts may be executed in line mode by preceding the name of the script to be run with the @ symbol. For example, to run a script called *demo.sql*, you'd enter the following line in Server Manager line mode:

```
@demo
```

The Future of Server Manager

Although Server Manager is shipping with Oracle8, Oracle's plan is to discontinue this product. The command-line functionality of Server Manager will soon be available in SQL*Plus, and the monitoring components are now available through Oracle Enterprise Manager.

SQLDBA

SQLDBA is an Oracle-supplied utility program that is similar in function to Server Manager. SQLDBA was supplied with Oracle Version 6, but was made obsolete with the introduction of Server Manager with Oracle7 Version 7.0. SQLDBA was supplied, for compatibility purposes, through Oracle7 Version 7.2.

Functionally, SQLDBA is much like the newer Server Manager. It provides the ability to execute SQL statements as well as to perform monitoring of the Oracle database to which it is attached. SQLDBA is a character-mode application; there is no graphical version, although some basic character-mode graphics are used where available.

There are a number of differences between SQLDBA and the newer Server Manager; some of them are operational, but most are cosmetic. One of the most notable differences is the behavior of the STARTUP command. When you are using SQLDBA to start a database, any failure in the startup process results in all operations being backed out and the database being shut down. When you are using Server Manager, however, failure of any step of the startup leaves the database in its current state. For example, if an error occurs after mounting the database, Server Manager will leave the database mounted, while SQLDBA will dismount the database and shut down Oracle.

For more information about differences between SQLDBA and Server Manager, see Oracle Corporation's online *SQLDBA to Oracle Server Manager Migration Guide.*

Oracle Network Manager

Oracle Network Manager, introduced in Chapter 5, *Oracle Networking*, is an Oracle-supplied tool that allows the DBA to create and maintain the configuration files required by the Oracle networking products SQL*Net and Net8. Oracle Network Manager will configure the following products:

*SQL*Net Version 2.0 and later, and Net8*
> Provides client-server and server-server communication.

MultiProtocol Interchange
> Provides application connectivity across protocols.

Oracle Names
> Provides name resolution services for SQL*Net and Net8.

SNMP
> Enables the monitoring of network objects using third-party tools.

Oracle Advanced Networking Option (ANO)
> Provides a variety of add-on features, including security enhancements, DCE integration, native naming adapters, and SNMP support.

For more information on Network Manager and the Net8 Assistant, which provides similar functionality beginning with Oracle8, see Chapter 5, *Oracle Networking*.

SQL*Loader

SQL*Loader is an Oracle-supplied tool that provides a reliable method of bulk loading data into the database from almost any type of external non-database file. The file containing the data to be loaded can contain either fixed- or variable-length records, and the fields in the records can be fixed or variable length as well. The actual data may be character, date, or any of several formats of numeric, including packed decimal and floating-point binary.

SQL*Loader provides the ability to selectively load data based on the values of data elements, and can load multiple tables simultaneously. Records that are not loaded due to errors or improper data values may be placed in a separate discard file for later processing.

The following tasks can be accomplished by SQL*Loader:

- Load data from multiple files, which can be of different file types.

- Load data from fixed-format, delimited-format (e.g., comma-delimited), or variable-length records.

- Perform manipulation of data fields with SQL statements before storing this data in the database.

- Load from a variety of datatypes, including DATE, BINARY, PACKED DECIMAL, and ZONED DECIMAL.

- Combine multiple records into a single database row.

- Create multiple database rows from a single input record.

- Generate unique key values for columns as data is loaded.

Conventional and Direct Path Loading

Data can be loaded into the database using either the conventional path or direct path methods. When using *conventional path loading*, data is loaded into a bind array, which is then written to the database when the bind array is full, or when there is no data remaining in the input file. Conventional path loading uses the standard SQL INSERT command to place data into the database.

When using *direct path loading*, data rows are placed into formatted database blocks and are then written directly to the database. This process bypasses most RDBMS processing, and results in a significantly faster load. However, there are several restrictions associated with direct path loading:

- Tables and associated indexes will be locked for the duration of the load.

- SQL*Net access is available only under limited circumstances, and its use will slow performance.

- Clustered tables cannot be loaded using direct path.

- Constraints that depend on other tables are disabled during the load and are then applied to the table when the load is completed.

- SQL functions are not available when using the direct path.

- Only the version of SQL*Loader that exactly matches the database version can be used for direct path loads; for example, you cannot use SQL*Loader Version 8.0.3 to load data into an Oracle database running Version 8.0.4.

SQL*Loader Files

SQL*Loader uses several different operating system files, including:

Control file
> This input file contains all information regarding the load, including the names, locations, characteristics, and formats of input datafiles, the datatypes and locations of all data fields, and the tables and columns to be loaded. In addition, detailed selection criteria can be specified in the control file.

Log file
> This output file contains a detailed description of the load, including details of all load specifications and any errors encountered. The log file is always created, although it may simply be written to the default output device, usually the screen.

Bad file
> This output file, which retains the same format as the input file, contains any records that cannot be loaded into the database due to improper input format or violation of a database integrity constraint (e.g., the required field is NULL or the field contains invalid data for the Oracle datatype).

Discard file
> If a data record is otherwise acceptable but is filtered out of the load because it does not match the selection criteria specified in the control file, then that record will be placed in the discard file. Like the bad file, the discard file is written in the same format as the original datafile.

For detailed information on the syntax of the SQL*Loader command line and control file, see Chapter 16, *Tools and Utilities*.

Oracle Enterprise Manager

Oracle Enterprise Manager (OEM) is a tool supplied by Oracle that provides an easy-to-use, graphical approach to managing one or more databases. It combines a number of distinct facilities into an integrated platform for managing Oracle products. From the Oracle Enterprise Manager's console, the DBA may be able to:

- Administer, diagnose, and tune one or more databases

- Distribute software to multiple servers and clients

- Schedule jobs on multiple nodes at varying times

- Monitor objects and events throughout the Oracle network

- Customize the display using graphic maps and groups of network objects such as nodes and databases

- Administer Oracle parallel servers

- Integrate participating Oracle or third-party tools

 Although Oracle Enterprise Manager is shipped with the Oracle database product, some features of the Enterprise Manager (for example, the Performance Pack) are separately licensed and may only be used with an appropriate license.

The client/server architecture of Oracle Enterprise Manager consists of a centralized console, common services, and intelligent agents running on the managed nodes. Various applications reside on top of the common services, performing system management tasks.

The Oracle Enterprise Manager Console is a graphical user interface that provides menus, toolbars, launch palettes, and the framework to allow access to Oracle tools, plus utilities available through other vendors. The windows provide access to several components:

Navigator

Discovers and displays a tree list of all the objects in a network, such as user-defined groups, nodes, listeners, name servers, and databases, plus the objects they contain.

Map

Provides a means to create, save, modify, and recall views of the network. Objects can be dragged and dropped from the Navigator into the Map view to create groups to be monitored.

Console menu bar

Provides access to the Navigator, Map, Job, Event, and database administration applications.

Oracle Enterprise Manager has a set of common services that help manage nodes throughout the Oracle network. Key to these services is the *repository*. The Oracle Enterprise Manager repository is a set of tables in an Oracle database. Each administrator is associated with a specific repository in a database, and any information related to the tasks performed by the administrator is stored in that repository. The repository provides a centralized location for storing information on configurations, jobs and events, historical collections, tuning recommendations, the preferred credentials for each user, and other information associated with the DBA user. The repository tables can be installed in any database accessible in the Oracle network, and a DBA can log on to the repository database from any machine.

The Job Scheduling System allows the management of job scheduling among the databases, listeners, and nodes being administered. Jobs can be scheduled and run on remote sites throughout the network at various times, such as daily or weekly, and at single or multiple destinations.

The Event Management System allows tracking and display of the status of events occurring on the databases, listeners, and nodes in the Oracle network. A job can be specified that will take corrective action when a particular event is detected.

Oracle Enterprise Manager uses intelligent agents and a communication daemon to manage Console tasks such as scheduling and running remote jobs and monitoring events on remote sites. The intelligent agent is a process that runs on remote nodes in the network and functions as the executor of jobs and events sent by the Console via the communication daemon. The agent can function regardless of the status of the Console or network connections.

Access to Oracle services on the network is controlled by a set of user-defined, preferred credentials for the available nodes and services. Oracle Enterprise Manager encrypts the user authentication information in the repository and provides it as part of the connection request from the Console or Console-launched applications.

Oracle Enterprise Manager includes a set of standard integrated database administration applications. These applications are specialized management tools that can be launched directly from the Console or the Administration toolbar. Third parties can write applications that integrate into the Console and use the available common services, and these applications can be launched directly from the Console.

A command-line interface is sometimes necessary or desirable, so Oracle Server Manager provides a conversational line mode. In line mode, DBA commands can be explicitly executed on a command line.

Third-Party Tools

While Oracle provides a wide array of tools for use with the Oracle database, the popularity of Oracle and the need for specific capabilities has given rise to a variety of tools from third-party vendors. These tools range from useful utilities distributed at no charge by Oracle user groups to full-featured, integrated management tools costing tens of thousands of dollars. A listing of these tools is beyond the scope of this book, but timely information on Oracle-related vendors and their products is often available at local user group meetings, as well as at the larger Oracle OpenWorld and user group conferences and tradeshows.

II

DBA Reference

This part of the book provides detailed reference information you will need to perform Oracle database administration, including extensive statement syntax and parameter settings.

- Chapter 10, *The Oracle Instance*, describes the elements of the Oracle instance—in particular, the various Oracle processes and memory structures.

- Chapter 11, *The Oracle Database*, describes the elements of the database (physical files and tablespaces) and storage allocation.

- Chapter 12, *Initialization Parameters*, provides a quick reference to the Oracle initialization parameters stored in the *INIT.ORA* file.

- Chapter 13, *SQL Statements for the DBA*, provides a quick reference to the SQL statements used by the DBA.

- Chapter 14, *The Oracle Data Dictionary*, provides a quick reference to the data dictionary views used by the DBA.

- Chapter 15, *System Privileges and Initial Roles*, provides a quick reference to the system privileges implemented by Oracle and to the initial, or default, roles created by Oracle.

- Chapter 16, *Tools and Utilities*, provides a quick reference to the commands and parameters used with the tools most often used by the DBA: SQL*Plus, Export, Import, and SQL*Loader.

- *Appendix: Resources for the DBA*, summarizes the books, magazines, organizations, web sites, discussion groups, and list servers that DBAs should find helpful sources of additional information.

In this chapter:
- *Elements of the Instance*
- *About Processes*
- *About Memory Structures*

10

The Oracle Instance

The terms *Oracle instance* and *Oracle database* are often used interchangeably; however, there is a definite distinction between them. The term *instance* refers to the memory structures and background processes that allow access to the physical files that make up the *database*. This chapter presents the elements of the instance, and Chapter 11, *The Oracle Database*, will provide information on database structures.

Elements of the Instance

The Oracle instance consists of the Oracle processes and the associated memory structures required both to access the files that make up an Oracle database and to give Oracle users access to the data. Figure 10-1 shows a simple Oracle instance.

Processes

Simply put, a *process* is a "thread of control," or a mechanism within an operating system that can execute a series of steps. In other words, a process is a program running on a computer, under the control of that computer's operating system. In most cases, the process (also called a *job* or a *task*) runs in its own memory space.

Oracle creates and uses two types of processes: Oracle processes and user processes. Oracle processes are created by Oracle to perform functions on its behalf. They can be further divided into two general categories: background processes and server processes.

Background processes

These processes consolidate tasks that would otherwise need to be performed by each user process connected to the instance. Background processes perform a variety of tasks, including system monitoring and control and

Software Code (Oracle Executable)		
Background Processes	DBWR	
	LGWR	
	SMON	
	PMON	
	etc.	
System Global Area (SGA)	Database Buffer Cache	
		Library Cache
		Dictionary Cache (shared SQL area)
	Shared Pool	Control Structures
Server Process 1	Program Global Area PGA	Sort Area
Server Process 2	Program Global Area PGA	Sort Area

Figure 10-1. A simple Oracle instance

asynchronous I/O. Specific background processes include the Database Writer (DBWR), the Log Writer (LGWR), and a number of others. See the "Standard Background Processes" section, later in this chapter, for a summary.

Server processes

These processes are created by Oracle specifically to handle requests made by connected user processes. A server process handles communication with the user process and interacts with Oracle to carry out specific requested tasks. The correspondence between server processes and user processes varies depending on whether the Multi-Threaded Server (MTS) is configured and in use, as described in the "Server Processes" section, later in this chapter.

User processes

User processes are created to execute the code of an application program (for example, SQL*Plus or a Pro*C program) and to handle communications between the application program and the server process. User processes make use of the program interface, which is a standardized mechanism for communication with Oracle. The "User Processes" section, later in this chapter, describes the different ways in which a user process connects to the Oracle instance.

Memory Structures

Oracle uses memory structures to buffer data, execute code, and share data among Oracle and user processes. There are three categories of memory structures:

1. System Global Area (SGA), consisting of:

   - Database buffer cache

   - Redo log buffer

   - Shared pool, consisting of:

     Library cache (shared SQL area)
     Dictionary cache
     Control structures

2. Program Global Area (PGA)

3. Sort area

The "About Memory Structures" section, later in this chapter, describes these categories in some detail.

About Processes

Oracle uses a number of processes to manipulate and access the data contained in an Oracle database. Some of these processes are required in all cases, while others apply only to specific Oracle options.

Standard Background Processes

Depending on the options installed and the specific configuration of an Oracle installation, many background processes may be required. There is, however, a core set of background processes required for every Oracle instance, which are found in any machine on which Oracle is running, from Personal Oracle on an Intel-based PC to the largest Unix server. The failure of any one of these processes indicates failure of the entire Oracle instance; when such failures occur, the instance must be restarted.

The standard background processes include:

- Database Writer (DBWR or DBW*n*)

- Log Writer (LGWR)

- System Monitor (SMON)

- Process Monitor (PMON)

- Checkpoint (CKPT)

- Archiver (ARCH)

- Shared Server (S*nnn*)

- Dispatcher (D*nnn*)

- Recoverer (RECO)

- Lock (LCK*n*)

- Parallel Query (P*nnn*)

- Queue Monitor (QMN*n*) (Oracle8 only)

- Job Queue (SNP*n*)

The following sections briefly describe these processes.

DBWR—the Database Writer

The Database Writer process is responsible for the actual writing of data to Oracle's physical database files at the operating system level. An important part of this responsibility is the management of the database buffer cache (described under "Database buffer cache").

When an application makes a change to data contained in an Oracle database, that change, including inserts and deletes, is first made to a memory buffer. When data is written to a memory buffer, it is marked as "dirty," as opposed to "clean" or "free." The DBWR process (and DBWR I/O slaves in Oracle8) is responsible for writing the contents of dirty buffers to the physical disk files, thereby keeping the buffer cache clean. This action has the effect of maintaining an adequate supply of free buffers for use when a user process needs to read data from disk. To accomplish this, the DBWR process utilizes a LRU (least recently used) algorithm to keep the most recently accessed buffers in memory, thereby minimizing I/O, while writing buffers that will not be needed again to disk.

Buffers are written to disk when:

- A checkpoint is signaled.

- The dirty list reaches a threshold length, controlled by the *INIT.ORA* parameter DB_BLOCK_MAX_DIRTY_TARGET.

- No free or reusable buffers are available.

At least one DBWR process (DBWR in Oracle7, DBW0 in Oracle8) is required, and on many platforms additional DBWR processes can be created. In Oracle7, these additional processes are named DBW1 through DBW9, and the number is configured with the *INIT.ORA* parameter DB_WRITERS. In Oracle8, the additional processes are controlled by the *INIT.ORA* parameter DB_WRITER_PROCESSES (see Chapter 12, *Initialization Parameters*). The use of multiple DBWR processes up to the number of individual physical disk devices usually improves overall performance by permitting multiple independent writes to disk at the same time, even on systems that perform asynchronous I/O.

LGWR—the Log Writer

The Log Writer process is responsible for writing the contents of the redo log buffer to the log file on disk, and for management of the log buffer. Redo log data is always written first to a buffer in memory, then written to disk by the LGWR process when:

- LGWR is not active for three seconds.
- The redo log buffer becomes one-third full.
- The DBWR process writes dirty buffers to disk.

The LGWR process is also responsible for the following:

- Writing commit records to the log file when a transaction is committed. Multiple commits (known as *group commits*) may be written in a single operation when database activity is high.
- Recording a system change number (SCN) to each committed transaction, for use in recovery operations when running Parallel Server.
- Updating the headers of all datafiles when a checkpoint occurs, unless the CKPT process (described under "CKPT—the Checkpoint process," later in this chapter) is active.

SMON—the System Monitor

The System Monitor is responsible for performing the following operations:

- Instance recovery at startup
- Cleanup of unneeded temporary segments
- Coalescing of contiguous free extents
- Instance recovery for a failed CPU or instance in a Parallel Server environment

The SMON process "wakes up" on a regular basis to check whether any of these operations are required. In addition, other background processes can wake up SMON if they require one of these services.

PMON—the Process Monitor

The Process Monitor is responsible for performing the following operations:

- Process recovery when a user process fails, including cache cleanup and the freeing of resources the process was using
- Rollback of uncommitted transactions
- Release of locks held by failed or terminated processes
- Restart of failed dispatcher and shared server processes

The PMON process wakes up on a regular basis to check whether any of these operations are required. In addition, other background processes can wake up PMON if they require one of these services.

Other Background Processes

Other background processes may be active, depending on the Oracle options installed and the specific configuration of the instance. Most Oracle instances include one or more of these processes, which are often used by Oracle to implement features or improve performance.

CKPT—the Checkpoint process

The CKPT process, which always exists in Oracle8 but is optional in Oracle7, is responsible for updating the headers of all Oracle datafiles at the time of a checkpoint. In Oracle7, this task may be performed by the LGWR process, but if there are many datafiles in the database then LGWR performance may be reduced. In such a case, the CKPT process can be enabled to perform this task through the use of the CHECKPOINT_PROCESS parameter in *INIT.ORA* (see Chapter 12, *Initialization Parameters*). Note that the CKPT process does not actually write the updated header records to disk; that is still the responsibility of the DBWR process.

ARCH—the Archiver process

The ARCH process is used to copy the contents of an online log file to another location, typically a disk file, when that log file becomes full. Oracle uses the online log files in a "round robin" fashion—that is, when all available online log files become full, the first file is reused. The mode of operation whereby the contents of each file are saved prior to reuse is called *archivelog mode*, and is controlled by the ARCHIVELOG parameter in the ALTER DATABASE statement. The ARCH process runs only when the instance is running in archivelog mode. For an additional discussion of archivelog mode, see Chapter 4, *Preventing Data Loss*.

Snnn—the Shared Server process

When utilizing the Multi-Threaded Server (MTS) configuration of Oracle, one or more Shared Server processes are created with names S001, S002, and so on. These processes allow many user processes (discussed later in this chapter) to create connections to the Oracle instance, thereby reducing the system overhead while increasing the number of users that can be supported. When running without Multi-Threaded Server, and thus without any S*nnn* processes, each user connection to the database requires a dedicated server connection to the instance, which can quickly consume available resources (especially memory) and limit the number of user connections possible. The initial number of Shared Server processes created is controlled by the MTS_SERVERS parameter in *INIT.ORA*, and the total number is limited by the parameter MTS_MAX_SERVERS. Note that due to the nature of Shared Server processes, user-related data is not contained in the Program Global Area (PGA). Instead, this data is stored in the System Global Area (SGA).

Dnnn—the Dispatcher process

When running Oracle Multi-Threaded Server, one or more dispatcher processes (named D001, D002, and so on) are responsible for receiving connection requests from the listener and directing each request to the least busy Shared Server process. If the listener cannot find an available D*nnn* process, a dedicated server process is created instead. The actual number of Dispatcher processes running is determined by the setting of the *INIT.ORA* parameter MTS_MAX_DISPATCHERS.

RECO—the Recoverer process

The Recoverer process is used by the Oracle distributed transaction facility to recover from failures involving distributed transactions by:

- Connecting to other databases involved in the distributed transaction
- Removing rows corresponding to any in-doubt transaction from each database's transaction table

If a database is not available when RECO attempts to connect, it automatically attempts to connect again after waiting a predetermined interval.

LCKn—the Lock process

One or more Lock processes (named LCK0, LCK1, and so on) are used by Oracle running with the Parallel Server Option to provide inter-instance locking. For most Oracle instances, a single process, LCK0, is sufficient.

Pnnn—the Parallel Query process

Parallel Query processes are responsible for executing SQL statements to perform the following actions:

- Parallel query
- Parallel index creation
- Parallel data loading
- Parallel CREATE TABLE AS SELECT...

When the Oracle instance is started, the number of Parallel Query processes specified by the *INIT.ORA* parameter PARALLEL_MIN_SERVERS will be started. If the volume of SQL statements being processed requires additional P*nnn* processes, they will be created up to the value of the *INIT.ORA* parameter PARALLEL_MAX_SERVERS. As P*nnn* processes become idle for the period of time specified by the

INIT.ORA parameter PARALLEL_SERVER_IDLE_TIME, they will be terminated until only PARALLEL_MIN_SERVERS processes remain. If no additional P*nnn* processes can be created because PARALLEL_MAX_SERVERS has been reached, then additional queries will be processed in non-parallel (sequential) mode.

QMNn—the Queue Monitor process

This optional process, which exists only in Oracle8, is used by the Oracle Advanced Queuing Option to monitor message queues. Up to 10 Queue Monitor processes (QMN0 through QMN9) may be configured using the *INIT.ORA* parameter AQ_TM_PROCESSES. Note that a failure of a QMN*n* process will not cause the instance to fail.

SNPn—the Job Queue process

This process (called the Snapshot Refresh process in Oracle7) is used when snapshots are implemented in an Oracle database running with the Distributed Option. There may be up to 10 of these processes (SNP0 through SNP9) in Oracle7, and up to 36 (SNP0 through SNP9, SNPA through SNPZ) in Oracle8. The number of SNP*n* processes is controlled by the *INIT.ORA* parameter SNAPSHOT_REFRESH_PROCESSES in Oracle7 or JOB_QUEUE_PROCESSES in Oracle8. These processes are responsible for automatically refreshing table snapshots, and they wake up periodically to perform this action. If more than one SNP*n* process is running, the automatic update tasks are shared among the processes. Note that failure of an SNP*n* process will not cause the instance to fail.

Server Processes

There are actually two types of server processes that may be created by Oracle, depending on whether the Multi-Threaded Server is configured. The Shared Server process, described earlier, is used whenever a Dispatcher process requests a connection for a user process. An MTS configuration allows a configurable number of user processes to share a single server process. When Multi-Threaded Server is not being used, either because it has not been configured or because no Dispatcher process is available, a dedicated server process is started. This server process is used to connect the user process (client) to the Oracle instance via the SGA. In this scenario, there is a one-to-one correspondence between user process and server process.

Note that on some systems, when running in dedicated server configuration on the same machine, the user process and the server process are combined into a single service.

User Processes

When a user runs an application program, a user process is created to connect that application to the Oracle instance. This user process then establishes a connection to the Oracle instance via the SGA. There are three different ways in which the user process connects to the Oracle instance, depending on the particular configuration in use; these are described in the following sections.

Single task (non-SQL*Net)

In operating systems that can maintain a separation between the database application and the Oracle code in a single process (e.g., VAX VMS), a single user process is created for each user, and this process connects directly to the Oracle instance via the SGA.

Two task (with dedicated servers)

In operating systems such as Unix, a user process is created to execute application code, and a separate server process is created to connect to the Oracle instance via the SGA. In this configuration, which is used whenever the Multi-Threaded Server is not used, each user process also requires a corresponding server process, which is automatically created for each client requesting a connection. This is a common configuration, and is used even when the application (client) code and the Oracle server code are running on the same machine, where interprocess communication mechanisms (IPCs) are used.

Multi-Threaded Server

When Oracle's Multi-Threaded Server is configured, each user process connects to a Shared Server process via a Dispatcher process (see the previous discussion of Shared Server and Dispatcher processes). SQL*Net is always required to use the Multi-Threaded Server, even if the client code and Oracle server code are running on the same machine.

About Memory Structures

Along with processes, memory structures are fundamental components of an Oracle instance. These memory structures store:

- Code being executed
- Data needed by code being executed
- Information about sessions
- Information shared among processes
- Cached information

The structures supporting each of these functions are described in the following sections.

Software Code Areas

The software code areas are segments of either real or virtual memory used to store Oracle's executable code. These areas are typically in a protected location, separate and distinct from any code being executed by the user (client) process. Software code areas are normally loaded at the first instance startup on the host machine, and are loaded as sharable, read-only code whenever possible. For example, a Unix machine running two Oracle instances loads only a single copy of the Oracle server code into memory, even though each instance will have its own set of processes and other memory structures.

System Global Area (SGA)

The System Global Area (SGA) is the most important memory structure of Oracle and consists of several different components. The SGA is a shared memory structure, and contains all memory-resident data and control information for a single Oracle instance (each instance must have its own SGA). Because the SGA data is shared among all users of the instance, it is sometimes called the Shared Global Area. Note that Oracle processes may both read from and write to the SGA.

Memory for the SGA is allocated when the instance is started and released when the instance is shut down. The size of the SGA is controlled primarily by various *INIT.ORA* parameters.

The SGA contains several components, described in the following sections.

Database buffer cache

The largest component of the SGA is usually the database buffer cache, which is the part of the SGA that holds copies of blocks of data read from the Oracle datafiles on disk. The size of the database buffer cache is controlled by the *INIT.ORA* parameter DB_BLOCK_BUFFERS, which specifies the number of database blocks that will be contained in the database buffer cache. Since this is expressed as database blocks, the size of the database buffer cache is the value of DB_BLOCK_BUFFERS multiplied by the DB_BLOCK_SIZE. For example, if a database has been created with a DB_BLOCK_SIZE of 8192 (8K) and DB_BLOCK_BUFFERS is set to 1000, then the database buffer cache component of the SGA would be 8192×1000 or 8,192,000 bytes.

When a user process needs data from the database, Oracle first checks to see if the required block is already in the database buffer cache. If it is, it is retrieved from the cache and a disk I/O operation is avoided. Oracle maintains an LRU (least recently used) list of blocks in the cache; when a block is read, its identifier is moved to the end of the list, making it the last block to be purged from the cache. One exception to this rule is that blocks read as the result of a full table scan are placed at the top of the LRU list; the assumption is that they are unlikely to be requested again soon. This behavior may be overridden by using the CACHE clause when creating or updating a table.

If the requested block is not resident in the database buffer cache, then a free block must be located. If the cache is full, then the block at the top of the LRU list is removed, and the requested block is read from disk. If the block at the top of the LRU is a "dirty" block—meaning that its data has been modified—then the identifier for that block is moved to the dirty list to await processing by the DBWR process. If a free buffer block cannot be located, the DBWR process is notified that its services are required, and the dirty blocks are written to disk.

When a block of data is not available in the database buffer cache and must be read from disk, it is considered a *cache miss*. Likewise, when a block is available in the buffer, it is considered a *cache hit*. The ratio of these two occurrences, called the *hit/miss ratio*, is an important metric for Oracle database tuning. The larger the size of the database buffer cache, the more likely it is that a particular block resides in cache memory, and the better the hit/miss ratio will be. Since memory access is orders of magnitude faster than disk access, most Oracle databases are configured with the largest possible database buffer cache.

Be extremely careful not to set DB_BLOCK_BUFFERS so high that paging results, since paging degrades the performance of the database much more than Oracle I/O operations from disk.

Redo log buffer

The redo log buffer is an area of memory within the SGA that holds information about changes to the database, called *redo log entries*. These entries are used if database recovery is necessary, and they contain information required to reconstruct changes made by INSERT, UPDATE, DELETE, CREATE, DROP, or ALTER statements.

The redo log buffer is circular—that is, when it is full, entries are written to it from the beginning. As discussed earlier, the LGWR process writes the contents of the redo log buffer to the active redo log file on disk. The size of the redo log buffer is determined by the *INIT.ORA* parameter LOG_BUFFER, which is expressed in bytes. The default value of this size is four times the DB_BLOCK_SIZE, but it is often desirable to set this value higher, particularly if there are many or long transactions generating high rates of redo generation.

Shared pool

The shared pool is an area of the SGA that, in turn, consists of three distinct areas: the library cache, the dictionary cache, and control structures. The overall size of the shared pool is controlled by the *INIT.ORA* parameter SHARED_POOL_SIZE.

Library cache. The library cache area of the shared pool holds SQL and PL/SQL code and control structures. SQL code may be contained in the shared SQL area, which contains both the parse tree and the execution plan for a SQL statement. When more than one user needs to execute a particular SQL statement, the parsed version is executed from the shared SQL area. In addition, each user has information related to the SQL statement in the private SQL area, which is contained in the Program Global Area (PGA). The private SQL area contains information unique to each user, such as bind variables and runtime buffers and is, in turn, associated with the shared SQL area that contains the actual parsed SQL code.

When a SQL statement is first executed, it is parsed and placed in the shared SQL area. Subsequent execution of that statement by any user will be faster, since reparsing is not necessary. Oracle maintains SQL statements in the shared SQL area using an LRU algorithm. If a SQL statement is removed from the shared SQL area, it must be reparsed and reinserted into the shared SQL area the next time it is executed. When a SQL statement is executed by a user process, the following steps take place:

1. Oracle checks to see if the SQL statement is already in the shared SQL area. If so, the parsed version is used for execution. If not, the statement is parsed and placed in the shared SQL area.

2. A private SQL area is allocated and assigned to the user process.

The private SQL area is maintained by the user process. The number of SQL statements that can be maintained in the private SQL area is limited by the *INIT.ORA* parameter OPEN_CURSORS, which has a default value of 50.

Note that if a user process is connected to the instance via a dedicated server process (i.e., the Multi-Threaded Server is not in use), the private SQL area is allocated in the user's PGA, not in the SGA. However, if the process is connected via a Shared Server process, the private SQL area will be allocated in the SGA.

PL/SQL program units (procedures, functions, packages, and triggers) are handled similarly to SQL statements. A shared area of the library cache is allocated to hold the parsed unit, and a private area is allocated for values associated with the specific session executing the PL/SQL unit. SQL statements contained within PL/SQL units are handled like any other SQL statement, even though they originate in a block of PL/SQL code. That is, the parsed SQL is placed in the shared SQL area, and a private SQL area is allocated for session data associated with that statement.

Dictionary cache. Oracle maintains its metadata—data about itself—in a series of tables called the *data dictionary*. The data dictionary consists of a number of tables and views containing information about the structure and contents of the database. Because the information from the data dictionary is used so often by Oracle, information read from these tables and views is stored in the dictionary cache (also called the *row cache*), where it can be shared with all Oracle processes. Like the database buffer cache, the dictionary cache is managed using an LRU algorithm that replaces infrequently accessed information with data that has been accessed more recently.

Control structures. The SGA contains other data required for the operation and control of the Oracle instance, including information about the state of the database, the instance, locks, and individual processes. This information is shared across all processes for the instance. No user data is stored in this area.

Program Global Area (PGA)

The Program Global Area (PGA) is a non-shared, writable memory area associated with a user process. Although the mechanism varies somewhat by operating system, the PGA is typically allocated when a server process establishes a connection to the instance via the SGA. There is a single PGA associated with each server process, and this area of memory is accessed only by Oracle code acting on behalf of this process.

The PGA always contains stack space for a session, which holds variables and other information associated with a session. The PGA may also contain session-specific information if the session is not established using the Multi-Threaded Server. If the Multi-Threaded Server is used, the session-specific information will be stored in the SGA.

The size of the PGA is determined automatically by Oracle and varies by operating system. The PGA size is affected by the following *INIT.ORA* parameters:

* OPEN_LINKS
* DB_FILES
* LOG_FILES

Sort Areas

Sort areas are memory structures used by Oracle to sort data. The sort area is allocated progressively at the time a sort is requested. It is created in the memory space of the user process that requests the sort when the user is not connected via the Multi-Threaded Server, and in the SGA if the MTS is in use. If multiple users are performing sort operations, multiple sort areas will exist in memory.

The maximum size of the sort area is controlled by the *INIT.ORA* parameter SORT_ AREA_SIZE, which is expressed in bytes. If the data to be sorted does not fit in the sort area, it is broken into multiple pieces that do fit, which are sorted separately. The results of these sorts are written to temporary segments in the database, then merged at the completion of the sort.

The size of the sort area may be decreased by Oracle under some circumstances. When this occurs, data is written to temporary segments, and the sort area is decreased to the value specified by the *INIT.ORA* parameter SORT_AREA_ RETAINED_SIZE. Memory released in this way is available to the user process, but is not released back to the operating system until the session terminates.

11

The Oracle Database

In Chapter 10, *The Oracle Instance*, we introduced the Oracle instance, and explained that the terms *instance* and *database* are often used interchangeably. This chapter provides information about the physical structures that make up an Oracle database, which is accessed by means of the Oracle instance.

Types of Database Files

The Oracle database consists of a number of physical files, often referred to as *operating system files*, since they are usually created and maintained by the host operating system. These physical files are used by Oracle for parameter storage, database coordination, and data storage. The files shown in the following list, which are described in the following sections, are unique to a particular database; that is, each mounted and opened database must have all of these files, and the files are not shared across instances except in the special case of the Oracle Parallel Server, whose purpose is to share datafiles.

- Parameter storage files:
  — Initialization file (*INIT.ORA*)
  — Configuration file (*CONFIG.ORA*)
- Database coordination files:
  — Control files
  — Redo log files
- Data storage files

Parameter Storage Files

Two types of parameter storage files are used by Oracle: the *INIT.ORA* file and the optional *CONFIG.ORA* file. These files, described in the following sections, collectively contain information provided by the DBA to configure and tune a particular Oracle instance.

Initialization file

The initialization file, usually referred to as the *INIT.ORA* file, is the primary file that contains configuration and tuning parameters. For detailed information on these parameters, see Chapter 12, *Initialization Parameters.* An *INIT.ORA* file must exist for each Oracle instance. This file is used by Oracle when starting the database, and therefore must be located in a known location, or Oracle must be told where it is located through the use of a command-line parameter to Server Manager. In Unix systems, this file is found in the *$ORACLE_HOME/dbs* directory.

The *INIT.ORA* file is one of only two Oracle files (the other is the *CONFIG.ORA* file) that can be directly read and manipulated by a user—in this case, by the DBA. The *INIT.ORA* file is stored as plain text—ASCII on most systems—and is typically edited by the DBA, using a text editor. The file format is straightforward: it consists of multiple lines, each of which specifies a parameter in the following format:

```
parameter_name = parameter_value
```

parameter_name
> Is the name of the parameter to be assigned a value.

parameter_value
> Is the value to be assigned—either numeric or text.

The following rules apply to entries in the *INIT.ORA* table:

- Parameter names are not case-sensitive. For example, the name "DB_Block_Buffers" is the same as "DB_BLOCK_BUFFERS" or "DB_block_buffers".

- There may be any number of spaces around the "=" sign.

- Parameter names must be spelled exactly; misspellings will result in errors.

- Text values may be provided without quotes.

- Parameters must be specified one per line.

- Comments begin with the # character (and are encouraged!).

Because the *INIT.ORA* file is a plain text file, it should not contain any special formatting, graphic, or control characters other than the newline character. Do not edit the *INIT.ORA* file with a word processing program, since these programs usually store extra control characters that will prevent the *INIT.ORA* file from being read properly by Oracle. Note that any error in the *INIT.ORA* file will prevent the database from being started.

> Be sure that the *INIT.ORA* file ends with a newline character. If it does not, a syntax error will be indicated, and this error will be very difficult to find.

Configuration file

The configuration file, usually referred to as the *CONFIG.ORA* file, is an optional file that contains parameters, just like the *INIT.ORA* file. In fact, the *CONFIG.ORA* file is a subset of the *INIT.ORA* file, and can only be used if the *INIT.ORA* file contains an "include" line specifying the name of the *CONFIG.ORA* file. Since the *CONFIG.ORA* file is actually merged into the *INIT.ORA* file prior to processing by Oracle, all of the same syntax rules apply.

The *CONFIG.ORA* file is primarily used to segregate a particular set of standard initialization parameters. For example, when running the Oracle Parallel Server, there are many initialization parameters that must be set identically for each instance, and these are stored in a separate *CONFIG.ORA* file. Similarly, several Oracle instances running on the same host may share a common subset of parameters that is stored in a single *CONFIG.ORA* file, while each instance also has a set of specific initialization parameters stored in its *INIT.ORA* file.

> At some Oracle installations, the database is configured differently for transaction processing (during the day, for example) and for batch processing (at night). In this case, the database is restarted with a different *INIT.ORA* file for each time period, but a single *CONFIG.ORA* file contains all common initialization parameters.

Database Coordination Files

Two types of database coordination files must exist for every Oracle instance: control files and redo log files. These files are critical to the operation of Oracle, and the loss of or damage to either file could have catastrophic effects on the database.

Control files

Every Oracle instance must have one or more control files. The control file is a binary file that is critical to Oracle, but is not directly readable by a user, nor is it editable by a text editor. The control file can be thought of as a software "boot-strap" file; it contains information that Oracle requires to start. Information stored in the control file includes:

- Names and locations of data files

- Names and locations of redo log files

- Information on the status of archived log files

- The current redo log sequence number

- Redo log information required for recovery

- Backup history (Oracle8 only)

- Timestamp information on the instance creation and startup/shutdown

- Essential parameters specified at database creation (e.g., MAXDATAFILES)

The information stored in the control file is so critical that if the control file is lost or damaged, the only options available for recovery are either to create a new control file (assuming that the DBA has access to all pertinent information required) or to rebuild the database and restore from a backup. Because of the critical nature of the control file, Oracle allows the DBA to maintain multiple mirrored control files, as specified by the CONTROL_FILES parameter in the *INIT.ORA* file. For example, the following line from *INIT.ORA* specifies two control files:

```
CONTROL_FILES = (/disk00/oracle/control01.ctl,/disk02/oracle/control02.ctl)
```

We strongly recommend that you maintain multiple mirrored control files on separate disks in case disk failure occurs, and, where possible, on different disk controllers in case controller failure occurs. Three or more mirrored control files are not unusual at well-administered Oracle installations.

Since the control file is not human readable, and is used only by Oracle itself, we recommend that, for operating systems with file protection, the control file be made readable only by the Oracle owner. In Unix, control files should be owned by Oracle, be assigned to group DBA, and have a protection of 600, which gives read/write access to the owner, but no access to the group or world.

Although the control file is in a binary format and is readable only by Oracle, a method is provided to create a script containing SQL statements that can be used to recreate a control file. This text version may be edited and used to create a new control file with modified values.

To create a text version of the control file, the DBA may use this command:

```
ALTER DATABASE BACKUP CONTROLFILE TO TRACE NORESETLOGS;
```

After execution of this command, a trace file will be created in a directory specified by the *INIT.ORA* parameter BACKGROUND_DUMP_DEST; by default, this will
usually be *$ORACLE_HOME/rdbms/log*. You must go to the directory containing
trace files and look for a file with an extension of *.trc* and a date/time stamp at the
time you executed the ALTER DATABASE command. This trace file will be similar
to the one shown in the following sample, which was created with Oracle Version 7.3.4 on an HP platform, and will contain the SQL statements required to create a new control file and restart the database.

```
Dump file /disk00/oracle/product/7.3.4/rdbms/log/DW1/ora_13607.trc
Oracle7 Server Release 7.3.4.2.0 - Production
With the distributed, replication and parallel query options
PL/SQL Release 2.3.4.2.0 - Production
ORACLE_HOME = /disk00/oracle/product/7.3.4
System name:      HP-UX
Node name:        datasrv2
Release:          B.10.20
Version:          E
Machine:          9000/800
Instance name: DW1
Redo thread mounted by this instance: 1
Oracle process number: 24
UNIX process pid: 13607, image: oracleDW1


*** SESSION ID:(33.132) 1998.09.20.20.10.16.174
*** 1998.09.20.20.10.16.173
# The following commands will create a new control file and use it
# to open the database.
# No data other than log history will be lost. Additional logs may
# be required for media recovery of offline data files. Use this
# only if the current versions of all online logs are available.
STARTUP NOMOUNT
CREATE CONTROLFILE REUSE DATABASE "DW1" NORESETLOGS NOARCHIVELOG
     MAXLOGFILES 32
     MAXLOGMEMBERS 2
     MAXDATAFILES 1000
     MAXINSTANCES 2
     MAXLOGHISTORY 200
LOGFILE
  GROUP 1 '/disk07/oracle/oradata/DW1/log01.log'   SIZE 2M,
  GROUP 2 '/disk10/oracle/oradata/DW1/log02.log'   SIZE 2M,
  GROUP 3 '/disk07/oracle/oradata/DW1/log03.log'   SIZE 2M,
  GROUP 4 '/disk10/oracle/oradata/DW1/log03.log'   SIZE 2M
DATAFILE
  '/disk00/oracle/oradata/DW1/system01.dbf',
  '/disk05/oracle/oradata/DW1/temp01',
  '/disk00/oracle/oradata/DW1/tools01.dbf',
  '/disk04/oracle/oradata/DW1/ldata01.dbf',
  '/disk08/oracle/oradata/DW1/ldata02.dbf',
  '/disk07/oracle/oradata/DW1/user01.dbf',
  '/disk09/oracle/oradata/DW1/rbs01.dbf',
  '/disk14/oracle/oradata/DW1/data01.dbf',
```

```
        '/disk15/oracle/oradata/DW1/data02.dbf',
        '/disk02/oracle/oradata/DW1/index01.dbf'
    ;
    # Recovery is required if any of the datafiles are restored backups,
    # or if the last shutdown was not normal or immediate.
    RECOVER DATABASE
    # Database can now be opened normally.
    ALTER DATABASE OPEN;
```

This SQL text file may then be edited (carefully!) by the DBA. You might change the value of one of the configuration parameters (MAXDATAFILES, for example), or perhaps change the name or location of a LOGFILE. To replace a control file, perform the following steps:

1. Use the ALTER DATABASE BACKUP CONTROLFILE TO TRACE command to create a control file trace (*.trc*) file.

2. Locate the *.trc* file in the BACKGROUND_DUMP_DEST directory, and rename it to something meaningful.

3. Perform a NORMAL or IMMEDIATE shutdown of the database. It is best if all tablespaces are online at the time of the shutdown; otherwise, recovery will be required after the control file is recreated.

4. Edit the *.trc* file created in step 1. Be sure to remove the documentation lines at the top of the file.

5. Using Server Manager or SQL*DBA, CONNECT AS INTERNAL.

6. Execute the edited file, which will recreate the control file and start the database.

Since this is a critical operation and an error may result in a database that cannot be opened, we highly recommend that you back up the database prior to creating a new control file.

Redo log files

Redo log files are operating system files used by Oracle to maintain logs of all transactions performed against the database. The primary purpose of these log files is to allow Oracle to recover changes made to the database in the case of a failure.

An Oracle database must have at least two redo log files, and most databases have more than two. These files are written by the LGWR process in a circular fashion; that is, when the last log file is filled, the first log file is reused. For example, if a database has three redo log files, blocks will be written to file1 until it is filled; then that file is closed, and LGWR begins writing to file2 (this is called a *log switch*). When file2 is filled, LGWR switches to file3. When file3 is filled, file1 is reused, and so on.

If the database is being operated in archivelog mode, then at the time of a log switch, the ARCH process copies the contents of the log file just filled to the ARCHIVE_LOG_DEST directory, giving the archived log file a unique name using a sequential number. These archived log files may be used during a database recovery to restore transactions made after the last complete backup of the database. If the ARCH process cannot finish copying before Oracle needs to use the log file again, all database activity stops until archiving is finished. Since this can have a significant effect on performance, make sure to create enough log files to prevent this from happening.

Because redo log files are so critical to database recovery, you must protect redo log files from loss due to a hardware failure. There are two ways this can be accomplished. One method is to replace redo log files with mirrored devices; with this method, the hardware or operating system (or both) ensures that redundant copies of the files are written simultaneously. The other method is to use redo log groups, a mechanism provided by Oracle. With redo log groups, the LGWR process writes to each member of the current redo log group at the same time, without incurring a significant amount of operating system overhead or degradation of overall performance. Place members of redo log groups on separate disks in order to avoid loss due to failure of a single disk device and to reduce I/O contention, since redo log files are written to sequentially.

Data Storage Files

The bulk of the storage allocated to any Oracle database is dedicated to (no surprise here) data. Data storage is arguably the most important component of the Oracle database, and it may be the most complex as well.

Oracle differs from other database management systems in many ways: one of the most important differences is the way Oracle allocates and manages data storage. In many systems, storage is maintained by the operating system and allocated to a database as required. In an Oracle database, the DBA allocates one or more blocks of storage to Oracle in the form of one or more operating system files, and Oracle itself then manages the allocation of this storage. In fact, the physical operating system files that make up the database are invisible to database user—only the DBA knows the physical makeup of the database. In order to control storage allocation, Oracle manages the physical disk space by dividing it into *Oracle blocks*, and uses logical constructs called *tablespaces,* described in some detail in the next section. Figure 11-1 illustrates the relationships within Oracle's data storage structure.

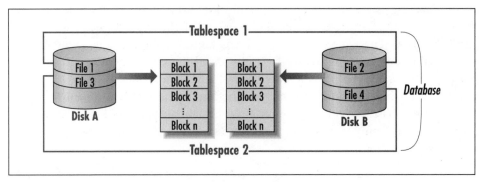

Figure 11-1. Data storage components of an Oracle database

Oracle Tablespaces

The tablespace is a logical construct used by Oracle to manage disk space. Tablespaces store various types of objects, including:

- Tables
- Indexes
- Stored procedures, functions, and packages (in the SYSTEM tablespace)
- Rollback segments
- Temporary segments

A tablespace is constructed by Oracle from one or more operating system files through the use of the CREATE TABLESPACE command. Every Oracle database consists of at least one tablespace, called SYSTEM.

When a tablespace is created, the names of the operating system files that will make up that tablespace are specified. For example, suppose that the following command is executed in a Unix environment:

```
CREATE TABLESPACE user_data
DATAFILE '/disk05/oracle/oradata/userdata01.dbf' SIZE 50M;
```

A datafile called *userdata01.dbf* will be created in */disk05/oracle/oradata*. This file will have a size of 50 megabytes and will be initialized by Oracle into Oracle blocks. The size of each Oracle block is determined by the parameter DB_BLOCK_SIZE, which is specified at the time the database is created. This is one of the only database parameters that cannot be changed, so take care when specifying the blocksize.

Once the tablespace is created, all access to the underlying datafiles is controlled by Oracle. No user has any reason to read from or write to Oracle datafiles, so file protections should be set so that only the Oracle owner account has access to these files. In a Unix environment, Oracle datafiles should be owned by the account "oracle", assigned to group DBA, and have their protection mode set to 700.

Oracle Blocks

When a datafile is assigned to a tablespace, Oracle formats the file into *blocks* for the actual storage of data. The size of each Oracle block is determined by the DB_BLOCK_SIZE parameter, which is specified when the database is created. The Oracle block is the basic unit of storage into which all Oracle objects (tables, indexes, rollback segments, etc.) are stored.

The Oracle block is divided into three distinct segments:

- The fixed block header
- The variable block header
- The data storage area

Figure 11-2 illustrates the structure of an Oracle block.

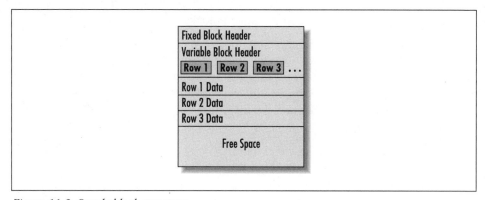

Figure 11-2. Oracle block structure

Fixed block header

The fixed block header will be exactly the same size for every block of a table, regardless of the Oracle blocksize. The size of the fixed block header will be:

    57 + (23 × INITRANS)

where INITRANS is the value specified for the INITRANS parameter in the CREATE TABLE statement when the table is created (the default value is 1).

Variable block header

The variable block header immediately follows the fixed block header in the block, and is dependent on the number of rows stored in the block. The size of the variable block header may be calculated as:

4 + (2 × number of rows in the block)

The initial 4 bytes contain the table directory, and there is a 2-byte row directory entry for each stored row.

As you can see, the fixed portion of the block header remains a constant size for every block of a particular table, and, in reality, for most tables, unless INITRANS is specified. The variable portion, however, is dynamic, and depends on the number of rows stored. More, smaller rows in a table will result in less available space in the remainder of the block than will fewer, larger rows. In addition, since the fixed portion is indeed fixed, better utilization of blocks can be expected with larger blocksizes. For example, a database having an Oracle blocksize of 2048 (2K) will lose about 3.9% of each block (57 + 23 bytes) to the fixed block header, while a database having an Oracle blocksize of 8192 (8K) will lose only .97% of each block. This is one way in which larger Oracle blocksizes may be more efficient.

Data storage area

The balance of the block is used for data storage—for example, to store the actual rows of a table. The calculation of the available storage in each block is not straightforward, since it is dependent on several factors, including:

* Oracle blocksize (DB_BLOCK_SIZE)
* Percent free space (PCTFREE)
* Average row length
* Number of rows stored per block

The average row length can be estimated as:

3 bytes row header
+ 1 byte per non-LONG column
+ 3 bytes per LONG column
+ average length of all table columns

The header space per row can be calculated as:

3 + (number of non-LONG columns) +
3 × (number of LONG columns)

The number of rows per block can then be calculated as:

((blocksize – (57 + 23 × INITRANS))
– (blocksize – (57 + 23 × INITRANS))
×(PCTFREE/100) – 4 – 2 × rows per block)
/ (average row length + header space per row)

Finally, the available space in the block can be calculated as:

(blocksize – (57 + 23 × INITRANS))
– ((blocksize – (57 + 23 × INITRANS)) × PCTFREE × 100)
– 4 – 2 × rows per block

Even this description simplifies the calculations a bit, since we do not take into account the possibility of trailing NULLs, LONG strings, and so on, which may have an impact on the exact calculation.

Storage Allocation Parameters

As you can see from the formulas presented above, the utilization of space within an Oracle block is complex. One major factor in the use of this space is the value set for PCTFREE. This parameter, which is normally set when an object is created but can be modified later, controls how much empty space is reserved in each block when a row is inserted. PCTFREE is specified as a percentage of the data storage area of a block reserved for future updates to rows in that block.

For example, a PCTFREE value of 10 would reserve 10% of the space remaining in a block after allocation of block headers for updates (note that this is not 10% of the total blocksize). This space is used by Oracle to allow rows stored in the block to grow in size. If there is not enough space left in a block to contain all of the data for an updated row, Oracle must allocate an additional block to hold the overflow. This is called *row chaining*, and should be avoided, since multiple, non-sequential I/Os will be required to read a single row of data. Of course, it is possible to have a single row, or even a single column, that is larger than the available space in a block. In this situation, block chaining is inevitable, although the DBA might consider a larger DB_BLOCK_SIZE, if warranted.

How Oracle Allocates Storage

Although Oracle stores rows of data in Oracle blocks, which exist in the context of a particular operating system file, the DBA has little control over which particular block is used for a particular database object. However, the DBA does control which tablespace an object is created in and how much space within that tablespace is allocated to the object.

When creating an object in the database, the CREATE statement usually specifies the tablespace in which the object will be stored (see the TABLESPACE clause of the CREATE commands in Chapter 13, *SQL Statements for the DBA*). If a TABLESPACE clause is not included in the CREATE command, the default tablespace for that user will be used for object creation.

As a DBA, you should be careful always to specify a DEFAULT TABLESPACE for each user, since Oracle will assign the SYSTEM tablespace as the default if you omit the specification, and in most cases you will not want non-system objects created in the SYSTEM tablespace.

Oracle allocates storage in logical units called *extents*. An extent is simply an amount of storage that is rounded up to the next multiple of the Oracle blocksize. When an object is created, that object has associated with it, either explicitly or implicitly, the amount of storage to be allocated upon object creation (the INITIAL extent) and the amount of space to be allocated when the INITIAL allocation is used and more space is required (the NEXT extent). A typical CREATE command contains a STORAGE clause in the following format:

```
STORAGE (INITIAL i  NEXT n  MINEXTENTS m  PCTINCREASE p)
```

The following sections examine each parameter of the STORAGE clause for this statement.

INITIAL

The INITIAL parameter in the STORAGE clause determines how much space will be allocated to the first extent when an object is created. This parameter may be specified in bytes, kilobytes, or megabytes. For example, the following all specify the same amount of storage to be allocated to the INITIAL extent:

```
INITIAL 1048576
INITIAL 1024K
INITIAL 1M
```

The default value for INITIAL is the INITIAL value established in the DEFAULT STORAGE for the tablespace in which the object is being created.

Extent sizes should be specified as integer multiples of the Oracle blocksize; otherwise, the allocation is rounded up to the next Oracle block. For example, with a 2K (2048) blocksize, a request for INITIAL 4097 results in three Oracle blocks being allocated.

NEXT

The NEXT parameter in the STORAGE clause determines how much space will be allocated for the second and subsequent extents allocated for an object. The NEXT parameter is specified in the same way as the INITIAL parameter. Although this parameter may be set to a specific value, that value may be modified dynamically if the PCTINCREASE parameter is set to a non-zero value. The default value for NEXT is the NEXT value established in the DEFAULT STORAGE for the tablespace in which the object is being created.

MINEXTENTS

The MINEXTENTS parameter in the STORAGE clause determines how many storage extents will be allocated to the object at the time of initial creation. Typically, this parameter is set to 1, but if it is set to a value greater than 1, the second and subsequent extents will use the NEXT parameter and will be subject to dynamic modification if PCTINCREASE is set to a non-zero value. The default value for MINEXTENTS is the MINEXTENTS value established in the DEFAULT STORAGE for the tablespace in which the object is being created.

PCTINCREASE

The PCTINCREASE parameter in the STORAGE clause determines the degree to which Oracle will automatically increase the size of subsequent extent allocations. This value is expressed as an integer percentage, and is applied to the then-current value of the NEXT parameter. For example, if an object is created with INITIAL 81920, NEXT 81920, and PCTINCREASE 10, this means that after each new extent is allocated, Oracle will dynamically increase the value of the NEXT parameter for that object by 10%. Table 11-1 illustrates the situation in a database with a 2048-byte blocksize.

Table 11-1. How Oracle Allocates Extents

Extent	Size in Bytes	Size in Blocks	Comment
Initial extent	81920	40 blocks	Uses INITIAL parameter
2nd extent	81920	40 blocks	Uses specified NEXT value
3rd extent	90112	40 blocks	NEXT increased by 10%
4th extent	100352	49 blocks	NEXT increased by another 10% and rounded to next block

If the default PCTINCREASE for a tablespace is set to 0, Oracle will *not* automatically coalesce smaller but contiguous extents back into larger extents in that tablespace. As a result, Oracle may be unable to allocate a particular extent even when sufficient contiguous blocks are available. Setting PCTINCREASE to a value of 1 will overcome this problem.

A Space Allocation Example

Consider the following SQL statement:

```
CREATE TABLE dept (
deptno              NUMBER(4),
deptname            VARCHAR(30)
location            VARCHAR(20))
TABLESPACE users
PCTFREE 10
STORAGE (INITIAL 8K NEXT 4K MINEXTENTS 1 PCTINCREASE 10)
```

Oracle will allocate space for the DEPT table as follows:

1. Oracle will look in the free space pool for 8K of space to assign as the INITIAL extent for the table. Assuming a database with a 4K blocksize, two blocks would be allocated.

2. After providing for the block headers, 10% of the remaining space would be reserved for growth of data rows, as indicated by the PCTFREE 10 parameter.

3. Once the INITIAL extent is filled (in this case, both blocks are filled), Oracle looks to the NEXT extent parameter to determine how much additional space to allocate. In this case, a value of 4K is specified. Since this database has a blocksize of 4K, a single block will be allocated and added to this table's space allocation. After this extent is allocated, the value of NEXT will be dynamically increased to 4506 because PCTINCREASE is set to 10 (4096×1.10).

4. When the third block is filled, additional space is required. This time Oracle allocates two blocks, since the current value of NEXT is 4506, and this value is rounded up to the next Oracle block.

Object Storage Sizing

One particularly important task for the DBA is to properly size the storage of objects in the database. This sizing primarily deals with the number and size of extents occupied. There is a widely held myth that multiple extents have a negative effect on performance; however, this is not necessarily the case. In fact, multiple extents, when properly planned and sized in a Parallel Query environment, can dramatically improve the overall performance of the database.

Free lists

When an object (for example, a table) is created, one or more Oracle blocks are allocated to that object; as we've mentioned, each allocation is called an extent. Storage is allocated according to the current STORAGE parameters. Oracle maintains a list of blocks available in each tablespace called the *free block list*. As blocks are added to a table, either through the allocation of an additional extent or by deleting data from an existing block, they are added to the end of the free block list. Since Oracle allocates data to blocks by searching for a free block starting at the beginning of the free block list, these newly freed or allocated blocks will be the last blocks used.

The highwater mark

For each object, Oracle also maintains a record of the highest relative block of the table used to hold data. This *highwater mark* is maintained in multiples of five blocks and is not reset unless the TRUNCATE command is executed.

When Oracle performs operations requiring a full table scan, such as SELECT COUNT(*), all blocks up to and including the highwater mark are read. If a table is created with 50,000 rows occupying 10,000 blocks, and those rows are subsequently deleted, the highwater mark will remain at 10,000, and a SELECT COUNT(*) command will read all 10,000 blocks even though they are all empty.

An even worse scenario is possible. Suppose that a table contains 50,000 rows, and the first 49,000 rows are then deleted. The blocks corresponding to the deleted data are placed at the end of the free block list. When the next INSERT statement is executed, Oracle finds the first block on the free block list, which is beyond the highwater mark. The effect is that all the free space (49,000 rows worth) is ignored, and the physical table becomes bigger. Full table scans and other similar operations still have to read all the empty blocks, and performance is significantly impacted. If you use SQL*Loader with the direct path option, these loads always begin at the highwater mark, so the table size may grow while leaving significant amounts of free space unused.

To easily determine the current value of the highwater mark, use the following formula after analyzing the table:

highwater mark = total blocks – empty blocks – 1

Total blocks for a table can be obtained by using the following query:

```
SELECT blocks
FROM dba_segments
WHERE owner='&Owner'
AND segment_name='Tablename';
```

Likewise, the number of empty blocks (blocks above the highwater mark) can be obtained with this query:

```
SELECT empty_blocks
FROM dba_tables
WHERE owner='&Owner'
AND segment_name='Tablename';
```

Disk Allocation

In a typical installation, Oracle tends to be I/O bound. Database transactions are slowed by waiting for one or more input/output operations, rather than by waiting for the CPU to complete an operation. Because the database is so dependent on I/O, overall Oracle performance can be improved, sometimes dramatically, by improving the overall performance of the I/O system on the host server. While there are several ways I/O performance may be improved (for example, by using faster disk drives or more controllers), one relatively easy way to improve I/O is by carefully allocating physical disk resources to Oracle.

Each time an Oracle table is updated, the following I/O operations are performed:

- The write to the table
- Reads and writes to any indexes
- Reads and writes to the temporary tablespace if large sorts or joins are involved
- Writes to the rollback segment for the table
- Writes to the rollback segment for any indexes
- Writes of the redo log buffer to disk for the table
- Writes of the redo log buffer to disk for any indexes
- Writes to the data dictionary if new extents are needed

In addition, if the database is running in archivelog mode, then at any given time the ARCH process may read from one of the online redo log files and write a copy to the archive log destination.

Disk Layout

The more independent physical disks that can be dedicated to Oracle files, the better the I/O operation of the system is likely to be. Carefully planning the location of each Oracle file will yield significant improvements in the performance of the database. Use the following guidelines when laying out the disk subsystem:

- Allocate separate disks for data, redo logs, and archive files.
- Keep data and index segments for a given table in separate tablespaces, on separate disks.
- Use a separate disk for rollback segments.
- Keep the system tablespace on a separate disk or on a lightly used disk.
- Try to keep Oracle files on different disks from user filesystems.

An ideal disk layout might look like the layout shown in Table 11-2.

Table 11-2. Ideal Disk Layout

Disk	Contents
01 Controller A	Oracle software (*$ORACLE_HOME*), control file 1
02 Controller A	SYSTEM tablespace
03 Controller A	DATA tablespace
04 Controller A	Redo log group 1, member 1 Redo log group 3, member 1
05 Controller A	Redo log group 2, member 1 Redo log group 4, member 1
06 Controller A	Redo log group 1, member 2 Redo log group 3, member 2
07 Controller A	Redo log group 2, member 2 Redo log group 4, member 2
08 Controller B	TOOLS tablespace
09 Controller B	TEMP tablespace, control file 2
10 Controller B	ROLLBACK tablespace
11 Controller B	INDEX tablespace
12 Controller B	Archivelog destination
13 Controller B	Application software
14 Controller B	User files, exports, etc.

Since this system has two controllers, we have made the following decisions:

1. Locate the INDEX tablespace on a different controller from the DATA tablespace.

   Rationale: During inserts and updates, there will be heavy activity as rows are inserted and indexes are updated. Distributing I/O across two controllers provides more I/O bandwidth.

2. Locate the ROLLBACK tablespace on a different controller from the DATA tablespace.

   Rationale: During heavy inserts and updates, there will be a significant number of rollback records written, so placing the ROLLBACK tablespace on a separate controller improves I/O bandwidth.

3. Allocate two members for each log group.

   Rationale: This protects against the loss of a log file by providing Oracle log file mirroring.

4. Alternate the locations of each log group across two different disks.

Rationale: While one log file is being archived, the next file can be written to without I/O contention.

5. Locate the archive log destination on a different controller from the online log files.

   Rationale: When running in archivelog mode, the ARCH process can read the online log file from one controller while writing to the archive log destination with the other controller.

About RAID

Recently, there has been a high degree of interest in the use of RAID (redundant arrays of inexpensive disks) technology over a wide range of server configurations. A variety of RAID implementations, or levels, is now available, as summarized in Table 11-3.

Table 11-3. RAID Implementations

RAID Level	Description	Advantages	Disadvantages
RAID-0	Block striping, no parity	Faster reads	No recovery from disk failure
RAID-1	One-to-one disk mirroring	Fully protected from single disk failure, no degradation of I/O speed	Twice as many disks are required
RAID-0+1	One-to-one mirroring with striping	Faster reads, fully protected from single disk failure	Twice as many disks are required
RAID-3	Byte-level striping with dedicated parity disk	Faster reads, fully protected from single disk failure, only one extra disk required per array	Slower writes, slower recovery from failure
RAID-4	Block-level striping with dedicated parity disk	Faster reads, only one extra disk required per array	Slower writes, slower recovery from disk failure
RAID-5	Block-level striping with distributed parity	Faster reads, fully protected from single disk failure, only one disk required per array, faster recovery from disk failure	Slower writes
RAID-6	Block-level striping with dual distributed parity	Faster reads, fully protected from failure of any two disks	Slower writes, requires two extra disks for each array, slower recovery from disk failure

Table 11-3. RAID Implementations (continued)

RAID Level	Description	Advantages	Disadvantages
RAID-7	Performance-enhanced RAID-5	Faster reads, fully protected from single disk failure, only one disk required per array, faster recovery from disk failure	Slower writes
RAID-8	Performance-enhanced RAID-5	Faster reads, fully protected from single disk failure, only one disk required per array, faster recovery from disk failure	Slower writes

A careful examination of this table suggests that there is no clear choice of RAID technologies, nor is it even clear that RAID should be used. In general, RAID-5 is the most popular RAID level, since it is supported by a wide range of hardware manufacturers and is relatively inexpensive to implement. However, RAID-5 has a performance penalty associated with it. In most RAID-5 implementations, there is a significant performance degradation when performing write operations, due primarily to the need to read, recalculate, and write the distributed parity information. While RAID-5 may be appropriate for fairly static tablespaces used primarily for read operations, avoid the use of RAID-5 disks for files with high write rates. These include the rollback segments, TEMPORARY tablespace, SYSTEM tablespace, redo logs, and tables with high amounts of inserts, updates, and deletes.

With the falling price of disk drives, RAID-0+1 may be the best all-around choice for both performance and protection from failure. Although twice as many disk devices are required as for traditional non-RAID disk implementation, the increases possible in read performance, combined with the ability to recover from a disk failure, makes this level attractive.

Some operating systems, for example, Windows NT, provide RAID capability as an operating system feature. While these RAID implementations may be attractive, they come at a very high resource cost. Since these RAID configurations are implemented in software, rather than by using specialized RAID hardware, they consume a large amount of CPU, memory, and controller capacity.

One word of caution when using RAID: do not create, or allow creation of, multiple logical disks on a single RAID array. While this may be practical for a file server configuration, use of such a configuration in an Oracle database environment will result in overall poor performance.

12

Initialization Parameters

In this chapter:
- *Dynamically Modifiable Parameters*
- *Platform-Specific Parameters*
- *Summary of Initialization Parameters*
- *Parameters Used Only in Oracle7*
- *Parameters New in Oracle8*

When you purchased your Oracle database software, the salesperson very likely told you that Oracle is preconfigured and should work perfectly right out of the box, with no tuning or configuration necessary. You might then have attended a local user group meeting, where a grizzled veteran Oracle database administrator told you that Oracle requires constant tuning and attention, and that you need to hire a consultant (maybe that same grizzled DBA!) to keep your database tuned and operating properly. Well, the truth lies somewhere between these positions.

Oracle is designed to be very flexible and configurable. This is actually an absolute necessity for a database that can be run on dozens of different hardware platforms in a multitude of configurations, supporting an almost infinite variety of applications and users. In order to achieve this flexibility, Oracle must provide the DBA with a method of specifying certain operational characteristics of the database in a clear and consistent manner. In Oracle, this is done through *initialization parameters*. Each of these parameters controls a specific aspect of the Oracle server. There are numerous initialization parameters—some documented, some not—and they are powerful and must be used with care. As the DBA, you will frequently specify or change initialization parameters in order to get your particular database running at peak performance. This chapter provides a comprehensive list of initialization parameters, along with some practical guidelines for their use.

Initialization parameters are specified in what is known as the Oracle *INIT.ORA* file, which we discussed in Chapter 11, *The Oracle Database*. This file is usually named *INITsid.ORA*, where *sid* is the SID (name) for the Oracle instance. For example, for an instance called TEST, the initialization parameters would be found in the file *INITTEST.ORA*. The default location of this file varies with operating system. Table 12-1 shows the location of this file for some popular operating systems.

Table 12-1. Default Locations of INIT.ORA Files

Operating System	Location
Unix	*$ORACLE_HOME/dbs*
Windows NT	*\orant\dbs*
Windows 95/98 (Personal Oracle)	*\orawin95\dbs*
VMS	*ORA_ROOT:[DB_dbname]*

There are two categories of initialization parameters:

Dynamically modifiable parameters
> Parameters that can be changed dynamically while the instance is up and the database is open

Static parameters
> Parameters whose values must be specified in the *INIT.ORA* file before the instance is started and cannot be changed during database operation

The next section lists the dynamically modifiable parameters. At the end of this chapter, you will also find listings of those parameters that may only be specified for a certain version of Oracle (Oracle7 or Oracle8).

Dynamically Modifiable Parameters

While most initialization parameters are static—that is, they take their values from the *INIT.ORA* file when the instance is started—some may be dynamically modified while the instance is up and the database is open. Tables 12-2 and 12-3 list the tables that may be modified dynamically for Oracle7 and Oracle8, respectively. These tables consist of three columns:

Parameter Name
> The name of the parameter, which must be specified in the *INIT.ORA* file.

Session Modifiable
> Indicates whether a parameter may be modified using an ALTER SESSION command.

System Modifiable
> Indicates whether a parameter may be modified using an ALTER SYSTEM command. IMMEDIATE indicates that the change takes place immediately, while DEFERRED indicates that the change is deferred until the next session.

Table 12-2. Dynamically Modifiable Initialization Parameters in Oracle7

Parameter Name	Session Modifiable	System Modifiable
B_TREE_BITMAP_PLANS	Yes	No
DB_FILE_MULTIBLOCK_READ_COUNT	Yes	Immediate

Table 12-2. Dynamically Modifiable Initialization Parameters in Oracle 7 (continued)

Parameter Name	Session Modifiable	System Modifiable
HASH_AREA_SIZE	Yes	No
HASH_JOIN_ENABLED	Yes	No
HASH_MULTIBLOCK_IO_COUNT	Yes	Immediate
LOG_CHECKPOINT_INTERVAL	No	Immediate
LOG_CHECKPOINT_TIMEOUT	No	Immediate
LOG_SMALL_ENTRY_MAX_SIZE	No	Immediate
MAX_DUMP_FILE_SIZE	Yes	No
OPTIMIZER_PERCENT_PARALLEL	Yes	No
OPTIMIZER_SEARCH_LIMIT	Yes	No
PARALLEL_MIN_PERCENT	Yes	No
PARTITION_VIEW_ENABLED	Yes	No
SORT_AREA_RETAINED_SIZE	Yes	Deferred
SORT_AREA_SIZE	Yes	Deferred
SORT_DIRECT_WRITES	Yes	Deferred
SORT_READ_FAC	Yes	Deferred
SORT_WRITE_BUFFERS	Yes	Deferred
SORT_WRITE_BUFFER_SIZE	Yes	Deferred
TEXT_ENABLE	Yes	No
TIMED_STATISTICS	Yes	Immediate
USER_DUMP_DEST	No	Immediate

Table 12-3. Dynamically Modifiable Initialization Parameters in Oracle 8

Parameter Name	Session Modifiable	System Modifiable
ALLOW_PARTIAL_SN_RESULTS	Yes	Deferred
AQ_TM_PROCESSES	No	Immediate
BACKGROUND_DUMP_DEST	No	Immediate
BACKUP_DISK_IO_SLAVES	No	Deferred
BACKUP_TAPE_IO_SLAVES	No	Deferred
B_TREE_BITMAP_PLANS	Yes	No
CLOSE_CACHED_OPEN_CURSORS	Yes	No
COMPLEX_VIEW_MERGING	Yes	No
CONTROL_FILE_RECORD_KEEP_TIME	No	Immediate
CORE_DUMP_DEST	No	Immediate
DB_BLOCK_CHECKPOINT_BATCH	No	Immediate
DB_BLOCK_CHECKSUM	No	Immediate
DB_BLOCK_MAX_DIRTY_TARGET	No	Immediate

Table 12-3. Dynamically Modifiable Initialization Parameters in Oracle8 (continued)

Parameter Name	Session Modifiable	System Modifiable
DB_FILE_DIRECT_IO_COUNT	No	Deferred
DB_FILE_MULTIBLOCK_READ_COUNT	Yes	Immediate
FIXED_DATE	No	Immediate
FAST_FULL_SCAN_ENABLED	No	Immediate
FREEZE_DB_FOR_FAST_INSTANCE_RECOVERY	No	Immediate
GC_DEFER_TIME	No	Immediate
GLOBAL_NAMES	Yes	Immediate
HASH_AREA_SIZE	Yes	No
HASH_JOIN_ENABLED	Yes	No
HASH_MULTIBLOCK_IO_COUNT	Yes	Immediate
JOB_QUEUE_PROCESSES	No	Immediate
LICENSE_MAX_SESSIONS	No	Immediate
LICENSE_MAX_USERS	No	Immediate
LICENSE_SESSIONS_WARNING	No	Immediate
LOG_ARCHIVE_DUPLEX_DEST	No	Immediate
LOG_ARCHIVE_MIN_SUCCEED_DEST	No	Immediate
LOG_CHECKPOINT_INTERVAL	No	Immediate
LOG_CHECKPOINT_TIMEOUT	No	Immediate
LOG_SMALL_ENTRY_MAX_SIZE	No	Immediate
MAX_DUMP_FILE_SIZE	Yes	Immediate
MTS_DISPATCHERS	No	Immediate
MTS_SERVERS	No	Immediate
NLS_CALENDAR	Yes	No
NLS_CURRENCY	Yes	No
NLS_DATE_FORMAT	Yes	No
NLS_DATE_LANGUAGE	Yes	No
NLS_ISO_CURRENCY	Yes	No
NLS_LANGUAGE	Yes	No
NLS_NUMERIC_CHARACTERS	Yes	No
NLS_SORT	Yes	No
NLS_TERRITORY	Yes	No
OBJECT_CACHE_MAX_SIZE_PERCENT	Yes	Deferred
OBJECT_CACHE_OPTIMAL_SIZE	Yes	Deferred
OPS_ADMIN_GROUP	Yes	Immediate
OPTIMIZER_INDEX_CACHING	Yes	No
OPTIMIZER_INDEX_COST_ADJ	Yes	No

Table 12-3. *Dynamically Modifiable Initialization Parameters in Oracle8 (continued)*

Parameter Name	Session Modifiable	System Modifiable
OPTIMIZER_MAX_PERMUTATIONS	Yes	No
OPTIMIZER_MODE	Yes	No
OPTIMIZER_PERCENT_PARALLEL	Yes	No
OPTIMIZER_SEARCH_LIMIT	Yes	No
PARALLEL_ADAPTIVE_MULTI_USER	Yes	No
PARALLEL_BROADCAST_ENABLED	Yes	No
PARALLEL_INSTANCE_GROUP	Yes	Immediate
PARALLEL_MIN_PERCENT	Yes	No
PARALLEL_TRANSACTION_RESOURCE_ TIMEOUT	No	Immediate
PARTITION_VIEW_ENABLED	Yes	No
PLSQL_V2_COMPATIBILITY	Yes	Immediate
PUSH_JOIN_PREDICATE	Yes	No
REMOTE_DEPENDENCIES_MODE	Yes	Immediate
RESOURCE_LIMIT	No	Immediate
SESSION_CACHED_CURSORS	Yes	No
SORT_AREA_RETAINED_SIZE	Yes	Deferred
SORT_AREA_SIZE	Yes	Deferred
SORT_DIRECT_WRITES	Yes	Deferred
SORT_READ_FAC	Yes	Deferred
SORT_WRITE_BUFFERS	Yes	Deferred
SORT_WRITE_BUFFER_SIZE	Yes	Deferred
SPIN_COUNT	No	Immediate
STAR_TRANSFORMATION_ENABLED	Yes	No
TEXT_ENABLE	Yes	Immediate
TIMED_OS_STATISTICS	No	Immediate
TIMED_STATISTICS	Yes	Immediate
TRANSACTION_AUDITING	No	Deferred
USER_DUMP_DEST	No	Immediate

Platform-Specific Parameters

In addition to the initialization parameters listed in the next section, which apply to most Oracle systems, there are some parameters that are specific to particular hardware platforms or operating systems. These parameters are documented in the *Installation and User Guide* and *Release Notes* for each individual release of Oracle. We recommend that you carefully review these additional parameters before you configure an Oracle instance.

Summary of Initialization Parameters

The following initialization parameters are documented by Oracle, and are presented here in alphabetical order. Both Oracle7 and Oracle8 parameters are listed—those that are specific to a single version are noted. We've provided brief descriptions of all parameters, along with allowable values and defaults; for complete details, see the appropriate *Oracle Server Reference Manual* for your release of Oracle.

Note that the parameter names are presented here in uppercase for readability, but parameters may appear in upper-, lower-, or mixed case when they appear in the actual *INIT.ORA* parameter file.

ALLOW_PARTIAL_SN_RESULTS

Values: TRUE or FALSE
Default: FALSE
Multiple Instances: Should have the same value

A Parallel Server parameter that allows queries to global performance tables (GV$) to return partial results, even if a slave could not be allocated on the instance. If the value of MAX_PARALLEL_SERVERS equals 0, a query on the global performance table reverts to a sequential query on the local instance. If the value of MAX_PARALLEL_SERVERS is greater than 0 and a slave cannot be allocated on an instance in a GV$ query, then whether the query returns partial results or a failure is determined by the value of ALLOW_PARTIAL_SN_RESULTS. If ALLOW_PARTIAL_SN_RESULTS is TRUE, the query succeeds and returns results from all instances that were able to allocate a slave for the query. If ALLOW_PARTIAL_SN_RESULTS is FALSE, the query fails and returns an error message.

ALWAYS_ANTI_JOIN

Values: NESTED_LOOPS, MERGE, or HASH
Default: NESTED_LOOPS

Sets the type of antijoin algorithm used by the Oracle Server. The system checks to verify that it is legal to perform an antijoin and, if it is, uses the value of this parameter to determine how it will process the subquery. When this parameter is set to the value NESTED_LOOPS, the Oracle Server evaluates the subquery using a nested loop antijoin algorithm. When it is set to the value MERGE, the Oracle Server uses the sort merge antijoin algorithm. When it is set to the value HASH, the Oracle Server uses the hash antijoin algorithm.

AQ_TM_PROCESSES (Oracle8 Only)

Values: 0 or 1
Default: 0

Toggles whether Oracle creates a time manager. If AQ_TM_PROCESSES is set to 1, Oracle creates one time manager process to monitor the messages. If AQ_TM_ PROCESSES is not specified or is set to 0, no time manager will be created. The parameter cannot be set to a value greater than 1 or an error will result and no time manager will be created.

ARCH_IO_SLAVES (Oracle8 Only)

Values: 0 to 15
Default: 0

Specifies the number of I/O slaves the ARCH process uses to archive redo log files. The ARCH process and its slaves always write to disk. By default, the value is 0 and the process does not use I/O slaves. Ordinarily, this parameter is adjusted when an I/O bottleneck has been detected in the ARCH process. Such I/O bottlenecks typically occur on platforms that do not support asynchronous I/O or that implement it inefficiently.

AUDIT_FILE_DEST

Values: Valid directory name
Default: *$ORACLE_HOME/RDBMS/AUDIT*

Specifies the directory in which Oracle stores auditing files.

AUDIT_TRAIL

Values: None
Default: NONE, DB, OS, TRUE, or FALSE

Enables or disables the writing of rows to the audit trail. If the value is set to NONE, or the parameter is not specified, audited records are not written. If this parameter is set to OS, system-wide auditing is enabled and audited records are written to the operating system's audit trail. If it is set to DB, system-wide auditing is enabled and audited records are written to the database audit trail (the SYS. AUD$ table). For backward compatibility, the parameter also supports TRUE and FALSE options. A TRUE setting is equivalent to DB, and a FALSE setting is equivalent to NONE. The SQL AUDIT statements can set auditing options regardless of the setting of this parameter.

B_TREE_BITMAP_PLANS

Values: TRUE or FALSE
Default: FALSE

Specifies that the optimizer considers a bitmap access path even when a table only has regular B-tree indexes. Do not change the value of this parameter unless Oracle Support instructs you to do so.

BACKGROUND_CORE_DUMP

Values: FULL or PARTIAL
Default: FULL

Specifies whether the System Global Area (SGA) is dumped as part of the generated core file. If BACKGROUND_CORE_DUMP is set to FULL, the SGA is dumped as part of the generated core file. If it is set to PARTIAL, the SGA is not dumped.

BACKGROUND_DUMP_DEST

Values: Valid directory name
Default: Operating system dependent

Specifies the directory in which debugging trace files for the background processes (LGWR, DBWR, and so on) are written. The ALERT file logs significant database events and messages in plain text format. The form taken by its filename depends on your operating system, but for platforms supporting multiple instances, it is *ALERT_sid.LOG.* Although the ALERT file grows slowly, there is no limit on this file, so you might want to delete it regularly—which can be done even when the database is running.

BACKUP_DISK_IO_SLAVES (Oracle8 Only)

Values: 0 to 15
Default: 0

Specifies the number of I/O slaves that Recovery Manager uses to back up, copy, or restore. Note that every Recovery Manager channel can get the specified number of I/O slave processes. I/O slaves are usually used to "simulate" asynchronous I/O on platforms that either do not support asynchronous I/O or that implement it inefficiently. However, I/O slaves can be used even when actual asynchronous I/O is being used. In that case, the I/O slaves will use asynchronous I/O. By default, the value is 0 and no I/O slaves are used.

BACKUP_TAPE_IO_SLAVES (Oracle8 Only)

Values: TRUE or FALSE
Default: FALSE

Specifies whether Recovery Manager uses I/O slaves to back up, copy, or restore data to tape. When BACKUP_TAPE_IO_SLAVES is set to TRUE, an I/O slave process is used to write to or read from a tape device. When this parameter is set to FALSE (the default), I/O slaves are not used for backups; instead, the shadow process engaged in the backup accesses the tape device. Typically, I/O slaves are used to simulate asynchronous I/O on platforms that either do not support asynchronous I/O or implement it inefficiently. However, I/O slaves can be used even when actual asynchronous I/O is being used. In that case, the I/O slaves will use asynchronous I/O.

BITMAP_MERGE_AREA_SIZE

Values: Operating system dependent
Default: 1000000

Specifies the amount of memory used to merge bitmaps retrieved from a range scan of the index. A larger value typically improves performance, since memory is needed to sort the bitmap segments before a merge into a single bitmap.

BLANK_TRIMMING

Values: TRUE or FALSE
Default: FALSE

Specifies the data assignment semantics of character datatypes. When BLANK_TRIMMING is set to TRUE, data assignment of a source character string or variable to a destination character column or variable is allowed, even though the source length is longer than the destination length, if the additional length over the destination length is comprised of all blanks. When set to FALSE, the data assignment is not allowed if the source length is longer than the destination length.

CACHE_SIZE_THRESHOLD

Values: 0 to DB_BLOCK_BUFFERS
Default: 0.1 × DB_BLOCK_BUFFERS
Multiple Instances: Should have the same value

Specifies the maximum size of a cached partition of a table that will be split among the caches of multiple instances. If the partition is larger than the value of this parameter, the table will not be split among the instances' caches. The default value of this parameter is one-tenth the number of database blocks in the buffer cache. This parameter can also be used to specify the maximum size of a cached partition for a single instance.

CHECKPOINT_PROCESS (Oracle7 Only)

Values: TRUE or FALSE

Default: FALSE

Enables the CKPT background process. CHECKPOINT_PROCESS should be set to TRUE only if the performance of the LGWR process decreases significantly during a checkpoint.

 Adjust all calculations that depend on the number of background processes to allow for the CKPT process. For example, increase the value of the PROCESSES parameter by one, and increase the values of other parameters whose default values are derived from PRO-CESSES if the default (derived) values are not used.

CLEANUP_ROLLBACK_ENTRIES

Values: Any integer

Default: 20

Specifies the number of undo records processed simultaneously when rolling back a transaction. This parameter is designed to prevent long transactions from freezing out shorter transactions that also need rolling back. Ordinarily, it will not need modification.

CLOSE_CACHED_OPEN_CURSORS

Values: TRUE or FALSE

Default: FALSE

Specifies whether cursors opened and cached in memory by PL/SQL are automatically closed at each COMMIT. A value of FALSE causes cursors opened by PL/SQL to be held open for use by subsequent executions. If PL/SQL cursors are reused frequently, this setting can speed up these subsequent executions. A value of TRUE causes open cursors to be closed at each COMMIT or ROLLBACK, and the cursor can then be reopened as needed. If cursors are rarely reused, setting the parameter to TRUE frees up memory the open cursor uses when idle.

COMMIT_POINT_STRENGTH

Values: 0 to 255
Default: Operating system dependent

Specifies a value that determines the commit point site in a distributed transaction. The commit point site is determined by the node in the transaction with the highest value for COMMIT_POINT_STRENGTH. A database's commit point strength should be set relative to the amount of critical shared data in the database. A database mounted on a mainframe, for example, ordinarily shares more data among users than does one mounted on a PC. Therefore, COMMIT_POINT_STRENGTH should be set to a higher value for the mainframe. In general, set COMMIT_POINT_STRENGTH to a higher value on machines that are more generally available.

COMPATIBLE

Values: 7.0.0 to current Oracle release
Default: Current Oracle release
Multiple Instances: Must have the same value

Allows the use of a new release, while maintaining backward compatibility with an earlier release. This parameter specifies the release with which the Oracle Server must maintain compatibility, causing some features on the current release to be restricted. When using the standby database feature, this parameter must have the same settings on the primary and standby databases, and the value must be 7.3.0.0.0 or higher.

COMPATIBLE_NO_RECOVERY

Values: Default Oracle release to current Oracle release
Default: Release dependent
Multiple Instances: Must have the same value

Functions in the same way as the COMPATIBLE parameter, except that the earlier release specified may not be usable on the current database if recovery is needed. The default value is the earliest release with which compatibility can be maintained. In some cases, this release may be an earlier release than can be specified with the COMPATIBLE parameter.

COMPLEX_VIEW_MERGING

Values: TRUE or FALSE
Default: FALSE

Specifies the method used to handle complex views. When this parameter is set to TRUE, complex views or subqueries are merged. When set to FALSE, this parameter causes complex views or subqueries to be evaluated before the referencing query.

CONTROL_FILE_RECORD_KEEP_TIME (Oracle8 Only)

Values: 0 to 365
Default: 7

Specifies the minimum age, in days, that certain records in the control file must attain before they can be reused. Records in some sections on the control file are circularly reusable, while records in other sections are never reused. CONTROL_FILE_RECORD_KEEP_TIME applies to the reusable sections. Ordinarily, when a new record needs to be added to a reusable section and the oldest record has not aged enough, the record section expands. When this parameter is set to 0, reusable sections never expand and records are reused as needed. The reusable sections of the control file are:

```
ARCHIVED LOG
BACKUP CORRUPTION
BACKUP DATAFILE
BACKUP PIECE
BACKUP REDO LOG
BACKUP SET
COPY CORRUPTION
DATAFILE COPY
DELETED OBJECT
LOGHISTORY
OFFLINE RANGE
```

CONTROL_FILES

Values: 1 to 8 filenames
Default: Operating system dependent

Specifies one or more names of control files, each name separated by commas. You should provide multiple files on different devices or mirror the file at the operating system level.

CORE_DUMP_DEST

Values: Valid directory name
Default: *$ORACLE_HOME/DBS/*

Specifies the directory into which Oracle dumps core files.

CPU_COUNT

Values: 0 to unlimited

Default: 0 or actual number of CPUs

Specifies the number of CPUs Oracle can use. Oracle uses this value to determine the default value of the LOG_SIMULTANEOUS_COPIES parameter. CPU_COUNT is set to 0 on single-CPU computers.

 On most platforms, Oracle automatically sets the value of CPU_COUNT to the number of CPUs available to the Oracle instance, and the value of CPU_COUNT should not be changed. If there is heavy contention for latches, change the value of LOG_SIMULTANEOUS_COPIES to twice the number of CPUs available, but do not change the value of CPU_COUNT.

CREATE_BITMAP_AREA_SIZE

Values: Operating system dependent

Default: 8 Mb

Specifies the amount of memory Oracle allocates for bitmap creation, with a default value of 8 Mb. A larger value usually leads to faster index creation. If cardinality is very small, a small value can be set for this parameter. For example, if cardinality is only 2, the value can be in kilobytes rather than megabytes. As a general rule, the higher the cardinality, the more memory is needed for optimal performance.

CURSOR_SPACE_FOR_TIME

Values: TRUE or FALSE

Default: FALSE

Controls how Oracle uses memory to store cursors. If the value of CURSOR_SPACE_FOR_TIME is TRUE, the database saves time by using more space for cursors. Shared SQL areas are kept pinned in the shared pool when this parameter is set to TRUE. As a result, shared SQL areas are not aged out of the pool as long as there is an open cursor that references them.

This increases execution speed, since each active cursor's SQL area is present in memory. However, because the shared SQL areas never leave memory while they are in use, this parameter should be set to TRUE only when the shared pool is large enough to hold all open cursors at the same time. Setting this parameter to TRUE also retains each cursor's private SQL area between executes instead of discarding it after cursor execution, thus saving cursor allocation and initialization time.

DB_BLOCK_BUFFERS

Values: 4 to operating system dependent

Default: 50

Specifies the number of database buffers available for use in the buffer cache. DB_BLOCK_BUFFERS is one of the primary parameters that contribute to the total memory requirements of the SGA on the instance. This parameter, together with the DB_BLOCK_SIZE parameter, determines the total size of the buffer cache. Using the buffer cache effectively can substantially reduce the I/O load on the database.

DB_BLOCK_CHECKPOINT_BATCH

Values: 0 to derived

Default: 8

Specifies the number of buffers added to each batch of buffers that DBWR writes in order to advance checkpoint processing. When set to a low value, DB_BLOCK_CHECKPOINT_BATCH prevents the I/O system from being flooded with checkpoint writes, thus allowing other modified blocks to be written to disk. Increasing this parameter allows checkpoints to complete more quickly.

Generally, this parameter should be set to a value that allows the checkpoint to complete before the next log switch takes place. If a log switch takes place every 20 minutes, for example, this parameter should be set to a value that allows checkpointing to complete within 20 minutes. Setting DB_BLOCK_CHECKPOINT_BATCH to 0 causes the default value to be used. If the value specified for this parameter is overly large, Oracle limits it (without notification) to the number of blocks that can be written in a DBWR write batch.

DB_BLOCK_CHECKSUM

Values: TRUE or FALSE

Default: FALSE

Specifies whether DBWR and the direct loader will store a calculated checksum in the cache header of every data block while writing the data block to disk. If the value of DB_BLOCK_CHECKSUM is TRUE, the checksum will be calculated and stored; if the parameter is set to FALSE, the checksum will not be calculated.

 Setting DB_BLOCK_CHECKSUM to TRUE can lead to performance overhead. Set this parameter to TRUE only on the advice of Oracle Support personnel while diagnosing data corruption problems.

DB_BLOCK_LRU_EXTENDED_STATISTICS

Values: 0 to value dependent on system memory
Default: 0

Allows or disallows compilation of statistics to measure the effects of an increased number of buffers in the buffer cache of the SGA. When enabled, this facility keeps track of the number of disk accesses that would be saved were additional buffers to be allocated. A value greater than 0 specifies the number of additional buffers (above those specified in DB_BLOCK_BUFFERS) for which statistics are kept. When compiling statistics, set this parameter to the maximum size desired in order to evaluate the buffer cache. At other times, set it to 0.

 Setting this parameter can cause a large performance loss, so set it only when the system is lightly loaded, and turn it off during normal operation.

DB_BLOCK_LRU_LATCHES

Values: 1 to number of CPUs
Default: CPU_COUNT / 2

Specifies the upper boundary for the number of LRU (least recently used) latch sets. When this parameter is set to the desired number of LRU latch sets, Oracle will decide whether to use this value or reduce it based on a number of internal checks. If DB_BLOCK_LRU_LATCHES is not specified, Oracle calculates its own value, which is ordinarily sufficient. You should increase this parameter only if misses in V$LATCH are higher than 3%.

DB_BLOCK_LRU_STATISTICS

Values: TRUE or FALSE
Default: FALSE

Allows or disallows compiling of statistics in the X$KCBCBH table, measuring the effect of fewer buffers in the SGA buffer cache. Setting this parameter to TRUE enables compilation of statistics for the X$KCBCBH table; otherwise, it should be left set to FALSE. This parameter is a tuning tool and should be set to FALSE during normal operation.

 Setting this parameter can cause a large performance loss, so set it only when the system is lightly loaded.

DB_BLOCK_MAX_DIRTY_TARGET (Oracle8 Only)

Values: 100 to all buffers in the cache
Default: All buffers in the cache

Specifies the number of buffers allowed to be dirty (i.e., modified and different from what is on disk). If the number of dirty buffers in a buffer cache exceeds this value, DBWR attempts to write out buffers in order to keep the number of dirty buffers below the specified value. Note that this parameter does not impose a hard limit on the number of dirty buffers, and DBWR will *not* stop or slow database activity if the number of dirty buffers exceeds this value.

DB_BLOCK_MAX_DIRTY_TARGET can be used to affect the amount of time Oracle takes to perform instance recovery, since recovery is related to the number of dirty buffers at the time of the crash. The smaller the value of this parameter, the faster the instance recovery. Note, however, that this increase in recovery time comes at the expense of writing more buffers during normal processing. Setting this parameter to a very small value might impair performance if the workload modifies large numbers of buffers. Setting this value to 0 disables writing of buffers for incremental checkpointing purposes; all other write activity continues normally (in other words, it is unaffected by setting this parameter to 0).

DB_BLOCK_SIZE

Values: 2048 to 32768
Default: Operating system dependent
Multiple Instances: Must have the same value

Establishes the size, in bytes, of Oracle database blocks. The value of this parameter is determined when the database is created, and must at all times be set to the original value. This parameter influences the maximum value of the FREELISTS storage parameter for tables and indexes.

DB_DOMAIN

Values: Any legal string of name components, separated by periods and up to 128 characters long
Default: WORLD
Multiple Instances: Must have the same value

Specifies the extension components of a global database name, consisting of valid identifiers separated by periods. For example, this parameter allows one department to create a database without any danger of using the name of a database created by another department. If one sales department's DB_DOMAIN = "US. JACKSON.COM", its SALES database (SALES.US.JACKSON.COM) is distinguished from another database whose DB_NAME = "SALES" but whose DB_DOMAIN = "FRANCE.JACKSON.COM". The domain name for the database may consist of any alphabetic and numeric characters, underscore (_), and pound (#).

DB_FILE_DIRECT_IO_COUNT (Oracle8 Only)

Values: Operating system dependent

Default: 64

Specifies the number of blocks to be used for I/O operations performed by backup, restore, or direct path read and write functions. The I/O buffer size is a product of DB_FILE_DIRECT_IO_COUNT and DB_BLOCK_SIZE, and it cannot exceed the maximum I/O size for the platform. Increasing the value of this parameter allows greater use of PGA or SGA memory.

DB_FILE_MULTIBLOCK_READ_COUNT

Values: Operating system dependent

Default: 8

Establishes the maximum number of blocks read in one I/O operation during a sequential scan. The total number of I/Os needed to perform a full table scan depends on factors that include the size of the table and the value of MULTI_BLOCK_READ_COUNT, and on whether Parallel Query is being utilized for the operation. Batch environment values for this parameter ordinarily range from 4 to 16. Data warehouse database environments tend to benefit from maximizing the value for this parameter. The actual maximum varies by operating system and is always less than the operating system's maximum I/O size expressed as Oracle blocks (maximum I/O size / DB_BLOCK_SIZE). If you set this parameter to a value greater than the maximum, the maximum value will be used.

DB_FILE_NAME_CONVERT (Oracle8 Only)

Values: Two valid datafile names

Converts the filename of a new datafile on the primary database to a filename on the standby database when the standby database is updated. Adding a datafile to the primary database necessitates adding a corresponding file to the standby database. The file must exist and be writable on the standby database; otherwise, the recovery process will halt with an error. Set the value of this parameter to two strings: the first string is the pattern found in the datafile names on the primary database; the second string is the pattern found in the datafile names on the standby database. For example:

```
DB_FILE_NAME_CONVERT = ("/oracle/prod/datafile", "/oracle/standby/datafile")
```

This parameter replaces the DB_FILE_STANDBY_NAME_CONVERT parameter in Oracle7.

DB_FILE_SIMULTANEOUS_WRITES

Values: 1 to 4 × number of disks in a striped file, or 4 if no striping
Default: 4

Specifies the maximum number of simultaneous writes allowed for a given database file. Oracle also uses this parameter to compute various internal parameters that affect read and write operations to database files. Increasing the value of this parameter is beneficial in environments where the database files reside on RAM devices or which use disk striping at the operating system level. If striped files are used, Oracle recommends that the value of this parameter be set to four times the maximum number of disks in the file that is striped the most. This parameter is also used to determine the number of reads per file in the redo read-ahead when reading redo during recovery.

If an excessively large value is specified for this parameter, significant delays in performing read and write operations to a given database file might occur, because I/O requests get queued in the disk. If the value set is too small, the number of I/Os that can be issued to a given database file will be limited.

DB_FILE_STANDBY_NAME_CONVERT (Oracle7 Only)

Values: Two valid datafile names

Converts the filename of a new datafile on the primary database to a filename on the standby database. Adding a datafile to the primary database necessitates adding a corresponding file to the standby database. When the standby database is updated, this parameter is used to convert the datafile name on the primary database to a datafile name on the standby database. The file must exist and be writable on the standby database; if it is not, the recovery process will halt with an error. Set the value of this parameter to two strings: the first string is the pattern found in the datafile names on the primary database; the second string is the pattern found in the datafile names on the standby database. For example:

```
DB_FILE_STANDBY_NAME_CONVERT = ("/oracle/prod/datafile",
                                "/oracle/standby/datafile")
```

This parameter has been replaced by DB_FILE_NAME_CONVERT in Oracle8.

DB_FILES

Values: Minimum is the current actual number of datafiles in the database; maximum is operating system dependent, and can be no greater than the value that was specified in the MAXDATAFILES clause the last time CREATE DATABASE or CREATE CONTROLFILE was executed.

Default: Operating system dependent

Multiple Instances: Must have the same value

Specifies the number of database files that can be opened for this database. This parameter is normally set to the maximum number of files, subject to operating system constraints, that will ever be specified for the database, including files to be added by the ADD DATAFILE statement. If the value of this parameter is increased, all instances accessing the database must be shut down and restarted before the new value will be valid.

DB_NAME

Values: Any valid database name up to 8 characters

Default: NULL

Multiple Instances: Must have the same value, or else the same value must be specified in STARTUP OPEN *db_name* or ALTER DATABASE *db_name* MOUNT.

Specifies a database identifier of up to eight characters. This parameter is optional, but if used, the name specified must correspond to the name specified in the CREATE DATABASE statement. If this parameter is not used, a database name must appear on either the STARTUP or the ALTER DATABASE MOUNT command line for each instance of the parallel server. The following are the only valid characters usable in a database name: alphabetic and numeric characters, underscore (_), pound (#), and dollar symbol ($). Double quotation marks are removed before processing the database name, and they cannot be used to embed other characters in the name. The name is not case-sensitive; lowercase letters are interchangeable with their uppercase counterparts.

DB_WRITERS (Oracle7 Only)

Values: 0 to operating system dependent

Default: 0

Specifies the number of additional DBWR processes to be used to provide supplementary resources to perform disk writes and simulate asynchronous I/O on platforms that do not support asynchronous I/O or implement it inefficiently. These processes, which are named DB01, DB02, and so on, are also useful in database environments with very large I/O throughput, even if asynchronous I/O is enabled. For best performance, specify one DB_WRITER for each disk device used. In Oracle8, this parameter has been replaced by DBWR_IO_SLAVES.

DBLINK_ENCRYPT_LOGIN

Values: TRUE or FALSE
Default: FALSE

Specifies whether passwords used to connect to other Oracle servers through database links should be encrypted. When an attempt is made to connect to a database using a password, the password is encrypted before it is sent to the database. If the DBLINK_ENCRYPT_LOGIN parameter is set to TRUE, and the connection fails, Oracle does not reattempt the connection. If this parameter is FALSE, Oracle tries to connect again using an unencrypted version of the password.

DBWR_IO_SLAVES (Oracle8 Only)

Values: 0 to operating system dependent
Default: 0

Specifies the number of I/O slaves the DBWR process uses to perform writes to disk and to simulate asynchronous I/O on platforms that do not support asynchronous I/O or implement it inefficiently. I/O slaves are also useful in database environments with very large I/O throughput, even if asynchronous I/O is enabled. For best performance, specify one DBWR_IO_SLAVE for each disk device used. This Oracle8 parameter replaces the DB_WRITERS parameter used in Oracle7.

DELAYED_LOGGING_BLOCK_CLEANOUTS

Values: TRUE or FALSE
Default: TRUE

Toggles the delayed block cleanout feature on or off, reducing pinging in Oracle Parallel Server. Keeping this feature set to TRUE sets a fast path in which Oracle does not log block cleanout at commit time. Logging block cleanout occurs when the block is subsequently changed. This generally improves Oracle Parallel Server performance, especially when block pings are a problem.

DISCRETE_TRANSACTIONS_ENABLED

Values: TRUE or FALSE
Default: FALSE

Implements a faster and less complicated rollback procedure that improves performance for certain kinds of transactions. Oracle places strict limits on the types of transactions allowed in discrete mode, but using this parameter can lead to greater efficiency for these transactions.

DISK_ASYNCH_IO (Oracle8 Only)

Values: TRUE or FALSE
Default: TRUE

Controls whether I/O to datafiles, control files, and log files is asynchronous. If a platform supports asynchronous I/O to disk, leave this parameter set at its default value of TRUE. However, if the asynchronous I/O implementation is not stable, set this parameter to FALSE to disable asynchronous I/O. If a platform does not support asynchronous I/O to disk, this parameter has no effect. If DISK_ASYNCH_IO is set to FALSE, then DBWR_IO_SLAVES should also be set to FALSE.

DISTRIBUTED_LOCK_TIMEOUT

Values: 1 to unlimited
Default: 60

Specifies the amount of time, in seconds, that distributed transactions should wait for locked resources.

DISTRIBUTED_RECOVERY_CONNECTION_HOLD_TIME

Values: 0 to 1800
Default: 200

Specifies the length of time, in seconds, that a remote connection will be held open after a distributed transaction fails, in hopes that communication will be restored without having to reestablish the connection. Larger values decrease reconnection time, but they also consume local resources over a long period of time. Values larger than 1800 seconds specify that the connection never closes, since the reconnection and recovery process runs every 30 minutes (1800 seconds) whether or not a failure occurs.

DISTRIBUTED_TRANSACTIONS

Values: 0 to TRANSACTIONS
Default: Operating system dependent

Limits the maximum number of distributed transactions in which the database can participate concurrently. This parameter cannot be set to a value greater than that of the parameter TRANSACTIONS. If network failures are occurring with abnormal frequency, causing many in-doubt transactions, consider temporarily decreasing the value of this parameter. This decrease limits the number of concurrent distributed transactions, which then reduces the number of in-doubt transactions, thus reducing the amount of blocked data and possible heuristic decision-making. If DISTRIBUTED_TRANSACTIONS is set to 0, distributed transactions are not allowed at all for the database, and the recovery (RECO) process does not start when the instance starts up.

DML_LOCKS

Values: 0 or 20 to unlimited

Default: 4 × TRANSACTIONS

Multiple Instances: Must all have positive values or must all be 0

Specifies the maximum number of DML locks—one for each table modified in a transaction. The value should be set equal to the grand total of locks on all tables currently referenced by all users. For example, if five users are modifying data in one table, five entries would be required. If three users are modifying data in two tables, six entries would be required. The default value assumes an average of four tables referenced per transaction. For some systems, this value may not be enough. Setting the value to 0 disables enqueues and slightly increases performance. However, you cannot use DROP TABLE, CREATE INDEX, or explicit lock statements such as LOCK TABLE IN EXCLUSIVE MODE.

ENQUEUE_RESOURCES

Values: 10 to 65535

Default: Derived from the SESSIONS parameter

Specifies the number of resources that can be locked concurrently by the lock manager. The default value of this parameter is derived from the SESSIONS parameter. For three or fewer sessions, the default value is 20; for 4 to 10 sessions, the default value is ((SESSIONS − 3) × 5) + 20; and for more than 10 sessions, it is ((SESSIONS − 10) × 2) + 55. These values should be adequate as long as DML_LOCKS + 20 is less than ENQUEUE_RESOURCES. If this parameter is explicitly set to a value higher than DML_LOCKS + 20, the value provided is used. If there are many tables, the value may be increased by 1 for each resource added (regardless of the number of sessions or cursors using that resource), not by 1 for each lock. You should only increase this parameter if Oracle returns an error specifying that enqueues are exhausted.

EVENT

Used to debug the system. Usually this parameter should only be set according to instructions of Oracle Support personnel.

FAST_FULL_SCAN_ENABLED

Values: TRUE or FALSE
Default: FALSE

Specifies whether fast full scans, a useful alternative to full table scans, are enabled. Fast full scans require an index containing all the columns that are needed for the query. In addition, at least one column of the table must be NOT NULL.

FIXED_DATE

Values: Valid Oracle date
Default: NULL

Sets a specific date that SYSDATE will always return instead of the current date. The format for this parameter is:

    YYYY-MM-DD-HH24:MI:SS

This parameter also accepts the default Oracle date format, without a time. Specify the value with double quotes, or without quotes, but not with single quotes; for example, FIXED_DATE = "14-feb-99" or FIXED_DATE = 14-feb-99. This parameter is primarily used for testing.

FREEZE_DB_FOR_FAST_INSTANCE_RECOVERY (Oracle8 Only)

Values: TRUE or FALSE
Default: See description
Multiple Instances: Must have identical values

A Parallel Server parameter that sets whether the entire database is frozen during instance recovery. When this parameter is set to TRUE, Oracle freezes the entire database during instance recovery, which stops all disk activities except those necessary for instance recovery, allowing the recovery process to complete faster.

When the parameter is set to FALSE, Oracle does not freeze the entire database unless Oracle is responsible for resilvering some of the mirrored datafiles. *Resilvering* means ensuring data consistency of mirrored datafiles after a node crash. If all online datafiles use hash locks, the default value is FALSE. If any datafiles use fine-grain locks, the default is TRUE.

GC_DB_LOCKS (Oracle7 Only)

Values: 1 to unlimited
Default: 0
Multiple Instances: Must have identical values

Specifies the total number of PCM locks covering data blocks cached in the multiple SGAs of a parallel server. This parameter must be set to a value greater by at least 1 than the sum of the locks set with the GC_FILES_TO_LOCKS initialization parameter. GC_DB_LOCKS is always rounded up to the next prime number in order to ensure that PCM locks are available for datafiles not specified in GC_FILES_TO_LOCKS.

GC_DEFER_TIME (Oracle8 Only)

Values: Any positive integer
Default: 0

Specifies the amount of time, in hundredths of a second, that the server waits, or defers, before responding to forced-write requests for hot blocks from other instances. Specifying this parameter makes it more likely that buffers will be properly cleaned out before being written, making them more useful when read by other instances. It also improves the chance of hot blocks being used multiple times within an instance between forced writes. The default value is 0, meaning that the feature is disabled and the server will not defer.

GC_FILES_TO_LOCKS

Values: See description
Multiple Instances: Must have identical values

A Parallel Server parameter that controls the mapping of PCM locks to datafiles. GC_FILES_TO_LOCKS should be set to cover as many files as possible. Thus, to avoid performance problems, it should always be changed to correspond to changes in the size of datafiles or to accommodate new datafiles that are added. Changing the parameter requires a shutdown and restart of the parallel server. GC_FILES_TO_LOCKS uses the following syntax:

```
GC_FILES_TO_LOCKS = "{file_list=lock_count[!blocks][EACH]}[:]..."
```

file_list
> One or more datafiles listed by their file numbers or ranges of file numbers, with comma separators (*filenumber[-filenumber][,filenumber[-filenumber]]* ...).

lock_count
> The number of PCM locks assigned to *file_list*. If *lock_count* is set to 0, fine-grain locking is used for these files.

!blocks

Optionally indicates the number of contiguous blocks covered by one lock.

EACH

Optionally specifies that each datafile in *file_list* is assigned a separate set of *lock_count* PCM locks; the default is noncontiguous blocks.

For example:

```
GC_FILES_TO_LOCKS = "1-4 = 64  EACH : 5-6 = 32 EACH"
```

If the number of PCM locks allocated to a datafile is less than or equal to the number of blocks contained in a datafile, each of these locks will cover a number of contiguous blocks within the datafile equal to *!blocks*. If the number of PCM locks assigned to the datafile is larger than the number of blocks it contains, resources will be wasted, since there will be locks that are not covering any blocks. The datafiles not specified in GC_FILES_TO_LOCKS are covered, by default, by releasable locks. These locks are controlled by a different parameter, GC_RELEASABLE_LOCKS.

To find the correspondence between filenames and file numbers, query the data dictionary view DBA_DATA_FILES.

GC_LCK_PROCS

Values: 1 to 10, or 0 for a single instance running in exclusive mode
Default: 1
Multiple Instances: Must have identical values

Specifies the number of background lock processes (LCK0 through LCK9) for an instance in a parallel server. The default of 1 is typically adequate, but the value can be increased if the distributed lock request rate saturates the lock process (i.e., becomes CPU bound). You should increase the value of the PROCESSES parameter by one for each LCK*n* process, and also increase the values of other parameters whose default values are derived from PROCESSES if the defaults are not used.

GC_RELEASABLE_LOCKS

Values: 0 to unlimited
Default: DB_BLOCK_BUFFERS

Sets a value used to allocate space for fine-grain locking. The maximum value for this parameter is only imposed by memory restrictions. GC_RELEASABLE_LOCKS is specific to the Oracle Parallel Server in shared mode.

GC_ROLLBACK_LOCKS

Values: 1 to unlimited
Default: 20
Multiple Instances: Must have identical values

For each rollback segment, sets the number of distributed locks available for concurrently modified rollback segment blocks for Oracle Parallel Server. The default is sufficient for most applications. These instance locks are acquired in exclusive mode by the instance that acquires the rollback segment, and are used to force the instance to write rollback segment blocks to disk when another instance requires a read-consistent version of a block.

GC_ROLLBACK_SEGMENTS (Oracle7 Only)

Values: 2 to unlimited
Default: 20
Multiple Instances: Must have identical values

Specifies the maximum number of system-wide rollback segments when running Oracle Parallel Server. Set this parameter to the total number of rollback segments acquired by all instances in a parallel server, including the SYSTEM rollback segment. To provide for additional instances in the future, or additional rollback segments for the current instances, this parameter can be set to a higher value. Each rollback segment requires one distributed lock, specified by this parameter, in addition to the number specified by the GC_ROLLBACK_LOCKS parameter. The total number of distributed locks for rollback segments is:

$$GC\_ROLLBACK\_SEGMENTS \times (GC\_ROLLBACK\_LOCKS + 1)$$

GC_SAVE_ROLLBACK_LOCKS (Oracle7 Only)

Values: 2 to unlimited
Default: 20
Multiple Instances: Must have identical values

Reserves distributed locks for deferred rollback segments, which contain rollback entries for transactions in tablespaces that were taken offline. The default is sufficient for one or two instances, but should be increased to 10 per instance for more instances or if tablespaces need to be taken offline while Oracle is running in parallel mode.

GC_SEGMENTS (Oracle7 Only)

Values: 2 to unlimited
Default: 10
Multiple Instances: Must have identical values

Specifies the maximum number of segments in the system that may have space management activities performed simultaneously by different instances. The default is sufficient for most applications. If tables acquire new extents frequently, the value can be increased to two or three times the number of tables that different instances extend simultaneously. Approximately nine distributed locks dedicated to coordinating space management activities are required by each segment that undergoes simultaneous space management in a parallel server. The total number of distributed locks reserved by this parameter is therefore approximately 9 × GC_SEGMENTS.

GC_TABLESPACES (Oracle7 Only)

Values: 2 to unlimited
Default: 5
Multiple Instances: Must have identical values

Sets the maximum number of tablespaces in a parallel server that can be brought from offline to online, or vice versa, simultaneously.

GLOBAL_NAMES

Values: TRUE or FALSE
Default: FALSE

Specifies whether a database link must have the same name as the database to which it connects. If GLOBAL_NAMES is set to FALSE, then no check is performed. Setting this parameter to TRUE ensures the use of consistent naming conventions for databases and links. If using distributed processing, you should set GLOBAL_NAMES to TRUE to ensure a unique identifying name for each database in a networked environment.

HASH_AREA_SIZE

Values: 0 to system-dependent value
Default: 2 × SORT_AREA_SIZE

Sets the maximum amount of memory, in bytes, to be used for hash joins.

HASH_JOIN_ENABLED

Values: TRUE or FALSE

Values: TRUE

Specifies whether the optimizer should consider using a hash join as a join method. When this parameter is set to FALSE, hash join is turned off and is not available as a join method to the optimizer. When the parameter is set to TRUE, the optimizer will compare the cost of a hash join to other types of joins, and choose it if it gives the best cost.

HASH_MULTIBLOCK_IO_COUNT

Values: Operating system dependent

Default: 1

Specifies how many sequential blocks a hash join reads and writes in one I/O. However, when Oracle is operating in Multi-Threaded Server mode, this parameter is ignored and a value of 1 is used even if the parameter is set to another value. The maximum value is always less than the operating system's maximum I/O size expressed as Oracle blocks.

 This parameter strongly affects performance because it controls the number of partitions into which the input is divided. If the parameter value is changed, the following formula should remain true:

$$R \ / \ M <= Po2(M/C)$$

where:

R = size of left input to the join

M = HASH_AREA_SIZE × 0.9

Po2(*n*) = largest power of 2 that is smaller than *n*

C = HASH_MULTIBLOCK_IO_COUNT × DB_BLOCK_SIZE

IFILE

Values: Valid filename

Default: NULL

Embeds parameter file within the current parameter file. For example:

```
IFILE = COMMON.ORA
```

Up to three levels of nesting are allowed. Multiple parameter files may be included in one parameter file by listing IFILE several times with different values.

INSTANCE_GROUPS (Oracle8 Only)

Values: A string of group names, separated by commas

A Parallel Server parameter that assigns the current instance to the groups specified. INSTANCE_GROUPS must be specified as a comma-separated list of instance groups, which are used when allocating query slaves for a parallel operation. This parameter is usable only in parallel mode. See also PARALLEL_INSTANCE_GROUP.

INSTANCE_NUMBER

Values: 1 to maximum number of instances specified in CREATE DATABASE statement

Default: Lowest available number (depends on instance startup order and on the INSTANCE_NUMBER values assigned to other instances)

Multiple Instances: Must have different values

A Parallel Server parameter that specifies a unique number that maps the instance to one group of free space lists for each table created with the FREELIST GROUPS storage option. The INSTANCE option of the ALTER TABLE ALLOCATE EXTENT statement assigns an extent to a particular group of free lists. If the INSTANCE_ NUMBER parameter is set to the value specified for the INSTANCE option, the instance uses that extent for inserts and for updates that expand rows.

JOB_QUEUE_INTERVAL

Values: 1 to 3600

Default: 60

Sets the interval, in seconds, between wake-ups for the SNPn background processes of the instance. This parameter is used for managing snapshots as well as jobs submitted via the DBMS_JOB built-in package.

JOB_QUEUE_PROCESSES

Values: 0 to 36

Default: 0

Specifies the number of SNPn background processes per instance, where n is 0 to 9 followed by A to Z. (See Chapter 10, *The Oracle Instance*, for more information on SNPn processes.) This parameter should be set to a value of 1 or higher if snapshots are to be updated automatically. One process is usually adequate unless there are many snapshots that refresh at the same time. Job Queue processes are also used to process requests created by DBMS_JOB_QUEUE.

LARGE_POOL_MIN_ALLOC (Oracle8 Only)

Values: 16K to 64M
Default: 16K

Sets the minimum allocation size from the large pool. This parameter can be set in bytes, megabytes (M), or kilobytes (K).

LARGE_POOL_SIZE (Oracle8 Only)

Values: 0 or 300K to 2GB (or higher; maximum is operating system dependent)
Default: 0

Specifies the size of the large pool allocation heap. If this parameter is used, the minimum size is 300K or LARGE_POOL_MIN_ALLOC, whichever is larger. The value can be specified in bytes, kilobytes (K), or megabytes (M). The large pool, if specified, is used for session memory with the Multi-Threaded Server, and for I/O buffers during backup operations.

LGWR_IO_SLAVES (Oracle8 Only)

Values: 0 to operating system dependent
Default: 0

Sets the number of I/O slaves that the LGWR process uses. Typically, I/O slaves are used to simulate asynchronous I/O on platforms that do not support asynchronous I/O or implement it inefficiently. The LGWR process can use I/O slaves even when actual asynchronous I/O is being used. In that case, the I/O slaves will use asynchronous I/O.

LICENSE_MAX_SESSIONS

Values: 0 to number of session licenses
Default: 0

Limits the maximum number of user sessions allowed to run concurrently. When this limit is reached, only users with the RESTRICTED SESSION privilege can connect to the server. All other users will receive a warning message indicating that the system has reached maximum capacity. When this parameter is set to 0, concurrent session licensing is not enforced. Concurrent usage licensing and user licensing should not both be enabled; thus, either LICENSE_MAX_SESSIONS or LICENSE_MAX_USERS should always be set to 0. Multiple instances can have different values, but the total for all instances mounting a database should not be greater than the total number of sessions licensed for that database.

If this parameter is set to a non-zero number, you must also set LICENSE_SESSIONS_WARNING.

LICENSE_MAX_USERS

Values: 0 to number of user licenses
Default: 0
Multiple Instances: Must have the same values

Limits the maximum number of users to be created in the database. When this limit is reached, additional users cannot be created until the limit is increased. Concurrent usage (session) licensing and user licensing should not both be enabled; either LICENSE_MAX_SESSIONS or LICENSE_MAX_USERS, or both, should be set to 0. When running Oracle Parallel Server, the value for this parameter in the first instance to mount the database takes precedence where different instances contain different settings for this parameter.

LICENSE_SESSIONS_WARNING

Values: 0 to LICENSE_MAX_SESSIONS
Default: 0

Sets a warning limit on the number of concurrent user sessions. Additional users can still connect after this limit is reached, but a message is written in the ALERT file for each new connection. Users with the RESTRICTED SESSION privilege connecting after the limit is reached receive a message warning that the system is nearing maximum capacity. If the value of LICENSE_SESSIONS_WARNING is 0, no warning is given when approaching the concurrent usage (session) limit. If this parameter is set to a non-zero number, LICENSE_MAX_SESSIONS should also be set.

LM_LOCKS (Oracle8 Only)

Values: 512 to available shared memory
Default: 12000
Multiple Instances: Must have the same value

Specifies the number of locks Oracle will configure for the lock manager when running Oracle Parallel Server. The number of locks can be expressed by the following equation:

$$L = R + (R \times (N - 1))/N$$

where:

- L is the total number of locks.
- R is the number of resources.
- N is the total number of nodes.

Note that since lock configurations are per lock manager instance, this parameter must be the same for all lock manager instances.

LM_PROCS (Oracle8 Only)

Values: 36 to PROCESSES + maximum number of instances + safety factor
Default: 64 + maximum instances supported
Multiple Instances: Must have the same value

A Parallel Server parameter that specifies the value of the PROCESSES parameter plus the maximum number of instances. Note that since PROCESSES are configured per lock manager instance, the value for LM_PROCS must be the same for all lock manager instances.

LM_RESS (Oracle8 Only)

Values: 256 to available shared memory
Default: 6000
Multiple Instances: Must have the same value

A Parallel Server parameter that specifies the number of resources allowed to be locked by each lock manager instance. The value specified for LM_RESS should be substantially less than twice the value of DML_LOCKS, plus an overhead of about 20 locks. LM_RESS covers the number of lock resources allocated for DML, DDL (data dictionary locks), data dictionary cache locks, and library cache locks, plus the file and log management locks.

LOCAL_LISTENER (Oracle8 Only)

Values: Valid listener specification
Default: See description

Identifies local Net8 listeners so they can complete client connections to dedicated servers. This parameter sets the network name of either a single address or an address list of Net8 listeners, which must be running on the same machine as the instance. When present, this parameter overrides the MTS_LISTENER_ ADDRESS and MTS_MULTIPLE_LISTENERS parameters. The default value for LOCAL_LISTENER is:

```
(ADDRESS_LIST = (ADDRESS = (PROTOCOL = TCP) (HOST=localhost) (Port=1521))
                (ADDRESS =(PROTOCOL = IPC)
                (KEY= dbname)))
```

LOCK_NAME_SPACE (Oracle8 Only)

Values: 1–8 characters, no special characters allowed

Specifies the name space used by the distributed lock manager (DLM) to generate lock names. This parameter may be necessary if a standby or clone database contains the same database name on the same cluster.

LOG_ARCHIVE_BUFFER_SIZE

Values: 1 to operating system dependent
Default: Operating system dependent

Establishes the size of each archival buffer, listed in terms of redo log blocks (operating system blocks). The default should be sufficient for most applications. This parameter can be used along with LOG_ARCHIVE_BUFFERS to tune archiving.

LOG_ARCHIVE_BUFFERS

Values: Operating system dependent
Default: Operating system dependent

Specifies the number of buffers allocated for archiving. The default should be sufficient for most applications. This parameter can be used along with LOG_ARCHIVE_BUFFER_SIZE to tune archiving so that it runs as fast as necessary, but not so fast that system performance is impaired.

LOG_ARCHIVE_DEST

Values: Valid path or device name
Default: Operating system dependent

Specifies the default location of the disk file directory or tape device when archiving redo log files during archivelog mode. Note that not all operating systems support archiving to tape.

On some platforms (e.g., Windows NT) the LOG_ARCHIVE_DEST parameter specifies the name of a directory, while on others (e.g., Unix) it specifies a directory and filename prefix. Be sure to check the documentation for your operating system to determine the exact format to use.

LOG_ARCHIVE_DUPLEX_DEST (Oracle8 Only)

Values: Valid path or device name or a NULL string

Default: NULL string

Specifies a second, or duplex, destination of the directory or tape device used for archiving files. This duplex archive destination can be either a must-succeed or a best-effort archive destination, depending on how many archive destinations must succeed (see LOG_ARCHIVE_MIN_SUCCEED_DEST). If this parameter is set to be a NULL string (`""` or `' '`), no duplex archive destination is activated. This parameter is similar to the initialization parameter LOG_ARCHIVE_DEST.

LOG_ARCHIVE_FORMAT

Values: Valid filename

Default: Operating system dependent

Multiple Instances: May have different values, but it is recommended that identical values be used.

Specifies the default filename format for archiving redo log files in archivelog mode. Oracle appends the string generated from this format to the string specified in the LOG_ARCHIVE_DEST parameter. LOG_ARCHIVE_FORMAT can contain the following variables:

%s Log sequence number

%t Thread number

Using uppercase letters (for example, %S) for the variables causes the value to be a fixed length padded to the left with zeros. The following is an example of the specification of the archive redo log filename format:

```
LOG_ARCHIVE_FORMAT = "LOG%s_%t.ARC"
```

LOG_ARCHIVE_MIN_SUCCEED_DEST (Oracle8 Only)

Values: 1 or 2

Default: 1

Specifies the minimum number of archive log destinations that must succeed when running archivelog mode. When automatic archiving is enabled, the allowable values are 1 and 2. If the value of this parameter is 1, LOG_ARCHIVE_DEST is a must-succeed destination and LOG_ARCHIVE_DUPLEX_DEST is a best-effort destination. If the value of this parameter is 2, both LOG_ARCHIVE_DEST and LOG_ARCHIVE_DUPLEX_DEST are must-succeed destinations.

LOG_ARCHIVE_START

Values: TRUE or FALSE
Default: FALSE

Sets whether archiving should be automatic or manual when the instance starts up in archivelog mode. TRUE sets archiving to be automatic, and FALSE allows the DBA to archive filled redo log files manually. The Server Manager command ARCHIVE LOG START or STOP overrides this parameter.

To use archivelog mode while creating a database, set this parameter to TRUE. Normally, a database is created in noarchivelog mode, then altered to archivelog mode after creation.

LOG_BLOCK_CHECKSUM

Values: TRUE or FALSE
Default: FALSE

Sets Oracle to give every log block a checksum before writing it to the current log.

Setting LOG_BLOCK_CHECKSUM to TRUE can cause performance problems due to increased overhead. Set this parameter to TRUE only under the advice of Oracle Technical Support personnel when diagnosing data corruption problems.

LOG_BUFFER

Values: Operating system dependent
Default: Operating system dependent

Specifies the amount of memory, in bytes, used to buffer redo entries to a redo log file. Redo log entries are written from the log buffer to a redo log file by the LGWR process. In general, larger values for this parameter reduce redo log file I/O, especially when dealing with many transactions or long transactions. In a busy system, LOG_BUFFER should be set to a value of 65536 or higher.

LOG_CHECKPOINT_INTERVAL

Values: 0 to unlimited
Default: Operating system dependent

Specifies the frequency of checkpoints in terms of the number of redo log file blocks (note that these are operating system blocks, not Oracle blocks) that are written between consecutive checkpoints. Regardless of this value, a checkpoint always occurs when switching from one online redo log file to another. If the value exceeds the actual redo log file size, checkpoints occur only when switching logs.

Extremely frequent checkpointing can cause excessive writes to disk, possibly impacting transaction performance, and if the intervals are so close together that the interval checkpoint requests are arriving at a rate faster than the rate at which Oracle can satisfy these requests, Oracle may choose to ignore some of these requests in order to avoid excessive checkpointing activity.

Specifying a value of 0 for the interval might cause interval checkpoints to be initiated very frequently, since a new request will be started even if a single redo log buffer has been written since the last request was initiated.

LOG_CHECKPOINT_TIMEOUT

Values: 0 to unlimited
Default: 0

Specifies the maximum amount of time, in seconds, before another checkpoint occurs. The time begins at the start of the previous checkpoint. Specifying a value of 0 disables time-based checkpoints, so setting the value to 0 is not recommended.

LOG_CHECKPOINTS_TO_ALERT

Values: TRUE or FALSE
Default: FALSE

Specifies that checkpoints are to be logged to the alert file. This parameter is useful in determining if checkpoints are occurring at the desired frequency.

LOG_FILE_NAME_CONVERT (Oracle8 Only)

Values: *"filename1","filename2"*

Converts the filename of a new log file on the primary database to the filename of a log file on the standby database. Adding a log file to the primary database necessitates adding a corresponding file to the standby database. When the standby database is updated, this parameter is used to convert the log file name on the primary database to the log file name on the standby database. The file must exist and be writable on the standby database or the recovery process will halt with an error.

Set the value of this parameter to two strings: the first string is the pattern found in the log file names on the primary database; the second string is the pattern found in the log file names on the standby database. For example:

```
LOG_FILE_NAME_CONVERT = ("/oracle/prod/redo1.log",
                         "/oracle/standby/redo1.log")
```

This parameter replaces the LOG_FILE_STANDBY_NAME_CONVERT parameter in Oracle7.

LOG_FILE_STANDBY_NAME_CONVERT (Oracle7 Only)

Values: *"filename1"*, *"filename2"*

Converts the filename of a new log file on the primary database to the filename of a log file on the standby database. Adding a log file to the primary database necessitates adding a corresponding file to the standby database. When the standby database is updated, this parameter is used to convert the log file name on the primary database to the log file name on the standby database. The file must exist and be writable on the standby database, or the recovery process will halt with an error.

Set the value of this parameter to two strings: the first string is the pattern found in the log file names on the primary database; the second string is the pattern found in the log file names on the standby database. For example:

```
LOG_FILE_STANDBY_NAME_CONVERT = ("/oracle/prod/redo1.log",
                                 "/oracle/standby/redo1.log")
```

This parameter has been replaced by LOG_FILE_NAME_CONVERT in Oracle8.

LOG_FILES

Values: 2 to 255
Default: 255
Multiple Instances: Must have the same value

Specifies the maximum log group number. This value specifies the maximum number of redo log files that can be opened at runtime for the database, and sets the upper limit on the group numbers that can be specified when issuing log-related commands. Reduce the value only if SGA space is needed and there are fewer redo log files than the current value of LOG_FILES.

LOG_SIMULTANEOUS_COPIES

Values: 0 to unlimited
Default: CPU_COUNT

Specifies the maximum number of redo buffer copy latches available to write log entries simultaneously. For good performance, up to twice as many redo copy latches as CPUs may be specified. For a single-processor system, set this parameter to 0 so that all log entries are copied on the redo allocation latch. If it is set to 0, redo copy latches are turned off, and the parameters LOG_ENTRY_PREBUILD_ THRESHOLD and LOG_SMALL_ENTRY_MAX_SIZE are ignored.

LOG_SMALL_ENTRY_MAX_SIZE

Values: Operating system dependent
Default: Operating system dependent

Specifies the size, in bytes, of the largest copy to the log buffers that can be made under the redo allocation latch without obtaining the redo buffer copy latch. This parameter is ignored if the LOG_SIMULTANEOUS_COPIES parameter is 0.

MAX_COMMIT_PROPAGATION_DELAY

Values: 0 to 90000
Default: 90000
Multiple Instances: Must have identical values

A Parallel Server parameter that specifies the maximum amount of time, in hundredths of a second, allowed before LGWR refreshes the System Change Number (SCN) held in the SGA of an instance. This parameter determines whether the local SCN should be refreshed from the lock value when acquiring the snapshot SCN for a query. Under rare circumstances involving rapid updates and queries of the same data from different instances, the SCN might not be refreshed in a timely manner. Setting this parameter to 0 causes the LGWR to refresh the SCN immediately after a commit. The default value of 90,000 hundredths of a second, or 15 minutes, is an upper bound allowing the preferred existing high performance mechanism to remain in place. This parameter should not be changed except under a limited set of circumstances specific to the Parallel Server (for example, when it is absolutely necessary to see the most current version of the database when performing a query).

MAX_DUMP_FILE_SIZE

Values: 0 to unlimited
Default: 10000

Limits the maximum size of trace files to be written by Oracle. This limit should be changed if there is a concern that trace files may take up too much space. MAX_ DUMP_FILE_SIZE can be set in the form of a number, or a number followed by the suffix "K" or "M". A number specifies the maximum size in operating system blocks; a number followed by a "K" or "M" suffix specifies the file size in kilobytes or megabytes, respectively. This parameter can also be set to the value string UNLIMITED, meaning that there is no upper limit on the trace file size.

MAX_ENABLED_ROLES

Values: 0 to 148
Default: 20

Limits the maximum number of database roles, in addition to the user's own role and PUBLIC, that may be enabled by a user.

MAX_ROLLBACK_SEGMENTS

Values: 2 to 65535
Default: 30

Limits the maximum size of the rollback segment cache in the SGA, which also designates the maximum number of rollback segments allowed to be kept online (with a status of INUSE) by one instance concurrently.

MAX_TRANSACTION_BRANCHES

Values: 1 to 32
Default: 8

Sets the number of branches in a distributed transaction. Allows Oracle to use up to 32 servers or server groups per instance to work on a single distributed transaction.

MTS_DISPATCHERS

Values: Valid dispatcher specification
Default: NULL

Enables certain attributes for each dispatcher. In Oracle 7.3, this parameter specifies a protocol and an initial number of dispatchers in a position-dependent, comma-separated string assigned to MTS_DISPATCHERS. For example:

```
MTS_DISPATCHERS = "TCP, 3"
```

While the parsing software in Oracle8 remains backward compatible with this format, it also supports a name-value syntax (similar to the syntax used by Net8) to enable specification of existing and additional attributes in a position-independent, case-insensitive manner. For example:

```
MTS_DISPATCHERS = "(PROTOCOL=TCP)(DISPATCHERS=3)"
```

This format requires that you specify one and only one of the following attributes: ADDRESS, DESCRIPTION, or PROTOCOL. For detailed information about this parameter, refer to Oracle's *Net8 Administrator's Guide* and the *Oracle8 Server Reference Manual*.

MTS_LISTENER_ADDRESS

Values: Valid MTS_LISTENER_ADDRESS specification
Default: NULL

Specifies an address to be used by the listener process, which listens for connection requests for each network protocol that is used on the system. Addresses are specified as the Net8 description of the connection address, but each address is specified with its own parameter (this differs from the Net8 syntax). Multiple MTS_ LISTENER_ADDRESS parameters must be adjacent to each other in the initialization file.

Note that this parameter is obsolete beginning with Oracle8, but is supported for backward compatibility. It has been replaced by the LOCAL_LISTENER parameter and the listener attribute of the MTS_DISPATCHERS parameter.

MTS_MAX_DISPATCHERS

Values: Operating system dependent
Default: Greater of 5 or number of dispatchers

Sets the maximum number of dispatcher processes able to run at the same time.

MTS_MAX_SERVERS

Values: Operating system dependent
Default: Greater of 20 or 2 × MAX_SERVERS

Sets the maximum number of shared server processes able to run at the same time.

MTS_MULTIPLE_LISTENERS

Values: TRUE or FALSE
Default: FALSE

Controls the syntax of the MTS_LISTENER_ADDRESS parameter. This parameter is obsolete for Oracle8, but is supported for backward compatibility. It has been replaced by the LOCAL_LISTENER parameter and the LISTENER attribute of the MTS_DISPATCHERS parameter.

MTS_RATE_LOG_SIZE (Oracle8 Only)

Values: See description
Default: 10 for each name listed

Specifies the sample size that Oracle uses to calculate dispatcher rate statistics. This size determines the amount of memory to be used and the frequency with which maximum rates will be determined. The memory used by each dispatcher is about 8 bytes per statistic multiplied by the sample size specified by this parameter. Dispatcher rate statistics themselves are calculated by first logging a sample of events (the size of which is specified by this parameter) and the times at which the events occur. This sample is then used to calculate the rates.

The syntax for MTS_RATE_LOG_SIZE consists of a string of one or more name=value sections, with the values being shared among all dispatchers. The following example directs each dispatcher to log 4 inbound connections, 32 buffers to go either to the client or the server, and 16 events for unspecified statistics:

```
MTS_RATE_LOG_SIZE="(IN_CONNECTS=4)(TOTAL_BUFFERS=32)(DEFAULTS=16)"
```

Valid names for MTS_RATE_LOG_SIZE are listed Table 12-4.

Table 12-4. Valid MTS_RATE_LOG_SIZE Names

Name	Description
DEFAULTS	Overrides 10 as the number of events to log for unspecified statistics
EVENT_LOOPS	Number of event loops to log
MESSAGES	Number of messages to log
SERVER_BUFFERS	Number of buffers going to the server to log
CLIENT_BUFFERS	Number of buffers going to the client to log
TOTAL_BUFFERS	Number of buffers going in either direction to log
IN_CONNECTS	Number of inbound connections to log
OUT_CONNECTS	Number of outbound connections to log
RECONNECTS	Number of connection pool reconnections to log

MTS_RATE_SCALE (Oracle8 Only)

Values: See description

Default: See description

Specifies the scale at which Oracle reports dispatcher rate statistics. The values are specified in hundredths of a second, so the following specification means that the event loops statistic will be reported on a once-per-minute interval:

```
MTS_RATE_SCALE = "(EVENT_LOOPS=6000)"
```

The syntax for MTS_RATE_SCALE consists of a string of one or more name=value sections. Valid names and default values are listed in Table 12-5.

Table 12-5. Valid MTS_RATE_SCALE Names and Defaults

Name	Default	Description
DEFAULTS	None	Scale for statistics not otherwise specified
EVENT_LOOPS	6000	Scale in which to report event loops

Table 12-5. Valid MTS_RATE_SCALE Names and Defaults (continued)

Name	Default	Description
MESSAGES	100	Scale in which to report messages
SERVER_BUFFERS	10	Scale in which to report buffers going to the server
CLIENT_BUFFERS	10	Scale in which to report buffers going to the client
TOTAL_BUFFERS	10	Scale in which to report buffers going in either direction
IN_CONNECTS	6000	Scale in which to report inbound connections
OUT_CONNECTS	6000	Scale in which to report outbound connections
RECONNECTS	6000	Scale in which to report connection pool reconnections

MTS_SERVERS

Values: Operating system dependent

Default: 0

Specifies the number of server processes created when an instance is started.

MTS_SERVICE

Values: Service name

Default: NULL

Sets the name of the service to be associated with the dispatcher (e.g., prod). Users may use this name in a connect string to connect to an instance through a dispatcher. Oracle always checks for such a service before it establishes a normal database connection. The name specified should not be enclosed in quotation marks, and it must be unique. If not specified, this parameter defaults to the value specified by DB_NAME. If DB_NAME is also not specified, the Oracle Server returns an error at startup indicating that the value for this parameter is missing.

Make the MTS_SERVICE name the same as the instance name, so that if the dispatcher is unavailable for any reason, the connect string will still connect the user to the database.

NLS_CURRENCY

Values: Any valid character string, with a maximum of 10 bytes

Default: Derived from the NLS_TERRITORY parameter

Establishes the string used as the local currency symbol for the L number format element. The NLS_TERRITORY parameter determines the default value of this parameter.

NLS_DATE_FORMAT

Values: Any valid date format mask
Default: Derived from the NLS_TERRITORY parameter

Establishes the default date format for use with the TO_CHAR and TO_DATE functions, in the following format:

```
NLS_DATE_FORMAT = "MM/DD/YYYY"
```

The value must be enclosed in double quotation marks, and can be any valid date format mask. The NLS_TERRITORY parameter determines the default value of this parameter.

NLS_DATE_LANGUAGE

Values: Any valid NLS_LANGUAGE value
Default: Value for NLS_LANGUAGE

Establishes the language used to spell day and month names and date abbreviations (AM, PM, AD, BC).

NLS_ISO_CURRENCY

Values: Any valid NLS_LANGUAGE value
Default: Derived from the NLS_TERRITORY parameter

Establishes the string used as the international currency symbol for the C number format element. The NLS_TERRITORY parameter determines the default value of this parameter.

NLS_LANGUAGE

Values: Any valid language name
Default: Operating system dependent

Establishes the default language for the database. This language is used for messages, day and month names, symbols for AD, BC, AM, and PM, and the default sorting mechanism. For example:

```
NLS_LANGUAGE = AMERICAN
```

Other supported languages include FRENCH, SPANISH, and JAPANESE. This parameter determines the default values of the parameters NLS_DATE_LANGUAGE and NLS_SORT. For a complete list of languages, see the *Oracle Server Reference Manual* and the server *Release Notes*.

NLS_NUMERIC_CHARACTERS

Values: See description

Default: Derived from the NLS_TERRITORY parameter

Sets the characters to use as the group separator and decimal and overrides those defined implicitly by NLS_TERRITORY. The group separator is the character that separates integer groups, that is, the thousands, millions, billions, and so on. The decimal separates the integer portion of a number from the decimal portion.

Both characters must be single-byte characters, and they can't be the same character. Prohibited values for these characters include all numeric characters and the plus (+), hyphen (-), less than sign (<), and greater than sign (>) characters. The format for this parameter is as follows:

```
NLS_NUMERIC_CHARACTERS = "<decimal_character><group_separator>"
```

For example, the following:

```
NLS_NUMERIC_CHARACTERS = ",^"
```

specifies that the decimal character will be a comma, and the group separator will be a caret. The parameter NLS_TERRITORY determines the default value of this parameter.

NLS_SORT

Values: BINARY or valid language name

Default: Derived from the NLS_LANGUAGE parameter

Specifies the collating sequence for ORDER BY queries. If the value is BINARY, the collating sequence for ORDER BY queries is based on the numeric value of characters, which requires less system overhead. If the value of this parameter is a designated language, sorting is based on the order of the linguistic sort defined. The NLS_LANGUAGE parameter determines the default value of this parameter.

Setting NLS_SORT to anything other than BINARY causes a sort to use a full table scan, regardless of the path chosen by the optimizer. BINARY is the exception, because indexes are built according to a binary order of keys, so the optimizer can use an index to satisfy the ORDER BY clause.

The NLS_SORT operator must be used with comparison operations if the linguistic sort behavior is desired.

NLS_TERRITORY

Values: Any valid territory name
Default: Operating system dependent

Specifies the name of the territory whose conventions are used for day and week numbering. Supported territories include America, France, Japan, and so on. For a complete list of territories, see "Supported Territories" in the *Oracle Server Reference Manual*. Also specifies the default date format, the default decimal character and group separator, and the default ISO and local currency symbols, which can be changed using the following parameters: NLS_CURRENCY, NLS_ISO_CURRENCY, NLS_DATE_FORMAT, and NLS_NUMERIC_CHARACTERS.

O7_DICTIONARY_ACCESSIBILITY (Oracle8 Only)

Values: TRUE or FALSE
Default: TRUE

Controls restrictions on SYSTEM privileges. If the value of this parameter is TRUE, access to objects in the SYS schema is allowed (Oracle7 behavior). If the value is FALSE, privileges allowing access to objects in other schemas do not allow access to objects in the SYS schema.

OBJECT_CACHE_MAX_SIZE_PERCENT (Oracle8 Only)

Values: 0 to operating system dependent
Default: 10

Sets the percentage of the optimal cache size that the session object cache can grow past the optimal size. The maximum size is equal to the optimal size plus the designated percentage of the optimal size. When the cache size exceeds this maximum size, Oracle will try to shrink the cache to the optimal size.

OBJECT_CACHE_OPTIMAL_SIZE (Oracle8 Only)

Values: 10K to operating system dependent
Default: 100K

Specifies the size to which the session object cache will shrink when the size of the cache exceeds the maximum size.

OPEN_CURSORS

Values: 1 to operating system dependent
Default: 50

Specifies the maximum number of cursors (context areas) that a session can have open at one time, thereby preventing a session from opening an excessive number of cursors. If a session does not open the number of cursors specified by OPEN_CURSORS, no overhead is added by setting this value too high. This parameter also limits the size of the PL/SQL cursor cache that PL/SQL uses to avoid reparsing as statements are executed again by a user.

Make sure the value of OPEN_CURSORS is set high enough to prevent an application from running out of open cursors. The number will vary from one application to another.

OPEN_LINKS

Values: 0 to 255
Default: 4

Sets the maximum number of connections to remote databases allowed to be open concurrently in one session. The value should be equal to or should exceed the number of databases referred to in a single SQL statement that references multiple databases using database links, so all the databases can be open to execute the statement.

If multiple databases are accessed during a session connection, but are not accessed in the same SQL statement, it may still be worthwhile increasing the value of OPEN_LINKS. Otherwise, for example, if queries alternately access databases A, B, and C, and OPEN_LINKS is set to 2, time is spent waiting while one connection is closed and another opened.

OPEN_LINKS_PER_INSTANCE (Oracle8 Only)

Values: 0 to 255
Default: 4

Sets the maximum number of open connections that can be migrated. XA transactions use migratable open connections so that the connections are cached after a transaction is committed. Another transaction can use the connection, assuming that the user who created the connection is the same as the user who owns it. OPEN_LINKS_PER_INSTANCE differs from the OPEN_LINKS parameter in that OPEN_LINKS indicates the number of connections from a session, and the OPEN_LINKS parameter is not applicable to XA applications.

OPS_ADMIN_GROUP (Oracle8 Only)

Values: Valid group name
Default: All active instances

Allows instances to be partitioned in an Oracle Parallel Server environment for monitoring or administration purposes. The database must be mounted in Parallel Server mode (that is, PARALLEL_SERVER=TRUE). This parameter determines the instances that return information in a GV$ fixed-view query.

OPTIMIZER_FEATURES_ENABLE

Values: 8.0.0, 8.0.3, 8.0.4
Default: 8.0.0

Specifies whether *INIT.ORA* parameters that control the optimizer's behavior can be changed. The parameters affected are PUSH_JOIN_PREDICATE, FAST_FULL_SCAN_ENABLED, COMPLEX_VIEW_MERGING, and B_TREE_BITMAP_PLANS. The values 8.0.0 and 8.0.3 set those parameters to FALSE; 8.0.4 sets them to TRUE. However, regardless of the setting, you can change each parameter individually.

OPTIMIZER_MODE

Values: RULE, CHOOSE, FIRST_ROWS, or ALL_ROWS
Default: CHOOSE

Specifies the behavior of the optimizer. When set to RULE, this parameter instructs the optimizer to use rule-based optimization unless hints are specified in the query. When set to CHOOSE, this parameter instructs the optimizer to use the cost-based approach for a SQL statement if the dictionary contains statistics for at least one table accessed in the statement. (Otherwise, the optimizer uses the rule-based approach.) FIRST_ROWS instructs the cost-based optimizer to choose execution plans that minimize response time. ALL_ROWS instructs the cost-based optimizer to choose execution plans that minimize total execution time.

Cost-based optimization will always be used for any query that references an object with a non-zero degree of parallelism. For such queries, a RULE hint or optimizer mode or goal will be ignored. Use of a FIRST_ROWS hint or optimizer mode will override a non-zero setting of OPTIMIZER_PERCENT_PARALLEL.

OPTIMIZER_PERCENT_PARALLEL

Values: 0 to 100
Default: 0

Sets the amount of parallelism used by the optimizer in its cost functions. The default of 0 instructs the optimizer to choose the best serial plan. A value of 100 instructs the optimizer to use each object's degree of parallelism in determining the cost of a full table scan operation. Low values favor indexes, and high values favor table scans.

OPTIMIZER_SEARCH_LIMIT

Values: 0 to 10
Default: 5

Specifies the search limit for the optimizer.

ORACLE_TRACE_COLLECTION_NAME

Values: Valid name up to 16 characters
Default: NULL

Specifies the Oracle Trace collection name. The output filenames (collection definition file, *.CDF*, and datafile, *.DAT*) also use this parameter. Be forewarned that some operating systems may limit the length of this name to less than the maximum 16 characters.

ORACLE_TRACE_COLLECTION_PATH

Values: Valid directory pathname
Default: Operating system dependent

Specifies the directory where Oracle Trace collection definition and datafiles can be found. If the default is accepted, the complete file specification is generally *$ORACLE_HOME/rdbms/log/collectionname.cdf* and *collectionname.dat*, where *collectionname* is the value of ORACLE_TRACE_COLLECTION_NAME.

ORACLE_TRACE_COLLECTION_SIZE

Values: 0 to 4294967295
Default: 5242880

Sets the maximum size, in bytes, of the Oracle Trace collection file. The collection is disabled once the collection file reaches this size.

ORACLE_TRACE_ENABLE

Values: TRUE or FALSE
Default: FALSE

Enables the Oracle Trace collections for the server. When set to TRUE, this parameter allows Oracle Trace to be used for that server, though it does not immediately start an Oracle Trace collection. Oracle Trace can be started by using the Oracle Trace Manager component of the Oracle Enterprise Manager, or by specifying a name in the ORACLE_TRACE_COLLECTION_NAME parameter.

ORACLE_TRACE_FACILITY_NAME

Values: Valid name up to 16 characters
Default: Operating system dependent

Specifies the Oracle Trace product definition file (*.FDF* file). The file must be located in the directory designated by the ORACLE_TRACE_FACILITY_PATH parameter. The product definition file contains definition information for all the events and data items that can be collected for a product that uses the Oracle Trace data collection API.

ORACLE_TRACE_FACILITY_PATH

Values: Valid pathname
Default: Operating system dependent

Specifies the directory pathname where Oracle Trace facility definition files can be found.

OS_AUTHENT_PREFIX

Values: Any valid string
Default: OPS$

Specifies the prefix concatenated to the beginning of every user's operating system username to allow authentication of the operating system account name and password for users connecting to the server. Oracle compares the value of this prefixed username with the Oracle usernames in the database when a connection request is attempted. For example, if an Oracle account is created with username OPS$DAVE IDENTIFIED EXTERNALLY, and a user with an operating system username DAVE then attempts to log into Oracle, the prefix OPS$ will be appended; thus, the operating system name OPS$DAVE matches the Oracle username OPS$DAVE, and Oracle allows DAVE to log in.

The default value of this parameter is OPS$ to allow backward compatibility with previous versions. Note that this mechanism has no effect on Oracle accounts that are not IDENTIFIED EXTERNALLY. (See the description of the CREATE USER and ALTER USER commands in Chapter 13, *SQL Statements for the DBA.*)

OS_ROLES

Values: TRUE or FALSE
Default: FALSE

Specifies whether Oracle allows the operating system to identify each username's roles. If the value of this parameter is TRUE, when a user attempts to create a session, the username's security domain is initialized using the roles identified by the operating system. If this parameter is set to FALSE, the database identifies and manages roles.

 If OS_ROLES is set to TRUE, the operating system completely manages the role grants for all database usernames. Any revokes of roles granted by the operating system are ignored, and any previously granted roles are ignored.

PARALLEL_DEFAULT_MAX_INSTANCES

Values: 0 to number of instances
Default: Operating system dependent
Multiple Instances: Should have the same value

Sets the default number of instances across which to split a table for parallel query processing. The value of this parameter is used if the INSTANCES DEFAULT is specified in the PARALLEL clause of a table's definition.

PARALLEL_INSTANCE_GROUP (Oracle8 Only)

Values: Valid group name
Default: Group consisting of all instances currently active

Identifies the parallel instance group used to spawn parallel query slaves. Parallel operations will spawn parallel query slaves only on instances that specify a matching group in their INSTANCE_GROUPS parameter. If name of the group specified in the PARALLEL_INSTANCE_GROUP parameter does not exist, no parallelism is used and the operation runs serially.

PARALLEL_MAX_SERVERS

Values: 0 to 256

Default: Operating system dependent

Multiple Instances: Must have either a value of 0 or the same value as all other instances

Sets the maximum number of parallel query servers or parallel recovery processes for an instance. As required by demand, Oracle will increase the number of query servers from the number created at instance startup up to this value. If this parameter is set too low, then a query server may not be available to some queries during query processing. If the parameter is set too high, memory resource shortages may occur during peak periods, which can degrade performance. Setting this parameter to 0 disables the Parallel Query option.

PARALLEL_MIN_MESSAGE_POOL (Oracle8 Only)

Values: 0 to SHARED_POOLSIZE × .90

Default: CPUs × PARALLEL_MAX_SERVERS × 1.5 × (OS message buffer size) or CPUs × 5 × 1.5 × (OS message size)

Specifies the minimum permanent amount of memory to be allocated from the shared pool for use by messages in parallel execution. This memory is allocated at startup time if PARALLEL_MIN_SERVERS is set to a non-zero value, or when the server is first allocated. PARALLEL_MIN_MESSAGE_POOL should be changed only if the default formula is known to be significantly inaccurate, since setting this parameter too high will lead to memory shortage for the shared pool, and setting it too low will lead to costlier memory allocation during parallel execution. This parameter cannot be set higher than 90% of the shared pool.

PARALLEL_MIN_PERCENT

Values: 0 to 100

Default: 0

Specifies the minimum percent of threads required for parallel query. Setting this parameter ensures that a parallel query will only be executed sequentially if adequate resources are available. The default value of 0 means that this parameter is not used. If too few query slaves are available, the query is not executed, and an error message is displayed. For example, specify the following settings:

```
PARALLEL_MIN_PERCENT = 50
PARALLEL_MIN_SERVERS = 5
PARALLEL_MAX_SERVERS = 10
```

In a system with 20 instances running, the system would have a maximum of 200 query slaves available. If 190 slaves are already in use and a new process wants to run a query with 40 slaves (for example, degree 2 instances 20), an error message would be returned because 20 slaves (that is, 50% of 40) are not available.

PARALLEL_MIN_SERVERS

Values: 0 to PARALLEL_MAX_SERVERS
Default: 0

Sets the minimum number of query server processes for an instance, which is also the number of query server processes created when the instance is started.

PARALLEL_SERVER (Oracle8 Only)

Values: TRUE or FALSE
Default: FALSE
Multiple Instances: Must have the same value

Enables, when set to TRUE, the Parallel Server option for this instance.

PARALLEL_SERVER_IDLE_TIME

Values: 0 to operating system dependent
Default: Operating system dependent

Specifies the amount of idle time, in minutes, after which Oracle will terminate a query server process.

PARALLEL_TRANSACTION_RESOURCE_TIMEOUT (Oracle8 Only)

Values: 0 to operating system dependent
Default: 300
Multiple Instances: May have different values, but it is recommended that the same value be used across all instances.

Specifies the maximum amount of time a session executing a parallel operation will wait for a resource held by another session in an incompatible lock mode before timing out. When set to 0, this parameter allows a the maximum wait time to be effectively infinite.

PARTITION_VIEW_ENABLED

Values: TRUE or FALSE
Default: FALSE

Establishes optimizer behavior for partitioned views. If set to TRUE, this parameter instructs the optimizer to prune or skip unnecessary table accesses in a partition view. It also changes the way the cost-based optimizer computes statistics on a partition view from statistics on underlying tables.

PLSQL_V2_COMPATIBILITY (Oracle8 Only)

Values: TRUE or FALSE

Default: FALSE

Sets the compatibility level for PL/SQL. If the value of this parameter is FALSE, PL/SQL V2 is not allowed, and V3 behavior is enforced. If it is TRUE, the following PL/SQL V2 behaviors are accepted when running PL/SQL V3:

- PL/SQL will allow elements of an index table passed in as an IN parameter to be modified or deleted.

- The PL/SQL compiler will allow OUT parameters to be used in expression contexts in some cases, for example, in dot-qualified names on the right-hand side of assignment statements. This behavior is restricted to fields of OUT parameters that are records, and OUT parameters referenced in the FROM list of a SELECT statement.

- PL/SQL will allow OUT parameters in the FROM clause of a SELECT list, where their values are read.

- PL/SQL will allow the passing of an IN argument into another procedure as an OUT. This is restricted to fields of IN parameters that are records.

- PL/SQL will allow a type to be referenced earlier than its definition in the source.

PRE_PAGE_SGA

Values: TRUE or FALSE

Default: FALSE

If this parameter is set to TRUE, Oracle touches all the SGA pages during the instance startup, causing them to be brought into memory. This increases instance startup time and user login time, but can reduce the number of page faults following shortly thereafter. This reduction in faults allows the instance to reach its maximum performance capability quickly rather than through an incremental buildup. This parameter is of the most benefit on systems that have sufficient memory to hold all the SGA pages without a degradation of performance in other areas.

PROCESSES

Values: 6 to operating system dependent

Default: 30

Specifies the maximum number of operating system user processes allowed to connect to an Oracle server at the same time. When setting this value, allow for all background processes such as LCK processes, Job Queue processes, and Parallel

Query processes. Also, the value of this parameter determines the default value of the SESSIONS parameter; if the value of PROCESSES is changed, the value of SESSIONS may need to be adjusted as well.

PUSH_JOIN_PREDICATE

Values: TRUE or FALSE
Default: FALSE

Specifies whether push-join predicates will be enabled. This is a cost-based method of improving performance in certain queries by pushing individual join predicates into a view that is the right side of an outer join, thereby enabling a more efficient access path and join method. Examples are hash joins transforming into nested loop joins or full table scans becoming index scans.

RECOVERY_PARALLELISM

Values: 0 to PARALLEL_MAX_SERVERS

Designates the number of processes to participate in instance or media recovery. When set to 0 or 1, this parameter indicates that recovery is to be performed serially by one process.

REMOTE_DEPENDENCIES_MODE

Values: TIMESTAMP or SIGNATURE
Default: TIMESTAMP

Specifies how the database will handle dependencies upon remote stored procedures. If set to TIMESTAMP, this parameter instructs the client running the procedure to compare the timestamp recorded on the server-side procedure with the current timestamp of the local procedure. In this case, it will execute the procedure only if the timestamps match. If the parameter is set to SIGNATURE, the procedure is allowed to execute as long as the signatures are considered safe, which allows client PL/SQL applications to be run without recompilation.

REMOTE_LOGIN_PASSWORDFILE

Values: NONE, SHARED, or EXCLUSIVE
Default: NONE
Multiple Instances: Should have the same value

Specifies whether Oracle checks for a password file and how many databases can use the password file. When the parameter is set to NONE, Oracle ignores any password file (therefore, privileged users must be authenticated by the operating system). When set to EXCLUSIVE, the password file can be used by only one database and the password file can contain names other than SYS and INTERNAL. When set to SHARED, more than one database can use a password file, but the only users recognized by the password file are SYS and INTERNAL.

REMOTE_OS_AUTHENT

Values: TRUE or FALSE
Default: FALSE

When set to TRUE, allows authentication of remote clients with the value of OS_AUTHENT_PREFIX. If this parameter is set to FALSE, remote clients are not allowed to log into the database using operating system authentication.

REMOTE_OS_ROLES

Values: TRUE or FALSE
Default: FALSE

When set to TRUE, allows operating system roles for remote clients. If this parameter is set to FALSE, the database identifies and manages roles for remote clients.

REPLICATION_DEPENDENCY_TRACKING (Oracle8 Only)

Values: TRUE or FALSE
Default: TRUE

Establishes dependency tracking for read/write operations to the database, which is essential for the Replication Server to propagate changes in parallel. TRUE toggles dependency tracking on, while FALSE allows read/write operations to the database to run faster, but does not produce dependency information for the Replication Server to perform parallel propagations. Don't specify this value unless applications will perform absolutely no read/write operations to replicated tables.

RESOURCE_LIMIT

Values: TRUE or FALSE
Default: FALSE

Sets the enforcement status of resource limits in database profiles. A value of TRUE enables the enforcement of resource limits, while a value of FALSE, the default, disables enforcement.

ROLLBACK_SEGMENTS

Values: Rollback segment names
Default: NULL
Multiple Instances: Must have different values; different instances cannot specify the same rollback segment.

Specifies one or more rollback segments to allocate by name to this instance. If this parameter is set, an instance acquires all of the rollback segments named in this parameter, even if the number of rollback segments exceeds the minimum number required by the instance (calculated from the ratio TRANSACTIONS / TRANSACTIONS_PER_ROLLBACK_SEGMENT). Although this parameter usually specifies private rollback segments, it can also specify public rollback segments if not already in use. If this parameter is not set, the instance uses all public rollback segments as the default. This parameter has the following syntax:

```
ROLLBACK_SEGMENTS = (rbseg_name [, rbseg_name] ... )
```

 Never name the SYSTEM rollback segment as a value for the ROLLBACK_SEGMENTS parameter.

ROW_CACHE_CURSORS

Values: 10 to 3300
Default: 10

Sets the maximum number of cached recursive cursors used by the dictionary cache manager for selecting rows from the data dictionary. For most systems, the default value is ordinarily sufficient.

ROW_LOCKING

Values: ALWAYS, DEFAULT, or INTENT
Default: ALWAYS
Multiple Instances: Must have the same value

Specifies whether row locks are acquired when a table is updated. When this parameter is set to ALWAYS, the default, then only row locks are acquired when a table is updated. The value of DEFAULT is treated the same as ALWAYS. If this parameter is set to INTENT, then only row locks are used on a SELECT FOR UPDATE, but at update time table locks are acquired.

SEQUENCE_CACHE_ENTRIES

Values: 10 to 32000
Default: 10

Specifies the number of sequence values allowed to be cached in the SGA for immediate access. The highest concurrency is achieved by setting this value to the highest possible number of sequences that will be used on an instance at once. For a parallel server, each entry requires approximately 110 bytes in the SGA. Sequences created with the NOCACHE option do not reside in this cache, and must be written through to the data dictionary on every use.

SEQUENCE_CACHE_HASH_BUCKET

Values: 10 to SEQUENCE_CACHE_ENTRIES
Default: 7

Sets the number of buckets used to speed lookup for newly requested sequences in the cache, which is arranged as a hash table. Each bucket occupies eight bytes, and the value specified should be a prime number; if the value is not prime, Oracle will raise that value to the next prime number.

SERIAL_REUSE (Oracle8 Only)

Values: DISABLE, SELECT, DML, PLSQL, ALL, or NULL
Default: NULL

Specifies which types of SQL cursors will make use of the serial-reusable memory feature, which moves well-structured private cursor memory into the SGA (shared pool) so that it can be reused by sessions executing the same cursor. Setting the parameter to the default NULL value is equivalent to setting it to DISABLE. The allowable values are listed in Table 12-6.

Table 12-6. Valid SERIAL_REUSE Values

Value	Description
DISABLE	Disables the option for all SQL statement types. This value overrides any other values included in the list.
SELECT	Enables the option for SELECT statements.
DML	Enables the option for DML statements.
PLSQL	Currently has no effect (although PLSQL packages do support the serial-reuse memory option using PL/SQL pragmas).
ALL	Enables the option for both DML and SELECT statements. Equivalent to setting SELECT, DML, and PLSQL.

SESSION_CACHED_CURSORS

Values: 0 to operating system dependent
Default: 0

Sets the maximum number of session cursors Oracle keeps in the session cursor cache. Repeated parse calls of the same SQL statement cause the session cursor for that statement to be moved into the session cursor cache. Subsequent parse calls will find the cursor in the cache and need not reopen the cursor.

SESSION_MAX_OPEN_FILES (Oracle8 Only)

Values: 1 to the smaller of 50 or MAX_OPEN_FILES
Default: 10

Sets the maximum number of files allowed to be opened in any given session. Once this maximum is reached, subsequent attempts to open more files in the session by calling the built-in package procedures DBMS_LOB.FILEOPEN() or OCILobFileOpen() will fail. This parameter is also dependent on the equivalent parameter defined for the underlying operating system.

SESSIONS

Values: 12 to operating system dependent
Default: 1.1 × PROCESSES + 5

Specifies the total number of user and system sessions. The default value for this parameter is calculated to be greater than PROCESSES to allow for recursive sessions. The setting for this parameter also determines the default values of ENQUEUE_RESOURCES and TRANSACTIONS, so if the value of SESSIONS is altered, the values for these parameters should be adjusted as well. With the Multi-Threaded Server, the value of SESSIONS should be set to approximately 1.1 × total number of connections.

SHADOW_CORE_DUMP

Values: FULL or PARTIAL
Default: FULL

Determines whether to include the SGA in core dumps. If the value of this parameter is FULL, the SGA is included in the core dump. If the value is PARTIAL, the SGA is not included and not dumped.

SHARED_POOL_RESERVED_MIN_ALLOC

Values: 5000 to SHARED_POOL_RESERVED_SIZE
Default: 5000

Controls the allocation of reserved memory. Memory allocations larger than this value can allocate space from the reserved list if a chunk of memory of sufficient size is not found on the shared pool free lists. If the value is increased, the Oracle server will allow fewer allocations from the reserved list and will request more memory from the shared pool list. This parameter can be specified as a plain number or as a number followed by a "K" or an "M," meaning "multiply by 1,000" and "multiply by 1,000,000," respectively. For most systems, the default value is ordinarily sufficient.

SHARED_POOL_RESERVED_SIZE

Values: SHARED_POOL_RESERVED_MIN_ALLOC to SHARED_POOL_SIZE / 2
Default: SHARED_POOL_SIZE × .05

Specifies the portion of the shared pool space to be reserved for large contiguous requests for shared pool memory. This parameter, along with the SHARED_POOL_RESERVED_MIN_ALLOC parameter, can be used to avoid performance degradation in the shared pool in situations where pool fragmentation forces Oracle to search for and free chunks of unused pool to satisfy the current request. If the value for SHARED_POOL_RESERVED_SIZE exceeds half of the value for SHARED_POOL_SIZE, an error statement is returned. Ideally, this parameter should be large enough to handle any request scanning for memory on the reserved list without flushing objects from the shared pool. The amount of operating system memory, however, may constrain the size of the shared pool.

In general, SHARED_POOL_RESERVED_SIZE should be set to 10% of SHARED_POOL_SIZE. If the shared pool has been tuned, then for most systems this value will be sufficient. SHARED_POOL_RESERVED_SIZE can accept a plain number or a number followed by "K" or "M," meaning "multiply by 1,000" and "multiply by 1,000,000," respectively.

SHARED_POOL_SIZE

Values: 300 Kbytes to operating system dependent
Default: 3500000

Specifies the size of the shared pool, in bytes. The shared pool contains shared cursors and stored procedures. Larger values can improve performance in multiuser systems, while smaller values use less memory. SHARED_POOL_SIZE can accept a plain number or number followed by K or M, meaning "multiply by 1,000" and "multiply by 1,000,000," respectively.

SORT_AREA_RETAINED_SIZE

Values: DB_BLOCK_SIZE to SORT_AREA_SIZE
Default: SORT_AREA_SIZE

Sets the maximum amount, in bytes, of user memory retained after a completed sort run. The size of retained memory controls the size of the read buffer, which is used to maintain a portion of the sort in memory. Larger values permit more sorts to be performed in memory; however, multiple sort spaces of this size may be allocated.

SORT_AREA_SIZE

Values: 0 to operating system dependent
Default: Operating system dependent

Specifies the maximum amount, in bytes, of the portion of the Program Global Area (PGA) memory used for a sort. If the Multi-Threaded Server is enabled, the sort area is allocated from the System Global Area. Following completion of the sort and prior to fetching of the rows, the memory is released down to the size specified by SORT_AREA_RETAINED_SIZE. All memory is freed after the last row is fetched, and released back to the PGA, not to the operating system. Increasing SORT_AREA_SIZE size improves the efficiency of large sorts. Multiple allocations never exist; only one memory area of SORT_AREA_SIZE exists for each user process at any time. The default is usually adequate for most online transaction processing operations, but this parameter may be adjusted to handle decision support systems, batch jobs, or large CREATE INDEX operations.

SORT_DIRECT_WRITES

Values: AUTO, TRUE, or FALSE
Default: AUTO

Controls whether sort data will bypass the buffer cache to write intermediate sort results to disk. If memory and temporary space are plentiful on the system, this parameter can improve sort performance. When the parameter is set to the default of AUTO, and the value of the sort area size is greater than ten times the block size, memory for this function is allocated from the sort area. When the parameter is set to TRUE, additional buffers are allocated from memory during each sort, and additional temporary segment space can be required. When the parameter is set to FALSE, the sorts that write to disk write through the buffer cache.

SORT_READ_FAC

Values: Operating system dependent
Default: Operating system dependent

Sets, in terms of a ratio, the amount of time to read a single database block divided by the block transfer rate. For more information on SORT_READ_FAC, see the appropriate operating system specific Oracle documentation.

SORT_SPACEMAP_SIZE

Values: Operating system dependent
Default: Operating system dependent

Sets the size, in bytes, of the sort space map. This parameter should be changed only when very large indexes exist. In most cases, a sort automatically increases its space map when necessary, but it does not necessarily do so when it will make best use of disk storage. The sort makes optimal use of disk storage when the parameter is set to the following value:

$$((total\_sort\_bytes) / (SORT\_AREA\_SIZE)) + 64$$

where total_sort_bytes is:

number_of_records × (sum_of_average_column_sizes
+ (2 × number_of columns))

SORT_WRITE_BUFFER_SIZE

Values: 32768 to 65536
Default: 32768

Sets the size of the sort I/O buffer when the SORT_DIRECT_WRITES parameter is set to TRUE. SORT_WRITE_BUFFER_SIZE is recommended for use with symmetric replication.

SORT_WRITE_BUFFERS

Values: 1 to 8
Default: 1

Sets the number of sort buffers used by Oracle when the SORT_DIRECT_WRITES parameter is set to TRUE. SORT_WRITE_BUFFERS should be used with symmetric replication.

SPIN_COUNT

Values: 1 to 1000000
Default: 1

Specifies the number of times a process will request a latch until it successfully obtains one. Tuning this parameter can heighten performance in a multiprocessor environment. When the number of unsuccessful requests for a latch reaches SPIN_COUNT, the process sleeps, then tries to acquire the latch again. Since a latch is a low-level lock, a process does not hold it for long. Thus, the CPU time used by spinning a process is less expensive than that used by making a process sleep. The contention level of the latch can be monitored with the miss rate and sleep rate from the UTLBSTAT and UTLESTAT scripts. Try reducing the sleep rate by tuning the spin count. If the contention level is high, increase the spin count to allow processes to spin longer before acquiring latches. Because increasing the spin count increases CPU usage, however, system throughput may decline at some point. The default value is ordinarily sufficient for almost all systems.

SQL_TRACE

Values: TRUE or FALSE
Default: FALSE

Disables or enables the SQL Trace facility. Setting this parameter to TRUE provides information on tuning that can be used to improve performance. Because the SQL Trace facility causes system overhead, however, the database should be run with the facility only when it is important to collect statistics. The value of this parameter can also be changed using the DBMS_SYSTEM built-in package.

SQL92_SECURITY

Values: TRUE or FALSE
Default: FALSE

Specifies whether table-level SELECT privileges are necessary in order to execute an update or delete that references table column values.

STAR_TRANSFORMATION_ENABLED (Oracle8 Only)

Values: TRUE or FALSE
Default: FALSE

Specifies whether a cost-based query transformation should be applied to star queries. If set to TRUE, this parameter instructs the optimizer to consider performing a cost-based query transformation on the star query. If the parameter is set to FALSE, the transformation will not be applied.

TAPE_ASYNCH_IO (Oracle8 Only)

Values: TRUE or FALSE
Default: TRUE

Controls whether I/O to sequential devices such as tape backup and restore of Oracle data is asynchronous. If a platform supports asynchronous I/O to sequential devices, leave this parameter at its default value of TRUE. However, if the asynchronous I/O implementation is not stable, a setting of FALSE can be used to disable its use. This parameter has no effect if a platform does not support asynchronous I/O to sequential devices.

TEMPORARY_TABLE_LOCKS

Values: 0 to operating system dependent
Default: SESSIONS

Sets the number of temporary tables allowed to be created in the temporary segment space. A temporary table lock is needed any time a sort is too large to hold in memory, either because of a SELECT on a large table with ORDER BY or as a result of sorting a large index. You may need to increase the value of this parameter on installations with many users of applications that perform several ordered queries on large tables at the same time. For most installations, the default should be sufficient.

THREAD

Values: 0 to maximum number of enabled threads
Default: 0
Multiple Instances: Must have different values

Sets the number of the redo thread that is to be used by the instance. THREAD is applicable only to instances that intend to run in parallel (shared) mode. Though any available redo thread number can be used, an instance cannot use the same thread number as another instance and cannot start when its redo thread is disabled. A value of 0 causes an available, enabled public thread to be chosen automatically.

Redo threads are specified with the THREAD option of the ALTER DATABASE ADD LOGFILE command and enabled with the ALTER DATABASE ENABLE [PUBLIC] THREAD command. The PUBLIC keyword signifies that the redo thread may be used by any instance, which is useful when running systems that have faster access to disks from certain nodes. Thread 1 is the default thread in exclusive mode, but an instance running in exclusive mode can specify THREAD to use the redo log files in a thread other than thread 1 if desired.

TIMED_OS_STATISTICS (Oracle8 Only)

Values: OFF, CALL, or LOGOFF
Default: OFF

Instructs the server when to collect operating system statistics. If the value of this parameter is CALL, operating system statistics are gathered at every push or pop call. Because this option implies significant overhead, however, it should be used with caution. If the value is LOGOFF, operating system statistics are gathered when the user logs off from an Oracle session. If the value is OFF, no operating system statistics are gathered. Note that operating system statistics are gathered only if the TIMED_STATISTICS parameter is set to TRUE.

TIMED_STATISTICS

Values: TRUE or FALSE
Default: FALSE

Specifies whether statistics related to time are collected. If this parameter is FALSE, the statistics are always 0 and the server avoids the overhead of requesting the time from the operating system. If TRUE, statistics are collected. Usually TIMED_ STATISTICS should be FALSE unless timing statistics are required.

TRANSACTION_AUDITING (Oracle8 Only)

Values: TRUE or FALSE
Default: TRUE

Specifies whether the transaction layer generates a special redo record that contains session and user information. When this parameter is TRUE, a record will be generated; when FALSE, no redo record is generated.

TRANSACTIONS

Values: Operating system dependent
Default: 1.1 × SESSIONS

Sets the maximum number of concurrent transactions. Greater values increase the size of the SGA and can increase the number of rollback segments allocated. The default value is calculated to be greater than SESSIONS (and, in turn, PROCESSES) to allow for recursive transactions.

TRANSACTIONS_PER_ROLLBACK_SEGMENT

Values: 1 to operating system dependent
Default: 21

Specifies the number of concurrent transactions allowed per rollback segment. At startup, the minimum number of rollback segments acquired is TRANSACTIONS divided by the value for this parameter, with fractions rounded up. For example, if TRANSACTIONS is 111 and this parameter is 10, the minimum number of rollback segments acquired would be the ratio 111/10, rounded up to 12.

USE_ISM (Oracle8 Only)

Values: TRUE or FALSE
Default: TRUE

Disables or enables the shared page table. If this parameter is set to TRUE, the shared page table is enabled; if it is FALSE, the shared page table is not enabled.

USER_DUMP_DEST

Values: Valid directory name
Default: Operating system dependent

Specifies the directory where the debugging trace files will be written on behalf of a user process.

UTL_FILE_DIR

Values: Valid directory name
Default: NULL

Specifies a directory or directories permitted for PL/SQL file I/O. Multiple directories may be specified, but each requires a separate UTL_FILE_DIR parameter in the *INIT.ORA* file. Note that all users can read or write all files specified in these parameters; therefore, all PL/SQL users must be trusted with the information in the directory or directories specified.

Parameters Used Only in Oracle7

Following is a list of parameters that are used only in Oracle7. These parameters must not appear in the *INIT.ORA* file for an Oracle8 database. Note that some of the parameters listed are platform-specific parameters. We've noted those that have been replaced by equivalent parameters in Oracle8.

ASYNC_READ
ASYNC_WRITE

CCF_IO_SIZE

CHECKPOINT_PROCESS

DB_FILE_STANDBY_NAME_CONVERT (renamed to DB_FILE_NAME_CONVERT)

DB_WRITERS (renamed to DBWR_IO_SLAVES)

GC_DB_LOCKS

GC_ROLLBACK_SEGMENTS

GC_SEGMENTS

GC_TABLESPACES

LOG_FILE_STANDBY_NAME_CONVERT (renamed to LOG_FILE_NAME_CONVERT)

LM_DOMAINS

LM_NON_FAULT_TOLERANT

PARALLEL_DEFAULT_MAX_SCANS

PARALLEL_DEFAULT_SCAN_SIZE

SEQUENCE_CACHE_HASH_BUCKETS

SERIALIZABLE

SESSION_CACHED_CURSORS

SNAPSHOT_REFRESH_INTERVAL (renamed to JOB_QUEUE_INTERVAL)

SNAPSHOT_REFRESH_PROCESS (renamed to JOB_QUEUE_PROCESSES)

USE_ASYNC_IO

Parameters New in Oracle8

Following is a list of parameters that are new for Oracle8. These parameters must not appear in the *INIT.ORA* file for an Oracle7 database. We've noted the parameters that have replaced equivalent Oracle7 parameters.

ALLOW_PARTIAL_SN_RESULTS

AQ_TM_PROCESSES

ARCH_IO_SLAVES

BACKUP_DISK_IO_SLAVES

BACKUP_TAPE_IO_SLAVES

COMPLEX_VIEW_MERGING

CONTROL_FILE_RECORD_KEEP_TIME

DB_BLOCK_MAX_DIRTY_TARGET

DB_FILE_DIRECT_IO_COUNT

DB_FILE_NAME_CONVERT (replaces DB_FILE_STANDBY_NAME_CONVERT)

DBWR_IO_SLAVES (replaces DB_WRITERS)

DISK_ASYNCH_IO

FAST_FULL_SCAN_ENABLED

FREEZE_DB_FOR_FAST_INSTANCE_RECOVERY

GC_DEFER_TIME

HASH_JOIN_ENABLED

INSTANCE_GROUPS

JOB_QUEUE_INTERVAL (replaces SNAPSHOT_REFRESH_INTERVAL)

JOB_QUEUE_PROCESSES (replaces SNAPSHOT_REFRESH_PROCESS)

LARGE_POOL_MIN_ALLOC

LARGE_POOL_SIZE

LGWR_IO_SLAVES

LM_LOCKS

LM_PROCS

LM_RESS

LOCAL_LISTENER

LOCK_NAME_SPACE

LOG_ARCHIVE_DUPLEX_DEST

LOG_ARCHIVE_MIN_SUCCEED_DEST

LOG_FILE_NAME_CONVERT

MTS_RATE_LOG_SIZE

MTS_RATE_SCALE

O7_DICTIONARY_ACCESSIBILITY

OBJECT_CACHE_MAX_SIZE_PERCENT

OBJECT_CACHE_OPTIMAL_SIZE

OPEN_LINKS_PER_INSTANCE

OPS_ADMIN_GROUP

OPTIMIZER_FEATURES_ENABLE

PARALLEL_INSTANCE_GROUP

PARALLEL_MIN_MESSAGE_POOL

PARALLEL_SERVER

PARALLEL_TRANSACTION_RESOURCE_TIMEOUT

PLSQL_V2_COMPATIBILITY

PUSH_JOIN_PREDICATE

REPLICATION_DEPENDENCY_TRACKING

SERIAL_REUSE

SESSION_MAX_OPEN_FILES

STAR_TRANSFORMATION_ENABLED

TAPE_ASYNCH_IO

TIMED_OS_STATISTICS

TRANSACTION_AUDITING

USE_ISM

13

SQL Statements for the DBA

SQL, or Structured Query Language, is the de facto language of choice for most relational databases, including Oracle. As an Oracle database administrator, you'll find that virtually every action you perform on the database is accomplished by issuing a SQL command. This chapter provides a quick reference to the commands you will use most often as you administer an Oracle database.

SQL Commands by Task

One of the most frustrating and time-consuming aspects of database administration, particularly for the novice DBA, is finding the proper command to accomplish a particular task. In Table 13-1, we have listed most common database administration tasks along with the SQL commands used to accomplish these tasks. The detailed syntax of each command is listed later in this chapter.

Table 13-1. Common DBA Tasks and SQL Commands

If You Want to...	Use This Command
Add a column/integrity constraint to a table	ALTER TABLE
Add a comment to the data dictionary about a column	COMMENT
Add a comment to the data dictionary about a table or view	COMMENT
Add a comment to the data dictionary about a snapshot	COMMENT
Add or remove a resource limit to or from a profile	ALTER PROFILE
Add/drop/clear redo log file group members	ALTER DATABASE
Add/rename datafiles	ALTER TABLESPACE
Allocate an extent for a cluster	ALTER CLUSTER
Allocate an extent for the table	ALTER TABLE
Allow/disallow writing to a table	ALTER TABLE

Table 13-1. Common DBA Tasks and SQL Commands (continued)

If You Want to...	Use This Command
Allow/disallow writing to a tablespace	ALTER TABLESPACE
Back up the current control file	ALTER DATABASE
Begin/end a backup	ALTER TABLESPACE
Bring a rollback segment online/offline	ALTER ROLLBACK SEGMENT
Change a rollback segment's storage characteristics	ALTER ROLLBACK SEGMENT
Change a snapshot log's storage characteristics	ALTER SNAPSHOT LOG
Change a user's default role	ALTER USER
Change a user's default tablespace	ALTER USER
Change a user's password	ALTER USER
Change a user's profile	ALTER USER
Change a user's tablespace quotas	ALTER USER
Change a user's temporary tablespace	ALTER USER
Change default storage characteristics	ALTER TABLESPACE
Change the authorization needed to access a role	ALTER ROLE
Change a snapshot's storage, refresh time, or refresh mode	ALTER SNAPSHOT
Change the name of a database	CREATE CONTROL FILE
Change the name of a schema object	RENAME
Change the storage characteristics of a cluster	ALTER CLUSTER
Choose archivelog/noarchivelog mode	ALTER DATABASE
Choose auditing for specified SQL commands	AUDIT
Choose auditing for operations on schema objects	AUDIT
Collect performance statistics for a table, index, or cluster	ANALYZE
Convert an Oracle Version 6 data dictionary when migrating to Oracle7	ALTER DATABASE
Create a cluster that can contain one or more tables	CREATE CLUSTER
Create a database trigger	CREATE TRIGGER
Create a database	CREATE DATABASE
Create a directory database object (for BFILEs)	CREATE DIRECTORY
Create a library from which to call external 3GL functions and procedures	CREATE LIBRARY
Create a link to a remote database	CREATE DATABASE LINK
Create a new datafile	ALTER TABLESPACE
Create a new database user	CREATE USER
Create a new datafile in place of an old one for recovery purposes	ALTER DATABASE
Create a place in the database for storage of database objects	CREATE TABLESPACE

Table 13-1. Common DBA Tasks and SQL Commands (continued)

If You Want to...	Use This Command
Create a profile and specify its resource limits	CREATE PROFILE
Create a role	CREATE ROLE
Create a rollback segment	CREATE ROLLBACK SEGMENT
Create a sequence for generating sequential values	CREATE SEQUENCE
Create a snapshot log containing changes made to the master table	CREATE SNAPSHOT LOG
Create a snapshot of data from one or more remote master tables	CREATE SNAPSHOT
Create a stored function	CREATE FUNCTION
Create a stored procedure	CREATE PROCEDURE
Create a synonym for a schema object	CREATE SYNONYM
Create a table and define its columns, constraints, and storage	CREATE TABLE
Create an incomplete object type	CREATE TYPE
Create an index for a table or cluster	CREATE INDEX
Create an object type	CREATE TYPE
Create the body of a stored package	CREATE PACKAGE BODY
Create the specification of a stored package	CREATE PACKAGE
Define a view of one or more tables or views	CREATE VIEW
Delete all the rows from a table	TRUNCATE TABLE or DELETE FROM
Delete a user from the database	DROP USER
Disable auditing by reversing the effect of a prior AUDIT statement	NOAUDIT
Enable/disable a database trigger	ALTER TRIGGER
Enable/disable a thread of redo log file groups	ALTER DATABASE
Enable/disable all triggers on a table	ALTER TABLE
Enable/disable autoextending the size of datafiles	ALTER TABLESPACE
Enable/disable table locks on a table	ALTER TABLE
Enable/disable/drop an integrity constraint	ALTER TABLE
Grant system privileges, roles, and object privileges to users and roles	GRANT
Identify chained rows for a table, index, or cluster	ANALYZE
Issue multiple CREATE TABLE, CREATE VIEW, and GRANT statements	CREATE SCHEMA
Modify the degree of parallelism for a table	ALTER TABLE
Open/mount the database	ALTER DATABASE
Perform media recovery	ALTER DATABASE

Table 13-1. Common DBA Tasks and SQL Commands (continued)

If You Want to...	Use This Command
Prepare to downgrade to an earlier release of Oracle	ALTER DATABASE
Recompile a stored function	ALTER FUNCTION
Recompile a stored package	ALTER PACKAGE
Recompile a stored procedure	ALTER PROCEDURE
Recompile a view	ALTER VIEW
Recreate a control file	CREATE CONTROLFILE
Recreate SQL commands to build the database to the trace file	ALTER DATABASE
Redefine a column to change a table's storage characteristics	ALTER TABLE
Redefine an index's future storage allocation	ALTER INDEX
Redefine value generation for a sequence	ALTER SEQUENCE
Remove a cluster from the database	DROP CLUSTER
Remove a database link	DROP DATABASE LINK
Remove a directory object from the database	DROP DIRECTORY
Remove a library object from the database	DROP LIBRARY
Remove a profile from the database	DROP PROFILE
Remove a role from the database	DROP ROLE
Remove a rollback segment from the database	DROP ROLLBACK SEGMENT
Remove a sequence from the database	DROP SEQUENCE
Remove a snapshot from the database	DROP SNAPSHOT
Remove a snapshot log from the database	DROP SNAPSHOT LOG
Remove a stored function from the database	DROP FUNCTION
Remove a stored package from the database	DROP PACKAGE
Remove a stored procedure from the database	DROP PROCEDURE
Remove a synonym from the database	DROP SYNONYM
Remove a table from the database	DROP TABLE
Remove a tablespace from the database	DROP TABLESPACE
Remove a trigger from the database	DROP TRIGGER
Remove a user and the objects in the user's schema from the database	DROP USER
Remove a user-defined type from the database	DROP TYPE
Remove a view from the database	DROP VIEW
Remove all rows from a table or cluster and free the space that the rows used	TRUNCATE
Remove an index from the database	DROP INDEX
Rename a datafile/redo log file member	ALTER DATABASE
Resize one or more datafiles	ALTER DATABASE

Table 13-1. Common DBA Tasks and SQL Commands (continued)

If You Want to...	Use This Command
Revoke system privileges, roles, and object privileges from users and roles	REVOKE
Shrink a rollback segment to an optimal or given size	ALTER ROLLBACK SEGMENT
Specify a formula to calculate the total cost of resources used by a session	ALTER RESOURCE COST
Take a datafile online/offline	ALTER DATABASE
Take a tablespace online/offline	ALTER TABLESPACE
Validate structure of a table, index, or cluster	ANALYZE

SQL Command Syntax

This section provides a detailed reference to each of the SQL commands likely to be used by the DBA. Each command is listed in one or more of its forms, with the exact syntax of the command and its associated parameters, a short explanation of the purpose of the command, an example, and usage notes where applicable.

Many statements allow you to specify a schema name. For example, if you specify:

    CREATE TABLE *schema.table_name*

the table is created in the specified schema. If you simply specify:

    CREATE TABLE *table_name*

the table is created in the schema of the user executing the command.

ALTER CLUSTER

```
ALTER CLUSTER [schema.]cluster_name
   [PCTFREE integer]
   [PCTUSED integer]
   [SIZE integer[K | M]]
   [INITRANS integer]
   [MAXTRANS integer]
   [STORAGE (
      [NEXT integer[K | M] ]
      [MAXEXTENTS {integer | UNLIMITED} ]
      [PCTINCREASE integer]
      [FREELISTS integer]
      [FREELIST GROUPS integer]
      ) ]
   [ALLOCATE EXTENT
     (SIZE integer[K | M] [DATAFILE 'filename'] [INSTANCE integer])]
```

```
[DEALLOCATE UNUSED [KEEP integer[K | M]]
[PARALLEL ( {DEGREE {integer | DEFAULT} | INSTANCES {integer | DEFAULT} } ) ]
[NOPARALLEL]
```

Redefines future storage allocations or allocates an extent for a cluster (*cluster_name*).

Keywords

PCTFREE

Changes the percentage of space that will be kept free for future updates to the rows contained in this cluster. The value may be in the range 0–99 and defaults to 10.

PCTUSED

Changes the minimum percentage of used space that Oracle will maintain in each block. The value may be in the range 0–99 and defaults to 40.

SIZE

Determines how many cluster keys will be stored in each data block of this cluster. The value should be a divisor of the Oracle blocksize, and will be rounded up to the next larger divisor if necessary.

INITRANS

Changes the number of transaction entries allocated to each block in the cluster. The value may be in the range 1–255 and should not normally be changed from the default of 2.

MAXTRANS

Changes the maximum number of concurrent transactions that can update blocks of the cluster. The value may be in the range 1–255 and should not normally be changed from the default, which is a function of the Oracle blocksize.

STORAGE

Specifies the physical characteristics of the cluster as follows:

NEXT

Specifies the size of the next extent in bytes, kilobytes, or megabytes. If the value is not a multiple of the database blocksize, it will be rounded up to a multiple of the database blocksize.

MAXEXTENTS

Specifies the maximum number of extents that may be allocated for this cluster. The default will vary according to the database blocksize. Specify UNLIMITED for unlimited expansion.

PCTINCREASE

Specifies the percentage by which each extent will grow over the previous extent. The default is 50, which means that each extent will be one-and-one-half times larger than the previous extent.

FREELISTS

Specifies the number of free lists contained in each freelist group in this cluster. The default is 1 and the maximum depends on the database blocksize.

FREELIST GROUPS

Specifies the number of groups of free lists for this cluster. The default is 1. This parameter should be used only with the Parallel Server option running in parallel mode.

ALLOCATE EXTENT

Forces the immediate allocation of the next extent.

SIZE

Specifies the size of the new extent in bytes, kilobytes, or megabytes.

DATAFILE

Specifies the name of the operating system datafile (*filename*) in the tablespace in which this cluster resides to hold the new extent. If this value is omitted, Oracle will select a datafile.

INSTANCE

Makes the new extent available to the specified instance, which is identified by the initialization parameter INSTANCE_NUMBER. This parameter can only be used when running in parallel mode.

DEALLOCATE UNUSED

Releases storage above the highwater mark.

KEEP

Specifies the amount of storage above the highwater mark to keep.

PARALLEL

Specifies the level of parallelism to be supported, based on the following parameters:

DEGREE

Specifies the degree of parallelism. An integer value specifies how many slave processes can be used. Specify DEFAULT to use the default value specified for the tablespace.

INSTANCES

Specifies the number of instances that can be used to execute slave processes. Specify DEFAULT to use the default value specified for the tablespace.

NOPARALLEL
   Specifies that no parallel operations are to be performed.

Note

The cluster must be in your schema or you must have the ALTER ANY CLUSTER
privilege to issue this command.

Example

The following example alters an existing cluster to allocate 512 bytes per block to
cluster keys and allow a maximum of 20 extents for the cluster:

```
ALTER CLUSTER demo.employee
            SIZE 512
            STORAGE (MAXEXTENTS 20);
```

ALTER DATABASE ARCHIVELOG

ALTER DATABASE [*dbname*] ARCHIVELOG | NOARCHIVELOG

Specifies whether Oracle will attempt to archive redo log files for the database
dbname after a redo log switch.

Keywords

ARCHIVELOG
   Specifies that a redo log group must be archived before it can be reused. If the
   group has not been archived, the database halts until archiving occurs successfully. This mode is required in order to perform media recovery.

NOARCHIVELOG
   Specifies that redo log groups will not be archived and may be reused immediately by Oracle.

Notes

The database must be mounted in EXCLUSIVE mode and not open in order to
issue this command. You must have the OSDBA role to issue this command.

ALTER DATABASE MOUNT

ALTER DATABASE [*dbname*] MOUNT [EXCLUSIVE | PARALLEL]

Mounts the database *dbname* either in EXCLUSIVE or PARALLEL mode.

Keywords

EXCLUSIVE
   Mounts one instance at a time. This is the default.

PARALLEL

Used with the Parallel Server option; permits the database to be mounted by multiple instances concurrently.

Note

You must have the OSDBA role to issue this command.

ALTER DATABASE OPEN

```
ALTER DATABASE [dbname] OPEN [RESETLOGS | NORESETLOGS]
```

Opens the database *dbname* for normal use. The database must first be mounted.

Keywords

RESETLOGS

Resets the log sequence number to 1 and invalidates all redo entries in the existing online and archived log files.

NORESETLOGS

Makes no change to the status of the current log sequence number and redo log entries.

Notes

You must have the OSDBA role to issue this command. The RESETLOGS option can only be specified after performing incomplete media recovery; at all other times, NORESETLOGS should be used. The RESETLOGS option must be specified when opening the database after performing media recovery with a backup control file. If the database is opened with the RESETLOGS keyword, a complete backup of the database should be performed immediately.

ALTER FUNCTION

```
ALTER FUNCTION [schema.]function_name COMPILE
```

Recompiles a standalone function (*function_name*). The COMPILE keyword is required.

Notes

This command first recompiles all objects upon which this function depends; if any of those objects are invalid, the function being recompiled will also be marked invalid. The procedure must be in your schema or you must have the ALTER ANY PROCEDURE privilege to issue this command.

Example

The following example explicitly recompiles the function called midday in schema scott:

```
ALTER FUNCTION scott.midday COMPILE
```

ALTER INDEX

```
ALTER INDEX [schema.]index_name
   [PCTFREE   integer]
   [INITRANS integer]
   [MAXTRANS integer]
   [PARALLEL ( {DEGREE {integer | DEFAULT} | INSTANCES {integer | DEFAULT} } ) ]
   [NOPARALLEL]
   [LOGGING | NOLOGGING ]
   [UNUSABLE]
   [STORAGE (
      [NEXT integer[K | M] ]
      [MAXEXTENTS {integer | UNLIMITED} ]
      [PCTINCREASE integer]
      [FREELISTS integer]
      [FREELIST GROUPS integer]
      ) ]
   [ALLOCATE EXTENT
      (SIZE integer[K | M] [DATAFILE 'filename'] [INSTANCE integer])]
   [DEALLOCATE UNUSED [KEEP integer[K | M]]
   [UNUSABLE]
   [DROP PARTITION partition_name]
   [SPLIT PARTITION partition AT (valuelist) INTO (newpartition,newpartition)]
   [RENAME PARTITION partition_name TO newpartition]
   [RENAME TO newindex_name]
```

Changes characteristics of an index (*index_name*).

Keywords

PCTFREE

Specifies the amount of free space to leave in each data block for later updates and inserts.

INITRANS

Changes the initial number of transaction entries allocated to each block of the index.

MAXTRANS

Changes the maximum number of transaction entries allocated to each block of the index.

PARALLEL

Specifies the level of parallelism to be supported, based on the following parameters:

DEGREE

Specifies the degree of parallelism. An integer value specifies how many slave processes can be used. Specify DEFAULT to use the default value for the tablespace.

INSTANCES

Specifies the number of instances that can be used to execute slave processes. Specify DEFAULT to use the default value specified for the tablespace.

NOPARALLEL

Specifies that no parallelism is to be used.

LOGGING

Specifies that the operation is to be logged to the redo logs.

NOLOGGING

Specifies that nothing is to be written to the redo logs for this operation.

UNUSABLE

Specifies that the index is to be marked unusable.

STORAGE

Specifies the physical characteristics of the index as follows:

NEXT

Specifies the size of the next extent in bytes, kilobytes, or megabytes. If the value is not a multiple of the database blocksize, it will be rounded up to a multiple of the database blocksize.

MAXEXTENTS

Specifies the maximum number of extents that may be allocated for this index. The default will vary according to the database blocksize. Specify UNLIMITED for unlimited expansion.

PCTINCREASE

Specifies the percentage by which each extent will grow over the previous extent. The default is 50, which means that each extent will be one-and-one-half times larger than the previous extent.

FREELISTS

Specifies the number of free lists contained in each freelist group in this index. The default is 1 and the maximum depends on the database blocksize.

FREELIST GROUPS

Specifies the number of groups of free lists for this index. The default is 1. This parameter should be used only with the Parallel Server option running in parallel mode.

ALLOCATE EXTENT

Forces the immediate allocation of the next extent.

SIZE

Specifies the size of the new extent in bytes, kilobytes, or megabytes.

DATAFILE

Specifies the name of the operating system datafile, in the tablespace that holds this index, to hold the new extent. If the name is omitted, Oracle will select a datafile.

INSTANCE

Makes the new extent available to the specified instance, which is identified by the initialization parameter INSTANCE_NUMBER. This parameter can only be used when running in parallel mode.

DEALLOCATE UNUSED

Releases storage above the highwater mark.

KEEP

Specifies the amount of storage above the highwater mark to keep.

DROP PARTITION

Specifies that the specified partition is to be dropped.

SPLIT PARTITION

Specifies that the partition is to be split into two new partitions. AT specifies the new, noninclusive upper bound for the first new split partition. INTO specifies the names of the two new partitions into which *partition* is to be split.

RENAME PARTITION

Specifies that the partition is to be RENAMEd TO *newpartition*.

RENAME TO

Specifies that the index *index_name* is to be RENAMEd TO *newindex_name*.

Notes

The index to be altered must be in your schema, or you must have the ALTER ANY INDEX privilege to issue this command.

If storage options are omitted, Oracle will allocate storage for the index as follows:

- If the indexed table has no rows, the default storage values for the tablespace will be used.

- If the indexed table has rows and the resulting index can be contained in no more than 25 data blocks, a single extent will be allocated for this index.

- If the indexed table has rows and the resulting index is more than 25 data blocks, 5 equal-size extents will be allocated for this index.

Example

The following example alters the index named employee owned by scott so that new extents added for this index are 4K each and will not grow, and each data block added to this index contains 5 initial transaction entries:

```
ALTER INDEX scott.employee
        INITRANS 5
        STORAGE (NEXT 4096 PCTINCREASE 0);
```

ALTER INDEX REBUILD

```
ALTER INDEX [schema.]index_name REBUILD
    [INITRANS integer]
    [MAXTRANS integer]
    [PCTFREE integer]
    [LOGGING | NOLOGGING]
    [PARALLEL ( {DEGREE {integer | DEFAULT} | INSTANCES {integer | DEFAULT} } ) ]
    [NOPARALLEL]
    [REVERSE | NOREVERSE ]
    [TABLESPACE tablespace_name
    [STORAGE (
        [NEXT integer[K | M]  ]
        [MAXEXTENTS {integer | UNLIMITED} ]
        [PCTINCREASE integer]
        [FREELISTS integer]
        [FREELIST GROUPS integer]
        ) ]
```

Rebuilds the index (*index_name*) using information from the current index. Allows you to change the physical attributes of existing indexed information.

Keywords

REBUILD

Forces Oracle to rebuild the index using information in that index. No table accesses are required.

INITRANS

Changes the initial number of transaction entries allocated to each block of the index.

MAXTRANS

Changes the maximum number of transaction entries allocated to each block of the index.

PCTFREE

Specifies the amount of free space left in each block for inserts and updates.

LOGGING

Specifies that the operation is to be logged to the redo logs.

NOLOGGING

Specifies that nothing is to be written to the redo logs for this operation.

PARALLEL

Specifies the level of parallelism to be supported, based on the following parameters:

DEGREE

Specifies the degree of parallelism. An integer value specifies how many slave processes can be used. Specify DEFAULT to use the default value for the tablespace.

INSTANCES

Specifies the number of instances that can be used to execute slave processes. Specify DEFAULT to use the default value specified for the tablespace.

NOPARALLEL

Specifies that no parallelism is to be used.

REVERSE

Specifies that Oracle will store the bytes of the index key in reverse order. This is useful in situations where rows are always added in increasing order to allow the index to grow evenly rather than always at one end. It is also useful in a Parallel Server environment, allowing individual instances to insert information in different blocks, thus reducing pinging.

NOREVERSE

Specifies that Oracle will not store the bytes of the index key in reverse order.

TABLESPACE

Specifies a new tablespace (*tablespace_name*) for the rebuilt index.

STORAGE

Specifies the physical characteristics of the specified index as follows:

NEXT

Specifies the size of the next extent in bytes, kilobytes, or megabytes. If the value is not a multiple of the database blocksize, it will be rounded up to a multiple of the database blocksize.

MAXEXTENTS

Specifies the maximum number of extents that may be allocated for this index. The default will vary according to the database blocksize. Specify UNLIMITED for unlimited expansion.

PCTINCREASE

Specifies the percentage by which each extent will grow over the previous extent. The default is 50, which means that each extent will be one-and-one-half times larger than the previous extent.

FREELISTS

> Specifies the number of free lists contained in each freelist group in this index. The default is 1 and the maximum depends on the database block-size.

FREELIST GROUPS

> Specifies the number of groups of free lists for this index. The default is 1. This parameter should be used only with the Parallel Server option running in parallel mode.

ALTER INDEX REBUILD PARTITION

```
ALTER INDEX [schema.]index_name
REBUILD PARTITION partition_name
[INITRANS integer]
[MAXTRANS integer]
[PCTFREE integer]
[LOGGING | NOLOGGING]
[PARALLEL ( {DEGREE {integer | DEFAULT} | INSTANCES {integer | DEFAULT} } ) ]
[NOPARALLEL]
[REVERSE | NOREVERSE ]
[TABLESPACE tablespace_name
[STORAGE (
    [NEXT integer[K | M] ]
    [MAXEXTENTS {integer | UNLIMITED} ]
    [PCTINCREASE integer]
    [FREELISTS integer]
    [FREELIST GROUPS integer]
```

Rebuilds the index partition using information from the current index (*index_name*). Allows you to change the physical attributes of existing indexed information.

Keywords

REBUILD PARTITION

> Forces Oracle to rebuild the index partition.

INITRANS

> Changes the initial number of transaction entries allocated to each block of the index.

MAXTRANS

> Changes the maximum number of transaction entries allocated to each block of the index.

PCTFREE

> Specifies the amount of free space left in each block for inserts and updates.

LOGGING

> Specifies that the operation is to be logged to the redo logs.

NOLOGGING

Specifies that nothing is to be written to the redo logs for this operation.

PARALLEL

Specifies the level of parallelism to be supported, based on the following parameters:

DEGREE

Specifies the degree of parallelism. An integer value specifies how many slave processes can be used. Specify DEFAULT to use the default value for the tablespace.

INSTANCES

Specifies the number of instances that can be used to execute slave processes. Specify DEFAULT to use the default value specified for the tablespace.

NOPARALLEL

Specifies that no parallelism is to be used.

REVERSE

Specifies that Oracle will store the bytes of the index key in reverse order. This is useful in situations where rows are always added in increasing order to allow the index to grow evenly rather than only at one end. It is also useful in a Parallel Server environment, allowing individual instances to insert information in different blocks, thus reducing pinging.

NOREVERSE

Specifies that Oracle will not store the bytes of the index key in reverse order.

TABLESPACE

Specifies a new tablespace (*tablespace_name*) for the rebuilt index partition.

STORAGE

Specifies the physical characteristics of the index as follows:

NEXT

Specifies the size of the next extent in bytes, kilobytes, or megabytes. If the value is not a multiple of the database blocksize, it will be rounded up to a multiple of the database blocksize.

MAXEXTENTS

Specifies the maximum number of extents that may be allocated for this index. The default will vary according to the database blocksize. Specify UNLIMITED for unlimited expansion.

PCTINCREASE

Specifies the percentage by which each extent will grow over the previous extent. The default is 50, which means that each extent will be one-and-one-half times larger than the previous extent.

FREELISTS

Specifies the number of free lists contained in each freelist group in this index. The default is 1 and the maximum depends on the database block-size.

FREELIST GROUPS

Specifies the number of groups of free lists for this index. The default is 1. This parameter should be used only with the Parallel Server option running in parallel mode.

ALTER PACKAGE

```
ALTER PACKAGE [schema.]package_name COMPILE [PACKAGE | BODY]
```

Recompiles a stored package (*package_name*). The COMPILE keyword is required.

Keywords

PACKAGE

Recompiles the package body and specifications. This is the default.

BODY

Recompiles only the package body.

Notes

This command recompiles all objects contained in the package. The procedure must be in your schema or you must have the ALTER ANY PROCEDURE privilege to issue this command.

Example

The following example explicitly recompiles the specification and body of the reconcile package in schema scott:

```
ALTER PACKAGE scott.reconcile
    COMPILE PACKAGE
```

ALTER PROCEDURE

```
ALTER PROCEDURE [schema.]procedure_name COMPILE
```

Recompiles a standalone stored procedure (*procedure_name*). The COMPILE keyword is required.

Notes

This command first recompiles all objects upon which this procedure depends; if any of those objects are invalid, the procedure being recompiled will also be marked invalid. The procedure must be in your schema or you must have the ALTER ANY PROCEDURE privilege to issue this command.

Example

The following example explicitly recompiles the procedure called midday in schema scott:

```
ALTER PROCEDURE scott.midday COMPILE
```

ALTER PROFILE

```
ALTER PROFILE profile_name LIMIT
    [SESSIONS_PER_USER {integer | UNLIMITED | DEFAULT}]
    [CPU_PER_SESSION {integer | UNLIMITED | DEFAULT}]
    [CPU_PER_CALL {integer | UNLIMITED | DEFAULT}]
    [CONNECT_TIME {integer | UNLIMITED | DEFAULT}]
    [IDLE_TIME {integer | UNLIMITED | DEFAULT}]
    [LOGICAL_READS_PER_SESSION {integer | UNLIMITED | DEFAULT}]
    [LOGICAL_READS_PER_CALL {integer | UNLIMITED | DEFAULT}]
    [PRIVATE_SGA {integer[K | M] | UNLIMITED | DEFAULT}]
    [COMPOSITE_LIMIT {integer | UNLIMITED | DEFAULT}]
    [FAILED_LOGIN_ATTEMPTS {integer | UNLIMITED | DEFAULT}]
    [PASSWORD_LIFE_TIME {integer | UNLIMITED | DEFAULT}]
    [PASSWORD_LOCK_TIME {integer | UNLIMITED | DEFAULT}]
    [PASSWORD_GRACE_TIME {integer | UNLIMITED | DEFAULT}]
    [PASSWORD_REUSE_TIME {integer | UNLIMITED | DEFAULT}]
    [PASSWORD_REUSE_MAX {integer | UNLIMITED | DEFAULT}]
    [PASSWORD_VERIFY_FUNCTION {function | NULL | DEFAULT}]
```

Adds, changes, or removes a resource limit from an existing profile (*profile_name*). For many of the following keywords you can specify:

UNLIMITED
    Specifying this value means that no limit will be imposed on this resource.

DEFAULT
    Specifying this value means that the limit specified in the DEFAULT profile will be used for this resource.

Keywords

SESSIONS_PER_USER
    Limits the number of concurrent sessions for a user. Note that each slave process in a parallel query uses one slot.

CPU_PER_SESSION
    Limits the amount of CPU time (in hundredths of a second) that can be used in a session.

CPU_PER_CALL

Limits the amount of CPU time (in hundredths of a second) for a parse, execute, or fetch call.

CONNECT_TIME

Limits the total elapsed time (in minutes) for a session.

IDLE_TIME

Limits the amount of continuous inactive time (in minutes) during a session.

LOGICAL_READS_PER_SESSION

Limits the number of database blocks read in a session, including those read from memory and disk.

LOGICAL_READS_PER_CALL

Limits the number of database blocks read for a parse, execute, or fetch call.

PRIVATE_SGA

Limits the amount of memory (in bytes) a session can allocate in the shared pool of the SGA.

COMPOSITE_LIMIT

Limits the total resource cost (in service units) for a session. See ALTER RESOURCE COST for additional information.

FAILED_LOGIN_ATTEMPTS

Limits the number of failed login attempts before the account is locked.

PASSWORD_LIFE_TIME

Limits the lifetime of the password. The value is specified in fractions of a day.

PASSWORD_LOCK_TIME

Specifies the number of days for which the account will be locked after failed login attempts.

PASSWORD_GRACE_TIME

Specifies the number of days the user has to change the password after the password has expired.

PASSWORD_REUSE_TIME

Specifies the minimum number of days before a password can be reused. If this value is set, the PASSWORD_REUSE_MAX must be unlimited.

PASSWORD_REUSE_MAX

Specifies the number of password changes that must occur before the current password can be reused. If this value is set, the parameter PASSWORD_REUSE_TIME must be unlimited.

PASSWORD_VERIFY_FUNCTION

Specifies the name of a function that will validate a new password. The function must be owned by SYS.

Notes

This command will only affect subsequent sessions; sessions already established will not be subject to the new limits. You must have the ALTER PROFILE privilege to issue this command.

The parameters that support password aging are specified in days. You can specify a fraction of a day by using standard fraction notation. For example, you can use 1/24 to specify an hour.

Example

The following example defines a limit of 5 concurrent sessions and 10 minutes of inactivity to the admin profile:

```
ALTER PROFILE admin
     SESSIONS_PER_USER 5
     IDLE_TIME 10
```

ALTER RESOURCE COST

```
ALTER RESOURCE COST
   [CPU_PER_SESSION weight]
   [CONNECT_TIME weight]
   [LOGICAL_READS_PER_SESSION weight]
   [PRIVATE_SGA weight]
```

Modifies the formula used to calculate the total resource cost used in a session, which is then limited by the COMPOSITE_LIMIT parameter in a profile. For each resource, *weight* represents the integer weight of the resource.

Keywords

CPU_PER_SESSION
   The amount of CPU time (in hundredths of a second) used in a session.

CONNECT_TIME
   The total elapsed time (in minutes) for a session.

LOGICAL_READS_PER_SESSION
   The number of database blocks read in a session, including those read from memory and disk.

PRIVATE_SGA
   The amount of memory (in bytes) a session can allocate in the shared pool of the SGA. This only applies when using the Multi-Threaded Server and allocating private space in the SGA for the session.

Notes

The total resource cost is calculated by multiplying the amount of each resource used in the session by the weight assigned to that resource and adding together the products for all four resources. The result is expressed in service units. You must have the ALTER RESOURCE COST privilege to issue this command.

Example

The following example assigns weights to CPU_PER_SESSION and CONNECT_TIME:

```
ALTER RESOURCE COST
    CPU_PER_SESSION 100
    CONNECT_TIME 2
```

The resulting cost in service units is calculated as:

SU = (CPU_PER_SESSION × 100) + CONNECT_TIME × 2

ALTER ROLE

```
ALTER ROLE role_name
    {NOT IDENTIFIED |
     IDENTIFIED BY password |
     IDENTIFIED EXTERNALLY |
     IDENTIFIED GLOBALLY
    }
```

Changes the authorization level required to enable a role (*role_name*).

Keywords

NOT IDENTIFIED

> Specifies that a user granted the role does not need to be verified when enabling it.

IDENTIFIED BY

> Specifies that the *password* must be provided when enabling the role.

IDENTIFIED EXTERNALLY

> Specifies that the operating system verifies the user enabling the role.

IDENTIFIED GLOBALLY

> Specifies that the Oracle Security Server verifies the user enabling the role.

Note

You must have been granted the role via the WITH ADMIN OPTION or have the ALTER ANY ROLE privilege to issue this command.

Example

The following example assigns the password "dilbert" to the manager role:

```
ALTER ROLE manager IDENTIFIED BY dilbert
```

ALTER ROLLBACK SEGMENT

```
ALTER ROLLBACK SEGMENT segment_name
   [ONLINE | OFFLINE]
   [STORAGE (
      [NEXT integer[K | M] ]
      [MAXEXTENTS {integer | UNLIMITED} ]
      [PCTINCREASE integer]
      [FREELISTS integer]
      [FREELIST GROUPS integer]
      [OPTIMAL {integer[K | M] | NULL} ]
      ) ]
   [SHRINK TO integer[K | M] ]
```

Changes the online status of a rollback segment (*segment_name*) or modifies its storage characteristics.

Keywords

ONLINE

Specifies that the named rollback segment is to be brought online.

OFFLINE

Specifies that the named rollback segment is to be taken offline.

STORAGE

Specifies the physical characteristics of the rollback segment as follows:

NEXT

Specifies the size of the next extent in bytes, kilobytes, or megabytes. If the value is not a multiple of the database blocksize, it will be rounded up to a multiple of the database blocksize.

MAXEXTENTS

Specifies the maximum number of extents that may be allocated for this rollback segment. The default will vary according to the database blocksize. Specify UNLIMITED for unlimited expansion.

PCTINCREASE

Specifies the percentage by which each extent will grow over the previous extent. The default is 50, which means that each extent will be one-and-one-half times larger than the previous extent.

FREELISTS

Specifies the number of free lists contained in each freelist group in this rollback segment. The default is 1, and the maximum depends on the database blocksize.

FREELIST GROUPS

Specifies the number of groups of free lists for this rollback segment. The default is 1. This parameter should be used only with the Parallel Server option running in parallel mode.

OPTIMAL

Specifies the optimal size for this rollback segment. Oracle will attempt to maintain this size by deallocating unused extents. The default is NULL, which means no deallocation will ever take place.

SHRINK TO

Specifies that the named rollback segment should be reduced in size TO the size specified (in kilobytes or megabytes), or to the OPTIMAL size if no size is specified.

Note

You must have the ALTER ROLLBACK SEGMENT privilege to issue this command.

Examples

The following example takes rollback segment RBS02 offline:

```
ALTER ROLLBACK SEGMENT RBS02 OFFLINE
```

The following example changes the storage allocation for RBS02 so that each extent will be 30K, its optimal size will be 60K, and a maximum of 10 extents will be permitted:

```
ALTER ROLLBACK SEGMENT RBS02
        STORAGE (NEXT 30K MAXEXTENTS 10 OPTIMAL 60K)
```

ALTER SEQUENCE

```
ALTER SEQUENCE [schema.]sequence_name
    [INCREMENT BY integer]
    [MAXVALUE integer | NOMAXVALUE]
    [MINVALUE integer | NOMINVALUE]
    [CYCLE | NOCYCLE]
    [CACHE integer | NOCACHE]
    [ORDER | NOORDER]
```

Changes the characteristics of an Oracle sequence (*sequence_name*), including starting sequence number, range, number of sequence numbers cached in memory, and whether sequential order is preserved.

Keywords

INCREMENT BY

Specifies the increment between sequence numbers; can be positive or negative (but not 0). The default is 1.

MAXVALUE

Specifies the largest value the sequence number can reach. The default is NOMAXVALUE, which means the maximum value is 10^{27}.

MINVALUE

Specifies the smallest value the sequence number can reach. The default is NOMINVALUE, which means the minimum value is 1.

CYCLE

Specifies that when sequence numbers reach MAXVALUE they will begin again at MINVALUE.

NOCYCLE

Specifies that after reaching the maximum value no additional sequence numbers will be generated. This is the default.

CACHE

Specifies how many sequence numbers Oracle will pregenerate and keep in memory. Note that when the database is shut down, unused sequence numbers stored in the cache will be lost. The default is 20.

NOCACHE

Specifies that no sequence numbers are pregenerated to memory.

ORDER

Specifies that sequence numbers are guaranteed to be issued in order of request.

NOORDER

Specifies that sequence numbers are not guaranteed to be generated in the order of request. This is the default.

Notes

The generation of a sequence number is not affected by the subsequent rollback of the transaction; once generated, that sequence number will not be available again, so gaps can occur. Sequence numbers are accessed by using the pseudocolumns CURRVAL and NEXTVAL.

Example

The following example modifies scott's sequence ord_seq so that the next sequence number generated will be 10001, and order is guaranteed:

```
ALTER SEQUENCE scott.ord_seq
    MINVALUE 10001
    ORDER
```

ALTER SESSION

```
ALTER SESSION
  [SET
      [ALLOW_PARTIAL_SN_RESULTS = {TRUE | FALSE} ]
      [B_TREE_BITMAP_PLANS = {TRUE | FALSE} ]
      [CLOSE_CACHED_OPEN_CURSORS = {TRUE | FALSE} ]
      [CONSTRAINT = {IMMEDIATE | DEFERRED | DEFAULT} ]
      [DB_FILE_MULTIBLOCK_READ_COUNT = integer]
      [FLAGGER = {ENTRY | INTERMEDIATE | FULL | OFF} ]
      [GLOBAL_NAMES = {TRUE | FALSE} ]
      [HASH_AREA_SIZE = integer]
      [HASH_JOIN_ENABLED = {TRUE | FALSE} ]
      [HASH_MULTIBLOCK_IO_COUNT = integer]
      [INSTANCE = integer]
      [ISOLATION_LEVEL = {SERIALIZABLE | READ COMMITTED} ]
      [MAX_DUMP_FILE_SIZE = {size | UNLIMITED} ]
      [NLS_LANGUAGE = language]
      [NLS_TERRITORY = territory]
      [NLS_DATE_FORMAT = 'date_format']
      [NLS_DATE_LANGUAGE = language]
      [NLS_NUMERIC_CHARACTERS = 'text']
      [NLS_ISO_CURRENCY = territory]
      [NLS_CURRENCY = 'text']
      [NLS_CALENDAR = 'text']
      [NLS_SORT = sort | BINARY]
      [OBJECT_CACHE_MAX_SIZE_PERCENT = integer]
      [OBJECT_CACHE_OPTIMAL_SIZE = integer]
      [OPS_ADMIN_GROUP = 'text']
      [OPTIMIZER_MODE = {ALL_ROWS | FIRST_ROWS | RULE | CHOOSE} ]
      [OPTIMIZER_PERCENT_PARALLEL = integer]
      [OPTIMIZER_SEARCH_LIMIT = integer]
      [PARALLEL_INSTANCE_GROUP = 'text' ]
      [PARALLEL_MIN_PERCENT = integer]
      [PARTITION_VIEW_ENABLED = {TRUE | FALSE} ]
      [PLSQL_V2_COMPATIBILITY = {TRUE | FALSE} ]
      [REMOTE_DEPENDENCIES_MODE = {TIMESTAMP | SIGNATURE} ]
      [SESSION_CACHED_CURSORS = integer]
      [SQL_TRACE = {TRUE | FALSE}]
      [SKIP_UNUSABLE_INDEXES = {TRUE | FALSE} ]
      [SORT_AREA_SIZE = integer]
      [SORT_AREA_RETAINED_SIZE = integer]
      [SORT_DIRECT_WRITES = {AUTO | TRUE | FALSE} ]
      [SORT_READ_FAC = integer]
      [SORT_WRITE_BUFFERS = integer]
```

```
      [SORT_WRITE_BUFFER_SIZE = integer]
      [SPIN_COUNT = integer]
      [STAR_TRANSFORMATION_ENABLED = {TRUE | FALSE} ]
      [TEXT_ENABLED = {TRUE | FALSE} ]
      [TIMED_STATISTICS = {TRUE | FALSE} ]
   ]
   [ADVISE {COMMIT | ROLLBACK | NOTHING}]
   [CLOSE DATABASE LINK dblink
   [ENABLE COMMIT IN PROCEDURE]
   [DISABLE COMMIT IN PROCEDURE]
   [ENABLE PARALLEL DML]
   [DISABLE PARALLEL DML]
   [FORCE PARALLEL DML]
```

Changes the functional characteristics of the current database session, including several National Language Support (NLS) characteristics.

Keywords

SET

Indicates that one or more keywords will follow.

ALLOW_PARTIAL_SN_RESULTS

Allows you to override the *INIT.ORA* parameter ALLOW_PARTIAL_SN_ RESULTS for the current session. A value of TRUE allows results to be retrieved in the GV$ views even if a slave process cannot be created for one or more instances.

B_TREE_BITMAP_PLANS

Allows you to override the *INIT.ORA* parameter B_TREE_BITMAP_PLANS for the current session. A value of TRUE allows the optimizer to use a B-tree index as if it were a bitmap index.

CLOSE_CACHED_OPEN_CURSORS

Controls whether PL/SQL cursors are closed or left open after a commit or rollback.

CONSTRAINT

Specifies how deferrable constraints are enforced, as follows:

IMMEDIATE

Specifies that all deferrable constraints are checked after each DML statement. This is equivalent to using the SET CONSTRAINTS ALL IMMEDIATE command at the start of every transaction.

DEFERRED

Specifies that all deferrable constraints are checked when the transaction is committed. This is equivalent to using the SET CONSTRAINTS ALL DEFERRED command at the start of every transaction.

DEFAULT

Specifies that all deferrable constraints are checked according to their individual specifications.

DB_FILE_MULTIBLOCK_READ_COUNT

Allows you to override the *INIT.ORA* parameter DB_FILE_MULTIBLOCK_READ_COUNT for the current session. This specifies the target number of database block buffers to read in at a time during sequential scans of a table.

FLAGGER

Specifies how to flag the use of extensions to the ANSI/ISO SQL standard (FIPS 127-2). Oracle is fully compatible with the Entry Level standard. Depending upon the level chosen, Oracle will flag the use of extensions to that level. In Oracle7, Oracle treats ENTRY, INTERMEDIATE, and FULL as the same.

ENTRY

Flags the use of statements not included in the Entry Level specification.

INTERMEDIATE

Flags the use of statements not included in the Intermediate Level specification.

FULL

Flags the use of statements not included in the Full Language specification.

OFF

Does not flag extensions to the SQL standard. This is the default.

GLOBAL_NAMES

Controls whether global name resolution will be enforced for this session.

HASH_AREA_SIZE

Specifies in bytes the amount of memory to be used for hash joins. The default is two times the value of SORT_AREA_SIZE.

HASH_JOIN_ENABLED

Determines whether hash joins are allowed in queries. The default is TRUE.

HASH_MULTIBLOCK_IO_COUNT

Specifies the number of database blocks to be read or written during hash I/O operations.

INSTANCE

Specifies that a different instance in a Parallel Server environment should attempt to process queries for this session.

ISOLATION_LEVEL

Specifies how Oracle should conform to the ANSI SQL92 Serializable Transaction specification for the remainder of the session.

SERIALIZABLE

Specifies that Oracle should conform to the ANSI SQL92 Serializable Transaction specification and roll back transactions that attempt to update rows being updated by another transaction.

READ COMMITTED

Specifies that Oracle should continue to use its default processing and wait for the rows to be unlocked before continuing.

MAX_DUMP_FILE_SIZE

Allows you to override the *INIT.ORA* parameter MAX_DUMP_FILE_SIZE for the current session. The integer specified is the maximum number of operating system blocks to be used for a trace file. A value of UNLIMITED specifies that no limit is to be imposed.

NLS_LANGUAGE

Specifies the language for Oracle messages, day and month names, and sort sequences.

NLS_TERRITORY

Specifies the values of the default date format, numeric decimal and group separator, and local and ISO currency symbols. This parameter may override the defaults set by NLS_LANGUAGE.

NLS_DATE_FORMAT

Specifies the default date format. The *'date_format'* must be a valid Oracle date format mask. This parameter may override the defaults set by NLS_TERRITORY.

NLS_DATE_LANGUAGE

Specifies the language for day and month names as well as other spelled date values. This parameter may override the defaults set by NLS_LANGUAGE.

NLS_NUMERIC_CHARACTERS

Specifies the decimal character and group separator. The value of *'text'* must be in the form *'dg'*, where *d* is the decimal character, and *g* is the group character. This parameter may override the defaults set by NLS_TERRITORY.

NLS_ISO_CURRENCY

Specifies the territory whose ISO currency symbol should be used. This parameter may override the defaults set by NLS_TERRITORY.

NLS_CURRENCY

Specifies the local currency symbol. This parameter may override the defaults set by NLS_TERRITORY.

NLS_CALENDAR

Specifies which of the standard calendars to use for dates. Currently supported values are:

ARABIC HIJRAH
ENGLISH HIJRAH
GREGORIAN
JAPANESE IMPERIAL
PERSIAN
ROC OFFICIAL
THAI BUDDHA

NLS_SORT

Specifies the collating sequence for character sorts. BINARY specifies a binary sort, while *sort* specifies the name of a specific sort sequence.

OBJECT_CACHE_MAX_SIZE_PERCENT

Allows you to override the *INIT.ORA* parameter OBJECT_CACHE_MAX_SIZE_PERCENT for this session. This value is the percent by which the object cache can exceed the optimal size. When this value is exceeded, the cache will be reduced to the optimal size.

OBJECT_CACHE_OPTIMAL_SIZE

Allows you to override the *INIT.ORA* parameter OBJECT_CACHE_OPTIMAL_SIZE for this session. This specifies the size to which the object cache is reduced when the object cache exceeds its maximum value.

OPS_ADMIN_GROUP

Allows you to override the *INIT.ORA* parameter OPS_ADMIN_GROUP for this session. In a Parallel Server environment, the instances can be divided into one or more groups to ease administration. The effect of this parameter is to limit the instances reflected in the GV$ views.

OPTIMIZER_MODE (OPTIMIZER_GOAL in Oracle 7.3)

Specifies the optimization goal for this session, as follows:

ALL_ROWS

Optimize for best overall throughput.

FIRST_ROWS

Optimize for best response time.

RULE

Use rule-based optimization.

CHOOSE

Use rule-based or cost-based optimization, if available.

OPTIMIZER_PERCENT_PARALLEL

Allows you to override the *INIT.ORA* parameter OPTIMIZER_PERCENT_ PARALLEL for this session. A value of 0 tells the optimizer to use no parallelism, while a value of 100 forces the optimizer to fully use the degrees of parallelism specified for each object.

OPTIMIZER_SEARCH_LIMIT

Allows you to override the *INIT.ORA* parameter OPTIMIZER_SEARCH_LIMIT for this session. The value specifies the search limit for the optimizer. The default value is 5.

PARALLEL_INSTANCE_GROUP

Allows you to override the *INIT.ORA* parameter PARALLEL_INSTANCE_ GROUP for this session. This specifies the instance groups to which parallel query slaves can be spawned.

PARALLEL_MIN_PERCENT

Allows you to override the *INIT.ORA* parameter PARALLEL_MIN_PERCENT for this session. This specifies the minimum percent of parallel threads that must be available before a parallel query is performed. If the minimum percent of threads is not available, an error message is generated and the query is not run.

PARTITION_VIEW_ENABLED

A value of TRUE allows the optimizer to skip unnecessary table accesses in a partitioned view.

PLSQL_V2_COMPATIBILITY

Specifies whether PL/SQL V2 constructs that are no longer supported in Oracle8 PL/SQL V3 are to be supported.

REMOTE_DEPENDENCIES_MODE

Allows you to override the *INIT.ORA* parameter REMOTE_DEPENDENCIES_ MODE for this session. This specifies how PL/SQL will treat dependencies upon remote procedures:

TIMESTAMP

Specifies that timestamps are to be checked, and will execute the local procedure if the timestamp of the remote procedure matches. This is the default.

SIGNATURE

Specifies that the local procedure can continue to call the remote procedure if the signature is considered safe.

SESSION_CACHED_CURSORS

Specifies how many session cursors can be cached.

SQL_TRACE

Controls whether performance statistics will be generated. The initial value is set in the *INIT.ORA* file.

SKIP_UNUSABLE_INDEXES

Specifies whether DML operations are allowed against a table with an index marked UNUSABLE.

SORT_AREA_SIZE

Allows you to override the *INIT.ORA* parameter SORT_AREA_SIZE for this session. This specifies the amount of memory allocated out of the Program Global Area (PGA) (System Global Area, or SGA, in an MTS environment) for sorts.

SORT_AREA_RETAINED_SIZE

Allows you to override the *INIT.ORA* parameter SORT_AREA_RETAINED_SIZE for this session. This is the maximum size the sort area in the PGA retains between the sort completing and fetching the last row from the sort area.

SORT_DIRECT_WRITES

Allows you to override the *INIT.ORA* parameter SORT_DIRECT_WRITES for this session. The valid values are:

AUTO

Oracle will bypass the buffer pool under certain circumstances. This is the default.

TRUE

Oracle will bypass the buffer pool and write temporary segments directly to disk.

FALSE

Oracle will perform all read/writes to the temporary segments through the buffer cache.

SORT_READ_FAC

Allows you to override the *INIT.ORA* parameter SORT_READ_FAC for this session. This parameter provides Oracle with a ratio indicating relative disk performance. The default is operating system dependent.

SORT_WRITE_BUFFERS

Allows you to override the *INIT.ORA* parameter SORT_WRITE_BUFFERS for this session. This parameter specifies the number of sort buffers to use when SORT_DIRECT_WRITES is set to TRUE.

SORT_WRITE_BUFFER_SIZE

Allows you to override the *INIT.ORA* parameter SORT_WRITE_BUFFER_SIZE for this session. This parameter specifies the size of the sort write buffer to use when SORT_DIRECT_WRITES is set to TRUE.

SPIN_COUNT

Allows you to override the *INIT.ORA* parameter SPIN_COUNT for this session. This parameter specifies the number of times a process will wait on a latch before sleeping.

STAR_TRANSFORMATION_ENABLED

Allows you to override the *INIT.ORA* parameter STAR_TRANSFORMATION_ ENABLED for this session. This parameter determines whether the cost-based optimizer can use star transformation for queries.

TEXT_ENABLED

Allows you to override the *INIT.ORA* parameter TEXT_ENABLED for this session. This parameter determines whether to enable the CONTAINS clause in the Oracle ConText option or the Oracle ConText cartridge.

TIMED_STATISTICS

Allows you to override the *INIT.ORA* parameter TIMED_STATISTICS for this session. When set to TRUE, Oracle will call system services to determine the length of time required for most operations.

ADVISE

Sends advice for forcing a distributed transaction to a remote database by placing the value 'C' (COMMIT), 'R' (ROLLBACK), or ' ' (NOTHING) in the DBA_2PC_PENDING_ADVICE data dictionary view on the remote database.

CLOSE DATABASE LINK

Closes a connection to a remote database using the database link *dblink*. This command will succeed only if the database link is not in use and there is no pending commit across the link.

ENABLE COMMIT IN PROCEDURE

Specifies that procedures and stored functions can issue COMMIT and ROLLBACK statements.

DISABLE COMMIT IN PROCEDURE

Specifies that procedures and stored functions may not issue COMMIT and ROLLBACK statements.

ENABLE PARALLEL DML

Enables Parallel DML where parallellism has been specified at the table level or in a parallel hint.

DISABLE PARALLEL DML

Overrides any parallel hints or table specifications and forces all transactions to be executed serially.

FORCE PARALLEL DML

Forces all allowed operations to be executed in parallel. If no level of parallelism has been specified, default values are used.

Notes

SQL_TRACE and TIMED_STATISTICS should be set to FALSE except when perfor-mance statistics are desired, since this option will degrade database performance. The PARALLEL DML clauses can only be used in the first SQL statement following a commit or rollback.

Examples

The following example enables the SQL Trace facility for this session:

```
ALTER SESSION
    SET SQL_TRACE = TRUE
```

The following example sets the language to French, then overrides the date for-mat with an American-style four-digit year date format:

```
ALTER SESSION
    SET NLS_LANGUAGE = French
ALTER SESSION
    SET NLS_DATE_FORMAT = 'mm/dd/yyyy'
```

ALTER SNAPSHOT

```
ALTER SNAPSHOT [schema.]snapshot_name
    [PCTFREE integer]
    [PCTUSED integer]
    [INITRANS integer]
    [MAXTRANS integer]
    [LOGGING | NOLOGGING]
    [CACHE | NOCACHE]
    [STORAGE (
        [NEXT integer[K | M] ]
        [MAXEXTENTS {integer | UNLIMITED} ]
        [PCTINCREASE integer]
        [FREELISTS integer]
        [FREELIST GROUPS integer] ]
        ) ]
    [PARALLEL ( {DEGREE {integer | DEFAULT} | INSTANCES {integer | DEFAULT} } ) ]
    [NOPARALLEL]
    [USING INDEX
        [PCTFREE integer]
        [INITRANS integer]
        [MAXTRANS integer]
        [LOGGING | NOLOGGING]
        [STORAGE (
            [INITIAL integer[K | M] ]
            [NEXT integer[K | M] ]
            [MINEXTENTS integer]
            [MAXEXTENTS {integer | UNLIMITED} ]
            [PCTINCREASE integer]
            [FREELISTS integer]
            [FREELIST GROUPS integer]
              ) ]
```

```
]
[REFRESH
   [FAST | COMPLETE | FORCE]
   [START WITH date]
   [NEXT date]
   [WITH PRIMARY KEY]
   [USING DEFAULT [MASTER | LOCAL ] ROLLBACK SEGMENT] |
   [USING [MASTER | LOCAL] ROLLBACK SEGMENT rollback_segment]
]
```

Changes the storage characteristics or automatic refresh characteristics of a snapshot (*snapshot_name*).

Keywords

PCTFREE

Specifies the percentage of space to be reserved in each data block for future updates to rows contained in that block. Valid values are 0–99, and the default value is 10.

PCTUSED

Specifies the minimum percentage of space that will be maintained as used in each data block. Valid values are 1–99, and the default value is 40.

INITRANS

Specifies the initial number of transaction entries allocated to each block.

MAXTRANS

Specifies the maximum number of transaction entries allocated to each block.

LOGGING

Specifies that the operation is to be logged to the redo logs.

NOLOGGING

Specifies that nothing is to be written to the redo logs for this operation.

CACHE

Specifies how many sequence numbers Oracle will pregenerate and keep in memory. Note that when the database is shut down, unused sequence numbers stored in cache will be lost. The default is 20.

NOCACHE

Specifies that no sequence numbers are pregenerated to memory.

STORAGE

Specifies the physical characteristics of the snapshot as follows:

NEXT

Specifies the size of the next extent in bytes, kilobytes, or megabytes. If the value is not a multiple of the database blocksize, it will be rounded up to a multiple of the database blocksize.

MAXEXTENTS

Specifies the maximum number of extents that may be allocated for this snapshot. The default will vary according to the database blocksize. Specify UNLIMITED for unlimited expansion.

PCTINCREASE

Specifies the percentage by which each extent will grow over the previous extent. The default is 50, which means that each extent will be one-and-one-half times larger than the previous extent.

FREELISTS

Specifies the number of free lists contained in each freelist group in this snapshot. The default is 1, and the maximum depends on the database blocksize.

FREELIST GROUPS

Specifies the number of groups of free lists for this snapshot. The default is 1. This parameter should be used only with the Parallel Server option running in parallel mode.

PARALLEL

Specifies the level of parallelism to be supported, based on the following parameters:

DEGREE

Specifies the degree of parallelism. An integer value specifies how many slave processes can be used. Specify DEFAULT to use the default value for the tablespace.

INSTANCES

Specifies the number of instances that can be used to execute slave processes. Specify DEFAULT to use the default value specified for the tablespace.

NOPARALLEL

Specifies that no parallel processing will be supported for the snapshot.

USING INDEX

Changes the value of the PCTFREE, INITRANS, MAXTRANS, and STORAGE parameters for the index Oracle uses to maintain the snapshot's data. If the index is being created, you can also specify:

INITIAL

Specifies the size of the first extent for this snapshot in bytes, kilobytes, or megabytes. If this value is not a multiple of the database blocksize, it will be rounded up to a multiple of the database blocksize.

MINEXTENTS

Specifies the number of extents to be allocated when this snapshot is created. The minimum and default value is 1.

REFRESH

Specifies the mode and times for automatic refreshes. FAST means use the snapshot log associated with the master table. COMPLETE means refresh by reexecuting the snapshot's query. FORCE is the default, and means that Oracle will either decide that a FAST refresh is possible or do a COMPLETE refresh.

START WITH

Specifies a date for the next automatic refresh time, using a standard Oracle date expression.

NEXT

Specifies a new date expression for calculating the interval between automatic refreshes.

USING DEFAULT ROLLBACK SEGMENT

Specifies the rollback segment to be used as a default if a rollback segment is not explicitly supplied. Select either MASTER (use the default rollback segment at the remote master for the individual snapshot) or LOCAL (use the default rollback segment for the local refresh group that contains the snapshot).

USING ROLLBACK SEGMENT rollback_segment

Specifies the rollback segment to use when refreshing the snapshot. Specify either MASTER (the rollback segment to be used at the remote master for the individual snapshot) or LOCAL (specifies the rollback segment to be used for the local refresh group that contains the snapshot).

Note

You must own the snapshot or have the ALTER ANY SNAPSHOT privilege to issue this command.

Example

The following example causes scott's snapshot dept_snap to be refreshed at midnight tomorrow, and then every week:

```
ALTER SNAPSHOT scott.dept_snap
   REFRESH COMPLETE
   START WITH SYSDATE+1
   NEXT SYSDATE+7
```

ALTER SNAPSHOT LOG

```
ALTER SNAPSHOT LOG ON [schema.]table_name
   [PCTFREE integer]
   [PCTUSED integer]
   [INITRANS integer]
   [MAXTRANS integer]
   [STORAGE (
```

```
    [NEXT integer[K | M] ]
    [MAXEXTENTS {integer | UNLIMITED} ]
    [PCTINCREASE integer]
    [FREELISTS integer]
    [FREELIST GROUPS integer] ]
    ) ]
```

Changes the storage characteristics of a snapshot log (*table_name*).

Keywords

PCTFREE

Specifies the percentage of space to be reserved in each data block for future updates to rows contained in that block. Valid values are 0–99, and the default value is 10.

PCTUSED

Specifies the minimum percentage of space that will be maintained as used in each data block. Valid values are 1–99, and the default value is 40.

INITRANS

Specifies the initial number of transaction entries allocated to each block.

MAXTRANS

Specifies the maximum number of transaction entries allocated to each block.

STORAGE

Specifies the physical characteristics of the snapshot log as follows:

NEXT

Specifies the size of the next extent in bytes, kilobytes, or megabytes. If the value is not a multiple of the database blocksize, it will be rounded up to a multiple of the database blocksize.

MAXEXTENTS

Specifies the maximum number of extents that may be allocated for this snapshot log. The default will vary according to the database blocksize. Specify UNLIMITED for unlimited expansion.

PCTINCREASE

Specifies the percentage by which each extent will grow over the previous extent. The default is 50, which means that each extent will be one-and-one-half times larger than the previous extent.

FREELISTS

Specifies the number of free lists contained in each freelist group in this snapshot log. The default is 1, and the maximum depends on the database blocksize.

FREELIST GROUPS

Specifies the number of groups of free lists for this snapshot log. The default is 1. This parameter should be used only with the Parallel Server option running in parallel mode.

Note

You must own the snapshot log or have the ALTER ANY TABLE privilege to issue this command.

Example

The following example changes the next extent size for scott's employee table to 50K:

```
ALTER SNAPSHOT LOG scott.employee
    STORAGE (NEXT 50K)
```

ALTER SYSTEM

```
ALTER SYSTEM
   [SET
      {
       [ALLOW_PARTIAL_SN_RESULTS = {TRUE | FALSE} ]
       [BACKUP_DISK_IO_SLAVES = integer DEFERRED]
       [BACKUP_TAPE_IO_SLAVES = integer DEFERRED]
       [CACHE_INSTANCES = integer]
       [CONTROL_FILE_RECORD_KEEP_TIME = integer DEFERRED]
       [DB_BLOCK_CHECKPOINT_BATCH = integer]
       [DB_BLOCK_CHECKSUM = {TRUE | FALSE} ]
       [DB_BLOCK_MAX_DIRTY_TARGET = integer]
       [DB_FILE_MULTIBLOCK_READ_COUNT = integer]
       [FIXED_DATE = {'DD_MM_YY' | 'YYYY_MM_DD_HH24_MI_SS'} ]
       [FREEZE_DB_FOR_FAST_INSTANCE_RECOVERY = {TRUE | FALSE } DEFERRED]
       [GC_DEFER_TIME = integer]
       [GLOBAL_NAMES = {TRUE | FALSE} ]
       [HASH_MULTIBLOCK_IO_COUNT = integer]
       [JOB_QUEUE_PROCESSES = integer]
       [LICENSE_MAX_SESSIONS = integer]
       [LICENSE_MAX_USERS = integer]
       [LICENSE_SESSIONS_WARNING = integer]
       [LOG_ARCHIVE_DUPLEX_DEST = 'text' ]
       [LOG_ARCHIVE_MIN_SUCCEED_DEST = integer]
       [LOG_CHECKPOINT_INTERVAL = integer]
       [LOG_CHECKPOINT_TIMEOUT = integer]
       [LOG_SMALL_ENTRY_MAX_SIZE = integer]
       [MAX_DUMP_FILE_SIZE = {size | UNLIMITED}]
       [MTS_DISPATCHERS = 'protocol, integer']
       [MTS_SERVERS = integer]
       [RESOURCE_LIMIT   {TRUE | FALSE} ]
       [OBJECT_CACHE_MAX_SIZE_PERCENT = integer]
       [OBJECT_CACHE_OPTIMAL_SIZE = integer]
```

```
        [OPS_ADMIN_GROUP = 'text' ]
        [PARALLEL_INSTANCE_GROUP = 'text' ]
        [PARALLEL_TRANSACTION_RESOURCE_TIMEOUT = integer]
        [PLSQL_V2_COMPATIBILITY = {TRUE | FALSE} ]
        [REMOTE_DEPENDENCIES_MODE = {TIMESTAMP | SIGNATURE} ]
        [RESOURCE_LIMIT = {TRUE | FALSE} ]
        [SCAN_INSTANCES = integer]
        [SORT_AREA_SIZE = integer]
        [SORT_AREA_RETAINED_SIZE = integer]
        [SORT_DIRECT_WRITES = {AUTO | TRUE | FALSE} ]
        [SORT_READ_FAC = integer]
        [SORT_WRITE_BUFFERS = integer]
        [SORT_WRITE_BUFFER_SIZE = integer]
        [SPIN_COUNT = integer]
        [TEXT_ENABLED = {TRUE | FALSE} ]
        [TIMED_STATISTICS = {TRUE | FALSE} ]
        [TIMED_OS_STATISTICS = integer]
        [TRANSACTION_AUDITING = {TRUE | FALSE} DEFERRED]
        [USER_DUMP_DEST = 'dirname']
        }
[ARCHIVE_LOG [THREAD integer]
    {
    [START [TO 'destination'] ]
    [STOP]
    [SEQ integer [TO 'destination'] ]
    [CHANGE integer [TO 'destination'] ]
    [CURRENT [TO 'destination'] ]
    [GROUP integer [TO 'destination'] ]
    [LOGFILE 'filename' [TO 'destination'] ]
    [NEXT [TO 'destination'] ]
    [ALL [TO 'destination'] ]
    }
[CHECKPOINT {GLOBAL | LOCAL} ]
[CHECK DATAFILES {GLOBAL | LOCAL} ]
[DISCONNECT SESSION 'sid_integer.session_integer' POST_TRANSACTION]
[ENABLE DISTRIBUTED RECOVERY]
[DISABLE DISTRIBUTED RECOVERY]
[ENABLE RESTRICTED SESSION]
[DISABLE RESTRICTED SESSION]
[FLUSH SHARED_POOL]
[SWITCH LOGFILE]
[KILL SESSION 'sid_integer, session_integer']
```

Makes dynamic changes to the database instance.

Keywords

SET

Indicates that one or more system-level keywords will follow.

ALLOW_PARTIAL_SN_RESULTS

Allows you to override the *INIT.ORA* parameter ALLOW_PARTIAL_SN_ RESULTS for the current instance. A value of TRUE allows results to be retrieved in the GV$ views even if a slave process cannot be created for one or more instances.

BACKUP_DISK_IO_SLAVES

Allows you to override the *INIT.ORA* parameter BACKUP_DISK_IO_SLAVES for the current instance. Specifies the number of I/O slaves used to back up, copy, or restore database files to disk.

BACKUP_TAPE_IO_SLAVES

Allows you to override the *INIT.ORA* parameter BACKUP_TAPE_IO_SLAVES for the current instance. Specifies the number of I/O slaves used to back up, copy, or restore database files to tape.

CACHE_INSTANCES

Specifies the number of instances in a Parallel Server environment that will cache a table. Note that this parameter is expected to be obsolete in a future release of Oracle.

CONTROL_FILE_RECORD_KEEP_TIME

Allows you to override the *INIT.ORA* parameter CONTROL_FILE_RECORD_ KEEP_TIME for the current instance. Specifies the minimum number of days a reusable entry is stored in the control file. If necessary, the control file will expand to include enough records.

DB_BLOCK_CHECKPOINT_BATCH

Allows you to override the *INIT.ORA* parameter DB_BLOCK_CHECKPOINT_ BATCH for this instance. Specifies a number of additional database buffer blocks that can be written out by DBWR when it writes buffers to disk, advancing checksum processing.

DB_BLOCK_CHECKSUM

Allows you to override the *INIT.ORA* parameter DB_BLOCK_CHECKSUM for the current instance. Specifies whether DBWR is to calculate and record a checksum with every database buffer block written. The checksum is then calculated and compared on reads. The default is FALSE.

DB_BLOCK_MAX_DIRTY_TARGET

Allows you to override the *INIT.ORA* parameter DB_BLOCK_MAX_DIRTY_ READ_COPY for this instance. Specifies a target maximum number of dirty blocks. When this value is reached, DBWR starts writing additional blocks in an attempt to bring the number of dirty blocks down.

DB_FILE_MULTIBLOCK_READ_COUNT

Allows you to override the *INIT.ORA* parameter DB_FILE_MULTIBLOCK_ READ_COUNT for the current instance. This specifies the target number of database block buffers to read in at a time during sequential scans of a table.

FIXED_DATE

Allows you to override the *INIT.ORA* parameter FIXED_DATE for this instance. This provides a fixed value that is always returned by SYSDATE for testing.

FREEZE_DB_FOR_FAST_INSTANCE_RECOVERY

Allows you to override the *INIT.ORA* parameter FREEZE_DB_FOR_FAST_INSTANCE_RECOVERY for this database. A value of TRUE freezes the entire database during an instance recovery. This causes the database to appear to hang for current users, but makes the instance recovery complete faster. FALSE does not freeze the database, and DEFERRED defers it.

GC_DEFER_TIME

Allows you to override the *INIT.ORA* parameter GC_DEFER_TIME for this instance. Specifies how many hundredths of a second the instance will wait or defer before writing out buffers when a forced write is signaled from another instance.

GLOBAL_NAMES

Specifies whether global naming will be enforced (TRUE) or not enforced (FALSE).

HASH_MULTIBLOCK_IO_COUNT

Specifies the number of database blocks to be read or written during hash I/O operations.

JOB_QUEUE_PROCESSES

Allows you to override the *INIT.ORA* parameter JOB_QUEUE_PROCESSES for this instance. Specifies the maximum number of SNP background processes. The allowed values are between 0 and 36.

LICENSE_MAX_SESSIONS

Specifies the maximum number of sessions permitted on this instance. A value of 0 indicates that there is no limit.

LICENSE_MAX_USERS

Specifies the maximum number of users in this database. A value of 0 indicates that there is no limit.

LICENSE_SESSIONS_WARNING

Specifies the maximum number of sessions permitted on this instance before a warning message is written to the alert file. A value of 0 indicates that there is no limit.

LOG_ARCHIVE_DUPLEX_DEST

Overrides the *INIT.ORA* parameter LOG_ARCHIVE_DUPLEX_DEST for this instance. Specifies an additional archive log destination that is to be written to when redo logs are archived.

LOG_ARCHIVE_MIN_SUCCEED_DEST

Overrides the *INIT.ORA* parameter LOG_ARCHIVE_MIN_SUCCEED_DEST for this instance. Specifies the minimum number of archive file writes that have to succeed before the archive is considered complete.

LOG_CHECKPOINT_INTERVAL

Overrides the *INIT.ORA* parameter LOG_CHECKPOINT_INTERVAL for this instance. Specifies the number of redo log blocks that can be written before a checkpoint is forced.

LOG_CHECKPOINT_TIMEOUT

Overrides the *INIT.ORA* parameter LOG_CHECKPOINT_TIMEOUT for this instance. Specifies in seconds the maximum amount of time between checkpoints. This can be used to force a checkpoint on a periodic basis even when there is minimal database activity.

LOG_SMALL_ENTRY_MAX_SIZE

Overrides the *INIT.ORA* parameter LOG_SMALL_ENTRY_MAX_SIZE for this instance. Specifies the largest copy of log buffers that can be performed using the log allocation latch without resorting to using the log buffer copy latch.

MAX_DUMP_FILE_SIZE

Allows you to override the *INIT.ORA* parameter MAX_DUMP_FILE_SIZE for the current instance. The integer specified is the maximum number of operating system blocks to be used for a trace file. A value of UNLIMITED specifies that no limit is to be imposed.

MTS_DISPATCHERS

Changes the number of dispatcher processes for the named protocol. The database must be open to issue this command.

MTS_SERVERS

Changes the minimum number of shared MTS server processes.

RESOURCE_LIMIT

Specifies whether resource limits will be enforced (TRUE) or not enforced (FALSE).

OBJECT_CACHE_MAX_SIZE_PERCENT

Allows you to override the *INIT.ORA* parameter OBJECT_CACHE_MAX_SIZE_PERCENT for this instance. This value is the percent by which the object cache can exceed the optimal size. When this value is exceeded, the cache will be reduced to the optimal size.

OBJECT_CACHE_OPTIMAL_SIZE

Allows you to override the *INIT.ORA* parameter OBJECT_CACHE_OPTIMAL_SIZE for this instance. This specifies the size to which the object cache is reduced when it exceeds its maximum value.

OPS_ADMIN_GROUP

Allows you to override the *INIT.ORA* parameter OPS_ADMIN_GROUP for this instance. In a Parallel Server environment, the instances can be divided into one or more groups to ease administration. The effect of this parameter is to limit the instances reflected in the GV$ views.

PARALLEL_INSTANCE_GROUP

Allows you to override the *INIT.ORA* parameter PARALLEL_INSTANCE_GROUP for this instance. This specifies the instance groups to which parallel query slaves can be spawned.

PARALLEL_TRANSACTION_RESOURCE_TIMEOUT

Allows you to override the *INIT.ORA* parameter PARALLEL_TRANSACTION_RESOURCE_TIMEOUT for this instance. This Parallel Server parameter specifies how many seconds a session will wait on an object locked by another session.

PLSQL_V2_COMPATIBILITY

Specifies whether to support, for compatibility reasons, PL/SQL V2 constructs that are no longer supported in Oracle8 PL/SQL V3.

REMOTE_DEPENDENCIES_MODE

Allows you to override the *INIT.ORA* parameter REMOTE_DEPENDENCIES_MODE for this session. This specifies how PL/SQL will treat dependencies upon remote procedures:

TIMESTAMP

Specifies that timestamps are to be checked, and will execute the local procedure if the timestamp of the remote procedure matches. This is the default.

SIGNATURE

Specifies that the local procedure can continue to call the remote procedure if the signature is considered safe.

RESOURCE_LIMIT

Allows you to override the *INIT.ORA* parameter RESOURCE_LIMIT for this instance. A value of TRUE enables enforcement of resource limits as specified in user profiles.

SCAN_INSTANCES

Specifies how many instances are to participate in parallelized operations. This parameter will become obsolete in the next major release of Oracle.

SORT_AREA_SIZE

Allows you to override the *INIT.ORA* parameter SORT_AREA_SIZE for this session. This specifies the amount of memory allocated out of the PGA (the SGA in an MTS environment) for sorts.

SORT_AREA_RETAINED_SIZE

Allows you to override the *INIT.ORA* parameter SORT_AREA_RETAINED_SIZE for this session. This is the maximum size that the sort area in the PGA retains between the sort completing and fetching the last row from the sort area.

SORT_DIRECT_WRITES

Allows you to override the *INIT.ORA* parameter SORT_DIRECT_WRITES for this session. The valid values are:

AUTO

Oracle will bypass the buffer pool under certain circumstances. This is the default.

TRUE

Oracle will bypass the buffer pool and write temporary segments directly to disk.

FALSE

Oracle will perform all reads and writes to the temporary segments through the buffer cache.

SORT_READ_FAC

Allows you to override the *INIT.ORA* parameter SORT_READ_FAC for this instance. This parameter provides Oracle with a ratio indicating relative disk performance. The default is operating system dependent.

SORT_WRITE_BUFFERS

Allows you to override the *INIT.ORA* parameter SORT_WRITE_BUFFERS for this instance. This parameter specifies the number of sort buffers to use when SORT_DIRECT_WRITES is set to TRUE.

SORT_WRITE_BUFFER_SIZE

Allows you to override the *INIT.ORA* parameter SORT_WRITE_BUFFER_SIZE for this instance. This parameter specifies the size of the sort write buffer to use when SORT_DIRECT_WRITES is set to TRUE.

SPIN_COUNT

Allows you to override the *INIT.ORA* parameter SPIN_COUNT for this instance. This parameter specifies the number of times a process will wait on a latch before sleeping.

TEXT_ENABLED

Allows you to override the *INIT.ORA* parameter TEXT_ENABLED for this instance. This parameter determines whether to enable the CONTAINS clause in the Oracle ConText option or the Oracle ConText cartridge.

TIMED_STATISTICS

Allows you to override the *INIT.ORA* parameter TIMED_STATISTICS for this instance. When this parameter is set to TRUE, Oracle will call system services to determine the length of time required for most operations.

TIMED_OS_STATISTICS

Allows you to override the *INIT.ORA* parameter TIMED_OS_STATISTICS for this instance. Specifies the number of seconds between calls to collect operating system statistics.

TRANSACTION_AUDITING

Allows you to override the *INIT.ORA* parameter TRANSACTION_AUDITING for the current instance. A value of TRUE causes Oracle to write information into the redo log to identify the user and instance responsible for individual modifications to the database. FALSE causes Oracle not to write information, and DEFERRED defers the operation.

USER_DUMP_DEST

Allows you to override the *INIT.ORA* parameter USER_DUMP_DEST for the current instance. Specifies a directory in which trace files are written.

ARCHIVE_LOG

Manually archives redo log file groups; enables or disables automatic archiving as follows:

THREAD

Specifies the thread containing the redo log file group to be archived. This parameter is only required when running the Parallel Server option in parallel mode.

START

Enables automatic archiving of redo log groups.

STOP

Disables automatic archiving of redo log groups.

SEQ

Specifies the log sequence number of the redo log file group to be manually archived. The database must be mounted but may be open or closed to issue this command.

CHANGE

Manually archives the online redo log file group containing the redo log entry with the system change number (SCN) specified by *integer*. If the SCN is the current log group, a log switch is performed. The database must be open to use this parameter.

CURRENT

Manually forces a log switch and archives the current redo log file group. The database must be open to use this parameter.

GROUP

Manually archives the online redo log file group with the specified GROUP value, which can be found in DBA_LOG_FILES. The database must be mounted but may be open or closed to issue this command.

LOGFILE

Manually archives the online redo log file group containing the log file member identified by *filename*. The database must be mounted but may be open or closed to issue this command.

NEXT

Manually archives the next online redo log file group that is full but has not yet been archived. The database must be mounted but may be open or closed to issue this command.

ALL

Manually archives all online redo log file groups that are full but have not been archived. The database must be mounted but may be open or closed to issue this command.

CHECKPOINT

Causes Oracle to perform a checkpoint. The database may be open or closed to issue this command. You may specify:

GLOBAL

Performs a checkpoint for all instances that have opened the database.

LOCAL

Performs a checkpoint only for this instance.

CHECK DATAFILES

Verifies access to online datafiles. The database may be open or closed to issue this command. You may specify:

GLOBAL

Verifies that all instances that have opened the database can access the datafiles.

LOCAL

Verifies that this instance can access the datafiles.

DISCONNECT SESSION

Disconnects a session in the current instance using SID and SESSION# from V$SESSION. The current transaction is allowed to complete, and, since the session is only disconnected, it becomes a candidate for application failover (if configured) to another instance in a Parallel Server environment.

ENABLE DISTRIBUTED RECOVERY

Specifies that distributed recovery is to be enabled and—in a single-process environment—used to initiate distributed recovery.

DISABLE DISTRIBUTED RECOVERY

Specifies that distributed recovery is to be disabled.

ENABLE RESTRICTED SESSION

Allows only users with the RESTRICTED SESSION privilege to log on to the instance.

DISABLE RESTRICTED SESSION

Allows any user with the CREATE SESSION privilege to log on to the instance.

FLUSH SHARED_POOL

Clears all data from the instance shared pool. The database may be dis-mounted or mounted, open or closed, to issue this command.

SWITCH LOGFILE

Causes Oracle to switch redo log file groups.

KILL SESSION

Terminates a session using SID and SESSION# from V$SESSION.

Notes

You must have the ALTER SYSTEM privilege to issue this command. In addition, the ARCHIVE LOG command requires that you have the OSDBA or OSOPER role enabled. Except as noted, the database may be mounted and open to issue these commands.

Examples

The following example changes the number of dispatcher processes for TCP to 10 and for DECNet to 8:

```
ALTER SYSTEM
    SET MTS_DISPATCHERS = 'TCP,10'
        MTS_DISPATCHERS = 'DECnet,8'
```

The following example sets the maximum number of sessions to 100, and sets the warning threshold to 80:

```
ALTER SYSTEM
    SET LICENSE_MAX_SESSIONS = 100
    LICENSE_SESSIONS_WARNING = 80
```

The following example archives log sequence number 123 to the specified location:

```
ALTER SYSTEM
    ARCHIVE LOG SEQ 123 TO '/disk09/oracle/archive'
```

ALTER TABLE

```
ALTER TABLE [schema.]table_name
  {
  [ADD (column datatype [DEFAULT expression] [column_constraint_clause] )]
  [MODIFY (column [datatype] [DEFAULT expression] [column_constraint_clause] }]
  [PCTFREE integer]
  [PCTUSED integer]
  [INITRANS integer]
  [MAXTRANS integer]
  [LOGGING | NOLOGGING]
  [STORAGE (
      [NEXT integer[K | M] ]
      [MAXEXTENTS {integer | UNLIMITED} ]
      [PCTINCREASE integer]
      [FREELISTS integer]
      [FREELIST GROUPS integer] ]
      ) ]

  [DROP {
      PRIMARY KEY [CASCADE] |
      UNIQUE (column[,column...] [CASCADE] |
      CONSTRAINT constraint_name [CASCADE]} ]
  [ALLOCATE EXTENT ([DATAFILE 'filename'] [SIZE integer[K | M] ]) ]
  [DEALLOCATE UNUSED [KEEP integer[K | M]]
  [CACHE | NOCACHE]
  [RENAME TO table_name]
  [PARALLEL ( {DEGREE {integer | DEFAULT} | INSTANCES {integer | DEFAULT} } ) ]
  [NOPARALLEL]
  [DROP PARTITION partition]
  [TRUNCATE PARTITION partition]
  [MODIFY PARTITION partition [REBUILD] UNUSABLE LOCAL INDEXES]
  [ADD PARTITION partition VALUES LESS THAN (valuelist)
  [RENAME PARTITION partition TO newpartition]
  [EXCHANGE PARTITION partition WITH TABLE table_name
  [ {INCLUDING | EXCLUDING} INDEXES ]
  [ {WITH | WITHOUT} VALIDATION ] ]
  }
  [ENABLE
    {
    ALL TRIGGERS |
    UNIQUE (column[, column...] [CASCADE] |
    PRIMARY KEY [CASCADE] |
    CONSTRAINT constraint_name |
    }]
  [DISABLE
    {
    ALL TRIGGERS |
    UNIQUE (column[, column...] [CASCADE] |
    PRIMARY KEY [CASCADE] |
    CONSTRAINT constraint_name
    }]
  [ENABLE TABLE LOCK]
  [DISABLE TABLE LOCK]
```

Modifies the column characteristics of a table (*table_name*), the storage characteristics of the table, or integrity constraints associated with the table or its columns.

Keywords

ADD

Adds a column or integrity constraint to the table with the specified *datatype*.

DEFAULT

Specifies a default value for the column. The specified *expression* must match
the datatype of the column.

column_constraint_clause

Adds or removes a column constraint, using the syntax shown in the later
column_constraint_clause section.

MODIFY

Changes the definition of an existing column in the table; you can optionally
change the datatype of the column, provide a default expression, and specify
column constraints.

PCTFREE

Specifies the percentage of space to be reserved in each data block for future
updates to rows contained in that block. The value may be in the range 0–99,
and the default value is 10.

PCTUSED

Specifies the minimum percentage of space that will be maintained as used in
each data block. The value may be in the range 1–99; the default value is 40.

INITRANS

Specifies the initial number of transaction entries allocated to each block.

MAXTRANS

Specifies the maximum number of transaction entries allocated to each block.

LOGGING

Specifies that future direct path DML operations are to be logged to the redo
logs.

NOLOGGING

Specifies that future direct path DML operations are not to be logged to the
redo logs.

STORAGE

Specifies the physical characteristics of the table as follows:

NEXT

Specifies the size of the next extent in bytes, kilobytes, or megabytes. If
the value is not a multiple of the database blocksize, it will be rounded up
to a multiple of the database blocksize.

MAXEXTENTS

Specifies the maximum number of extents that may be allocated for this table. The default will vary according to the database blocksize. Specify UNLIMITED for unlimited expansion.

PCTINCREASE

Specifies the percentage by which each extent will grow over the previous extent. The default is 50, which means that each extent will be one-and-one-half times larger than the previous extent.

FREELISTS

Specifies the number of free lists contained in each freelist group in this table. The default is 1 and the maximum depends on the database blocksize.

FREELIST GROUPS

Specifies the number of groups of free lists for this table. The default is 1. This parameter should be used only with the Parallel Server option running in parallel mode.

DROP PRIMARY KEY

Specifies that the table's primary key is to be dropped.

DROP UNIQUE

Specifies that the UNIQUE constraint on the specified columns is to be dropped.

DROP CONSTRAINT

Specifies that the named integrity constraint is to be dropped.

CASCADE

Specifies that all other integrity constraints that depend on the dropped integrity constraint should also be dropped.

ALLOCATE EXTENT

Explicitly allocates a new extent for the table; you can optionally specify a datafile and size.

DEALLOCATE UNUSED

Releases storage above the highwater mark.

KEEP

Specifies the amount of storage above the highwater mark to keep.

CACHE

Specifies that blocks retrieved from this table during full table scans are placed at the beginning of the least-recently-used (LRU) list. This allows small lookup tables to remain in the SGA.

NOCACHE

Specifies that blocks retrieved from this table during full table scans are placed at the end of the LRU list. This is the default behavior.

RENAME TO

Renames table to *table_name*.

PARALLEL

Specifies the level of parallelism to be supported, based on the following parameters:

DEGREE

Specifies the degree of parallelism. An integer value specifies how many slave processes can be used. Specify DEFAULT to use the default value for the tablespace.

INSTANCES

Specifies the number of instances that can be used to execute slave processes. Specify DEFAULT to use the default value specified for the tablespace.

NOPARALLEL

Specifies that no parallel operations are to be performed.

DROP PARTITION

Drops the specified partition, and all data contained in that partition, from the table.

TRUNCATE PARTITION

Truncates the specified partition.

MODIFY PARTITION

Changes the physical attributes of the specified partition.

REBUILD

When used with MODIFY PARTITION, tells Oracle to rebuild all local indexes associated with the partition.

UNUSABLE LOCAL INDEXES

When used with MODIFY PARTITION, tells Oracle to mark all local indexes associated with the partition as unusable.

ADD PARTITION

Adds a new partition at the high end of the partitions. Cannot be used if the existing top partition has the key word MAXVALUE.

VALUES LESS THAN

Specifies the upper bound for the new partition. The *valuelist* is a comma-separated, ordered list of literal values which must collate greater than the top boundary for the highest existing partition in the table.

RENAME PARTITION TO

Renames the specified *partition* TO *newpartition*.

EXCHANGE PARTITION

Specifies that the partition and table (specified in WITH TABLE *table_name*) are to be exchanged. The segments are kept intact, and only the data dictionary is modified.

INCLUDING INDEXES

Specifies that local indexes on the partition and indexes on the table are to be exchanged as well.

EXCLUDING INDEXES

Specifies that indexes are to be ignored.

WITH VALIDATION

Specifies that Oracle is to validate that all rows in the table are capable of being included in the partition.

WITHOUT VALIDATION

Specifies that the exchange is to occur without Oracle's verifying that all rows are legitimate.

ENABLE

Enables a single integrity constraint or all triggers associated with the table (see the definitions for the keywords under DROP). ALL TRIGGERS enables all triggers.

DISABLE

Disables a single integrity constraint or all triggers associated with the table (see the definitions for the keywords under DROP). ALL TRIGGERS disables all triggers.

ENABLE TABLE LOCK

Enables DML and DDL locks on a table in a Parallel Server environment.

DISABLE TABLE LOCK

Disables DML and DDL locks on a table in a Parallel Server environment.

column_constraint_clause

The following is the syntax for the *column_constraint_clause* in the ALTER TABLE statement:

```
{
[NULL | NOT NULL] |
[UNIQUE | PRIMARY KEY] |
[FOREIGN KEY (column [, column ...] )]
[REFERENCES [schema.]table_name[(column)] [ON DELETE CASCADE] ]
[CHECK (condition) ]
}
```

```
[USING INDEX
    [PCTFREE integer]
    [PCTUSED integer]
    [INITRANS integer]
    [MAXTRANS integer]
    [TABLESPACE tablespace_name]
    [STORAGE (
        [INITIAL integer [K | M]]
        [NEXT integer [K | M]]
        [MINEXTENTS integer [K | M]]
        [MAXEXTENTS {integer | UNLIMITED}]
        [PCTINCREASE integer]
        [FREELISTS integer]
        [FREELIST GROUPS integer]
        )
    [NOSORT]
    [LOGGING | NOLOGGING]
]
[EXCEPTIONS INTO [schema.]table_name]
[{ENABLE [VALIDATE  | NOVALIDATE] | DISABLE} ]
[[NOT] DEFERRABLE [INITIALLY {IMMEDIATE | DEFERRED}] ]
[[INITIALLY {IMMEDIATE | DEFERRED}] [[NOT] DEFERRABLE] ]
```

NULL

Specifies that the values in the column list may contain NULL.

NOT NULL

Specifies that the values in the column may not contain NULL.

UNIQUE

Specifies that the column list must be unique.

PRIMARY KEY

Specifies that the column list will be a primary key. A primary key can be referenced from another table with a foreign key. A primary key must also be UNIQUE and NOT NULL.

FOREIGN KEY

Requires that all values in the column list must be either NULL or found in the referenced table's defined primary key or the specified column list.

REFERENCES

Specifies the table that is referenced.

ON DELETE CASCADE

Specifies that any deletes to the referenced table are propagated down to this table through the foreign key.

CHECK

Allows you to specify an expression that a column value must satisfy.

USING INDEX

Specifies physical characteristics of the index created to support the UNIQUE or PRIMARY KEY constraint. The index will always be created.

PCTFREE

Specifies the percentage of space to be reserved in each data block for future updates to rows contained in that block. Valid values are 0–99, and the default value is 10.

PCTUSED

Specifies the minimum percentage of space that will be maintained as used in each data block. Valid values are 1–99, and the default value is 40.

INITRANS

Specifies the initial number of transaction entries allocated to each block.

MAXTRANS

Specifies the maximum number of transaction entries allocated to each block. Specify UNLIMITED for unlimited expansion.

TABLESPACE

Specifies the name of the tablespace where this object will be stored. If omitted, the default tablespace for the schema owner will be used.

STORAGE

Specifies the physical storage characteristics of this object. For keyword descriptions, see the STORAGE clause described earlier for this command.

NOSORT

Specifies that rows have been inserted into the database in sequential order; thus, no sorting is required when creating the index.

LOGGING

Specifies that redo log records will be written during index creation.

NOLOGGING

Specifies that redo log records will not be written during index creation. In case of a database failure, the index cannot be recovered by applying log files, and must be recreated. This option will speed the creation of indexes.

EXCEPTIONS INTO

Specifies the table to list the ROWIDs that violate the constraint at the time the constraint is enabled.

ENABLE

Specifies that the constraint is to be enabled at creation time.

VALIDATE

Specifies that all existing rows (and all new rows) must conform to the constraint at the time when it is enabled.

NOVALIDATE

Specifies that all new rows must conform to the constraint once it is enabled. Oracle will not verify that existing rows conform.

DISABLE

Specifies that the constraint is to be defined, but not initially enabled.

DEFERRABLE

Specifies that DML statements can be executed that violate the constraint as long as the constraint is enforceable by the time of the commit.

NOT DEFERRABLE

Specifies that the constraint is checked with each DML statement.

INITIALLY IMMEDIATE

Specifies that even though the constraint can be deferred, it is initially not deferred.

INITIALLY DEFERRED

Specifies for deferrable constraints that the constraint is deferred initially.

Note

You must own the table, have the ALTER privilege on the table, or have the ALTER ANY TABLE privilege to issue this command.

Examples

The following example adds a new column to scott's table emp:

```
ALTER TABLE scott.emp
    ADD (bonus NUMBER(7,2)
```

The following example increases the size of the bonus column to 9 digits:

```
ALTER TABLE scott.emp
    MODIFY (bonus NUMBER(9,2)
```

The following example adds a primary key constraint to scott's emp table:

```
ALTER TABLE scott.emp
    MODIFY (empno CONSTRAINT pk_emp PRIMARY_KEY)
```

ALTER TABLESPACE

```
ALTER TABLESPACE tablespace_name
    {
    [ADD DATAFILE filename [SIZE integer[K | M]] [REUSE] [autoextend_clause] ]
    [RENAME DATAFILE 'filename1' TO 'filename2']
    [DEFAULT STORAGE (
        [INITIAL integer[K | M] ]
        [NEXT integer[K | M] ]
        [MAXEXTENTS {integer | UNLIMITED} ]
```

```
      [PCTINCREASE integer]
      [FREELISTS integer]
      [FREELIST GROUPS integer] ]
      ) ]
   [ONLINE]
   [OFFLINE [NORMAL | TEMPORARY | IMMEDIATE]]
   [COALESCE]
   [MINIMUM EXTENT integer[K | M] ]
   [READ [ONLY | WRITE]
   [PERMANENT]
   [TEMPORARY]
   [LOGGING]
   [NOLOGGING]
   [BEGIN BACKUP]
   [END BACKUP]
 }
```

Changes an existing tablespace (*tablespace_name*) by adding or changing datafiles, changing storage parameters, taking the tablespace offline or putting it online, or starting and stopping backups.

Keywords

ADD DATAFILE

Adds a new operating system datafile to the existing tablespace. SIZE information is required unless the file already exists; in this case, the REUSE keyword must be specified.

autoextend_clause

Specifies whether a given datafile is able to be automatically extended when it runs out of free space. The syntax is shown in the later *autoextend_clause* section.

RENAME

Changes the name of a datafile as stored in the data dictionary. Note that the tablespace must be offline before this command is issued.

DEFAULT STORAGE

Changes the physical characteristics for objects subsequently created in this tablespace, as follows:

NEXT

Specifies the size of the next extent in bytes, kilobytes, or megabytes. If the value is not a multiple of the database blocksize, it will be rounded up to a multiple of the database blocksize.

MAXEXTENTS

Specifies the maximum number of extents that may be allocated for this index. The default will vary according to the database blocksize. Specify UNLIMITED for unlimited expansion.

PCTINCREASE

Specifies the percentage by which each extent will grow over the previous extent. The default is 50, which means that each extent will be one-and-one-half times larger than the previous extent.

FREELISTS

Specifies the number of free lists contained in each freelist group in this index. The default is 1 and the maximum depends on the database blocksize.

FREELIST GROUPS

Specifies the number of groups of free lists for this index. The default is 1. This parameter should be used only with the Parallel Server option running in parallel mode.

ONLINE

Brings a tablespace online.

OFFLINE

Takes a tablespace offline as follows:

NORMAL

The default; performs a checkpoint for all datafiles in this tablespace and ensures that each can be written. Note that this is the only mode allowed if the database is running in noarchivelog mode.

TEMPORARY

Performs a checkpoint for all datafiles in this tablespace, but does not ensure that each can be written, and therefore may require media recovery for offline files when bringing the tablespace back online.

IMMEDIATE

Does not perform a checkpoint and requires media recovery on the tablespace before bringing it back online.

COALESCE

Forces Oracle to coalesce all contiguous free extents into one large free extent.

MINIMUM EXTENT

Forces every extent created to be the size specified or a multiple of the size specified. This reduces fragmentation.

READ ONLY

Specifies that the tablespace is read only. That is, no more writes are allowed to the tablespace.

READ WRITE

Specifies that the tablespace is available for updates and writes.

PERMANENT

The default value. Allows permanent objects to be created in the tablespace.

TEMPORARY

Specifies that no permanent objects can be stored in the tablespace. Oracle then finds a more efficient access method when using the tablespace for temporary segments.

LOGGING

Specifies the default value of LOGGING for objects created in the tablespace; that is, redo log records will be written. This default value can be overridden for each object when the object is created.

NOLOGGING

Specifies the default value of NOLOGGING for objects created in the tablespace. This default value can be overridden for each object at the time the object is created. A value of NOLOGGING indicates that certain operations to the object are not logged to the redo log. This is a performance gain, but leaves the object vulnerable in the event that the tablespace has to be recovered.

BEGIN BACKUP

Signals Oracle that the tablespace is being backed up, thereby changing log file behavior to accumulate all transactions to this tablespace. Note that this command does not actually perform a backup; it signals Oracle that the backup is about to begin.

END BACKUP

Signals Oracle that the tablespace backup is complete, thereby restoring log file behavior to normal.

auto_extend_clause

The following is the syntax for the *autoextend_clause* in the ALTER TABLESPACE statement:

```
AUTOEXTEND
    {
    OFF |
    ON [NEXT integer[K | M]
        [MAXSIZE {UNLIMITED | integer [K | M] } ]
    }
```

OFF

Turns the AUTOEXTEND feature off.

ON

Turns the AUTOEXTEND feature on.

NEXT

Specifies the size of the next file extent allocated.

MAXSIZE

Specifies the maximum size to which the datafile can grow.

UNLIMITED

Specifies that the datafile size is unlimited, or rather, limited by operating system limits.

Notes

You must have the MANAGE TABLESPACE privilege to take the tablespace online or offline, or to begin or end the backup. You must have the ALTER TABLESPACE privilege to perform any other operation in this command.

Examples

The following example adds a new 25-megabyte datafile to the users tablespace:

```
ALTER TABLESPACE users
    ADD DATAFILE '/disk09/oracle/oradata/users02.dbf' SIZE 25M
```

The following example signals Oracle that a backup of the users tablespace is about to begin:

```
ALTER TABLESPACE users
    BEGIN BACKUP
```

ALTER TRIGGER

```
ALTER TRIGGER [schema.]trigger_name
  [ENABLE | DISABLE]
  [COMPILE [DEBUG] ]
```

Enables or disables a database trigger (*trigger_name*).

Keywords

ENABLE

Specifies that this trigger is to be fired when a triggering statement is issued.

DISABLE

Specifies that this trigger is not to be fired when a triggering statement is issued.

COMPILE

Specifies that the trigger is to be manually recompiled after it has become invalid.

DEBUG

Specifies that the PL/SQL compiler is to generate information for use by the PL/SQL debugger.

Notes

You must own this trigger or have the ALTER ANY TRIGGER privilege to issue this command. Unlike other ALTER commands, the ALTER TRIGGER statement does not change the definition or structure of a trigger; this must be done with a CRE-ATE OR REPLACE TRIGGER statement. Note that a trigger is automatically enabled when it is created. The ENABLE and DISABLE clauses of the ALTER TABLE statement may also be used to perform this function.

Example

The following example disables scott's trigger emp_aud:

```
ALTER TRIGGER scott.emp_aud ENABLE
```

ALTER USER

```
ALTER USER username
   [IDENTIFIED {BY password | EXTERNALLY | GLOBALLY} ]
   [DEFAULT TABLESPACE tablespace_name]
   [TEMPORARY TABLESPACE tablespace_name]
   [QUOTA [integer[K | M] | UNLIMITED] ON tablespace_name]
   [PROFILE profile_name]
   [DEFAULT ROLE {
      [role_name[,role_name ...]] |
      [ALL [EXCEPT role_name[,role_name ...]]] | NONE}
   [PASSWORD EXPIRE]
   [ACCOUNT {LOCK | UNLOCK}
```

Changes the security and storage characteristics of a user (*username*).

Keywords

IDENTIFIED BY

Specifies that the *password* must be provided when enabling the role.

IDENTIFIED EXTERNALLY

Specifies that the operating system verifies the user enabling the role.

IDENTIFIED GLOBALLY

Specifies that the Oracle Security Server verifies the user enabling the role.

DEFAULT TABLESPACE

Changes the name of the tablespace (*tablespace_name*) that will be used by default when this user creates a database object.

TEMPORARY TABLESPACE

Changes the name of the tablespace (*tablespace_name*) that will be used for the creation of temporary segments for operations like sorting that require more memory than is available.

QUOTA

Specifies the amount of space this user is permitted to use for object storage in the specified tablespace. UNLIMITED means there is no limit to the storage used, subject to the total size of the tablespace.

PROFILE

Changes the user's profile to *profile_name*, which subjects the user to the limits specified in that profile.

DEFAULT ROLE

Specifies the roles assigned to the user as default roles. ALL means that all roles granted to the user will be default roles except those specified in the EXCEPT clause, and NONE means that none of the roles granted to the user will be default roles.

PASSWORD EXPIRE

Causes the userid's password to expire. It will have to be reset before the user can connect to the database.

ACCOUNT LOCK

Causes the account to be locked and disabled. The account will have to be unlocked with the ALTER USER .... ACCOUNT UNLOCK command.

ACCOUNT UNLOCK

Causes the account to be unlocked. This is the default.

Note

You can change your own password, but you must have the ALTER USER privilege to use any other operations of this command.

Examples

The following example assigns a new password to scott:

```
ALTER USER scott IDENTIFIED BY lion
```

The following example changes the default and temporary tablespaces for user scott:

```
ALTER USER scott
    TEMPORARY TABLESPACE temp
    DEFAULT TABLESPACE users:
```

ALTER VIEW

```
ALTER VIEW [schema.]view_name COMPILE
```

Recompiles a view (*view_name*). The COMPILE keyword is required.

Notes

You must own this view or have the ALTER ANY VIEW privilege to issue this command. This command is recommended after changes are made to any of the underlying base tables.

Example

The following example recompiles scott's emploc view:

```
ALTER VIEW scott.emploc RECOMPILE
```

ANALYZE CLUSTER

```
ANALYZE CLUSTER [schema.]cluster_name
    {
    COMPUTE STATISTICS |
    ESTIMATE STATISTICS [SAMPLE integer ROWS | PERCENT]  |
    DELETE STATISTICS |
    VALIDATE STRUCTURE [CASCADE] |
    LIST CHAINED ROWS [INTO [schema.]table_name]
    }
```

Collects or deletes statistics about a cluster (*cluster_name*), validates the structure of the cluster, or identifies migrated and chained rows in the cluster.

Keywords

COMPUTE STATISTICS

Computes the exact statistics for the entire named object and stores them in the data dictionary.

ESTIMATE STATISTICS

Estimates statistics for the object named and stores them in the data dictionary. A SAMPLE may be specified: ROWS causes integer rows of a table or cluster, or *integer* entries from an index, to be sampled. PERCENT causes *integer* percent of the rows of a table or cluster or *integer* percent of the entries of an index to be sampled. The valid range for PERCENT is 1–99.

DELETE STATISTICS

Causes all statistics stored in the data dictionary for the named object to be deleted.

VALIDATE STRUCTURE

>Causes the structure of the named object to be validated. The CASCADE keyword causes any tables or indexes associated with the named object to also be validated.

LIST CHAINED ROWS

>Generates a list of chained and migrated rows for the named table or cluster (this operation is not permitted on an index). Entries are made in a table called CHAINED_ROWS, which is assumed to exist in the user's schema, unless the INTO clause specifies a different *table_name*.

Notes

You must own the object to be analyzed or have the ANALYZE ANY privilege to issue this command. If you want to use the LIST CHAINED ROWS operation to list into a table, that table must be in your schema or you must have the INSERT privilege on it. COMPUTE STATISTICS will result in more accurate statistics, but is likely to take longer. ESTIMATE STATISTICS will normally be much faster and almost as accurate. Statistics are stored in the DBA_CLUSTERS, DBA_TABLES, and DBA_INDEXES data dictionary views.

Example

The following example analyzes scott's empclus cluster using a 50% sample:

```
ANALYZE CLUSTER scott.empclus ESTIMATE STATISTICS SAMPLE 50 PERCENT
```

ANALYZE INDEX

```
ANALYZE INDEX [schema.]index_name [PARTITION (partition_name)]
    {
    COMPUTE STATISTICS |
    ESTIMATE STATISTICS [SAMPLE integer ROWS | PERCENT] |
    DELETE STATISTICS |
    VALIDATE STRUCTURE
    }
```

Collects or deletes statistics about an index (*index_name*), or validates the structure of the index.

Keywords

PARTITION

>Specifies one or more partitions (*partition_name*) to analyze in a partitioned index.

COMPUTE STATISTICS

>Computes the exact statistics for the entire named object and stores them in the data dictionary.

ESTIMATE STATISTICS

Estimates statistics for the named object and stores them in the data dictionary. A SAMPLE may be specified: ROWS causes *integer* rows of a table or cluster, or *integer* entries from an index, to be sampled. PERCENT causes *integer* percent of the rows of a table or cluster, or *integer* percent of the entries, of an index, to be sampled. The valid range for PERCENT is 1–99.

DELETE STATISTICS

Causes all statistics stored in the data dictionary for the named object to be deleted.

VALIDATE STRUCTURE

Causes the structure of the named object to be validated. Oracle will place a lock on the table during this operation.

Notes

You must own the object to be analyzed or have the ANALYZE ANY privilege to issue this command. COMPUTE STATISTICS will result in more accurate statistics, but is likely to take longer. ESTIMATE STATISTICS will normally be much faster and almost as accurate. Statistics are stored in the DBA_INDEXES, DBA_IND_PARTITIONS, and DBA_PART_INDEXES data dictionary views.

If you use the VALIDATE STRUCTURE clause, Oracle will also populate the INDEX_STATS data dictionary view.

Example

The following example analyzes scott's emppk index using a 50% sample:

```
ANALYZE INDEX scott.emppk ESTIMATE STATISTICS SAMPLE 50 PERCENT
```

ANALYZE TABLE

```
ANALYZE TABLE [schema.]table_name  [PARTITION (partition_name) ]
   {
   COMPUTE STATISTICS [for_clause] |
   ESTIMATE STATISTICS [for_clause] [SAMPLE integer ROWS | PERCENT] |
   DELETE STATISTICS |
   VALIDATE STRUCTURE [CASCADE] |
   VALIDATE REF UPDATE |
   LIST CHAINED ROWS [INTO [schema.]table_name]
   }
```

Collects or deletes statistics about a table (*table_name*), validates the structure of the table, or identifies migrated and chained rows in the table.

Keywords

PARTITION

Specifies one or more partitions to analyze in a partitioned index.

COMPUTE STATISTICS

Computes the exact statistics for the entire named object and stores them in the data dictionary.

ESTIMATE STATISTICS

Estimates statistics for the named object and stores them in the data dictionary. A SAMPLE may be specified: ROWS causes *integer* rows of a table or cluster, or *integer* entries from an index, to be sampled. PERCENT causes *integer* percent of the rows of a table or cluster, or *integer* percent of the entries of an index, to be sampled. The valid range for PERCENT is 1–99.

for_clause

Allows you to specify more granularity in the analyze. The syntax is shown in the later *for_clause* section.

DELETE STATISTICS

Causes all statistics stored in the data dictionary for the named object to be deleted.

VALIDATE STRUCTURE

Causes the structure of the named object to be validated. The CASCADE keyword causes any indexes associated with the named object also to be validated.

VALIDATE REF UPDATE

Causes the object references to be validated and updated, if necessary.

LIST CHAINED ROWS

Generates a list of chained and migrated rows for the named table or cluster (this operation is not permitted on an index). Entries are made in a table called CHAINED_ROWS that is assumed to exist in the user's *schema*, unless the INTO clause specifies a different *table_name*.

for_clause

The following is the syntax for the *for_clause* in the ANALYZE TABLE statement:

```
{
FOR TABLE |
FOR ALL [INDEXED] COLUMNS [SIZE integer] |
FOR COLUMNS column_name [SIZE integer] |
FOR ALL [LOCAL] INDEXES
}
```

FOR TABLE

Specifies that only the table is to be analyzed.

FOR ALL COLUMNS

> Specifies that, instead of the table, all columns are to be analyzed; if you specify INDEXED, all indexed columns will be analyzed. SIZE specifies the number of buckets to be generated when columns are being analyzed.

FOR COLUMNS

> Provides a list of columns to be analyzed.

FOR ALL INDEXES

> Specifies that, instead of the table, all indexes are to be analyzed. This is equivalent to executing an ANALYZE INDEX command for all indexes. If you specify LOCAL, all local indexes will be analyzed.

Notes

You must own the object to be analyzed or have the ANALYZE ANY privilege to issue this command. If you want to use the LIST CHAINED ROWS operation to list into a table, that table must be in your schema or you must have the INSERT privilege on it. COMPUTE STATISTICS will result in more accurate statistics, but is likely to take longer. ESTIMATE STATISTICS will normally be much faster and almost as accurate. Note that the object being analyzed will be locked while statistics are being collected, so the faster ESTIMATE STATISTICS may be preferable in a heavy transaction environment. Statistics are stored in the DBA_TABLES data dictionary view, and some column statistics are stored in the DBA_TAB_COLUMNS data dictionary view.

Example

The following example analyzes scott's emp table using a 50% sample:

```
ANALYZE TABLE scott.emp ESTIMATE STATISTICS SAMPLE 50 PERCENT
```

AUDIT (Schema Objects)

```
AUDIT object_privilege[,object_privilege ...] ON {[schema.]object_name | DEFAULT}
[BY SESSION [WHENEVER [NOT] SUCCESSFUL]
   [BY ACCESS [WHENEVER [NOT] SUCCESSFUL]
```

Sets up auditing for a specific schema object (*object_name*).

Keywords

object_privilege

> Indicates that a particular operation is to be audited. The following are valid operations: ALTER, AUDIT, COMMENT, DELETE, EXECUTE, GRANT, INDEX, INSERT, LOCK, RENAME, SELECT, and UPDATE. The keyword ALL is equivalent to specifying all of the operations listed.

DEFAULT

Establishes the specified object options as the default for objects that have not yet been created.

BY SESSION

Causes Oracle to write a single record for all SQL statements of the same type issued in the same session.

BY ACCESS

Causes Oracle to write a single record for each audited statement.

WHENEVER SUCCESSFUL

Chooses auditing only for SQL statements that complete successfully.

WHENEVER NOT SUCCESSFUL

Chooses auditing only for SQL statements that fail or result in errors.

Notes

You must own the object to be audited or have the AUDIT SYSTEM privilege to issue this command. Audit records are written to the audit trail, a database table containing audit records that can be accessed through data dictionary views. Note that auditing must be enabled using the *INIT.ORA* parameter AUDIT_TRAIL.

Examples

The following example audits for any UPDATE statement issued for scott's bonus table:

```
AUDIT UPDATE ON scott.bonus
```

The following example audits for any unsuccessful operation on scott's emp table:

```
AUDIT ALL ON scott.emp WHENEVER NOT SUCCESSFUL
```

AUDIT (SQL Statements)

```
AUDIT {system_privilege | sql_statement}[,{system_privilege | sql_statement ...}]
    [BY user[,user ...]]
    [BY SESSION [WHENEVER [NOT] SUCCESSFUL]
    [BY ACCESS [WHENEVER [NOT] SUCCESSFUL]
```

Sets up auditing for specific SQL statements in subsequent user sessions.

Keywords

system_privilege

Indicates that the SQL statement authorized by the named system privilege is to be audited.

sql_statement

Indicates that a set of SQL statements (e.g., SELECT, UPDATE) specified by the system option is to be audited.

BY user

Indicates that SQL statements issued by the particular user are to be audited.

BY SESSION

Causes Oracle to write a single record for all SQL statements of the same type issued in the same session.

BY ACCESS

Causes Oracle to write a single record for each audited statement.

WHENEVER SUCCESSFUL

Chooses auditing only for SQL statements that complete successfully.

WHENEVER NOT SUCCESSFUL

Chooses auditing only for SQL statements that fail or result in errors.

Notes

You must have the AUDIT SYSTEM privilege to issue this command. Audit records are written to the audit trail, a database table containing audit records, which can be accessed through data dictionary views. Note that auditing must be enabled using the *INIT.ORA* parameter AUDIT_TRAIL.

Example

The following example audits for any unsuccessful SELECT statement, which may indicate an attempt to read a table for which a user has not been granted access:

```
AUDIT SELECT TABLE
    WHENEVER NOT SUCCESSFUL
```

COMMENT

COMMENT ON TABLE | COLUMN [*schema.*]*name* IS '*text*'

Adds a comment about a table, view, snapshot, or column (identified by *name*) into the data dictionary. If you specify a column, it must be in the form *table_name.column_name*.

Keywords

TABLE

Specifies that the comment is to be associated with a table, view, or snapshot.

COLUMN

Specifies that the comment is to be associated with a column of a table, view, or snapshot.

text

The actual text of the comment to be inserted.

Notes

You must own the object to be commented or have the COMMENT ANY TABLE privilege to issue this command. A comment can be dropped by setting it to a null string (' ') using the COMMENT command.

Example

The following example adds a comment to the ename column of scott's emp table:

```
COMMENT ON COLUMN scott.emp.ename IS 'Last name from personnel records'
```

CREATE CLUSTER

```
CREATE CLUSTER [schema.]cluster_name
    (column datatype[, column datatype ...])
    [PCTFREE integer]
    [PCTUSED integer]
    [SIZE integer[K | M]]
    [INITRANS integer]
    [MAXTRANS integer]
    [TABLESPACE tablespace_name]
    [STORAGE (
        [INITIAL integer[K | M] ]
        [NEXT integer[K | M] ]
        [MINEXTENTS integer[K | M] ]
        [MAXEXTENTS {integer | UNLIMITED} ]
        [PCTINCREASE integer]
        [FREELISTS integer]
        [FREELIST GROUPS integer]
        ) ]
    [INDEX]
    [HASHKEYS integer [HASH IS column] ]
    [PARALLEL ( {DEGREE {integer | DEFAULT} | INSTANCES {integer | DEFAULT} } ) ]
    [NOPARALLEL]
    [CACHE | NOCACHE ]
```

Creates a cluster (*cluster_name*), which is a schema object that contains one or more tables with one or more columns (*column ...*) in common; you must specify a *datatype* for each column.

Keywords

PCTFREE

Changes the percentage of space that will be kept free for future updates to the rows contained in this cluster. The value may be in the range 0–99 and defaults to 10.

PCTUSED

Changes the minimum percentage of used space that Oracle will maintain in each block. The value may be in the range 0–99 and defaults to 40.

SIZE

Determines how many cluster keys will be stored in each data block of this cluster. The value should be a divisor of the Oracle blocksize, and will be rounded up to the next larger divisor, if necessary.

INITRANS

Changes the number of transaction entries allocated to each block in the cluster. The value may be in the range 1–255 and should not normally be changed from the default of 2.

MAXTRANS

Changes the maximum number of concurrent transactions that can update a block of the cluster. The value may be in the range 1–255 and should not normally be changed from the default, which is a function of the Oracle blocksize.

TABLESPACE

Specifies the tablespace (*tablespace_name*) where this cluster will be stored. If the name is omitted, the default tablespace for the schema owner will be used.

STORAGE

Specifies the physical characteristics of the specified cluster as follows:

INITIAL

Specifies the size of the first extent for this cluster in bytes, kilobytes, or megabytes. If the value is not a multiple of the database blocksize, it will be rounded up to a multiple of the database blocksize.

NEXT

Specifies the size of the next extent in bytes, kilobytes, or megabytes. If the value is not a multiple of the database blocksize, it will be rounded up to a multiple of the database blocksize.

MINEXTENTS

Specifies the number of extents to be allocated when this cluster is created. The minimum and default value is 1.

MAXEXTENTS

Specifies the maximum number of extents that may be allocated for this index. The default will vary according to the database blocksize. Specify UNLIMITED for unlimited expansion.

PCTINCREASE

Specifies the percentage by which each extent will grow over the previous extent. The default is 50, which means that each extent will be one-and-one-half times larger than the previous extent.

FREELISTS

Specifies the number of free lists contained in each freelist group in this index. The default is 1, and the maximum depends on the database blocksize.

FREELIST GROUPS

Specifies the number of groups of free lists for this index. The default is 1. This parameter should be used only with the Parallel Server option running in parallel mode.

INDEX

Specifies that an indexed column is to be created.

HASHKEYS

Creates a hash cluster and specifies the number of hash values for the cluster. If this value is omitted, an indexed cluster will be created by default.

HASH IS

Specifies that a column be used as the hash function for the hash cluster. If this value is omitted, an internal hash function is used.

PARALLEL

Specifies the level of parallelism to be supported, based on the following parameters:

DEGREE

Specifies the degree of parallelism. An integer value specifies how many slave processes can be used. Specify DEFAULT to use the default value for the tablespace.

INSTANCES

Specifies the number of instances that can be used to execute slave processes. Specify DEFAULT to use the default value specified for the tablespace.

NOPARALLEL

Specifies that no parallel operations are to be performed.

CACHE

> Specifies that blocks retrieved from this cluster during full table scans are placed at the beginning of the LRU list. This allows small lookup tables to remain in the SGA.

NOCACHE

> Specifies that blocks retrieved from this cluster during full table scans are placed at the end of the LRU list. This is the default behavior.

Notes

The cluster must be in your schema or you must have the CREATE ANY CLUSTER privilege to issue this command. Clustering can improve database performance and efficiency, since columns in common are stored only once, and data from all tables is normally stored contiguously.

Example

The following example creates a cluster in scott's schema that will allocate 512 bytes per block to cluster keys and allow a maximum of 20 extents for the cluster. All other values will be default:

```
CREATE CLUSTER demo.employee SIZE 512 STORAGE (MAXEXTENTS 20);
```

CREATE CONTROLFILE

```
CREATE CONTROLFILE [REUSE] [SET] DATABASE dbname
   LOGFILE [GROUP integer] (filespec[,[GROUP integer] filespec ...])
      RESETLOGS | NORESETLOGS
   DATAFILE (filespec[,filespec ...])
      [MAXLOGFILES integer]
      [MAXLOGMEMBERS integer]
      [MAXLOGHISTORY integer]
      [MAXDATAFILES integer]
      [MAXINSTANCES integer]
      [ARCHIVELOG | NOARCHIVELOG]
```

Recreates a control file for a specified database (*dbname*), allowing changes to some parameters.

Keywords

REUSE

> Specifies that one or more existing control files specified in the *INIT.ORA* file can be reused and overwritten. If this keyword is omitted and any of the control files named in *INIT.ORA* exist, an error will result.

SET

> Specifies that the supplied *dbname* will be a new name for the database. The database name may be 1–8 characters long and may not be a reserved word.

DATABASE

> Specifies the name of the database. Unless you use the SET command, this must be the current name of the database.

LOGFILE

> Specifies all members of all redo log file groups (each in a GROUP clause), which must all exist.

RESETLOGS

> Specifies that the contents of the log files listed in the LOGFILE clause are to be ignored. Each file listed in the LOGFILE clause must have a SIZE specified.

NORESETLOGS

> Specifies that all files listed in the LOGFILE clause (which must be current redo log files and not restored from backups) should be reused with their original sizes.

DATAFILE

> Specifies the names of all datafiles in the database, which must all exist.

MAXLOGFILES

> Specifies the maximum number of redo log file groups that can be created for the database. The default and maximum values are operating system dependent. This value must be at least 2, and should be at least 3.

MAXLOGMEMBERS

> Specifies the maximum number of copies of a redo log group that may exist in the database. The minimum is 1, and the default and maximum are operating system dependent.

MAXLOGHISTORY

> Specifies the maximum number of archived redo log file groups for automatic media recovery of the Parallel Server. The minimum value is 1, and the default and maximum are operating system dependent.

MAXDATAFILES

> Specifies the maximum number of datafiles that can be created for the database. The minimum is 1, but this value should never be set lower than the largest number of datafiles ever created in the database.

MAXINSTANCES

> Specifies the maximum number of instances that can have the database mounted and open. This parameter applies only to the Parallel Server.

ARCHIVELOG

Specifies that the database will be run in archivelog mode.

NOARCHIVELOG

Specifies that the database will not be run in archivelog mode, and that online redo log files will be reused. This option is the default.

Notes

You must have the OSDBA role enabled to issue this command, and the database must not be mounted. We strongly recommend that the entire database, including control files and redo log files, be backed up before issuing this command.

Example

The following example recreates a control file for the TEST database:

```
CREATE CONTROLFILE REUSE DATABASE TEST
    LOGFILE GROUP 1 ('/disk01/oracle/log1.log','/disk02/oracle/log1.log')
           GROUP 2 ('/disk03/oracle/log2.log','/disk04/oracle/log2.log')
    NORESETLOGS
    DATAFILE '/disk10/oradata/db01.dbs'
    MAXLOGFILES 6
    MAXDATAFILES 128
    ARCHIVELOG
```

CREATE DATABASE

```
CREATE DATABASE [dbname]
    CONTROLFILE [REUSE] (filespec [,filespec. . .])
    LOGFILE [GROUP integer] (filespec[,[GROUP integer] filespec ...])
        [MAXLOGFILES integer]
        [MAXLOGMEMBERS integer]
        [MAXLOGHISTORY integer]
        [MAXDATAFILES integer]
        [MAXINSTANCES integer]
        [ARCHIVELOG | NOARCHIVELOG]
    CHARACTER SET charset
    NATIONAL CHARACTER SET charset
    DATAFILE (filespec autoextend_clause[,filespec [autoextend_clause]...])
```

Creates a database (*dbname*) and specifies parameters associated with it. The database name may be 1 to 8 characters long, and may not be a reserved word.

Keywords

CONTROLFILE

Specifies the names of one or more control files to be used for this database.

REUSE

Specifies that one or more existing control files specified in *INIT.ORA* can be reused and overwritten. If this keyword is omitted and any of the control files named in *INIT.ORA* exists, an error will result. If the parameters specified require that the control file be larger than the current size, the command will fail. Note that this option is not normally used for new database creation.

filespec

Specifies an operating system file or raw partition. The syntax is shown later in the *filespec* section.

LOGFILE

Specifies the names of one or more redo log file GROUPs to be created.

MAXLOGFILES

Specifies the maximum number of redo log file groups that can ever be created for the database. The default and maximum values are operating system dependent. This value must be at least 2, and should be at least 3.

MAXLOGMEMBERS

Specifies the maximum number of copies of a redo log group that may exist in the database. The minimum is 1, and the default and maximum are operating system dependent.

MAXLOGHISTORY

Specifies the maximum number of archived redo log file groups for automatic media recovery of the Parallel Server. The minimum value is 1; the default and maximum are operating system dependent.

MAXDATAFILES

Specifies the maximum number of datafiles that can ever be created for the database. The minimum is 1, but should never be set lower than the largest number of datafiles ever created in the database.

MAXINSTANCES

Specifies the maximum number of instances that can have the database mounted and open. This parameter applies only to the Parallel Server.

ARCHIVELOG

Specifies that the database will be run in archivelog mode, which means that a redo log group must be archived before it can be reused. If the group has not been archived, the database will halt until archiving occurs successfully. This mode is required in order to perform media recovery.

NOARCHIVELOG

Specifies that redo log groups will not be archived, and may be reused immediately by Oracle. This is the default.

CHARACTER SET

Specifies the character set that the database will use to store data. This character set cannot be changed after database creation. The choices and default are operating system dependent.

NATIONAL CHARACTER SET

Specifies the character set that the database will use to store data in NCHAR, NCLOB, and NVARCHAR2 datatypes. This character set cannot be changed after database creation. If this parameter is not specified, it will default to the value specified for CHARACTER SET.

DATAFILE

Specifies the names of all datafiles in the database, which must all exist.

autoextend_clause

Specifies whether a given datafile is able to be automatically extended when it runs out of free space. The syntax is shown in the later *autoextend_clause* section.

filespec

The following is the syntax for *filespec* in the CREATE DATABASE statement:

```
'file_name' [SIZE integer[K | M] ] [REUSE]
```

SIZE

Specifies the size of the file. You can optionally specify K or M for kilobytes (1024) or megabytes (1024 × 1024)

REUSE

Specifies that if the file already exists, it can be used.

autoextend_clause

The following is the syntax for the *autoextend_clause* in the CREATE DATABASE statement:

```
AUTOEXTEND
    {
    OFF |
    ON [NEXT integer[K | M]
        [MAXSIZE {UNLIMITED | integer [K | M] } ]
    }
```

OFF

Turns the AUTOEXTEND feature off.

ON

Turns the AUTOEXTEND feature on.

NEXT

Specifies the size of the next file extent allocated.

MAXSIZE

Specifies the maximum size to which the datafile can grow.

UNLIMITED

Specifies that the datafile size is unlimited or, rather, limited by operating system limits.

Notes

You must have the OSDBA role enabled to issue this command. If any datafiles already exist, their contents will be erased. After completion, this command mounts the database in EXCLUSIVE mode and opens it for use.

Example

The following example creates a new database called TEST:

```
CREATE DATABASE TEST
LOGFILE GROUP 1 ('/disk01/oracle/log1.log','/disk02/oracle/log2.log')
     SIZE 50K,
GROUP 2 ('/disk03/oracle/log2.log','/disk04/oracle/log2.log') SIZE 50K
MAXLOGFILES 5
DATAFILE '/disk10/oradata/system01.dbf' SIZE 50M
MAXDATAFILES 100
ARCHIVELOG
```

CREATE DATABASE LINK

```
CREATE [SHARED] [PUBLIC] DATABASE LINK dblink
   [CONNECT TO {CURRENT USER | username IDENTIFIED BY password}
   [AUTHENTICATED BY username IDENTIFIED BY password]
   USING 'connect string'
```

Creates a database link (*dblink*), which allows access to objects on a remote database; *dblink* must be a valid Oracle object name.

Keywords

SHARED

Specifies that the database link will share a connection through the Multi-Threaded Server.

PUBLIC

Specifies that the database link will be available to all users. If PUBLIC is omitted, the database link is private and is available only to you.

CONNECT TO

Specifies the username and password used to connect to the remote database.

CURRENT USER

Creates a "current user database link" that can only be used by users authenticated globally by the Oracle Security Server.

IDENTIFIED BY

Specifies the *password* for the *username.*

AUTHENTICATED BY

Specifies the *username* and *password* on the remote database, used when a SHARED database link is specified.

USING

Specifies the SQL*Net database specification (*'connect_string'*) for the remote database.

Notes

You must have the CREATE DATABASE LINK privilege to create a private database link. You must have the CREATE PUBLIC DATABASE LINK privilege to create a public database link. In addition, you must have the CREATE SESSION privilege on the remote database, and SQL*Net must be operating on both the local and remote databases.

Examples

The following example creates a public database link to scott's account on the TEST database:

```
CREAT PUBLIC DATABASE LINK testscott
CONNECT TO scott IDENTIFIED BY tiger
USING 'TEST'
```

Any user on the local database may now access any of scott's objects for which they have privileges on the TEST database. For example, to select the emp table on the remote database, specify the following SQL statement:

```
SELECT * FROM emp@testscott
```

CREATE DIRECTORY

```
CREATE [OR REPLACE] DIRECTORY directory_name AS 'path_name'
```

Creates a database directory object (*directory_name*) that is used to store binary large object (BLOB) files.

Keywords

OR REPLACE

Can be used to redefine a directory object. If you use the OR REPLACE function, all grants on the directory object are maintained.

AS *path_name*

> Specifies a valid filesystem directory on the current machine.

Notes

Oracle does not verify that the specified *path_name* exists. Oracle will maintain the value of *path_name* as specified for case-sensitive filesystems.

Example

The following example creates a directory object named blob_dir:

```
CREATE DIRECTORY blob_dir AS '/u01/app/oracle/local/blob_dir'
```

CREATE FUNCTION

```
CREATE [OR REPLACE] FUNCTION [schema.]function_name
[(argument [IN] datatype[,argument [IN] datatype.)]
RETURN datatype {IS | AS}
pl/sql_function_code
```

Creates a standalone function (*function_name*).

Keywords

OR REPLACE

> Specifies that if the function exists, it is to be replaced.

argument

> Specifies the name of an argument to the function.

IN

> Specifies that a value must be supplied for the argument when calling the function.

datatype

> Specifies the datatype of the argument; this can be any PL/SQL datatype.

RETURN

> Specifies the *datatype* (any PL/SQL datatype) of the function code (*pl/sql_ function_code*). You must specify either the IS or AS keyword.

pl/sql_function_code

> Specifies the function code, written in PL/SQL.

Notes

This command creates a function as a standalone object in the specified (or default) schema. To include the function in a package, see the CREATE PACKAGE command. You must have the CREATE PROCEDURE or CREATE ANY PROCEDURE privilege to issue this command.

Example

The following example creates a function named get_balance:

```
CREATE function get_balance (acct VARCHAR2)
    RETURN NUMBER;
    AS
        acct_balance  NUMBER (12,2);
    BEGIN
        SELECT balance
        INTO acct_balance
        FROM account_master
        WHERE account_no = acct;
    RETURN acct_balance;
END;
```

CREATE INDEX

```
CREATE [UNIQUE | BITMAP]  INDEX [schema.]index_name
   ON {[schema.]table_name (column [ASC | DESC][,column [ASC | DESC] ...] |
       CLUSTER [schema.]cluster_name }
   [global_index_clause]
   [local_index_clause]
   [INITRANS integer]
   [MAXTRANS integer]
   [TABLESPACE tablespace_name]
   [STORAGE (
      [INITIAL integer[K | M] ]
      [NEXT integer[K | M] ]
      [MINEXTENTS integer]
      [MAXEXTENTS {integer | UNLIMITED} ]
      [PCTINCREASE integer]
      [FREELISTS integer]
      [FREELIST GROUPS integer]
      ) ]
   [PCTFREE integer]
   [NOSORT | REVERSE]
   [LOGGING | NOLOGGING]
   [UNRECOVERABLE]
```

Creates an index (*index_name*) on one or more columns of a table (*table_name*)
or cluster (*cluster_name*).

Keywords

UNIQUE

Specifies that the index will be unique. That is, every row must have a unique
value across all columns in the index.

BITMAP

Specifies that the index is to be created as a bitmap index; you can specify
ASC (ascending) or DESC (descending) for compatibility with DB2 syntax, but
these have no effect.

CLUSTER

Specifies the cluster for which the index is to be created.

global_index_clause

Specifies that the index is to be a global partitioned index; the syntax is shown later in the *global_index_clause* section.

local_index_clause

Specifies that the index is to be a local partitioned index. The syntax is shown later in the *local_index_clause* section.

INITRANS

Changes the number of transaction entries allocated to each block in the index. The value may be in the range 1–255 and should not normally be changed from the default of 2.

MAXTRANS

Changes the maximum number of concurrent transactions that can update a block of the index. The value may be in the range 1–255 and should not normally be changed from the default, which is a function of the Oracle blocksize.

TABLESPACE

Specifies the name of the tablespace where this index will be stored. If this parameter is omitted, the default tablespace for the schema owner will be used.

STORAGE

Specifies the physical characteristics of the index as follows:

INITIAL

Specifies the size of the first extent for this index in bytes, kilobytes, or megabytes. If the value is not a multiple of the database blocksize, it will be rounded up to a multiple of the database blocksize.

NEXT

Specifies the size of the next extent in bytes, kilobytes, or megabytes. If the value is not a multiple of the database blocksize, it will be rounded up to a multiple of the database blocksize.

MINEXTENTS

Specifies the number of extents to be allocated when this index is created. The minimum and default value is 1.

MAXEXTENTS

Specifies the maximum number of extents that may be allocated for this index. The default will vary according to the database blocksize. Specify UNLIMITED for unlimited expansion.

PCTINCREASE

Specifies the percentage by which each extent will grow over the previous extent. The default is 50, which means that each extent will be one-and-one-half times larger than the previous extent.

FREELISTS

Specifies the number of free lists contained in each freelist group in this index. The default is 1 and the maximum depends on the database block-size.

FREELIST GROUPS

Specifies the number of groups of free lists for this index. The default is 1. This parameter should be used only with the Parallel Server option running in parallel mode.

PCTFREE

Changes the percentage of space in each data block that will be kept free for future updates to this index. The value may be in the range 0–99 and defaults to 10.

NOSORT

Specifies that rows have been inserted into the database in sequential order, thus, no sorting is required when creating the index. NOSORT cannot be specified with REVERSE.

REVERSE

Specifies that Oracle will store the bytes of the index key in reverse order. This is useful in situations where rows are always added in increasing order to allow the index to grow evenly rather than only at one end. It is also useful in a Parallel Server environment, allowing individual instances to insert information in different blocks, thus reducing pinging. REVERSE cannot be specified with NOSORT.

LOGGING (Oracle8 only)

Specifies that redo log records be written during index creation.

NOLOGGING (Oracle8 only)

Specifies that redo log records not be written during index creation. In case of a database failure, the index cannot be recovered by applying log files, and must be recreated. This option will speed the creation of indexes.

UNRECOVERABLE (Oracle7 only)

Specifies that redo log records not be written during index creation. In the case of a database failure, the index cannot be recovered by applying log files, and must be recreated. This option will speed the creation of indexes.

global_index_clause

The following is the syntax for the *global_index_clause* in the CREATE INDEX statement. Parameters not already described in this section are described following the syntax.

```
GLOBAL PARTITION BY RANGE (column_list)
(PARTITION [partition_name] VALUES LESS THAN (value_list)
  [TABLESPACE tablespace_name]
  [LOGGING | NOLOGGING]
  [INITRANS integer]
  [MAXTRANS integer]
  [STORAGE (
      [INITIAL integer[K | M] ]
      [MINEXTENTS integer]
      [MAXEXTENTS {integer | UNLIMITED} ]
      [PCTINCREASE integer]
      [FREELISTS integer]
      [FREELIST GROUPS integer]
      ) ] )
```

PARTITION

Specifies the partition (*partition_name*) for this index.

VALUES LESS THAN

Specifies the upper bound for the new partition. The *value_list* is a comma-separated, ordered list of literal values which must collate greater than the partition bound for the highest existing partition in the table.

local_index_clause

The following is the syntax for the *local_index_clause* in the CREATE INDEX statement. For an explanation of the parameters, refer to the descriptions earlier in this section.

```
LOCAL
(
  [PARTITION [partition_name]
  [TABLESPACE tablespace_name]
  [LOGGING | NOLOGGING]
  [INITRANS integer]
  [MAXTRANS integer]
  [STORAGE (
      [INITIAL integer[K | M] ]
      [MINEXTENTS integer]
      [MAXEXTENTS {integer | UNLIMITED} ]
      [PCTINCREASE integer]
      [FREELISTS integer]
      [FREELIST GROUPS integer]
      ) ]
  ] )
```

Notes

The index must be in your schema, or you must have the CREATE ANY INDEX privilege and the INDEX privilege on the table to be indexed to issue this command. If storage options are omitted, Oracle will allocate storage for the index as follows:

- If the indexed table has no rows, the default storage values for the tablespace will be used.

- If the indexed table has rows and the resulting index can be contained in no more than 25 data blocks, a single extent will be allocated for this index.

- If the indexed table has rows and the resulting index is more than 25 data blocks, 5 equal-size extents will be allocated for this index.

Example

The following example creates an index on the empno and ename columns of scott's emp table, with the indicated storage parameters:

```
CREATE INDEX emp_ndx ON scott.emp(empno,ename)
    STORAGE (INITIAL 50K NEXT 10K PCTINCREASE 0 MAXEXTENTS 10)
    TABLESPACE users
    PCTFREE 20
```

CREATE LIBRARY

```
CREATE [OR REPLACE ]  LIBRARY [schema.] library_name {IS | AS} 'filespec'
```

Defines a library (*library_name*) to hold external stored procedures. You must specify the IS or AS keyword.

Keywords

filespec
> Specifies an operating system file or raw partition. The syntax is:

> ```
> 'file_name' [SIZE integer[K | M] ] [REUSE]
> ```

> *SIZE*
>> Specifies the size of the file. You can optionally specify K or M for kilobytes (1024) or megabytes (1024×1024).

> *REUSE*
>> Specifies that if the file already exists, it can be used.

Notes

You must have the CREATE LIBRARY system privilege to create a library database object in your schema. You must have the CREATE ANY LIBRARY system privilege to create a library database object in another schema.

Example

The following example creates a library named "carnegie":

```
CREATE LIBRARY carnegie AS '/u01/app/oracle/local/carnegie.so'
```

CREATE PACKAGE

```
CREATE [OR REPLACE] PACKAGE [schema.]package_name
{IS | AS}
pl/sql_package_spec
```

Creates the specification for a stored package (*package_name*).

Keywords

OR REPLACE
> Specifies that if the package exists, it is to be replaced.

pl/sql_package_spec
> The package specification, written in PL/SQL. You must specify the IS or AS keyword.

Notes

This command creates only the package specification. You must use the CREATE PACKAGE BODY command to create the package body. You must have the CREATE PROCEDURE or CREATE ANY PROCEDURE privilege to issue this command.

Example

The following example creates the package specification for my_pkg:

```
CREATE PACKAGE my_pkg AS
    FUNCTION getbal (sale_amt NUMBER, acct VARCHAR2)
        RETURN NUMBER;
    PROCEDURE drop_acct (acct VARCHAR2);
    PROCEDURE add_credit (add_amt NUMBER, acct VARCHAR2);
END my_pkg;
```

CREATE PACKAGE BODY

```
CREATE [OR REPLACE] PACKAGE BODY [schema.]package_name
{IS | AS}
pl/sql_package_body
```

Creates the body for a stored package (*package_name*).

Keywords

OR REPLACE
> Specifies that if the package body exists, it is to be replaced.

pl/sql_package_body
> The package body, written in PL/SQL. You must specify the IS or AS keyword.

Notes

This command creates only the package body. You must use the CREATE PACKAGE command to create the package specification. You must have the CREATE PROCEDURE or CREATE ANY PROCEDURE privilege to issue this command.

CREATE PROCEDURE

```
CREATE [OR REPLACE] PROCEDURE [schema.]procedure_name
[(argument [IN | OUT | IN OUT] datatype[,argument [IN | OUT | IN OUT] datatype.)]
{IS | AS}
pl/sql_subprogram
```

Creates a standalone stored procedure (*procedure_name*).

Keywords

OR REPLACE
> Specifies that if the procedure exists, it is to be replaced.

argument
> Specifies the name of an argument to the procedure.

IN
> Specifies that a value must be supplied for *argument* when calling the procedure.

OUT
> Specifies that the procedure will pass a value for *argument* back to the calling environment.

IN OUT
> Specifies that a value must be supplied for *argument* when calling the procedure, and that the procedure will pass a value for *argument* back to the calling environment.

pl/sql_subprogram
> Specifies the procedure code, written in PL/SQL. You must specify either the IS or AS keyword.

Notes

This command creates a procedure as a standalone object in the specified or default schema. To include the procedure in a package, see the CREATE PACKAGE command. You must have the CREATE PROCEDURE or CREATE ANY PROCEDURE privilege to issue this command.

Example

The following example creates a procedure named "post" in scott's schema:

```
CREATE PROCEDURE scott.post (acct IN NUMBER, amt IN NUMBER)
AS BEGIN
    UPDATE account_master
    SET bal = bal + amt
    WHERE account_no = acct;
END;
```

CREATE PROFILE

```
CREATE PROFILE profile_name LIMIT
    [SESSIONS_PER_USER {integer | UNLIMITED | DEFAULT} ]
    [CPU_PER_SESSION {integer | UNLIMITED | DEFAULT} ]
    [CPU_PER_CALL {integer | UNLIMITED | DEFAULT} ]
    [CONNECT_TIME {integer | UNLIMITED | DEFAULT} ]
    [IDLE_TIME {integer | UNLIMITED | DEFAULT}]
    [LOGICAL_READS_PER_SESSION {integer | UNLIMITED | DEFAULT} ]
    [LOGICAL_READS_PER_CALL {integer | UNLIMITED | DEFAULT} ]
    [PRIVATE_SGA {integer[K | M] | UNLIMITED | DEFAULT} ]
    [COMPOSITE_LIMIT {integer | UNLIMITED | DEFAULT} ]
    [FAILED_LOGIN_ATTEMPTS {integer | UNLIMITED | DEFAULT} ]
    [PASSWORD_LIFE_TIME {integer | UNLIMITED | DEFAULT} ]
    [PASSWORD_LOCK_TIME {integer | UNLIMITED | DEFAULT} ]
    [PASSWORD_GRACE_TIME {integer | UNLIMITED | DEFAULT} ]
    [PASSWORD_REUSE_TIME {integer | UNLIMITED | DEFAULT} ]
    [PASSWORD_REUSE_MAX {integer | UNLIMITED | DEFAULT} ]
    [PASSWORD_VERIFY_FUNCTION {function | NULL | DEFAULT} ]
```

Creates a profile (*profile_name*) to set limits on database resources. For many of the following keywords, you can specify:

UNLIMITED

Specifying this value means that no limit will be imposed on this resource.

DEFAULT

Specifying this value means that the limit specified in the DEFAULT profile will be used for this resource.

Keywords

SESSIONS_PER_USER

Limits the number of concurrent sessions for a user.

CPU_PER_SESSION

Limits the amount of CPU time (in hundredths of a second) that can be used in a session.

CPU_PER_CALL

Limits the amount of CPU time (in hundredths of a second) for a parse, execute, or fetch call.

CONNECT_TIME

Limits the total elapsed time (in minutes) for a session.

IDLE_TIME

Limits the amount of continuous inactive time (in minutes) during a session.

LOGICAL_READS_PER_SESSION

Limits the number of database blocks read in a session, including those read from memory and disk.

LOGICAL_READS_PER_CALL

Limits the number of database blocks read for a parse, execute, or fetch call.

PRIVATE_SGA

Limits the amount of memory (in bytes) a session can allocate in the shared pool of the SGA.

COMPOSITE_LIMIT

Limits the total resource cost (in service units) for a session. See ALTER RESOURCE COST, earlier in this chapter, for additional information.

FAILED_LOGIN_ATTEMPTS

Limits the number of failed login attempts allowed before the account is locked.

PASSWORD_LIFE_TIME

Limits the lifetime of the password. The value is specified in fractions of a day.

PASSWORD_LOCK_TIME

Specifies the number of days for which the account will be locked after failed login attempts.

PASSWORD_GRACE_TIME

Specifies the number of days after the password has expired within which the user must change the password.

PASSWORD_REUSE_TIME

Specifies the minimum number of days before a password can be reused. If this value is set, PASSWORD_REUSE_MAX must be unlimited.

PASSWORD_REUSE_MAX

Specifies the number of password changes that must occur before the current password can be reused. If this value is set, the parameter PASSWORD_REUSE_TIME must be unlimited.

PASSWORD_VERIFY_FUNCTION

Specifies the name of a function that will validate a new password. The function must be owned by SYS.

Notes

You must have the CREATE PROFILE privilege to issue this command. To apply the limits associated with the profile to a specific user, you must assign the profile to the user with the CREATE USER or ALTER USER command. In addition, resource limits must be enabled either via the *INIT.ORA* parameter RESOURCE_LIMIT, or by using the ALTER SYSTEM command.

The parameters that support password aging are specified in days. You can specify a fraction of a day by using standard fraction notation. For example, you can use 1/24 to specify an hour.

Example

The following example defines a limit of 5 concurrent sessions and 10 minutes of inactivity to the profile:

```
CREATE PROFILE admin
    SESSIONS_PER_USER  5
    IDLE_TIME  10
```

CREATE ROLE

```
CREATE ROLE role_name
   {NOT IDENTIFIED |
    IDENTIFIED BY password |
    IDENTIFIED EXTERNALLY |
    IDENTIFIED GLOBALLY
    }
```

Creates a role (*role_name*), which is a set of privileges that can be granted to users.

Keywords

NOT IDENTIFIED

Specifies that a user granted the role does not need to be verified when enabling it.

IDENTIFIED BY

Specifies that a *password* must be provided when enabling the role.

IDENTIFIED EXTERNALLY

Specifies that the operating system verifies the user enabling the role.

IDENTIFIED GLOBALLY

Specifies that the Oracle Security Service verifies the user enabling the role.

Notes

You must have the CREATE ROLE privilege to issue this command. When you create a role, you are automatically granted that role WITH ADMIN OPTION, which allows you to grant or revoke the role, or to modify it using the ALTER ROLE command.

Example

The following example creates a role called "manager" and assigns the password "dilbert" to the role:

```
ALTER ROLE manager IDENTIFIED BY dilbert
```

CREATE ROLLBACK SEGMENT

```
CREATE [PUBLIC] ROLLBACK SEGMENT segment_name
   TABLESPACE tablespace_name
   [STORAGE (
      [INITIAL integer[K | M] ]
      [NEXT integer[K | M] ]
      [MINEXTENTS integer[K | M] ]
      [MAXEXTENTS {integer | UNLIMITED} ]
      [PCTINCREASE integer]
      [FREELISTS integer]
      [FREELIST GROUPS integer] ]
      [OPTIMAL {integer[K | M] | NULL} ]
   ) ]
```

Creates a rollback segment (*segment_name*), which is used by Oracle to store data necessary to roll back changes made by transactions.

Keywords

PUBLIC
   Specifies that this rollback segment is available to any instance. If PUBLIC is omitted, it is only available to the instance naming it in the ROLLBACK_SEGMENTS parameter in the *INIT.ORA* file.

TABLESPACE
   Specifies the tablespace (*tablespace_name*) where this rollback segment will be created.

STORAGE
   Specifies the physical characteristics of the rollback segment as follows:

   INITIAL
      Specifies the size of the first extent for this rollback segment in bytes, kilobytes, or megabytes. If this value is not a multiple of the database blocksize, it will be rounded up to a multiple of the database blocksize.

NEXT

Specifies the size of the next extent in bytes, kilobytes, or megabytes. If this value is not a multiple of the database blocksize, it will be rounded up to a multiple the of database blocksize.

MINEXTENTS

Specifies the number of extents to be allocated when this rollback segment is created. The minimum number of extents for a rollback segment is 2, and this is the default.

MAXEXTENTS

Specifies the maximum number of extents that may be allocated for this rollback segment. The default will vary according to the database blocksize. Specify UNLIMITED for unlimited expansion.

PCTINCREASE

Specifies the percentage by which each extent will grow over the previous extent. The default is 50, which means that each extent will be one-and-one-half times larger than the previous extent. It is recommended that rollback segments use a PCTINCREASE value of 0, in order to allocate equal-size extents. Beginning with Oracle8, the PCTINCREASE parameter cannot be specified, and defaults to a value of 0.

FREELISTS

Specifies the number of free lists contained in each freelist group in this rollback segment. The default is 1, and the maximum depends on the database blocksize.

FREELIST GROUPS

Specifies the number of groups of free lists for this rollback segment. The default is 1. This parameter should be used only with the Parallel Server option running in parallel mode.

OPTIMAL

Specifies the optimal size for this rollback segment. Oracle will attempt to maintain this size by deallocating unused extents. The default is NULL, which means that no deallocation will ever take place.

Notes

You must have the CREATE ROLLBACK SEGMENT privilege to issue this command. The tablespace must be online for you to create a rollback segment in it. When it is created, the rollback segment will be offline and must be brought online by using the ALTER ROLLBACK SEGMENT statement or restarting the database with the rollback segment named in the *INIT.ORA* file.

Example

The following example creates a rollback segment rbs02:

```
CREATE ROLLBACK SEGMENT rbs02
    TABLESPACE rollback
    STORAGE (INITIAL 40K NEXT 40K PCTINCREASE 0)
```

CREATE SCHEMA

```
CREATE SCHEMA AUTHORIZATION schema
    [CREATE TABLE command]
    [CREATE VIEW command]
    [SQL_TRACE = {TRUE | FALSE} ]
    [GRANT command]
```

Creates multiple tables and views and performs multiple grants in a single transaction.

Keywords

CREATE TABLE

A CREATE TABLE command (described later in this chapter).

CREATE VIEW

A CREATE VIEW command (described later in this chapter).

SQL_TRACE

Controls whether performance statistics will be generated. The initial value is set in the *INIT.ORA* file.

GRANT

A GRANT command (described later in this chapter).

Notes

You must have the same privileges required for the CREATE TABLE, CREATE VIEW, and GRANT commands in order to issue this command. Individual commands within the CREATE SCHEMA command must not be terminated with the SQL termination character.

Example

The following example creates a schema for scott consisting of a table and a view, and grants privileges on the view to a role:

```
CREATE SCHEMA AUTHORIZATION scott
CREATE TABLE dept (
       deptno      NUMBER NOT NULL,
       dname       VARCHAR2(20),
       location    VARCHAR2(15),
       avg_salary  number  (9,2))
```

```
CREATE VIEW deptview AS SELECT deptno,dname,location FROM dept
GRANT SELECT ON deptview to non_admin
```

CREATE SEQUENCE

```
CREATE SEQUENCE [schema.]sequence_name
    [INCREMENT BY integer]
    [START WITH integer]
    [MAXVALUE {integer | NOMAXVALUE} ]
    [MINVALUE {integer | NOMINVALUE} ]
    [CYCLE | NOCYCLE]
    [CACHE integer | NOCACHE]
    [ORDER | NOORDER]
```

Creates an Oracle sequence which can be used to automatically generate sequential numbers during database operations.

Keywords

INCREMENT BY

Specifies the increment between sequence numbers, and can be positive or negative, but not 0. The default is 1.

START WITH

Specifies the first sequence number to be generated. The default is the MINVALUE for ascending sequences, and the MAXVALUE for descending sequences.

MAXVALUE

Specifies the largest value the sequence number can reach. The default is NOMAXVALUE, which sets the maximum value at 10^{27}.

MINVALUE

Specifies the smallest value the sequence number can reach. The default is NOMINVALUE, which sets the minimum value at 1.

CYCLE

Specifies that when sequence numbers reach MAXVALUE, they will begin again at MINVALUE. The default is NOCYCLE.

NOCYCLE

Specifies that after reaching the maximum value no additional sequence numbers will be generated.

CACHE

Specifies how many sequence numbers Oracle will pregenerate and keep in memory. Note that when the database is shut down, unused sequence numbers stored in the cache are lost. The default is 20.

NOCACHE

Specifies that no sequence numbers are pregenerated to memory.

ORDER

Specifies that sequence numbers are guaranteed to be issued in order of request. The default is NOORDER.

NOORDER

Specifies that sequence numbers are not guaranteed to be generated in the order of request.

Notes

You must have the CREATE SEQUENCE privilege to issue this command. The generation of a sequence number is not affected by the subsequent rollback of the transaction; once generated, that sequence number will not be available again, so gaps can occur. Sequence numbers are accessed by using the pseudocolumns CURRVAL and NEXTVAL.

Example

The following example creates a sequence ord_seq so that the next sequence number generated will be 101, and order will be guaranteed. The sequence will reach a maximum value of 9999, then recycle to 1:

```
ALTER SEQUENCE ord_seq
    START WITH 101
    MINVALUE 1
    CYCLE
    ORDER
```

CREATE SNAPSHOT

```
CREATE SNAPSHOT [schema.]snapshot_name
    [PCTFREE integer]
    [PCTUSED integer]
    [INITRANS integer]
    [MAXTRANS integer]
    [LOGGING | NOLOGGING]
    [CACHE | NOCACHE]
    [CLUSTER cluster_name (clustercolumnlist) ]
    [TABLESPACE tablespace_name]
    [STORAGE (
        [INITIAL integer[K | M] ]
        [NEXT integer[K | M] ]
        [MINEXTENTS integer[K | M] ]
        [MAXEXTENTS {integer | UNLIMITED} ]
        [PCTINCREASE integer]
        [FREELISTS integer]
        [FREELIST GROUPS integer]
        ) ]
```

```
     [NOPARALLEL]
     [PARALLEL ( {DEGREE {integer | DEFAULT} | INSTANCES {integer | DEFAULT} } ) ]
     [USING INDEX
        [TABLESPACE tablespace_name]
        [PCTFREE integer]
        [INITRANS integer]
        [MAXTRANS integer]
        [STORAGE (
            [INITIAL integer[K | M] ]
            [NEXT integer[K | M] ]
            [MINEXTENTS integer]
            [MAXEXTENTS {integer | UNLIMITED} ]
            [PCTINCREASE integer]
            [FREELISTS integer]
            [FREELIST GROUPS integer]
           ) ]
      ]
   [REFRESH
       [FAST | COMPLETE | FORCE]
       [START WITH date]
       [NEXT date]
       [WITH PRIMARY KEY]
       [WITH ROWID]
       [USING DEFAULT [MASTER | LOCAL ] ROLLBACK SEGMENT]
       [USING [MASTER | LOCAL] ROLLBACK SEGMENT rollback_segment]
   ]
[FOR UPDATE ] AS snapshot_query
```

Creates a snapshot (*snapshot_name*), which is the result of a query run against one or more tables or views.

Keywords

PCTFREE

Specifies the percentage of space to be reserved in each data block for future updates to rows contained in that block. Valid values are 0–99, and the default value is 10.

PCTUSED

Specifies the minimum percentage of space that will be maintained as used in each data block. The value may be in the range 1–99, and the default value is 40.

INITRANS

Specifies the initial number of transaction entries allocated to each block.

MAXTRANS

Specifies the maximum number of transaction entries allocated to each block.

LOGGING

Specifies that all changes to the snapshot are logged in the redo logs. This is the default.

NOLOGGING

Specifies that changes to the snapshot are not logged. This improves performance, but requires that the snapshot be recreated from the base tables in the event that the database must be rebuilt.

CACHE

Specifies that full table scans of the snapshot will be placed at the front of the LRU list. This is useful for small lookup or dimension tables.

NOCACHE

Specifies that full table scans of the snapshot will not place data blocks at the start of the LRU list. This is the default.

CLUSTER

Specifies that the snapshot is to be created in the specified cluster (*cluster_name*). Since the cluster has its own storage specifications, do not use the STORAGE clauses with the CLUSTER clause.

TABLESPACE

Specifies the name of the tablespace in which this snapshot will be created. The default is the default tablespace for the schema owner.

STORAGE

Specifies the physical characteristics of the snapshot as follows:

INITIAL

Specifies the size of the first extent for this snapshot in bytes, kilobytes, or megabytes. If this value is not a multiple of the database blocksize, it will be rounded up to a multiple of the database blocksize.

NEXT

Specifies the size of the next extent in bytes, kilobytes, or megabytes. If this value is not a multiple of the database blocksize, it will be rounded up to a multiple of the database blocksize.

MINEXTENTS

Specifies the number of extents to be allocated when this snapshot is created. The minimum and default value is 1.

MAXEXTENTS

Specifies the maximum number of extents that may be allocated for this snapshot. The default will vary according to the database blocksize. Specify UNLIMITED for unlimited expansion.

PCTINCREASE

Specifies the percentage by which each extent will grow over the previous extent. The default is 50, which means that each extent will be one-and-one-half times larger than the previous extent.

FREELISTS

Specifies the number of free lists contained in each freelist group in this snapshot. The default is 1 and the maximum depends on the database blocksize.

FREELIST GROUPS

Specifies the number of groups of free lists for this snapshot. The default is 1. This parameter should be used only with the Parallel Server option running in parallel mode.

NOPARALLEL

Specifies that no parallel processing will be supported for the snapshot.

PARALLEL

Specifies the level of parallelism to be supported, based on the following parameters:

DEGREE

Specifies the degree of parallelism. An integer value specifies how many slave processes can be used. Specify DEFAULT to use the default value for the tablespace.

INSTANCES

Specifies the number of instances that can be used to execute slave processes. Specify DEFAULT to use the default value specified for the tablespace.

USING INDEX

Specifies the storage parameters for the index that Oracle uses to maintain the snapshot. The TABLESPACE (TABLESPACE *tablespace_name*) and STORAGE parameters have the meanings shown earlier in the keyword list for the snapshot.

REFRESH

Specifies the mode and times for automatic refreshes. FAST uses the snapshot log associated with the master table; COMPLETE refreshes by reexecuting the snapshot's query; FORCE is the default, and means that Oracle will either decide that a FAST refresh is possible or do a COMPLETE refresh.

START WITH

Specifies a date for the next automatic refresh time, using a standard Oracle date expression.

NEXT

Specifies a new date expression for calculating the interval between automatic refreshes.

WITH PRIMARY KEY

Specifies that the snapshot is created as a primary key snapshot. That is, Oracle keeps track of the changes by using the primary key rather than ROWID. This allows the master table to be reorganized without impacting the ability to perform a fast refresh.

WITH ROWID

Specifies that the snapshot is created as a ROWID snapshot. This is for compatibility with Oracle 7.3.

USING DEFAULT ROLLBACK SEGMENT

Specifies the rollback segment to be used as a default if a rollback segment is not explicitly supplied. Select either MASTER (use the default rollback segment at the remote master for the individual snapshot) or LOCAL (use the default rollback segment for the local refresh group that contains the snapshot).

USING ROLLBACK SEGMENT rollback_segment

Specifies the rollback segment to use when refreshing the snapshot. Specify either MASTER (the rollback segment to be used at the remote master for the individual snapshot) or LOCAL (the rollback segment to be used for the local refresh group that contains the snapshot).

FOR UPDATE

Allows the simple snapshot to be updated. If used with Oracle8 replication, the changes will be propagated back to the master database.

AS snapshot_query

Provides the actual SQL query used to populate the snapshot, and is subject to the same restrictions as a view.

Notes

You must have the CREATE SNAPSHOT privilege to create a snapshot in your own schema, or the CREATE ANY SNAPSHOT privilege to create a snapshot in another schema. In addition, you must have sufficient privileges to create a table, view, and index, since these are created as part of the snapshot creation process, and the owner of the schema containing the snapshot must have appropriate privileges to execute the snapshot's query.

The script *dbmssnap.sql* must have been run by SYS to create the SNAPSHOT package before attempting to create a snapshot.

Since Oracle appends 7-character identifiers to the snapshot name when creating snapshot objects in the schema, you should limit the snapshot name to 27 characters or less.

Example

The following example creates a snapshot of scott's emp table, which is located on a server called UK. The snapshot will be populated tomorrow and then every seven days from today:

```
CREATE SNAPSHOT uk_emp
    REFRESH COMPLETE
    START WITH SYSDATE+1
    NEXT SYSDATE+7
    AS SELECT * FROM scott.emp@UK
```

CREATE SNAPSHOT LOG

```
CREATE SNAPSHOT LOG ON [schema.]table_name
    [PCTFREE integer]
    [PCTUSED integer]
    [INITRANS integer]
    [MAXTRANS integer]
    [TABLESPACE tablespace_name]
    [STORAGE (
        [INITIAL integer[K | M] ]
        [NEXT integer[K | M] ]
        [MINEXTENTS integer[K | M] ]
        [MAXEXTENTS {integer | UNLIMITED} ]
        [PCTINCREASE integer]
        [FREELISTS integer]
        [FREELIST GROUPS integer]
        ) ]
```

Creates a snapshot log (*table_name*), a table associated with the master table of a snapshot and used to control refreshes of snapshots.

Keywords

PCTFREE

Specifies the percentage of space to be reserved in each data block for future updates to rows contained in that block. Valid values are 0–99, and the default value is 10.

PCTUSED

Specifies the minimum percentage of space that will be maintained as used in each data block. Valid values are 1–99, and the default value is 40.

INITRANS

Specifies the initial number of transaction entries allocated to each block.

MAXTRANS

Specifies the maximum number of transaction entries allocated to each block.

TABLESPACE

Specifies the name of the tablespace in which this snapshot log will be created. The default is the default tablespace for the schema owner.

STORAGE

Specifies the physical characteristics of the snapshot log as follows:

INITIAL

Specifies the size of the first extent for this snapshot log in bytes, kilobytes, or megabytes. If this value is not a multiple of the database blocksize, it will be rounded up to a multiple of the database blocksize.

NEXT

Specifies the size of the next extent in bytes, kilobytes, or megabytes. If this value is not a multiple of the database blocksize, it will be rounded up to a multiple of the database blocksize.

MINEXTENTS

Specifies the number of extents to be allocated when this snapshot log is created. The minimum and default value is 1.

MAXEXTENTS

Specifies the maximum number of extents that may be allocated for this snapshot log. The default will vary according to the database blocksize. Specify UNLIMITED for unlimited expansion.

PCTINCREASE

Specifies the percentage by which each extent will grow over the previous extent. The default is 50, which means that each extent will be one-and-one-half times larger than the previous extent.

FREELISTS

Specifies the number of free lists contained in each freelist group in this snapshot log. The default is 1, and the maximum depends on the database blocksize.

FREELIST GROUPS

Specifies the number of groups of free lists for this snapshot. The default is 1. This parameter should be used only with the Parallel Server option running in parallel mode.

Note

You must have privileges sufficient to create a table in the master table's schema to issue this command.

Example

The following example creates a snapshot log on scott's emp table:

```
CREATE SNAPSHOT LOG ON scott.emp
    STORAGE (INITIAL 50K NEXT 50K PCTINCREASE 0)
    TABLESPACE USERS
```

CREATE SYNONYM

```
CREATE [PUBLIC]SYNONYM synonym_name
    FOR [schema.]object_name[@dblink]
```

Creates a public or private synonym (*synonym_name*) for a database object.

Keywords

PUBLIC

Specifies that this synonym will be available to all users. If PUBLIC is omitted, the synonym will be available only to the schema owner.

FOR object_name

Specifies the name of the object to which the synonym will refer. It may include a reference to a remote database by appending *@dblink*.

Notes

You must have the CREATE SYNONYM privilege to create a private synonym in your own schema, and CREATE ANY SYNONYM to create a synonym in another schema. You must have the CREATE PUBLIC SYNONYM privilege to create a public synonym. Oracle will resolve object names in the schema first, so a public synonym will only be used if the object name is not prefaced with a schema name or followed by *@dblink* and if the object name does not exist in the current schema.

Example

The following example creates a public synonym for scott's emp table on the UK database:

```
CREATE PUBLIC SYNONYM uk_emps
FOR scott.emp@UK
```

CREATE TABLE

```
CREATE TABLE [schema.]table_name
    (
    [table_constraint_clause]
    [table_ref_clause]
    [column datatype [DEFAULT expression]
        [column_ref_clause] [column_contraint_clause] ]
    )
```

```
{
[CLUSTER (column[,column ...]]
[ORGANIZATION INDEX index_organization_clause ]
[ORGANIZATION HEAP [segment_attrib_clause] ]
[segment_attrib_clause]
}
[partition_clause]
[PARALLEL ( {DEGREE {integer | DEFAULT} | INSTANCES {integer | DEFAULT} } ) ]
[NOPARALLEL]
[ENABLE
 {
   ALL TRIGGERS
   UNIQUE (column[, column...] [CASCADE]
   PRIMARY KEY [CASCADE]
   CONSTRAINT constraint_name
 }]
[DISABLE
 {
   ALL TRIGGERS
   UNIQUE (column[, column...] [CASCADE]
   PRIMARY KEY [CASCADE]
   CONSTRAINT constraint_name
 }]
[AS subquery]
[CACHE | NOCACHE]
```

Creates a table (*table_name*) either by specifying the structure or by referencing an existing table.

Keywords

table_constraint_clause

Specifies a table constraint; the syntax is shown in the later *table_constraint_clause* section.

table_ref_clause

Allows you to specify additional information about a column of type REF. The syntax is shown in the later *table_ref_clause* section.

column_ref_clause

Allows you to specify additional information about a column of type REF. The syntax is shown in the later *column_ref_clause* section.

column_constraint_clause

Adds or removes a column constraint; the syntax is shown in the later *column_constraint_clause* section.

CLUSTER

Specifies that the table is to be created in the specified cluster.

ORGANIZATION INDEX

Specifies that the table is to be an indexed organized table.

index_organization_clause

Specifies how the indexed organized table is to be created. The syntax is shown in the later *index_organization_clause* section.

ORGANIZATION HEAP

Specifies that the table is a tradition table. The table will default to ORGANIZATION HEAP if an organization is not specified.

segment_attrib_clause

Specifies the storage characteristics of the table; the syntax is shown in the later *segment_attrib_clause* section.

partition_clause

Specifies the partition key and the various partitions; the syntax is shown in the later *partition_clause* section.

PARALLEL

Specifies the level of parallelism to be supported, based on the following parameters:

DEGREE

Specifies the degree of parallelism. An integer value specifies how many slave processes can be used. Specify DEFAULT to use the default value for the tablespace.

INSTANCES

Specifies the number of instances that can be used to execute slave processes. Specify DEFAULT to use the default value specified for the tablespace.

NOPARALLEL

Specifies that no parallel processing will be supported for the table.

ENABLE ALL TRIGGERS

Enables all triggers associated with the table.

ENABLE UNIQUE

Enables the UNIQUE constraint on the specified columns.

ENABLE PRIMARY KEY

Enables the integrity constraints on the table's primary key.

ENABLE CONSTRAINT

Enables the named integrity constraint.

CASCADE

Specifies that all other constraints that depend on the enabled constraints should also be enabled.

DISABLE

Disables a single constraint or ALL TRIGGERS. See ENABLE for specific keywords.

AS

Specifies a *subquery* to be used to insert rows into the table upon creation. If column definitions are omitted from the CREATE TABLE statement, the column names, datatypes, and constraints will be copied from the table referenced in the *subquery.*

CACHE

Specifies that blocks retrieved from this table during full table scans are placed at the beginning of the least-recently-used (LRU) list. This allows small lookup tables to remain in the SGA.

NOCACHE

Specifies that blocks retrieved from this table during full table scans are placed at the end of the LRU list. This is the default behavior.

table_constraint_clause

The following is the syntax for the *table_constraint_clause* in the CREATE TABLE statement:

```
{
[NULL | NOT NULL] |
[UNIQUE | PRIMARY KEY] |
[FOREIGN KEY (column [, column ...] )] |
[REFERENCES [schema.]table_name[(column)] [ON DELETE CASCADE] ]
[CHECK (condition) ]
}
[USING INDEX
    [PCTFREE integer]
    [PCTUSED integer]
    [INITRANS integer]
    [MAXTRANS integer]
    [TABLESPACE tablespace_name]
    [STORAGE (
        [INITIAL integer [K | M]]
        [NEXT integer [K | M]]
        [MINEXTENTS integer [K | M]]
        [MAXEXTENTS {integer | UNLIMITED}]
        [PCTINCREASE integer]
        [FREELISTS integer]
        [FREELIST GROUPS integer]
        )
    [NOSORT]
    [LOGGING | NOLOGGING]
]
[EXCEPTIONS INTO [schema.]table_name]
[{ENABLE [VALIDATE  | NOVALIDATE] | DISABLE} ]
```

```
[[NOT] DEFERRABLE [INITIALLY {IMMEDIATE | DEFERRED}] ]
[[INITIALLY {IMMEDIATE | DEFERRED}] [[NOT] DEFERRABLE] ]
```

NULL

Specifies that the values in the column list may contain NULL.

NOT NULL

Specifies that the values in the column may not contain NULL.

UNIQUE

Specifies that the column list must be unique.

PRIMARY KEY

Specifies that the column list will be a primary key. A primary key can be referenced from another table with a foreign key. A primary key must also be UNIQUE and NOT NULL.

FOREIGN KEY

Requires that all values in the column list must be either NULL or found in the referenced table's defined primary key or the specified column list.

REFERENCES

Specifies the table that is referenced.

ON DELETE CASCADE

Specifies that any deletes to the referenced table are propagated down to this table through the foreign key.

CHECK

Allows you to specify an expression that a column value must satisfy.

USING INDEX

Specifies physical characteristics of the index created to support the UNIQUE or PRIMARY KEY constraint. The index will always be created.

PCTFREE

Specifies the percentage of space to be reserved in each data block for future updates to rows contained in that block. Valid values are 0–99, and the default value is 10.

PCTUSED

Specifies the minimum percentage of space that will be maintained as used in each data block. Valid values are 1–99, and the default value is 40.

INITRANS

Specifies the initial number of transaction entries allocated to each block.

MAXTRANS

Specifies the maximum number of transaction entries allocated to each block. Specify UNLIMITED for unlimited expansion.

TABLESPACE

Specifies the name of the tablespace where this object will be stored. If omitted, the default tablespace for the schema owner will be used.

STORAGE

Specifies the physical storage characteristics of this object. For keyword descriptions, see the STORAGE clause described earlier for this command.

NOSORT

Specifies that rows have been inserted into the database in sequential order; thus, no sorting is required when creating the index.

LOGGING

Specifies that redo log records will be written during index creation.

NOLOGGING

Specifies that redo log records will not be written during index creation. In case of a database failure, the index cannot be recovered by applying log files, and must be recreated. This option will speed the creation of indexes.

EXCEPTIONS INTO

Specifies the table to list the ROWIDs that violate the constraint at the time the constraint is enabled.

ENABLE

Specifies that the constraint is to be enabled at creation time.

VALIDATE

Specifies that all existing rows (and all new rows) must conform to the constraint at the time that it is enabled.

NOVALIDATE

Specifies that all new rows must conform to the constraint once it is enabled. Oracle will not verify that existing rows conform.

DISABLE

Specifies that the constraint is to be defined, but not initially enabled.

DEFERRABLE

Specifies that DML statements can be executed that violate the constraint as long as the constraint is enforceable by the time of the commit.

NOT DEFERRABLE

Specifies that the constraint is checked with each DML statement.

INITIALLY IMMEDIATE

Specifies that even though the constraint can be deferred, it is initially not deferred.

INITIALLY DEFERRED

Specifies for deferrable constraints that the constraint is deferred initially.

table_ref_clause

The following is the syntax for the *table_ref_clause* in the CREATE TABLE statement:

```
[SCOPE FOR ( [ref_column | ref_attribute] )
IS [schema.]scope_table_name]
[REF ( [ref_column | ref_attribute] ) WITH ROWID ]
```

SCOPE FOR ... IS

Restricts the scope of the *ref_column* or *ref_attribute* to *scope_table_name*.

REF ... WITH ROWID

References a row in an object table.

column_ref_clause

The following is the syntax for the column_ref_clause in the CREATE TABLE statement:

```
[WITH ROWID] [SCOPE IS [schema.]scope_table_name]
```

WITH ROWID

Stores the ROWID with the REF in the table. This usually results in better performance, but uses more space.

SCOPE IS

Restricts the scope of the *ref_column* or *ref_attribute* to *scope_table_name*.

column_constraint_clause

The following is the syntax for the *column_constraint_clause* in the CREATE TABLE statement. See the description of the keywords in the *table_constraint_clause* section.

```
{
[NULL | NOT NULL] |
[UNIQUE | PRIMARY KEY] |
[FOREIGN KEY (column[, column ...])]
[REFERENCES [schema.]table_name[(column)] [ON DELETE CASCADE] ]
[CHECK (condition)]
}
[USING INDEX
    [PCTFREE integer]
    [PCTUSED integer]
    [INITRANS integer]
    [MAXTRANS integer]
    [TABLESPACE tablespace_name]
    [STORAGE (
        [INITIAL integer [K | M]]
        [NEXT integer [K | M]]
```

```
        [MINEXTENTS integer [K | M]]
        [MAXEXTENTS {integer | UNLIMITED}]
        [PCTINCREASE integer]
        [FREELISTS integer]
        [FREELIST GROUPS integer]
        )
    [NOSORT]
    [LOGGING | NOLOGGING]
]
[EXCEPTIONS INTO [schema.]table_name]
[{ENABLE [VALIDATE  | NOVALIDATE] | DISABLE} ]
[[NOT] DEFERRABLE [INITIALLY {IMMEDIATE | DEFERRED}] ]
[[INITIALLY {IMMEDIATE | DEFERRED}] [[NOT] DEFERRABLE] ]
```

index_organization_clause

The following is the syntax for the *index_organization_clause* in the CREATE TABLE statement:

```
[segment_attrib_clause]
[PCTTHRESHOLD integer] [INCLUDING column] OVERFLOW [segment_attrib_clause]
```

PCTTHRESHOLD

Specifies the maximum percent of an index block that any one row can use. Larger rows are forced into the OVERFLOW area. Allowable values are between 0 and 50.

INCLUDING

Specifies the column after which the row is split when forced into the OVERFLOW area. The column must be the last column in the primary key or any column after the primary key.

OVERFLOW

Specifies the storage attributes of the OVERFLOW area.

segment_attrib_clause

The following is the syntax for the *segment_attrib_clause* in the CREATE TABLE statement:

```
        [PCTFREE integer]
        [PCTUSED integer]
        [INITRANS integer]
        [MAXTRANS integer]
        [TABLESPACE tablespace_name]
        [LOGGING | NOLOGGING]
        [STORAGE (
            [INITIAL integer[K | M] ]
            [MINEXTENTS integer]
            [MAXEXTENTS {integer | UNLIMITED} ]
            [PCTINCREASE integer]
            [FREELISTS integer]
            [FREELIST GROUPS integer]
            ) ]
```

PCTFREE

Specifies the percentage of space to be reserved in each data block for future updates to rows contained in that block. Valid values are 0–99, and the default value is 10.

PCTUSED

Specifies the minimum percentage of space that will be maintained as used in each data block. Valid values are 1–99, and the default value is 40.

INITRANS

Specifies the initial number of transaction entries allocated to each block.

MAXTRANS

Specifies the maximum number of transaction entries allocated to each block.

TABLESPACE

Specifies the tablespace for the table.

LOGGING

Specifies that the operation is to be logged to the redo logs.

NOLOGGING

Specifies that nothing is to be written to the redo logs for this operation.

STORAGE

Specifies the physical characteristics of the table as follows:

INITIAL

Specifies the size of the first extent for this table in bytes, kilobytes, or megabytes. If this value is not a multiple of the database blocksize, it will be rounded up to a multiple of the database blocksize.

NEXT

Specifies the size of the next extent in bytes, kilobytes, or megabytes. If this value is not a multiple of the database blocksize, it will be rounded up to a multiple of the database blocksize.

MINEXTENTS

Specifies the number of extents to be allocated when this table is created. The minimum and default value is 1.

MAXEXTENTS

Specifies the maximum number of extents that may be allocated for this table. The default will vary according to the database blocksize. Specify UNLIMITED for unlimited expansion.

PCTINCREASE

Specifies the percentage by which each extent will grow over the previous extent. The default is 50, which means that each extent will be one-and-one-half times larger than the previous extent.

FREELISTS

> Specifies the number of free lists contained in each freelist group in this table. The default is 1 and the maximum depends on the database block-size.

FREELIST GROUPS

> Specifies the number of groups of free lists for this table. The default is 1. This parameter should be used only with the Parallel Server option running in parallel mode.

partition_clause

The following is the syntax for the *partition_clause* in the CREATE TABLE statement:

```
PARTITION BY RANGE (column_list)
( PARTITION [partition_name] VALUES LESS THAN (value_list)
[segment_attrib_clause] )
```

PARTITION BY RANGE

> Specifies the columns (in the *column_list*) used to partition the table.

PARTITION

> Specifies the partition name.

VALUES LESS THAN

> > Specifies the values that all rows in the partition must be less than. Specify the keyword MAXVALUE to indicate that there is no maximum value.

Notes

You must have the CREATE TABLE privilege to create a table in your own schema, or the CREATE ANY TABLE privilege to create a table in any other schema. The schema owner must have either sufficient space quota on the tablespace where the table will be created, or the UNLIMITED TABLESPACE privilege.

Examples

The following example creates a new table dept in scott's schema:

```
CREATE TABLE scott.dept (
    DEPTNO  NUMBER(2) NOT NULL,
    DNAME   VARCHAR2(14),
    LOC     VARCHAR(15))
    TABLESPACE USERS
    STORAGE (INIITIAL 40K NEXT 4K PCTINCREASE 0)
    PCTFREE 15
```

The following example creates a copy of scott's emp table:

```
CREATE TABLE test_emp
    AS SELECT * FROM scott.emp
```

CREATE TABLESPACE

```
CREATE TABLESPACE tablespace_name
    DATAFILE 'filename' [SIZE integer[K | M]] [REUSE] [autoextend_clause]
    [DEFAULT STORAGE (
        [INITIAL integer[K | M] ]
        [NEXT integer[K | M] ]
        [MINEXTENTS integer]
        [MAXEXTENTS {integer | UNLIMITED} ]
        [PCTINCREASE integer]
        [FREELISTS integer]
        [FREELIST GROUPS integer]
        ) ]
    [ONLINE | OFFLINE ]
    [MINIMUM EXTENT integer[K | M] ]
    [PERMANENT | TEMPORARY]
    [LOGGING | NOLOGGING]
```

Creates a new tablespace (*tablespace_name*), optionally specifying default storage characteristics for objects subsequently created in the tablespace.

Keywords

DATAFILE

Specifies the name of the operating system datafile for this tablespace. SIZE is required unless the file already exists, in which case the REUSE keyword must be specified.

autoextend_clause

Specifies whether a given datafile is able to be automatically extended when it runs out of free space. The syntax is shown in the later *autoextend_clause* section.

DEFAULT STORAGE

Specifies the physical characteristics of the objects subsequently created in this tablespace that do not specify their own storage parameters, as follows:

INITIAL

Specifies the size of the first extent for this tablespace in bytes, kilobytes, or megabytes. If this value is not a multiple of the database blocksize, it will be rounded up to a multiple of the database blocksize.

NEXT

Specifies the size of the next extent in bytes, kilobytes, or megabytes. If this value is not a multiple of the database blocksize, it will be rounded up to a multiple of the database blocksize.

MINEXTENTS

Specifies the number of extents to be allocated when this tablespace is created. The minimum and default value is 1.

MAXEXTENTS

Specifies the maximum number of extents that may be allocated for this tablespace. The default will vary according to the database blocksize. Specify UNLIMITED for unlimited expansion.

PCTINCREASE

Specifies the percentage by which each extent will grow over the previous extent. The default is 50, which means that each extent will be one-and-one-half times larger than the previous extent.

FREELISTS

Specifies the number of free lists contained in each freelist group in this tablespace. The default is 1, and the maximum depends on the database blocksize.

FREELIST GROUPS

Specifies the number of groups of free lists for this tablespace. The default is 1. This parameter should be used only with the Parallel Server option running in parallel mode.

ONLINE

Brings the tablespace online after creation. This is the default.

OFFLINE

Leaves the tablespace offline after creation.

MINIMUM EXTENT

Forces every extent created to be the size specified or a multiple of the size specified. This reduces fragmentation.

PERMANENT

The default value. Allows permanent objects to be created in the tablespace.

TEMPORARY

Specifies that no permanent objects can be stored in the tablespace. Oracle will then find a more efficient access method when using the tablespace for temporary segments.

LOGGING

Specifies the default value of LOGGING for objects created in the tablespace. This default value can be overridden for each object when the object is created.

NOLOGGING

Specifies the default value of NOLOGGING for objects created in the tablespace. This default value can be overridden for each object when the object is created. A value of NOLOGGING indicates that certain operations to the object are not logged to the redo log. This is a performance gain, but leaves the object vulnerable in the event that the tablespace has to be recovered.

autoextend_clause

The following is the syntax for the *autoextend_clause* in the CREATE TABLESPACE statement:

```
AUTOEXTEND
    {
    OFF |
    ON [NEXT integer[K | M]
        [MAXSIZE {UNLIMITED | integer[K | M] } ]
    }
```

OFF

Turns the AUTOEXTEND feature off.

ON

Turns the AUTOEXTEND feature on.

NEXT

Specifies the size of the next file extent allocated.

MAXSIZE

Specifies the maximum size to which the datafile can grow.

UNLIMITED

Specifies that the datafile size is unlimited or, rather, limited by operating system limits.

Notes

You must have the CREATE TABLESPACE privilege to issue this command. At least one rollback segment (other than the SYSTEM rollback segment) must exist before this command may be issued.

Example

The following example creates a new 25-megabyte tablespace called "users":

```
CREATE TABLESPACE users
    DATAFILE '/disk09/oracle/oradata/users02.dbf' SIZE 25M
    DEFAULT STORAGE (INITIAL 500K NEXT 50K PCTINCREASE 0)
```

CREATE TRIGGER

```
CREATE [OR REPLACE]  TRIGGER [schema.]triggername
  {
  BEFORE {INSERT | DELETE | UPDATE [OF column[,column ...]} |
  AFTER {INSERT | DELETE | UPDATE [OF column[,column ...]} |
  INSTEAD OF {INSERT | DELETE | UPDATE [OF column[,column ...]} |
  }
  ON [schema.]table_name
  [REFERENCING {OLD [AS] old | NEW [AS] new}
  [FOR EACH ROW [WHEN (condition) ]]
  pl/sql_block
```

Creates a trigger (*trigger_name*), a stored PL/SQL block associated with a table that is automatically executed when a particular SQL statement is executed against that table.

Keywords

OR REPLACE

Specifies that if the trigger already exists, it is to be replaced.

BEFORE

Specifies that this trigger is to be fired before executing the triggering statement.

AFTER

Specifies that this trigger is to be fired after executing the triggering statement.

INSTEAD OF

Specifies that this trigger is to fire instead of the INSERT, UPDATE, or DELETE statement. Use this construct when you want to modify a view that is not normally modifiable.

INSERT

Specifies that this trigger is to be fired whenever an INSERT statement adds a row to the table.

DELETE

Specifies that this trigger is to be fired whenever a DELETE statement removes a row from the table.

UPDATE

Specifies that this trigger is to be fired whenever an UPDATE statement changes the value in one of the columns specified in the OF clause. If the OF clause is omitted, an UPDATE to any column will cause the trigger to fire.

ON

Specifies the name of the table (*table_name*) and optional *schema* on which the trigger is to be created.

REFERENCING

Specifies correlation names, which allow the PL/SQL block to refer to old and new values of the current row. The default values are OLD as *old* and NEW as *new.*

FOR EACH ROW

Specifies that this trigger is to be a row trigger fired once for each row that is affected by the triggering mechanism and that meets the conditions of the WHEN clause.

WHEN condition

Specifies a SQL condition that must be true in order to fire the trigger.

pl/sql_block

The PL/SQL block that will be executed when the trigger fires. This block may not contain COMMIT, ROLLBACK, or SAVEPOINT commands.

Notes

You must have the CREATE TRIGGER privilege to create a trigger on a table in your own schema, and you must have the CREATE ANY TRIGGER privilege to create a trigger on a table in any other schema. The SQL script *dbmsstdx.sql* must have been run by SYS prior to issuing this command.

Example

The following example creates a trigger that inserts a row into a table each time an INSERT, DELETE, or UPDATE performed on scott's emp table results in a salary increase:

```
CREATE TRIGGER scott.empaud
   BEFORE INSERT OR UPDATE OF sal
   ON scott.emp
   FOR EACH ROW WHEN (new.sal <> old.sal)
   DECLARE
      empno    number(6);
      oldsal   number(7.2);
      newsal   number(7.2);
   BEGIN
   /* First get the old salary and empno */
      SELECT empno,sal
      INTO empno,oldsal
      FROM scott.emp
      WHERE empno = :old.empno;
   /* Now write the record */
      INSERT INTO track_sal_changes
      VALUES (empno,oldsal);
   END;
```

CREATE USER

```
CREATE USER username
   [IDENTIFIED (BY password | EXTERNALLY | GLOBALLY} ]
   [DEFAULT TABLESPACE tablespace_name[
   [TEMPORARY TABLESPACE tablespace_name[
   [QUOTA [integer[K | M] | UNLIMITED] ON tablespace_name[
   [PROFILE profile_name]
   [DEFAULT ROLE {
      role_name[,role_name ...] |
      ALL [EXCEPT role_name[,role_name ...] ] |
      NONE
      }
   [PASSWORD EXPIRE]
   [ACCOUNT {LOCK | UNLOCK}
```

Creates a new database user (*username*); assigns security and storage properties.

Keywords

IDENTIFIED BY

Specifies that the *password* indicated must be provided when connecting as the user enabling the role.

IDENTIFIED EXTERNALLY

Specifies that the operating system validates the user enabling the role.

IDENTIFIED GLOBALLY

Specifies that the Oracle Security Service verifies the user enabling the role.

DEFAULT TABLESPACE

Changes the name of the tablespace that will be used by default when this user creates a database object.

TEMPORARY TABLESPACE

Changes the name of the tablespace that will be used for the creation of temporary segments for operations, like sorting, that require more memory than is available.

QUOTA

Specifies the amount of space that this user is permitted to use for object storage in the specified tablespace. UNLIMITED means there is no storage limit, subject to the total size of the tablespace.

PROFILE

Changes the user's profile to *profile_name*, which subjects the user to the limits specified in that profile.

DEFAULT ROLE

Specifies the roles (*role_name...*) assigned to the user as default roles. ALL means that all roles granted to the user will be default except those specified in the EXCEPT clause; NONE means that none of the roles granted to the user will be default roles.

PASSWORD EXPIRE

Causes the userid's password to be pre-expired. It must be reset before the user can connect to the database.

ACCOUNT LOCK

Causes the account to be created in a locked mode and disabled. The account must be unlocked with the ALTER USER ... ACCOUNT UNLOCK command.

ACCOUNT UNLOCK

Causes the account to be created in an unlocked mode. This is the default.

Notes

You must have the CREATE USER privilege to issue this command. If the user is authenticated EXTERNALLY, the *username* must be prefixed by the current *INIT. ORA* parameter OS_AUTHENT_PREFIX and must match an operating system account name.

Examples

The following example creates a new user scott:

```
CREATE USER scott IDENTIFIED BY tiger
    DEFAULT TABLESPACE users
    TEMPORARY TABLESPACE TEMP
    QUOTA 500K ON users
```

The following example creates the same user, but the account is authenticated by the operating system:

```
CREATE USER ops$scott IDENTIFIED EXTERNALLY
    DEFAULT TABLESPACE users
    TEMPORARY TABLESPACE TEMP
    QUOTA 500K ON users
```

CREATE VIEW (Object)

```
CREATE [OR REPLACE] [FORCE | NO FORCE] VIEW [schema.]view_name
OF [schema.]type_name
[WITH OBJECT OID [DEFAULT | (attribute)] ]
AS viewquery
[WITH READ ONLY]
[WITH CHECK OPTION [CONSTRAINT constraint]]
```

Creates an object view (*view_name*).

Keywords

OR REPLACE

Specifies that if the view already exists, it is to be replaced.

FORCE

Specifies that the view is to be created regardless of whether the view's base tables exist or whether the owner of the schema has privileges on them.

NO FORCE

Specifies that the view is to be created only if the base tables exist and the owner of the schema has privileges on them. This is the default.

OF

Specifies the object type (*type_name*) (and optional *schema*) of the view.

WITH OBJECT OID

Specifies the attributes of the object type that will be used to uniquely identified the rows in the object view. If this clause is omitted, the values default to the primary key of the base object table.

> *DEFAULT*
>
> Specifies that the OBJECT OID should default to the primary key of the base object view. This is equivalent to not including the WITH OBJECT OID clause at all.

> *attribute*
>
> List of columns in the view from which the object identifier is to be created.

AS viewquery

Any SQL SELECT statement without an ORDER BY or FOR UPDATE clause.

WITH READ ONLY

Specifies that the view cannot be used for inserts and updates.

WITH CHECK OPTION

Specifies that inserts and updates performed through the view must result in rows that the view query can select.

> *CONSTRAINT*
>
> Specifies a name for the CHECK OPTION constraint. The default is a system-assigned name in the form SYS_C*n*, where *n* is an integer resulting in a unique name.

Notes

You must have the CREATE VIEW privilege to create a view in your own schema, or you must have CREATE ANY VIEW to create a view in another schema. You must have the Oracle8 Object option installed to create an object view.

The owner of the schema containing the view must have the privileges required to perform requested operations on the tables or views upon which this view is based. These privileges must be granted directly, not through a role.

CREATE VIEW (Relational)

```
CREATE [OR REPLACE] [FORCE | NO FORCE] VIEW [schema.]view_name
[(alias[,alias ...]]
AS viewquery
[WITH READ ONLY]
[WITH CHECK OPTION [CONSTRAINT constraint]]
```

Creates a relational view (*view_name*).

Keywords

OR REPLACE

Specifies that if the view already exists, it is to be replaced.

FORCE

Specifies that the view is to be created regardless of whether the view's base tables exist or whether the owner of the schema has privileges on them.

NO FORCE

Specifies that the view is to be created only if the base tables exist and the owner of the schema has privileges on them. This is the default.

alias

One or more aliases that correspond to columns or expressions returned by the *viewquery*.

AS viewquery

Any SQL SELECT statement without an ORDER BY or FOR UPDATE clause.

WITH READ ONLY

Specifies that the view cannot be used for inserts and updates.

WITH CHECK OPTION

Specifies that inserts and updates performed through the view must result in rows that the *viewquery* can select.

CONSTRAINT

Specifies a name for the CHECK OPTION constraint. The default is a system-assigned name in the form SYS_Cn, where n is an integer resulting in a unique name.

Notes

You must have the CREATE VIEW privilege to create a view in your own schema, or you must have CREATE ANY VIEW to create a view in another schema. The owner of the schema containing the view must have the privileges required to perform requested operations on the tables or views upon which this view is based. These privileges must be granted directly, not through a role.

Example

The following example creates a view emploc:

```
CREATE OR REPLACE VIEW emploc
    (empno,lname,location) AS
SELECT empno,ename,loc
    FROM scott.emp,scott.dept
    WHERE emp.deptno = dept.deptno
```

DROP CLUSTER

```
DROP CLUSTER [schema.]cluster_name
    [INCLUDING TABLES]
    [CASCADE CONSTRAINTS]
```

Removes a cluster (*cluster_name*) from the database.

Keywords

INCLUDING TABLES
    Specifies that all tables belonging to the cluster are to be dropped.

CASCADE CONSTRAINTS
    Specifies that all referential integrity constraints from tables outside the cluster that refer to primary and unique keys in the tables of this cluster are to be dropped.

Notes

The cluster to be dropped must be in your schema or you must have the DROP ANY OBJECT privilege to remove an object from another schema.

Example

The following example removes a cluster and all the tables it contains from the database:

```
DROP CLUSTER demotables INCLUDING TABLES
```

DROP DATABASE LINK

```
DROP [PUBLIC] DATABASE LINK dblink
```

Removes a database link (*dblink*) from the database.

Keyword

PUBLIC

 Must be specified to drop a public database link.

Notes

The database link to be dropped must be in your schema, or you must have the
DROP PUBLIC DATABASE LINK privilege to remove a public database link.

Example

The following example removes the public database link emp_UK from the database:

```
DROP PUBLIC DATABASE LINK emp_UK
```

DROP DIRECTORY

```
DROP DIRECTORY directory_name
```

Removes the definition of a directory (*directory_name*) used to hold BLOB
objects.

Notes

You must have the DROP ANY DIRECTORY system privilege to execute this command.

Example

The following example shows how to drop the directory database object blob_
directory:

```
DROP DIRECTORY blob_directory;
```

DROP FUNCTION

```
DROP FUNCTION [schema.]function_name
```

Removes a function (*function_name*) from the database.

Note

The function to be dropped must be in your schema, or you must have the DROP
ANY PROCEDURE privilege to remove a function from another schema.

Example

The following example removes the function salcalc from the database:

```
DROP FUNCTION salcalc
```

DROP INDEX

```
DROP INDEX [schema.]index_name
```

Removes an index (*index_name*) from the database.

Note

The index to be dropped must be in your schema, or you must have the DROP ANY INDEX privilege to remove an object from another schema.

Example

The following example removes the index empno_ndx from scott's schema in the database. When an index is dropped, all of the space it previously occupied is returned to the free space pool:

```
DROP INDEX scott.empno_ndx
```

DROP LIBRARY

```
DROP LIBRARY [schema.]library_name
```

Drops an external procedure library (*library_name*) from the database.

Note

You must have the DROP ANY LIBRARY system privilege to drop a library owned by another schema.

Example

The following example drops the library "carnegie":

```
DROP LIBRARY carnegie
```

DROP PACKAGE

```
DROP PACKAGE [BODY][schema.]package_name
```

Removes a package (*package_name*) from the database.

Keyword

BODY

> Specifies that only the package body is to be dropped. If this keyword is omitted, both the package body and specification will be removed.

Note

The package to be dropped must be in your schema, or you must have the DROP ANY PROCEDURE privilege to remove a package from another schema.

Example

The following example removes the package salcalc from the database:

```
DROP PACKAGE salcalc
```

DROP PROCEDURE

```
DROP PROCEDURE [schema.]procedure_name
```

Removes a procedure (*procedure_name*) from the database.

Note

The procedure to be dropped must be in your schema, or you must have the DROP ANY PROCEDURE privilege to remove a procedure from another schema.

Example

The following example removes the procedure give_raise from the database:

```
DROP PROCEDURE give_raise
```

DROP PROFILE

```
DROP PROFILE profile_name [CASCADE]
```

Removes a profile (*profile_name*) from the database.

Keyword

CASCADE

> Specifies that this profile is to be deassigned from all users to whom it is assigned, and replaced with the DEFAULT profile.

Notes

You must have the DROP PROFILE privilege to remove a profile. You cannot remove the DEFAULT profile.

Example

The following example removes the admin profile from the database: '

```
DROP PROFILE admin
```

DROP ROLE

```
DROP ROLE role_name
```

Removes a role (*role_name*) from the database.

Note

You must have been granted the role via the WITH ADMIN OPTION, or you must have the DROP ANY ROLE privilege to remove a role.

Example

The following example removes the operator role from the database:

```
DROP ROLE operator
```

DROP ROLLBACK SEGMENT

```
DROP ROLLBACK SEGMENT segment_name
```

Removes a rollback segment (*segment_name*) from the database.

Notes

You must have the DROP ROLLBACK SEGMENT privilege to issue this command. The rollback segment must be taken offline using the ALTER ROLLBACK SEGMENT command before it can be dropped. When it is dropped, all space used by the rollback segment is returned to the free space pool.

Example

The following example removes the rollback segment RBS02 from the database:

```
DROP ROLLBACK SEGMENT RBS02
```

DROP SEQUENCE

```
DROP SEQUENCE [schema.]sequence_name
```

Removes a sequence (*sequence_name*) from the database.

Notes

The sequence to be dropped must be in your schema, or you must have the DROP ANY SEQUENCE privilege to remove a sequence from another schema.

This command can be combined with CREATE SEQUENCE to restart a sequence at a lower number.

Example

The following example removes the sequence order_seq from the scott schema in the database:

```
DROP SEQUENCE scott.order_seq
```

DROP SNAPSHOT

```
DROP SNAPSHOT [schema.]snapshot_name
```

Removes a snapshot (*snapshot_name*) from the database.

Notes

The snapshot to be dropped must be in your schema, or you must have the DROP ANY SNAPSHOT privilege to remove a snapshot from another schema. Note that if you drop the master table, the snapshot is not automatically dropped.

Example

The following example removes the snapshot emp_UK from the database:

```
DROP SNAPSHOT emp_UK
```

DROP SNAPSHOT LOG

```
DROP SNAPSHOT LOG ON [schema.]table_name
```

Removes a snapshot log from the database, where *table_name* is the name of the master table associated with the snapshot log to be dropped.

Notes

The master table must be in your schema, or you must have the DROP ANY TABLE, DROP ANY INDEX, and DROP ANY TRIGGER privileges to remove a snapshot log from another schema.

Example

The following example removes the snapshot log associated with scott's emp table from the database:

```
DROP SNAPSHOT LOG ON scott.emp
```

DROP SYNONYM

```
DROP [PUBLIC] SYNONYM [schema.]synonym_name
```

Removes a public or private synonym (*synonym_name*) from the database.

Keyword

PUBLIC
   Specifies that the synonym to be dropped is a public synonym.

Notes

The synonym to be dropped must be in your schema, or you must have the DROP ANY SYNONYM privilege to remove a synonym from another schema or the DROP ANY PUBLIC SYNONYM privilege to remove a public synonym.

Example

The following example removes the public synonym employee from the database:

```
DROP PUBLIC SYNONYM employee
```

DROP TABLE

```
DROP TABLE [schema.]table_name
   CASCADE CONSTRAINTS
```

Removes a table (*table_name*) from the database.

Keyword

CASCADE CONSTRAINTS
   Specifies that all referential integrity constraints that refer to primary and unique keys in the table to be dropped will also be dropped.

Notes

The table to be dropped must be in your schema, or you must have the DROP ANY TABLE privilege to remove a table from another schema. When you drop a table, all rows are deleted and any indexes on the table are automatically deleted, regardless of what schema created or owns them. If the table to be dropped is a base table for a view, or if it is referenced in any stored procedure, the view or procedure will be marked invalid, but not dropped. If the table is the master table for a snapshot, the snapshot is not dropped, and if the table has a snapshot log, that snapshot log is not dropped.

Example

The following example removes scott's emp table from the database:

```
DROP TABLE scott.emp
```

DROP TABLESPACE

```
DROP TABLESPACE tablespace_name
   [INCLUDING CONTENTS] [CASCADE CONSTRAINTS]
```

Removes a tablespace (*tablespace_name*) from the database.

Keywords

INCLUDING CONTENTS

Specifies that any objects contained in this tablespace are to be automatically dropped. If this keyword is not included and any objects exist in the tablespace, the command will fail.

CASCADE CONSTRAINTS

Specifies that any referential integrity constraints from tables outside this tablespace that refer to primary and unique keys in the tables of this tablespace will be dropped.

Note

You must have the DROP TABLESPACE privilege to remove a tablespace from the database.

Example

The following example removes the trial_and_error tablespace and all objects it contains from the database:

```
DROP TABLESPACE trial_and_error INCLUDING CONTENTS
```

DROP TRIGGER

```
DROP TRIGGER [schema.]trigger_name
```

Removes a trigger (*trigger_name*) from the database.

Note

The trigger to be dropped must be in your schema, or you must have the DROP ANY TRIGGER privilege, to remove a trigger from another schema.

Example

The following example removes the inventory_low trigger from the database:

```
DROP TRIGGER inventory_low
```

DROP USER

```
DROP USER username [CASCADE]
```

The DBA's favorite command, this statement removes a user (*username*) from the database.

Keyword

CASCADE
   Specifies that all objects in the user's schema will be dropped before removing the user. This keyword must be specified if the user schema contains any objects.

Notes

You must have the DROP USER privilege to remove a user from the database. Note that if you specify the CASCADE option, any referential integrity constraints on tables in other schemas that refer to primary and unique keys on tables in this schema will also be dropped. If tables or other database objects in this schema are referred to by views, synonyms, or stored procedures, functions, or packages in another schema, those referring objects will be marked invalid but not dropped.

Example

The following example removes the user debby and the contents of her schema from the database:

```
DROP USER debby CASCADE
```

DROP VIEW

```
DROP VIEW [schema.]view_name
```

Removes a view (*view_name*) from the database.

Note

The view to be dropped must be in your schema, or you must have the DROP ANY VIEW privilege to remove a view from another schema.

Example

The following example removes scott's emploc view from the database:

```
DROP VIEW scott.emploc
```

EXPLAIN PLAN

```
EXPLAIN PLAN
   SET STATEMENT_ID = 'text'
   [INTO [schema.]table_name[@dblink]]
   FOR sql_statement
```

Creates an explanation of the execution plan for a SQL statement.

Keywords

SET STATEMENT_ID

Specifies a text string (*'text'*) to be used to identify the result of this EXPLAIN PLAN statement. The default is NULL.

INTO

Specifies the location of the PLAN_TABLE (*table_name*). If you omit *schema*, the default is a PLAN_TABLE in your own schema. Specify *@dblink* to indicate a remote database.

FOR sql_statement

Specifies the SQL statement for which the plan is to be generated.

Notes

You must have the INSERT privilege on the destination table (specified by INTO) before issuing this command. The destination table is usually called PLAN_TABLE, and can be created by running the script *utlxplan.sql*. The value specified in the SET clause will appear in the STATEMENT_ID column of the destination table.

Example

The following example generates an execution plan for the SQL statement listed. The output will be placed in the PLAN_TABLE table in the current schema:

```
EXPLAIN PLAN
   SET STATEMENT_ID = 'Plan1'
   FOR
   SELECT ename,sal,comm,loc
   FROM emp,dept
   WHERE emp.deptno=dept.deptno
```

GRANT (Object Privileges)

```
GRANT {object_priv [(column_list) ][,object_priv [ (column_list) ]...] |
   ALL [PRIVILEGES] }
   {
   ON [schema.]object_name |
   ON DIRECTORY directory_name
   }
   TO {username | role | PUBLIC}
   [WITH GRANT OPTION]
```

Grants privileges on a database object to one or more users or roles.

Keywords

object_priv
> Specifies the name of the object privilege to be granted. Valid privileges are: ALTER, DELETE, EXECUTE, INDEX, INSERT, REFERENCES, SELECT, and UPDATE. ALL PRIVILEGES grants all privileges for the object that have been granted to the grantor.

column_list
> Specifies one or more columns in the object to which the object privilege applies.

object_name
> Specifies the name of the object on which privileges are being granted.

DIRECTORY
> Specifies an Oracle8 directory (*directory_name*) to be granted.

username
> Specifies the name of the user to whom the object privilege will be granted.

role
> Specifies the name of a role to which the object privilege will be granted.

PUBLIC
> Specifies that the object privilege will be granted to all current and future users.

WITH GRANT OPTION
> Specifies that the grantee of the privilege can grant the privilege to others.

Note

The object must be in your schema or you must have been granted the object privileges via the WITH GRANT OPTION.

Example

The following example grants INSERT and UPDATE privileges on scott's emp table to debby:

```
GRANT insert,update ON scott.emp TO debby
```

GRANT (System Privilege or Role)

```
GRANT {privilege | role][,[privilege | role] ...}
    TO {username | role_name | PUBLIC[,[username | role_name | PUBLIC] ...}
    [WITH ADMIN OPTION]
```

Grants a system privilege or role to one or more users or roles.

Keywords

privilege

Specifies a system privilege to be granted.

role

Specifies a role to be granted.

TO username

Specifies the name of a user who is granted a privilege or role.

TO role_name

Specifies the name of a role that is granted a privilege or role.

PUBLIC

Specifies that the granted privilege or role is to be granted to all users, including those not yet created.

WITH ADMIN OPTION

Specifies that the grantee of the privilege or role can grant the privilege or role to others, and may alter or drop the role.

Note

You must have the GRANT ANY PRIVILEGE privilege or have been granted the privilege or role WITH ADMIN OPTION to issue this command.

Example

The following example grants the account_admin role to scott and debby:

```
GRANT account_admin TO scott,debby
```

The following example grants CREATE USER and DROP USER privileges to the dba_assist role:

```
GRANT create user, drop user TO dba_assist
```

NOAUDIT

```
NOAUDIT {statement_opt | system_priv}[,{statement_opt | system_priv ...}
   [BY username[,username ...]
   [WHENEVER [NOT] SUCCESSFUL]
```

Stops auditing defined by a prior AUDIT statement.

Keywords

statement_opt
> Specifies a statement option for which auditing is to be stopped.

system_priv
> Specifies a system privilege for which auditing is to be stopped.

BY username
> Stops auditing only for SQL statements issued by a *username* in this list. The default is all users.

WHENEVER SUCCESSFUL
> Stops auditing only for SQL statements that complete successfully. If NOT is specified, auditing is stopped only for SQL statements that result in an error. If this clause is omitted, auditing is stopped for all SQL statements, successful or not.

Note

You must have the AUDIT ANY privilege to issue this command.

Example

The following example stops auditing of INSERT and DELETE statements issued by scott on the emp table:

```
NOAUDIT INSERT,DELETE ON scott.emp
```

RENAME

```
RENAME oldname TO newname
```

Changes the name of an existing table, view, sequence, or private synonym from *oldname* to *newname*.

Notes

The object to be renamed must be in your schema. Integrity constraints, indexes, and grants on the old object are automatically transferred to the new object. Objects that depend on the renamed object (e.g., views, synonyms, stored procedures, or functions) will be marked invalid.

Example

The following example changes the name of the emp table to employees:

```
RENAME emp TO employees
```

REVOKE (Object Privileges)

```
REVOKE {object_priv[,object_priv ...] | ALL [PRIVILEGES] }
    ON [schema.]object_name
    TO {username | role | PUBLIC}
```

Revokes privileges on a database object (*object_name*) for one or more users (*username*) or roles (*role*).

Keywords

object_priv

> Specifies the name of the object privilege to be revoked. Valid privileges are: ALTER, DELETE, EXECUTE, INDEX, INSERT, REFERENCES, SELECT, and UPDATE. ALL PRIVILEGES revokes all privileges granted for this object.

PUBLIC

> Specifies that the object privilege will be revoked for all current and future users.

Notes

The object must be in your schema or you must have been granted the object privileges via the WITH GRANT OPTION. If you revoke a privilege from a user who has granted that privilege to others, the revoke is cascaded, so the privilege is revoked from the other user.

Example

The following example revokes INSERT and UPDATE privileges from scott's emp table:

```
REVOKE insert,update ON scott.emp
```

REVOKE (System Privilege or Role)

```
REVOKE {privilege | role][,[privilege | role] ...}
    FROM {username | role_name | PUBLIC[,[username | role_name | PUBLIC] ...}
```

Removes a system privilege or role from one or more users or roles.

Keywords

privilege
> Specifies the name of a system privilege to be revoked.

role
> Specifies the name of a role to be revoked.

username
> Specifies the name of a user from whom a privilege or role is to be removed.

role_name
> Specifies the name of a role from which a privilege or role is to be removed.

PUBLIC
> Specifies that the granted privilege or role is to be removed from all users.

Notes

You must have been granted the privilege or role via the WITH ADMIN OPTION to issue this command. You can revoke any role if you have the GRANT ANY ROLE privilege.

Examples

The following example revokes the account_admin role from scott and debby:

```
REVOKE account_admin FROM scott,debby
```

The following example revokes CREATE USER and DROP USER from the dba_ assist role:

```
REVOKE create user, drop user FROM dba_assist
```

SET ROLE

```
SET ROLE {
    role [IDENTIFIED BY password][,role [IDENTIFIED BY password ...] |
    ALL [EXCEPT role[,role ...] |
    NONE
    }
```

Enables or disables roles (*role*) for the current session.

Keywords

IDENTIFIED BY
> Specifies the *password* for the role. This is required if the *role* is password protected.

ALL

Specifies that all roles granted to you are to be enabled. If the EXCEPT clause is included, the specified roles will not be enabled, but all other roles granted to you will be enabled.

NONE

Specifies that all roles granted to you are to be disabled for this session.

Note

You must already have been granted the roles named in this statement.

Example

The following example enables the DBA role for the current session:

```
SET ROLE dba IDENTIFIED BY manager
```

SET TRANSACTION

```
SET TRANSACTION
    [READ ONLY]
    [READ WRITE]
    [ISOLATION LEVEL [SERIALIZABLE | READ COMMITTED] ]
    [USE ROLLBACK SEGMENT seg_name]
```

Establishes the current transaction as read only or read and write, or specifies the rollback segment to be used by the transaction.

Keywords

READ ONLY

Specifies that the current transaction is read only.

READ WRITE

Specifies that the current transaction is read and write.

ISOLATION_LEVEL

Specifies how Oracle should conform to the ANSI SQL92 Serializable Transaction specification for the transaction; you may specify:

SERIALIZABLE

Specifies that Oracle should conform to the ANSI SQL92 Serializable Transaction specification and roll back transactions that attempt to update rows being updated by another transaction.

READ COMMITTED

Specifies that Oracle should continue to use its default processing and wait for the rows to be unlocked before continuing.

USE ROLLBACK SEGMENT

> Assigns this transaction to a specified rollback segment. This clause implies READ WRITE, and cannot be specified with READ ONLY.

Note

If used, this statement must be the first statement of your transaction. A transaction is ended with a COMMIT or COMMIT WORK statement.

Example

The following example specifies a rollback segment and performs an update transaction:

```
SET TRANSACTION                 ,
    USE ROLLBACK SEGMENT rbs99
/
UPDATE emp
SET SAL = SAL*1.1
/
COMMIT
/
```

TRUNCATE CLUSTER

```
TRUNCATE CLUSTER [schema.]cluster_name]
    [{DROP | REUSE} STORAGE]
```

Removes all rows from a cluster (*cluster_name*).

Keywords

DROP STORAGE

> Deallocates the storage used by the rows and returns the space to the free space pool. This is the default.

REUSE STORAGE

> Retains the space used by the deleted rows. This is useful if the table or cluster will be reloaded with data.

Notes

The cluster to be truncated must be in your schema, or you must have the DROP ANY TABLE privilege to truncate a cluster in another schema. The TRUNCATE command does not create rollback records, so it cannot be rolled back. This characteristic makes TRUNCATE extremely fast, and it is preferable to DELETE FROM unless the rollback capability is required. When a table is truncated and the DROP STORAGE clause is specified, only the initial extent of the table is retained; all other storage is deallocated.

Example

The following example removes all the rows from scott's empcluster cluster and deallocates the space used:

```
TRUNCATE CLUSTER scott.empcluster
```

TRUNCATE TABLE

```
TRUNCATE TABLE   [schema.] table_name
[{PRESERVE | PURGE} SNAPSHOT LOG
[{DROP | REUSE} STORAGE]
```

Removes all rows from a table (*table_name*).

Keywords

PRESERVE SNAPSHOT LOG

Keeps the contents of any snapshot log associated with the table. This allows you to reorganize the table without losing the snapshot log. This is the default.

PURGE SNAPSHOT LOG

Cleans out the snapshot log along with the table.

DROP STORAGE

Deallocates the storage used by the rows and returns the space to the free space pool. This is the default.

REUSE STORAGE

Retains the space used by the deleted rows. This is useful if the table or cluster will be reloaded with data.

Notes

The table to be truncated must be in your schema, or you must have the DROP ANY TABLE privilege to truncate a table in another schema. The TRUNCATE command does not create rollback records, so it cannot be rolled back. This characteristic makes TRUNCATE extremely fast, and it is preferable to DELETE FROM unless the rollback capability is required. When a table is truncated and the DROP STORAGE clause is specified, only the initial extent of the table is retained; all other storage is deallocated.

Example

The following example removes all the rows from scott's emp table and deallocates the space used:

```
TRUNCATE TABLE scott.emp
```

14

In this chapter:
- *Static Data Dictionary Views*
- *Dynamic Performance Data Dictionary Views*

The Oracle Data Dictionary

The Oracle data dictionary is a collection of tables and related views that enable you to see the inner workings and structure of the Oracle database. By querying these tables and views, you can obtain information about every object and every user of the database. For example, you can determine the amount of I/O to each datafile, the values of the *INIT.ORA* parameters, and much more. All of the Oracle monitoring tools look at the information available in the data dictionary and present it in an easy-to-use format.

Traditionally, the data dictionary has consisted of a series of views owned by SYS. These views, known as *static data dictionary views*, present information contained in tables that are updated when Oracle processes a DDL statement. The SYS tables and views, as well as a set of public synonyms for the views, are all created by the *catalog.sql* script. In addition, the installation of some Oracle features creates tables and views in the SYSTEM schema. In general, tables and views owned by SYSTEM exist to support functionality provided by PL/SQL stored procedures rather than fundamental Oracle functionality.

An additional set of views is composed of the *dynamic performance data dictionary views*, commonly referred to as the *V$ views* (or, mistakenly, as the V$ tables). These V$ views are based on a set of internal memory structures maintained by Oracle as virtual tables, which all begin with an "X$" prefix. Just as the static data dictionary views provide information about the database, the V$ views and the underlying X$ tables provide information about the instance.

Table 14-1 distinguishes between the types of information you will find in the static data dictionary views and in the dynamic performance data dictionary views.

Table 14-1. Basic Data Dictionary Divisions

If You Need to Find Information About...	Use These Data Dictionary Views
Database objects	Static data dictionary views
Instance objects	Dynamic performance data dictionary views
Database data files	Static data dictionary views
Archive log files	Dynamic performance data dictionary views
Users allowed to access the database	Static data dictionary views
Users currently connected to the database	Dynamic performance data dictionary views

Static Data Dictionary Views

The static data dictionary views have existed in their current format since Oracle Version 6. These are views owned by SYS that are built upon tables owned by SYS and give you the ability to find information about database objects. Table 14-2 shows which static data dictionary views should be used to find specific types of information.

Table 14-2. Static Data Dictionary Views

If You Need to Find Information About...	Use These Data Dictionary Views
Objects owned by you	Views that begin with USER_
Objects to which you have been granted access	Views that begin with ALL_
All objects in the database	Views that begin with DBA_
Tables	DBA_TABLES DBA_NESTED_TABLES DBA_OBJECT_TABLES DBA_PART_TABLES DBA_TAB_COMMENTS DBA_TAB_PARTITIONS DBA_TAB_HISTOGRAMS
Columns	DBA_CLU_COLUMNS DBA_COLL_TYPES DBA_COL_COMMENTS DBA_COL_PRIVS DBA_CONS_COLUMNS DBA_IND_COLUMNS DBA_TAB_COL_STATISTICS DBA_TAB_COLUMNS DBA_TRIGGER_COLS DBA_UPDATABLE_COLUMNS
Views	DBA_VIEWS

Table 14-2. Static Data Dictionary Views (continued)

If You Need to Find Information About...	Use These Data Dictionary Views
Tablespaces	DBA_TABLESPACES DB_TS_QUOTAS DBA_DATA_FILES
Constraints	DBA_CONSTRAINTS DBA_CONS_COLUMNS
Indexes	DBA_INDEXES DBA_IND_COLUMNS DBA_PART_INDEXES DBA_IND_PARTITIONS
Auditing	DBA_AUDIT_TRAIL DBA_AUDIT_SESSION DBA_EXITS DBA_AUDIT_OBJECT DBA_AUDIT_STATEMENT
Procedures/packages	DBA_SOURCE ALL_ARGUMENTS DBA_ERRORS DBA_OBJECT_SIZE DBA_LIBRARIES PUBLIC_DEPENDENCIES
Snapshots	DBA_REGISTERED_SNAPSHOTS DBA_SNAPSHOT_LOGS DBA_SNAPSHOT_REFRESH_TIMES DBA_SHAPSHOT_LOG_FILTER_COLS DBA_SNAPSHOTS
Sequences	DBA_SEQUENCES

Families of Views

Most of the data dictionary is constructed in a matrix fashion. The first way to categorize data dictionary views is by the breadth of information they cover. Views can be divided into four groups:

- Views that allow you to see objects you own. Most of these views begin with USER_.

- Views that allow you to see objects that you own or that were granted to you. Most of these views begin with ALL_.

- Views that allow you to see all objects in the database. These are primarily for use by the DBA. Most of these views begin with DBA_.

- A handful of other views that provide information of general interest about the database.

The second way to categorize data dictionary views is by content. Many of the USER_, ALL_, and DBA_ views are grouped in families, according to how their view names end (e.g., TABLES, COLUMNS, and so on). Groups of views provide information about various topics, including:

- Tables
- Storage
- Columns
- Views
- Objects
- Networking objects

As this is a book for DBAs, in this chapter we'll concentrate on the DBA_ views and the other views of interest to DBAs. The ALL_ views have the same structure as the DBA_ views. The USER_ views have the same structure as the DBA_ views with the exception that they do not include the OWNER column.

Commonly Used Data Dictionary Views

This section summarizes the static data dictionary views you'll commonly use. Views are divided into functional categories and arranged alphabetically by category.

Advanced Queuing

These views provide information about the message queues:

DBA_QUEUE_SCHEDULES
> Shows when particular queued messages are to be delivered.

DBA_QUEUE_TABLES
> Lists the tables used to hold the queues defined as part of the Advanced Queuing facility.

DBA_QUEUES
> Lists the queues defined as part of the Advanced Queuing facility.

Audit trail

These views (and some tables) provide information about the status of auditing and the actual audit trail. For further information, see Chapter 7, *Auditing.*

ALL_DEF_AUDIT_OPTS
> Lists the default auditing options in effect for new objects.

AUDIT_ACTIONS
> Lists the audit codes and descriptions.

DBA_AUDIT_EXISTS

Contains audit trail information generated by AUDIT EXISTS and AUDIT NOEXISTS.

DBA_AUDIT_OBJECT

Contains audit trail information for object auditing.

DBA_AUDIT_SESSION

Contains audit trail information for all connects and disconnects from the instance.

DBA_AUDIT_STATEMENT

Contains audit trail information for all audited statements.

DBA_AUDIT_TRAIL

Contains all audit trail information. The other DBA_AUDIT_ views are subsets of this view.

DBA_OBJ_AUDIT_OPTS

Lists all object auditing options in effect.

DBA_PRIV_AUDIT_OPTS

Lists all system privilege auditing options in effect.

DBA_STMT_AUDIT_OPTS

Lists all statement auditing options in effect.

STMT_AUDIT_OPTION_MAP

Lists the valid SQL statements that can be specified for statement auditing.

SYSTEM_PRIVILEGE_MAP

Lists the valid system privileges that can be specified for system privilege auditing.

TABLE_PRIVILEGE_MAP

Lists the valid object audit options that can be specified for schema object auditing.

Constraints

These views provide information about constraints and columns included in the constraints:

DBA_CONS_COLUMNS

Shows which columns are affected by each constraint.

DBA_CONSTRAINTS

Lists all constraints defined in the database.

Dictionary

These views provide information about the objects in the data dictionary:

DBA_CATALOG
Lists all tables, views, sequences, and synonyms in the database.

DBA_DEPENDENCIES
Lists dependencies between database objects. Used to determine which objects become invalid after other objects are altered or dropped.

DBA_OBJECTS
Lists all objects in the database. Note that this name predates the Objects Option and is not restricted to objects created using the Objects Option.

DICT_COLUMNS
Lists all columns defined in the data dictionary views.

DICTIONARY
Lists all data dictionary views.

Indexes

These views provide information about indexes and indexed columns:

DBA_IND_COLUMNS
Lists all indexed columns.

DBA_INDEXES
Lists all indexes.

INDEX_HISTOGRAM
Contains information about the distribution of index keys within the table. Populated for one index at a time by the ANALYZE INDEX ... VALIDATE STRUCTURE command.

INDEX_STATS
Contains information about the structure of an index. Populated for one index at a time by the ANALYZE INDEX ... VALIDATE STRUCTURE command.

Jobs

These views provide information about the job queues managed by the Oracle built-in DBMS_JOBS package. These job queues are used by the replication facilities and by Oracle Enterprise Manager, but are available for use by any application.

DBA_JOBS
Lists all jobs defined.

DBA_JOBS_RUNNING
Lists all currently running jobs.

Large objects (LOBs)

These views provide information about large objects (LOBs):

DBA_DIRECTORIES
    Lists all defined external directories. Directories are where BFILEs are stored.

DBA_LOBS
    Lists all large objects defined in the database.

Locks

These views provide information about the current status of locks in the database:

DBA_BLOCKERS
    Lists all sessions holding locks for whose release others are waiting.

DBA_DDL_LOCKS
    Lists all existing DDL locks.

DBA_DML_LOCKS
    Lists all existing DML locks.

DBA_KGLLOCK
    Lists all KGL (library cache) locks in the database.

DBA_LOCK_INTERNAL
    Contains internal information for each lock defined in DBA_LOCKS.

DBA_LOCKS
    Lists all locks held or requested in the database.

DBA_WAITERS
    Lists all sessions that are waiting on a lock held by another session.

DBMS_LOCK_ALLOCATED
    Shows which locks the current user has allocated.

Net8

These views provide information about the status of Net8 and remote databases. See Chapter 5, *Oracle Networking*, for more details on the use and implementation of Net8.

DBA_2PC_NEIGHBORS
    Contains information about the commit point for distributed transactions listed in DBA_2PC_PENDING.

DBA_2PC_PENDING
    Lists information about distributed transactions requiring recovery.

DBA_DB_LINKS
    Lists all database links.

DBA_PENDING_TRANSACTIONS

Contains further information used by XA for distributed transactions listed in DBA_2PC_PENDING.

GLOBAL_NAME

Shows the value of the global name. Can be used to determine which database the application is connected to.

TRUSTED_SERVERS

Specifies which servers have been identified as trusted.

Objects Option

These views provide information relating to objects created using Oracle's Objects Option:

DBA_COLL_TYPES

Lists collection types created.

DBA_METHOD_PARAMS

Lists all parameters for methods defined in DBA_TYPE_METHODS.

DBA_METHOD_RESULTS

Lists all method results for methods defined in DBA_TYPE_METHODS.

DBA_NESTED_TABLES

Lists all nested tables created using features from the Objects Option.

DBA_OBJECT_TABLES

Lists all tables created using features from the Objects Option.

DBA_REFS

Lists the REF columns and attributes for objects.

DBA_TYPE_ATTRS

Lists attributes of all types.

DBA_TYPE_METHODS

Lists methods created to support each type defined in DBA_TYPES.

DBA_TYPES

Lists all types created.

Partitioning

These views provide information about partitioned tables and indexes:

DBA_IND_PARTITIONS

Lists all index partitions. There is one row for each index partition.

DBA_PART_COL_STATISTICS

Contains distribution information about partitioned columns that have been analyzed; comparable to DBA_TAB_COL_STATISTICS for partitioned tables.

DBA_PART_HISTOGRAMS

Contains information about histograms created on individual partitions.

DBA_PART_INDEXES

Lists all partitioned indexes. There is one row for each partitioned index.

DBA_PART_KEY_COLUMNS

Lists the partition key columns for all partitions.

DBA_PART_TABLES

Lists all partitioned tables. There is one row for each partitioned table.

DBA_TAB_PARTITIONS

Lists all table partitions. There is one row for each table partition.

PL/SQL

These views provide information about PL/SQL functions, procedures, packages, and triggers:

ALL_ARGUMENTS

Lists all valid arguments for stored procedures and functions.

DBA_ERRORS

Shows all errors from compiling objects.

DBA_LIBRARIES

Lists the external libraries that can be called from PL/SQL packages, procedures, and functions.

DBA_OBJECT_SIZE

Shows the size of the compiled code for each PL/SQL package, procedure, function, and trigger.

DBA_SOURCE

Shows PL/SQL source for packages, procedures, and functions.

DBA_TRIGGER_COLS

Lists columns that are referenced in triggers.

DBA_TRIGGERS

Shows PL/SQL code for database triggers.

PUBLIC_DEPENDENCY

Lists dependencies using only object numbers.

Security

These views provide information about users and grants. Please refer to Chapter 6, *Security and Monitoring*, for more details on security.

DBA_COL_PRIVS
Lists all column grants made in the database.

DBA_PROFILES
Lists all defined profiles.

DBA_ROLE_PRIVS
Lists all roles granted to users and to other roles.

DBA_ROLES
Lists all roles.

DBA_SYS_PRIVS
Shows which system privileges have been assigned to which users.

DBA_TAB_PRIVS
Shows all object privileges. Includes not only tables but also views, sequences, packages, procedures, and functions.

DBA_USERS
Lists all users.

RESOURCE_COST
Shows the assigned cost of each resource for composite limits.

RESOURCE_MAP
Maps profile resource numbers to resource names.

ROLE_ROLE_PRIVS
Lists roles granted to other roles. A subset of DBA_ROLE_PRIVS.

ROLE_SYS_PRIVS
Lists system privileges granted to roles. A subset of DBA_SYS_PRIVS.

ROLE_TAB_PRIVS
Lists table grants granted to roles. A subset of DBA_TAB_PRIVS.

SESSION_PRIVS
Shows which system privileges are active for the current session.

SESSION_ROLES
Shows which roles are active for the current session

USER_PASSWORD_LIMITS
Shows the password limits in effect for the current session. There is no corresponding DBA_PASSWORD_LIMITS.

Sequences

This view provides information about sequences:

DBA_SEQUENCES
Lists all sequences in the database.

Server management

These views provide information about the current status of the database:

NLS_DATABASE_PARAMETERS
Shows the National Language Support (NLS) parameters in effect at the database level.

NLS_INSTANCE_PARAMETERS
Shows the NLS parameters in effect at the instance level.

NLS_SESSION_PARAMETERS
Shows the NLS parameters in effect at the session level.

PRODUCT_COMPONENT_VERSION
Shows the current release level of all installed Oracle options.

SM$VERSION
Oracle version level packaged for Server Manager to use.

Storage

These views provide information about internal storage in the database, including datafiles, tablespaces, free extents, used extents, and segments:

DBA_DATA_FILES
Lists all data files in use by the database.

DBA_EXTENTS
Lists every allocated extent for every segment.

DBA_FREE_SPACE
Lists every free extent. With DBA_EXTENTS, should account for all storage in DBA_DATA_FILES.

DBA_FREE_SPACE_COALESCED
Lists every extent that is at the start of a block of free extents.

DBA_ROLLBACK_SEGS
Lists all rollback segments.

DBA_SEGMENTS
Lists all segments.

DBA_TABLESPACES
Lists all tablespaces.

DBA_TS_QUOTAS
Shows the granted quota and used storage in tablespaces by user.

Synonyms

This view provides information about synonyms:

DBA_SYNONYMS
　Lists all synonyms in the database.

Tables, clusters, and views

These views provide information about tables, clusters, and views:

DBA_ALL_TABLES
　Lists all object and relational tables.

DBA_CLU_COLUMNS
　Lists all cluster keys.

DBA_CLUSTER_HASH_EXPRESSIONS
　Lists the hash values used for the optional cluster hash indexes.

DBA_CLUSTERS
　Lists all clusters in the database.

DBA_COL_COMMENTS
　Shows comments on all table and view columns.

DBA_TAB_COL_STATISTICS
　Contains column information about analyzed columns. This is a subset of the
　information available in DBA_TAB_COLUMNS.

DBA_TAB_COLUMNS
　Shows all table and view columns.

DBA_TAB_COMMENTS
　Shows all comments on tables and views.

DBA_TAB_HISTOGRAMS
　Shows all table histograms.

DBA_TABLES
　Shows all relational tables.

DBA_UPDATABLE_COLUMNS
　Lists columns in views with joins that can be updated.

DBA_VIEWS
　Shows all views.

Others

These other views and tables are used by individual users:

CHAINED_ROWS
Populated by the ANALYZE TABLE command to show all chained rows in a table. Created using the *utlchain.sql* script.

EXCEPTIONS
Contains a list of all rows that have a constraint violation. Populated when attempting to create or enable a constraint. Created using the *utlexcpt.sql* script.

PLAN_TABLE
Used by the EXPLAIN_PLAN process to show the execution plan for a SQL statement. Created using the *utlxplan.sql* script.

Other Static Data Dictionary Views

The following views show important information about the structure of the database, but are normally not referenced by DBAs directly. They are listed here for completeness.

Advanced replication

These views provide information used by Oracle's advanced replication facilities. Oracle currently recommends using the Replication Manager to obtain the information in these views.

```
DBA_ANALYZE_OBJECTS
DBA_REGISTERED_SNAPSHOT_GROUPS
DBA_REPAUDIT_ATTRIBUTE
DBA_REPAUDIT_COLUMN
DBA_REPCAT
DBA_REPCATLOG
DBA_REPCOLUMN
DBA_REPCOLUMN_GROUP
DBA_REPCONFLICT
DBA_REPDDL
DBA_REPGENERATED
DBA_REPGENOBJECTS
DBA_REPGROUP
DBA_REPGROUPED_COLUMN
DBA_REPKEY_COLUMNS
DBA_REPOBJECT
DBA_REPPARAMETER_COLUMN
```

DBA_REPPRIORITY
DBA_REPPRIORITY_GROUP
DBA_REPPROP
DBA_REPRESOL_STATS_CONTROL
DBA_REPRESOLUTION
DBA_REPRESOLUTION_METHOD
DBA_REPRESOLUTION_STATISTICS
DBA_REPSCHEMA
DBA_REPSITES
DEFCALLDEST

Export

These views provide information to the Export and Import utilities. Please refer to Chapter 4, *Preventing Data Loss*, for more information on these views.

DBA_EXP_FILES
DBA_EXP_OBJECTS
DBA_EXP_VERSION

Gateways

These views provide information needed to support foreign data sources (FDSs) or data gateways:

HS_ALL_CAPS
HS_ALL_DD
HS_ALL_INITS
HS_BASE_CAPS
HS_BASE_DD
HS_CLASS_CAPS
HS_CLASS_DD
HS_CLASS_INIT
HS_EXTERNAL_OBJECT_PRIVILEGES
HS_EXTERNAL_OBJECTS
HS_EXTERNAL_USER_PRIVILEGES
HS_FDS_CLASS
HS_FDS_INST
HS_INST_CAPS
HS_INST_DD
HS_INST_INIT

Oracle Parallel Server

These views provide information about the status of the Oracle Parallel Server environment:

    FILE_LOCK
    FILE_PING

Remote procedure calls

These views provide information about the status of remote procedure calls (RPCs):

    DEFCALL
    DEFDEFAULTDEST
    DEFERRCOUNT
    DEFERROR
    DEFLOB
    DEFPROPAGATOR
    DEFSCHEDULE
    DEFTRAN
    DEFTRANDEST
    ORA_KGLR7_DB_LINKS
    ORA_KGLR7_DEPENDENCIES
    ORA_KGLR7_IDL_CHAR
    ORA_KGLR7_IDL_SB4
    ORA_KGLR7_IDL_UB1
    ORA_KGLR7_IDL_UB2

Snapshots

These views provide information about snapshots:

    DBA_RCHILD
    DBA_REFRESH
    DBA_REFRESH_CHILDREN
    DBA_REGISTERED_SNAPSHOTS
    DBA_RGROUP
    DBA_SNAPSHOT_LOGS
    DBA_SNAPSHOT_REFRESH_TIMES
    DBA_SNAPSHOTS

SQL*Loader

These views provide information used by the SQL*Loader direct path option:

    LOADER_CONSTRAINT_INFO
    LOADER_FILE_TS

LOADER_PARAM_INFO
LOADER_PART_INFO
LOADER_TAB_INFO
LOADER_TRIGGER_INFO

Tablespace point-in-time recovery

These views provide information required for tablespace point-in-time recovery. See Chapter 4, *Preventing Data Loss,* for more information on these views.

STRADDLING_RS_OBJECTS
TS_PITR_CHECK
TS_PITR_OBJECTS_TO_BE_DROPPED

Trusted Oracle

This view provides information required by the Trusted Oracle product:

ALL_LABELS

Dynamic Performance Data Dictionary Views

The dynamic performance data dictionary views (the $V views) primarily cover information about the instance and information that the instance has about the database. These views are referred to as dynamic views because their contents change based upon how the instance is performing. The contents respond to the total workload, rather than to any one specific SQL statement or command.

Table 14-3 provides a quick reference for some commonly used dynamic performance data dictionary views.

Table 14-3. Commonly Used Dynamic Performance Data Dictionary Views

If You Need to Find Information About...	Use These Data Dictionary Views
List of features in use that preclude being able to downgrade Oracle releases	V$COMPATIBILITY V$COMPATSEG
Current Oracle options loaded	V$OPTION
Current Oracle release levels	V$VERSION
Parallel Query performance	V$PQ_TQSTAT
Active database pipes	V$DB_PIPES
Active database links	V$DBLINK
List of all background processes	V$BGPROCESS
Currently enabled privileges	V$ENABLEDPRIVS

Table 14-3. Commonly Used Dynamic Performance Data Dictionary Views (continued)

If You Need to Find Information About…	Use These Data Dictionary Views
List of all dynamic performance data dictionary views	V$FIXED_TABLE
Definitions of the dynamic performance data dictionary views	V$FIXED_VIEW_DEFINITIONS
List of all users defined in the password file	V$PWFILE_USERS
Contents of RMAN backup sets	V$BACKUP_DATAFILE
Location of archived redo logs	V$ARCHIVED_LOG
Location of RMAN backup sets	V$BACKUP_SET
Number of threads in the database	V$THREAD
Current usage of fixed resources specified in the *INIT.ORA* file.	V$RESOURCE_LIMIT
Information about active rollback segments	V$ROLLNAME V$ROLLSTAT
Current temporary segments used for sorting	V$SORT_SEGMENT V$SORT_USAGE
Information about who is currently connected to the instance	V$SESSION V$PROCESS
Size of the SGA	V$SGA
Allocation of space within the SGA	V$SGASTAT
Current SQL statements	V$SQLTEXT V$SQLTEXT_WITH_NEWLINES
Current values of *INIT.ORA* parameters	V$PARAMETER V$SYSTEM_PARAMETER
Current NLS parameters	V$NLS_PARAMETERS
List of all datafiles	V$DATAFILE
List of all outstanding locks and latches	V$LOCK V$LATCH
Multi-Threaded Server processes	V$DISPATCHER
Oracle Parallel Server locks	V$DLM_LOCKS V$DLM_LATCH

Availability of the Dynamic Performance Data Dictionary Views

Specific dynamic performance data dictionary views are available based on the status of the instance, as follows:

- Dynamic performance data dictionary views that provide information specifically about the instance (e.g., V$PARAMETER) are available immediately upon the instance being started. Table 14-4 lists these views.

- Dynamic performance data dictionary views that provide information stored in the control files (e.g., V$LOGHIST) are available once the database has been mounted. Table 14-5 lists these views.

- Dynamic performance data dictionary views that provide information about how the kernel is processing SQL statements (e.g., V$SQLAREA) are available once the database has been opened. Table 14-6 lists these views.

Table 14-4. Dynamic Performance Data Dictionary Views Available Immediately

V$ACCESS	V$ACTIVE_INSTANCES
V$ARCHIVE_DEST	V$BACKUP_DEVICE
V$BGPROCESS	V$BUFFER_POOL
V$CIRCUIT	V$CLASS_PING
V$COMPATIBILITY	V$COMPATSEG
V$CONTROLFILE	V$DB_OBJECT_CACHE
V$DB_PIPES	V$DBLINK
V$DISPATCHER	V$DISPATCHER_RATE
V$DLM_CONVERT_LOCAL	V$DLM_CONVERT_REMOTE
V$DLM_LOCKS	V$DLM_MISC
V$ENABLEDPRIVS	V$ENQUEUE_LOCK
V$EVENT_NAME	V$EXECUTION
V$FIXED_TABLE	V$FIXED_VIEW_DEFINITION
V$GLOBAL_TRANSACTION	V$INDEXED_FIXED_COLUMN
V$INSTANCE	V$LATCH_CHILDREN
V$LATCH_MISSES	V$LATCH_PARENT
V$LATCHHOLDER	V$LIBRARYCACHE
V$LICENSE	V$LOADCSTAT
V$LOADPSTAT	V$LOADTSTAT
V$LOCK	V$LOCK_ACTIVITY
V$LOCK_ELEMENT	V$LOCKED_OBJECT
V$LOCKS_WITH_COLLISIONS	V$MTS
V$MYSTAT	V$NLS_PARAMETERS
V$NLS_VALID_VALUES	V$OBJECT_DEPENDENCY
V$OPEN_CURSOR	V$OPTION
V$PARAMETER	V$PQ_SESSTAT
V$PQ_SLAVE	V$PQ_SYSSTAT
V$PQ_TQSTAT	V$PROCESS
V$PWFILE_USERS	V$QUEUE
V$RECOVERY_PROGRESS	V$RECOVERY_STATUS

Table 14-4. Dynamic Performance Data Dictionary Views Available Immediately (continued)

V$REQDIST	V$RESOURCE
V$RESOURCE_LIMIT	V$ROLLSTAT
V$ROWCACHE	V$SESSION
V$SESSION_CONNECT_INFO	V$SESSION_CURSOR_CACHE
V$SESSION_EVENT	V$SESSION_LONGOPS
V$SESSION_OBJECT_CACHE	V$SESSION_WAIT
V$SESSTAT	V$SGA
V$SGASTAT	V$SHARED_POOL_RESERVED
V$SHARED_SERVER	V$SORT_SEGMENT
V$SORT_USAGE	V$SQL
V$SQL_BIND_DATA	V$SQL_BIND_METADATA
V$SQL_CURSOR	V$SQL_SHARED_MEMORY
V$SQLTEXT	V$SQLTEXT_WITH_NEWLINES
V$STATNAME	V$SUBCACHE
V$SYSSTAT	V$SYSTEM_CURSOR_CACHE
V$SYSTEM_EVENT	V$SYSTEM_PARAMETER
V$TIMER	V$TRANSACTION
V$TRANSACTION_ENQUEUE	V$TYPE_SIZE
V$VERSION	V$WAITSTAT

Table 14-5. Dynamic Performance Data Dictionary Views Available After the Database Is Mounted

V$ARCHIVE	V$ARCHIVED_LOG
V$BACKUP	V$BACKUP_CORRUPTION
V$BACKUP_DATAFILE	V$BACKUP_PIECE
V$BACKUP_REDOLOG	V$BACKUP_SET
V$CONTROLFILE_RECORD_SECTION	V$COPY_CORRUPTION
V$DATABASE	V$DATAFILE
V$DATAFILE_COPY	V$DATAFILE_HEADER
V$DBFILE	V$DELETED_OBJECT
V$FILE_PING	V$FILESTAT
V$LATCHNAME	V$LOG
V$LOG_HISTORY	V$LOGFILE
V$LOGHIST	V$OFFLINE_RANGE
V$RECOVER_FILE	V$RECOVERY_FILE_STATUS
V$RECOVERY_LOG	V$TABLESPACE
V$THREAD	

*Table 14-6. Dynamic Performance Data Dictionary Views Available
After the Database Is Opened*

V$AQ	V$BH
V$CACHE	V$CACHE_LOCK
V$CURRENT_BUCKET	V$DLM_LATCH
V$FALSE_PING	V$LATCH
V$MLS_PARAMETERS	V$PING
V$RECENT_BUCKET	V$ROLLNAME
V$SESS_IO	V$SQLAREA

How the Dynamic Performance Data Dictionary Views Are Built

Unlike the static data dictionary views, which are views on existing tables, the dynamic performance data dictionary views are views on a set of tables that do not physically exist in the database; instead they are actually views of X$ tables, which are representations of internal memory structures in the Oracle instance. For example:

- V$DATABASE is a public synonym for the view SYS.V_$DATABASE.

- SYS.V_$DATABASE is a view on SYS.V$DATABASE.

- V$DATABASE (which is not defined in DBA.OBJECTS) is a view on the memory structure X$KCCDI.

The exact specification of how the V$ views are built is maintained within the Oracle kernel. The view V$FIXED_VIEW_DEFINITION defines all V$ views as views based upon the X$ tables.

How these views are built is important to understanding how they work. Initially defined within the Oracle kernel, these hardcoded V$ tables are accessible once the instance has been started or the database has been mounted. Once the database is opened, the normal SQL processing takes over, and the public synonyms referencing the views are used. With public synonyms, the same name is available whether you are CONNECTed INTERNAL before the database is opened, or are connected as a user with DBA privileges after the database is opened.

The relatively few V$ views that are only available once the database is open turn out to be true views, based upon X$ or other V$ tables.

The Global Dynamic Performance Data Dictionary Views (GV$ Views)

Effective with Oracle8, the dynamic performance data dictionary views (V$ views) have been augmented with a complementary set of global dynamic performance data dictionary views (GV$ views). The V$ views provide information about the instance to which you are connected and its management of the database. The GV$ views provide the same information for all other instances that have the same database mounted, and are primarily of interest in an Oracle Parallel Server environment. The global dynamic performance data dictionary views add the column INST_ID to their names, which allows you to identify the instance for which information is being provided.

New Views with Oracle8

In support of the new functionality delivered with Oracle8, additional dynamic performance data dictionary views have been provided. These are listed in Table 14-7. Most of the new dynamic performance data dictionary views support the new Recovery Manager (RMAN) or the integration of the Oracle Parallel Server's Distributed Lock Manager (DLM) into the Oracle kernel.

Table 14-7. New Dynamic Performance Data Dictionary Views in Oracle8

V$AQ	V$ARCHIVE_DEST
V$ARCHIVED_LOG	V$BACKUP
V$BACKUP_CORRUPTION	V$BACKUP_DATAFILE
V$BACKUP_DEVICE	V$BACKUP_PIECE
V$BACKUP_REDOLOG	V$BACKUP_SET
V$BUFFER_POOL	V$CLASS_PING
V$CONTROLFILE_RECORD_SECTION	V$COPY_CORRUPTION
V$CURRENT_BUCKET	V$DATAFILE_COPY
V$DATAFILE_HEADER	V$DELETED_OBJECT
V$DISPATCHER_RATE	V$DLM_CONVERT_LOCAL
V$DLM_CONVERT_REMOTE	V$DLM_LATCH
V$DLM_LOCKS	V$DLM_MISC
V$ENQUEUE_LOCK	V$EXECUTION
V$FILE_PING	V$GLOBAL_TRANSACTION
V$OFFLINE_RANGE	V$RECENT_BUCKET
V$RECOVERY_PROGRESS	V$RESOURCE_LIMIT
V$SESSION_LONGOPS	V$SESSION_OBJECT_CACHE
V$SORT_SEGMENT	V$SORT_USAGE
V$SQL_BIND_DATA	V$SQL_BIND_METADATA
V$SQL_CURSOR	V$SQL_SHARED_MEMORY
V$SUBCACHE	V$TABLESPACE
V$TRANSACTION_ENQUEUE	

Dynamic Views

This section summarizes the dynamic performance data dictionary views. For convenience, the dynamic performance data dictionary views have been divided into families based upon general areas of functionality, which are listed alphabetically.

 The breakdown of the dynamic performance data dictionary views into families is somewhat more arbitrary than the classification of the static data dictionary views. The static data dictionary views follow a naming convention, and are even created in families inside the *catalog.sql* script.

Advanced Queuing

This view provides throughput statistics for the Advanced Queuing facility:

V$AQ
> Provides message statistics for each of the Advanced Queuing message queues.

Configuration

These views provide information about the current configuration of the Oracle environment:

V$COMPATIBILITY
> Lists features in use by the current instance that would preclude reverting to a previous release of the Oracle software. Since these are instance based, some of the features may disappear if the database is shut down normally.

V$COMPATSEG
> Lists permanent features in the database that would preclude reverting to a previous release of the Oracle software.

V$EVENT_NAME
> Contains descriptive information about all possible wait events.

V$LICENSE
> Contains a single row specifying the maximum numbers of concurrent and named users allowed, as well as the highwater marks.

V$MLS_PARAMETERS
> Lists the initialization parameters and their current values for Trusted Oracle. The format is the same as V$PARAMETER.

V$NLS_PARAMETERS
> Contains the current values for each of the National Language Support (NLS) parameters.

V$NLS_VALID_VALUES
> Lists the valid values that each of the NLS parameters can take.

V$OPTION
> Lists the Oracle options that have been installed with the Oracle software.

V$PARAMETER
> Lists all *INIT.ORA* parameters and their current settings. It also indicates whether the current value is specified in the *INIT.ORA* file or is the default value, as well as whether the parameter is modifiable with an ALTER SYSTEM or ALTER SESSION command.

V$STATNAME
> Lists the name for each statistic stored in V$SYSSTAT and V$SESSTAT.

V$SYSTEM_PARAMETER
> Lists all *INIT.ORA* parameters and their current settings. It also indicates whether the current value is specified in the *INIT.ORA* file or is the default value, as well as whether the parameter is modifiable with an ALTER SYSTEM or ALTER SESSION command.

V$VERSION
> Lists current version numbers of the library components of the Oracle kernel.

Data dictionary cache

These views provide information about how the Oracle kernel is managing the data dictionary and library caches:

V$DB_OBJECT_CACHE
> Lists tables, indexes, clusters, synonyms, PL/SQL procedures, packages, and triggers that are in the library cache.

V$LIBRARYCACHE
> Contains statistics about library cache performance.

V$ROWCACHE
> Contains statistics about data dictionary cache performance.

V$SUBCACHE
> Lists each subordinate cache in the library cache.

Database

These views provide information about the physical database:

V$CONTROLFILE
> Provides the names of all control files.

V$CONTROLFILE_RECORD_SECTION
> Provides information about the amount of information stored in each section of the control file.

V$DATABASE

> Provides information about the database that is stored in the control file.

V$DATAFILE

> Contains information about each datafile, based upon information from the control file.

V$DATAFILE_HEADER

> Contains information about each datafile, based upon information in the datafile header.

V$DBFILE

> Contains the name for each datafile. Maintained for upward compatibility. Use V$DATAFILE instead.

V$OFFLINE_RANGE

> Provides information about the offline status of datafiles. The information is provided from the control file.

V$TABLESPACE

> Provides information about tablespaces, based upon information in the control file.

V$TYPE_SIZE

> Specifies the size in bytes for the various components of an Oracle data or index block.

Instance

These views provide information specifically geared toward the status of the instance:

V$BGPROCESS

> Provides information about each of the background processes.

V$INSTANCE

> Provides status information about the current instance.

Locks and latches

These views provide information about the status of locks and latches within the instance:

V$ACCESS

> Lists all locked objects in the database and the sessions accessing these objects.

V$BUFFER_POOL

> Provides information about the available buffer pools. The number of buffer pools is related to the *INIT.ORA* parameter DB_BLOCK_LRU_LATCHES.

V$ENQUEUE_LOCK

Lists all locks owned by enqueue state objects.

V$LATCH

Provides statistics for all latches. If the latch is a parent latch, provides a summation of the statistics for each of its children latches.

V$LATCH_CHILDREN

Provides statistics for all children latches.

V$LATCH_MISSES

Provides statistics about all failures to acquire a latch.

V$LATCH_PARENT

Provides statistics for all parent latches.

V$LATCHHOLDER

Provides information about current latch holders.

V$LATCHNAME

Provides a decoded latch name for every latch listed in V$LATCH. There is a one-to-one correspondence between these two views.

V$LOCK

Lists all locks held and all outstanding requests for locks or latches.

V$LOCKED_OBJECT

Lists all objects currently locked by transactions within the system.

V$RESOURCE

Contains the names, types, and addresses of all resources in the system.

Multi-Threaded Server

These views provide information on how the Multi-Threaded Server is configured and performing:

V$CIRCUIT

Contains information about the virtual circuits used to connect users to the instance.

V$DISPATCHER

Provides information about the various configured Dispatcher processes.

V$DISPATCHER_RATE

Provides statistics about the Dispatcher processes throughput.

V$MTS

Provides information about the overall activity of the Multi-Threaded Server.

V$QUEUE

Provides statistics about the multi-threaded message queue.

V$REQDIST

Provides a 12-bucket histogram of the distribution of request service times. This width-balanced histogram shows the number of hits in each of the 12 consistent times. The sizes of the buckets are allowed to change over time.

V$SHARED_SERVER

Shows the status of the each of the shared servers.

Oracle Parallel Server

These views are specific to an Oracle Parallel Server environment:

V$ACTIVE_INSTANCES

Lists all current instances that have the database mounted.

V$BH

Provides the status and pings of every data buffer in the System Global Area (SGA).

V$CACHE

Provides information about the block header of every object the current instance has in its SGA.

V$CACHE_LOCK

Provides the lock status of every data block the current instance has in its SGA.

V$CLASS_PING

Shows statistics on the number of pings per data block class.

V$DLM_CONVERT_LOCAL

Shows elapsed times for local DLM lock conversions.

V$DLM_CONVERT_REMOTE

Shows elapsed times for remote DLM lock conversions.

V$DLM_LATCH

Shows the total count and number of immediate gets of DLM latches acquired by latch type.

V$DLM_LOCKS

Shows all DLM locks and lock requests that are blocked or are blocking other lock requests.

V$DLM_MISC

Provides statistics on various DLM parameters.

V$FALSE_PING

Lists buffers that are getting excessive pings because they are covered under a different lock. Buffers that are identified can be remapped using the *INIT.ORA* parameter GC_FILES_TO_LOCKS.

V$FILE_PING

Shows the number of block pings per datafile.

V$LOCK_ACTIVITY

Provides an overall view of DLM locks within the current instance.

V$LOCK_ELEMENT

Provides information about each PCM lock in the data buffers.

V$LOCKS_WITH_COLLISIONS

Shows locks with high numbers of false pings.

V$PING

A subset of V$CACHE; shows only those buffers that have been pinged at least once.

Parallel Query

These views provide information in support of Parallel Query operations:

V$EXECUTION

Provides information about each Parallel Query execution.

V$PQ_SESSTAT

Provides statistics on Parallel Query activity for the current session.

V$PQ_SLAVE

Provides statistics on each of the Parallel Query servers (slaves) in the system.

V$PQ_SYSSTAT

Provides a summary of Parallel Query statistics for the entire system.

V$PQ_TQSTAT

Provides statistics for each Parallel Query session while it is active.

Recovery

These views provide information about the current status of the online and offline redo logs as well as backup processes controlled by the Recovery Manager (RMAN):

V$ARCHIVE

Lists redo logs that must be archived.

V$ARCHIVE_DEST

Shows the status of all archive log destinations specified for the instance. See the *INIT.ORA* parameters LOG_ARCHIVE_DEST, LOG_ARCHIVE_DUPLEX_DEST, and LOG_ARCHIVE_MIN_SUCCEED_DEST.

V$ARCHIVED_LOG

Provides information from the control file for all archive logs, using a time-based view of the log files.

V$BACKUP

Shows the backup status of all online datafiles. This is managed by RMAN.

V$BACKUP_CORRUPTION

Details any datafile corruption detected as part of a backup managed by RMAN.

V$BACKUP_DATAFILE

Shows the location of the backup datafile used by RMAN.

V$BACKUP_DEVICE

Provides a list of available backup devices supported by RMAN.

V$BACKUP_PIECE

Provides information about each backup piece. A backup piece is a subset of an RMAN backup set.

V$BACKUP_REDOLOG

Provides information about archived redo logs that have been backed up by RMAN.

V$BACKUP_SET

Provides information about all RMAN backup sets.

V$COPY_CORRUPTION

Details any datafile corruption detected as part of a datafile copy managed by RMAN.

V$DATAFILE_COPY

Provides information about datafile copies from the control file. This information is maintained by RMAN.

V$DELETED_OBJECT

Provides information about archived redo logs, datafile pieces, and datafile copies that have been deleted from the control file.

V$LOG

Contains information about the redo logs from the control file.

V$LOG_HISTORY

Contains information about archived redo logs from the control files. Provides an SCN view of the archived log files.

V$LOGFILE

Provides the current status of all redo logs.

V$LOGHIST

Contains redo log history from the control file. Use of V$LOG_HISTORY is recommended.

V$RECOVER_FILE

Lists datafiles used in media recovery.

V$RECOVERY_FILE_STATUS

Contains information relevant to the current file recovery process. The information is available only to the Recovery Manager process and is not available to users.

V$RECOVERY_LOG

Contains derived information from V$LOG_HISTORY that is useful to Recovery Manager. It returns no rows when queried directly by users.

V$RECOVERY_PROGRESS

A subset of V$SESSION_LONGOPS that provides current status of recovery operations.

V$RECOVERY_STATUS

Maintains current statistics for the recovery process. The information is only available to the Recovery Manager and will return zero rows when queried directly by users.

V$THREAD

Contains information about all current redo log threads from the control file.

Security

These views provide information about privileges:

V$ENABLEDPRIVS

Lists all system privileges that are enabled for the current session. Includes those explicitly granted and those available through a role.

V$PWFILE_USERS

Lists all users who have been identified in the password file as having SYSDBA or SYSOPER privileges.

Session

These views provide information about the current Oracle session:

V$MYSTAT

Provides information about current session statistics. There is one row for every entry in V$STATNAME.

V$PROCESS

Lists each process in the instance. You can join this table to V$SESSION to gain more information.

V$SESS_IO

Provides up-to-date I/O information for each session in the database.

V$SESSION

Lists each session in the instance.

V$SESSION_CONNECT_INFO

Provides information about the network connection of the current session.

V$SESSION_CURSOR_CACHE

Provides information about the current session's cursor usage.

V$SESSION_EVENT

Provides information about how much time each session spends waiting on each event specified in V$EVENT_NAME.

V$SESSION_LONGOPS

Provides information about the status of long-running operations for sessions. Details the number of work units already accomplished and the expected amount of work required to complete the operation.

V$SESSION_OBJECT_CACHE

Provides object cache statistics for the current session in the current instance.

V$SESSION_WAIT

Lists the resources upon which each active session is waiting, and how long each session has been waiting for each resource.

V$SESSTAT

Provides information about each session's session statistics. There is one row for each session for each statistic specified in V$STATNAME.

SGA

These views provide information about the System Global Area:

V$CURRENT_BUCKET

Lists the number of increased buffer misses if the value of DB_BLOCK_BUFF-ERS were to be reduced. See the *INIT.ORA* parameter DB_BLOCK_EXTENTED.

V$RECENT_BUCKET

Lists the number of increased buffer hits if the value of DB_BLOCK_BUFFERS were to be increased. See the *INIT.ORA* parameter DB_BLOCK_LRU_EXTENDED_STATISTICS.

V$SGA

Contains information about the size, in bytes, of each of the various SGA components.

V$SGASTAT

Provides more detailed information about SGA utilization than V$SGA. Shows the breakdown of the SHARED_POOL and LARGE_POOL areas.

V$SHARED_POOL_RESERVED

Contains statistics about the SHARED_POOL area of the SGA. Some of the columns are meaningful only if the *INIT.ORA* parameter SHARED_POOL_RESERVED_SIZE has been set.

SQL

These views provide information about the processing of all SQL statements in the instance:

V$OBJECT_DEPENDENCY

Lists all objects that a package, procedure, or cursor in the SGA is depending upon. This view can be joined to the V$SQL and V$SESSION views to obtain a list of all objects being referenced by a user.

V$OPEN_CURSOR

Lists all open cursors in the system.

V$SORT_SEGMENT

Provides information about all sort segments in tablespaces specified as TEMPORARY.

V$SORT_USAGE

Provides information about sort segments in all tablespaces.

V$SQL

Provides information about all SQL statements in the shared SQL area.

V$SQL_BIND_DATA

Provides information about the bind variables provided for each SQL statement.

V$SQL_BIND_METADATA

Provides metadata about all bind variables used in SQL statements.

V$SQL_CURSOR

Provides debugging information about every cursor in the shared SQL area.

V$SQL_SHARED_MEMORY

Provides information about how memory is allocated for every cursor in the shared SQL area.

V$SQLAREA

Provides information on all SQL statements in the shared SQL area.

V$SQLTEXT

Provides the text of all SQL statements in the shared SQL area. All newline and tab information is replaced by spaces.

V$SQLTEXT_WITH_NEWLINES

Provides the text of all SQL statements in the shared SQL area, but includes the original newline and tab characters.

SQL*Loader direct path

These views provide information relevant to the current SQL*Loader direct path operation:

V$LOADCSTAT

> View in which Oracle stores statistics about the number of rows processed during the current load. However, since you cannot query the view when the load is in progress, all queries of the view return no rows found.

V$LOADPSTAT

> View used by SQL*Loader to track statistics for the current direct load. Since this information applies only to the current session, it will always return 0 rows when queried by a user.

V$LOADTSTAT

> View in which Oracle stores additional statistics about the number of rows discarded during the current load. However, since you cannot query the view when the load is in progress, all queries of the view return no rows found.

System environment

These views provide miscellaneous information about the current environment:

V$DB_PIPES

> Provides information about database pipes currently defined in the database.

V$DBLINK

> Provides information about all currently open database links.

V$FILESTAT

> Provides information about the current read/write status of all datafiles.

V$FIXED_TABLE

> Lists all V$ and X$ tables defined in the kernel.

V$FIXED_VIEW_DEFINITION

> Provides a view definition for each dynamic performance view based upon the X$ tables.

V$GLOBAL_TRANSACTION

> Provides information on all current global transactions.

V$INDEXED_FIXED_COLUMN

> Lists each index column in the tables listed in V$FIXED_TABLE.

V$RESOURCE_LIMIT

> Shows the current utilization of system resources that can be specified in the *INIT.ORA* file. For each resource, the initial allocation, the current usage, and the maximum allowed value are specified.

V$ROLLNAME

Lists the names of all rollback segments.

V$ROLLSTAT

Provides statistics about each rollback segment.

V$SYSSTAT

Provides the current values for each of the system statistics defined in V$STAT-NAME.

V$SYSTEM_CURSOR_CACHE

Provides information about cursor usage across all sessions.

V$SYSTEM_EVENT

Provides information about time spent waiting for each system event defined in V$EVENT_NAME.

V$TIMER

Provides access to a timer that increments every $1/100$th of a second.

V$TRANSACTION

Lists all active transactions in the system.

V$TRANSACTION_ENQUEUE

Lists all enqueues held by active transactions in the system.

V$WAITSTAT

Provides information about the number of waits and how long the system had to wait for each class of data block.

15

System Privileges and Initial Roles

Privileges in Oracle are divided into two classes: system and object. *System privileges* define what actions you are allowed to take within the database. *Object privileges* define what you are allowed to do to a specific object, such as a table, a view, or a sequence. This chapter discusses the system privileges available in Oracle8. Object privileges are described in Chapter 6, *Security and Monitoring*.

In addition, Oracle recognizes certain *roles* that behave in a manner similar to system privileges, and this chapter discusses the six initial, or default, roles created with each database and the nine roles created by optional scripts during the standard database creation process.

Actions, Privileges, and Roles

Certain actions you might want to take in an Oracle database require that you have specific system privileges or initial roles. Table 15-1 summarizes the system privileges you need to perform some basic actions using the Oracle database.

Table 15-1. System Privileges Required to Perform Actions

If You Need to Perform This Type of Action...	You Need This System Privilege
Connect to the database	CREATE SESSION
Create an object in your schema	The corresponding CREATE ... system privilege
Create an object in someone else's schema	The corresponding CREATE ANY... system privilege
Drop an object in your schema	The corresponding DROP... system privilege
Drop an object in someone else's schema	The corresponding DROP ANY... system privilege

Table 15-1. System Privileges Required to Perform Actions (continued)

If You Need to Perform This Type of Action...	You Need This System Privilege
Manipulate the database	ALTER DATABASE
Manipulate the instance	ALTER SYSTEM
Manipulate a tablespace	ALTER/CREATE/DROP/MANAGE TABLESPACE
Change a user's password	ALTER USER
Change a user's default roles	ALTER USER
Exceed quotas in any tablespace	UNLIMITED TABLESPACE
Connect to an instance started in RESTRICTED mode	RESTRICTED SESSION

Table 15-2 summarizes the roles you need to perform the actions you are likely to perform with the Oracle database.

Table 15-2. Roles Required to Perform Actions

If You Need to Perform This Type of Action...	You Need This Role
Carry out DBA functions	DBA
Create objects in your own schema	CONNECT or RESOURCE
Export the entire database	EXP_FULL_DATABASE
Import from a full export	IMP_FULL_DATABASE
Manipulate data dictionary objects directly	SELECT_CATALOG_ROLE, EXECUTE_CATALOG_ROLE, DELETE_CATALOG_ROLE
Manage Advanced Queuing facility	AQ_ADMINISTRATOR_ROLE
Send or receive queued messages	AQ_USER_ROLE
Use the SQL*Plus AUTOTRACE facility	PLUSTRACE
Manage backups with RMAN	RECOVERY_CATALOG_OWNER
Run TKPROF	TKPROFER
Manage external data gateways	HS_ADMIN_ROLE

System Privileges

There are 90 distinct system privileges defined within the Oracle8 database. These values are hardcoded and are available immediately after the CREATE DATABASE command has completed. There are three types of system privileges:

- Privileges that allow you to perform some action to or in the database
- Privileges that allow you to create objects within your own schema
- Privileges that allow you to create, alter, or drop objects in any schema

For example, the CREATE TABLE system privilege allows you to create a table within your schema, while CREATE ANY TABLE allows you to create a table in any schema.

Privileges That Affect the Entire Database

Table 15-3 lists the privileges that are traditionally reserved to the database administrator and that have been granted to the DBA role. These privileges allow DBAs to alter the database, create new users, define public database links and synonyms, and grant any privilege or role without having first been granted the role with the WITH ADMIN OPTION option (see Chapter 13, *SQL Statements for the DBA*, for information about specifying that option).

Table 15-3. Privileges That Affect the Entire Database

ALTER DATABASE	ALTER PROFILE
ALTER RESOURCE COST	ALTER ROLLBACK SEGMENT
ALTER SYSTEM	ALTER TABLESPACE
ALTER USER	AUDIT SYSTEM
BECOME USER	CREATE LIBRARY
CREATE PROFILE	CREATE PUBLIC DATABASE LINK
CREATE PUBLIC SYNONYM	CREATE ROLE
CREATE ROLLBACK SEGMENT	CREATE TABLESPACE
CREATE USER	DROP PROFILE
DROP PUBLIC DATABASE LINK	DROP PUBLIC SYNONYM
DROP ROLLBACK SEGMENT	DROP TABLESPACE
DROP USER	GRANT ANY PRIVILEGE
GRANT ANY ROLE	MANAGE TABLESPACE
RESTRICTED SESSION	UNLIMITED TABLESPACE

Privileges That Allow You to Create Objects in Your Own Schema

Table 15-4 lists the privileges that allow you to create your own objects in the database. These privileges have been allocated to the CONNECT and RESOURCE roles. They allow you to connect to the database; to create a table, view, or snapshot; and to create a private database link, synonym, or snapshot.

Table 15-4. Privileges That Allow You to Create Objects in Your Own Schema

ALTER SESSION	CREATE CLUSTER
CREATE DATABASE LINK	CREATE PROCEDURE
CREATE SEQUENCE	CREATE SESSION
CREATE SNAPSHOT	CREATE SYNONYM

Table 15-4. Privileges That Allow You to Create Objects in Your Own Schema (continued)

CREATE TABLE	CREATE TRIGGER
CREATE TYPE	CREATE VIEW
FORCE TRANSACTION	

 You may need more than one system privilege to perform an action. For example, you cannot create a sequence if you do not first have the CREATE SESSION privilege, which allows you to connect to the database. Also, note that you cannot create a table or index unless you have a quota on a tablespace or have the UNLIMITED TABLESPACE system privilege.

Privileges That Allow You to Manipulate Objects in Any Schema

Table 15-5 lists the privileges that allow you to manipulate all other users' objects. If you have these privileges, you will not need to be granted object privileges on the objects themselves. The privileges in this category are intended to be used primarily by DBAs and support personnel and have been granted to the DBA role.

Table 15-5. Privileges That Allow You to Manipulate Objects in Any Schema

ALTER ANY CLUSTER	ALTER ANY INDEX
ALTER ANY LIBRARY	ALTER ANY PROCEDURE
ALTER ANY ROLE	ALTER ANY SEQUENCE
ALTER ANY SNAPSHOT	ALTER ANY TABLE
ALTER ANY TRIGGER	ALTER ANY TYPE
ANALYZE ANY	AUDIT ANY
BACKUP ANY TABLE	COMMENT ANY TABLE
CREATE ANY CLUSTER	CREATE ANY DIRECTORY
CREATE ANY INDEX	CREATE ANY LIBRARY
CREATE ANY PROCEDURE	CREATE ANY SEQUENCE
CREATE ANY SNAPSHOT	CREATE ANY SYNONYM
CREATE ANY TABLE	CREATE ANY TRIGGER
CREATE ANY TYPE	CREATE ANY VIEW
DELETE ANY TABLE	DROP ANY CLUSTER
DROP ANY DIRECTORY	DROP ANY INDEX
DROP ANY LIBRARY	DROP ANY PROCEDURE
DROP ANY ROLE	DROP ANY SEQUENCE
DROP ANY SNAPSHOT	DROP ANY SYNONYM

Table 15-5. Privileges That Allow You to Manipulate Objects in Any Schema (continued)

DROP ANY TABLE	DROP ANY TRIGGER
DROP ANY TYPE	DROP ANY VIEW
EXECUTE ANY LIBRARY	EXECUTE ANY PROCEDURE
EXECUTE ANY TYPE	FORCE ANY TRANSACTION
INSERT ANY TABLE	LOCK ANY TABLE
SELECT ANY SEQUENCE	SELECT ANY TABLE
UPDATE ANY TABLE	

Summary of System Privileges

This section contains a brief summary of all of Oracle's system privileges, listed in alphabetical order. Some system privileges are new in Oracle8; this is noted in the list. A complete list of new Oracle8 system privileges can also be found later in this chapter.

ALTER ANY CLUSTER

Allows you to execute the ALTER CLUSTER command for all clusters in the database.

ALTER ANY INDEX

Allows you to execute the ALTER INDEX command for all indexes in the database.

ALTER ANY LIBRARY (Oracle8)

Allows you to execute the CREATE OR REPLACE LIBRARY command to alter an existing external library in another schema.

ALTER ANY PROCEDURE

Allows you to execute the ALTER FUNCTION, ALTER PACKAGE, and ALTER PROCEDURE commands to recompile any function, package, or procedure in the database. Also allows you to execute the CREATE OR REPLACE FUNCTION, CREATE OR REPLACE PACKAGE, and CREATE OR REPLACE PROCEDURE commands on any existing function, package, or procedure in the database.

ALTER ANY ROLE

Allows you to execute the ALTER ROLE command to add, change, or remove a password on the role.

ALTER ANY SEQUENCE

Allows you to execute the ALTER SEQUENCE command on any sequence in the database.

ALTER ANY SNAPSHOT

Allows you to execute the ALTER SNAPSHOT command on any snapshot in the database.

ALTER ANY TABLE

> Allows you to execute the ALTER TABLE command on any table in the database. You must have the ALTER ANY TRIGGER privilege to execute the ALTER TABLE ... ENABLE/DISABLE ALL TRIGGERS command on tables outside your schema.

ALTER ANY TRIGGER

> Allows you to execute the ALTER TRIGGER command for all triggers in the database. With the ALTER ANY TRIGGER privilege, you can execute an ALTER TRIGGER ... ENABLE/DISABLE command, but you must also have the ALTER ANY TABLE privilege to execute the ALTER TABLE ... ENABLE/DISABLE ALL TRIGGERS command on tables outside your schema.

ALTER ANY TYPE (Oracle8)

> Allows you to execute the ALTER TYPE command on any user-defined type in any schema.

ALTER DATABASE

> Allows you to execute the ALTER DATABASE command.

ALTER PROFILE

> Allows you to execute the ALTER PROFILE command.

ALTER RESOURCE COST

> Allows you to execute the ALTER RESOURCE COST command.

ALTER ROLLBACK SEGMENT

> Allows you to execute the ALTER ROLLBACK SEGMENT command.

ALTER SESSION

> Allows you to execute the ALTER SESSION SET SQL_TRACE command.

ALTER SYSTEM

> Allows you to execute the ALTER SYSTEM command.

ALTER TABLESPACE

> Allows you to execute the ALTER TABLESPACE command.

ALTER USER

> Allows you to execute the ALTER USER command. You do not need the ALTER USER privilege to execute the ALTER USER *userid* IDENTIFIED BY *password* command to change your own password.

ANALYZE ANY

> Allows you to execute the ANALYZE command on all tables, clusters, and indexes in the database.

AUDIT ANY

> Allows you to execute the AUDIT command on any database object in any schema.

AUDIT SYSTEM

Allows you to execute the AUDIT command to audit SQL statements.

BACKUP ANY TABLE

Necessary to perform a full export.

BECOME USER

Necessary to import from a full export. There is no SQL statement that directly uses this privilege. However, there is an internal API (Application Programming Interface) that is used by the Import utility and checks for this privilege.

COMMENT ANY TABLE

Allows you to execute the COMMENT statement for all tables in the database.

CREATE ANY CLUSTER

Allows you to execute the CREATE CLUSTER statement and specify any schema as owner.

CREATE ANY DIRECTORY (Oracle8)

Allows you to execute the CREATE DIRECTORY statement. Since all BFILE directories are owned by SYS, there is no CREATE DIRECTORY privilege.

CREATE ANY INDEX

Allows you to execute the CREATE INDEX statement and specify any schema as owner.

CREATE ANY LIBRARY (Oracle8)

Allows you to define a library for external functions in any schema.

CREATE ANY PROCEDURE

Allows you to execute the CREATE FUNCTION, CREATE PROCEDURE, and CREATE PACKAGE statements and specify any schema as owner.

CREATE ANY SEQUENCE

Allows you to execute the CREATE SEQUENCE statement and specify any schema as owner.

CREATE ANY SNAPSHOT

Allows you to execute the CREATE SNAPSHOT statement and specify any schema as owner.

CREATE ANY SYNONYM

Allows you to execute the CREATE SYNONYM statement and specify any schema as owner.

CREATE ANY TABLE

Allows you to execute the CREATE TABLE statement and specify any schema as owner. You still must have a quota specified in the TABLESPACE clause.

CREATE ANY TRIGGER
> Allows you to execute the CREATE TRIGGER statement on any table in the database.

CREATE ANY TYPE (Oracle8)
> Allows you to create a user-defined type in any schema.

CREATE ANY VIEW
> Allows you to execute the CREATE VIEW statement and specify any schema as owner.

CREATE CLUSTER
> Allows you to create a cluster in your own schema.

CREATE DATABASE LINK
> Allows you to create a private database link.

CREATE LIBRARY (Oracle8)
> Allows you to execute the CREATE LIBRARY command to define a library in your schema for external procedures.

CREATE PROCEDURE
> Allows you to create a function, package, or procedure in your own schema.

CREATE PROFILE
> Allows you to execute the CREATE PROFILE command.

CREATE PUBLIC DATABASE LINK
> Allows you to execute the CREATE PUBLIC DATABASE LINK command. This is the one case in which there isn't a corresponding CREATE ANY version of the privilege. There is no CREATE ANY DATABASE LINK.

CREATE PUBLIC SYNONYM
> Allows you to execute the CREATE PUBLIC DATABASE LINK command.

CREATE ROLE
> Allows you to execute the CREATE ROLE command.

CREATE ROLLBACK SEGMENT
> Allows you to execute the CREATE ROLLBACK command.

CREATE SEQUENCE
> Allows you to create a sequence in your own schema.

CREATE SESSION
> Allows you to connect to the database.

CREATE SNAPSHOT
> Allows you to create a snapshot in your own schema.

CREATE SYNONYM
> Allows you to create a private synonym.

CREATE TABLE

Allows you to create a table in your own schema. You still must have a quota specified for the tablespace listed in the TABLESPACE clause.

CREATE TABLESPACE

Allows you to execute the CREATE TABLESPACE command.

CREATE TRIGGER

Allows you to create a trigger on a table in your schema.

CREATE TYPE (Oracle8)

Allows you to create a user-defined type in your schema.

CREATE USER

Allows you to execute the CREATE USER command.

CREATE VIEW

Allows you to execute the CREATE VIEW command within your schema.

DELETE ANY TABLE

Allows you to execute the DELETE statement against any table in the database.

DROP ANY CLUSTER

Allows you to execute the DROP CLUSTER command for all clusters in the database.

DROP ANY DIRECTORY (Oracle8)

Allows you to execute the DROP DIRECTORY command. Since all BFILE directories are owned by SYS, there is no DROP DIRECTORY privilege.

DROP ANY INDEX

Allows you to execute the DROP INDEX command for all indexes in the database.

DROP ANY LIBRARY (Oracle8)

Allows you to execute the DROP LIBRARY command for any library in the database.

DROP ANY PROCEDURE

Allows you to execute the DROP FUNCTION, DROP PACKAGE, and DROP PROCEDURE commands for all functions, packages, and procedures in the database.

DROP ANY ROLE

Allows you to execute the DROP ROLE command.

DROP ANY SEQUENCE

Allows you to execute the DROP SEQUENCE command for any sequence in any schema.

DROP ANY SNAPSHOT

Allows you to execute the DROP SNAPSHOT command for any snapshot in the database.

DROP ANY SYNONYM

Allows you to execute the DROP SYNONYM command for any synonym in the database.

DROP ANY TABLE

Allows you to execute the DROP TABLE command for any table in the database. You need the DROP ANY TABLE privilege to truncate a table that is not in your schema.

DROP ANY TRIGGER

Allows you to execute the DROP TRIGGER command for all triggers in the database.

DROP ANY TYPE (Oracle8)

Allows you to drop any user-defined type in any schema.

DROP ANY VIEW

Allows you to execute the DROP VIEW command for all views in the database.

DROP PROFILE

Allows you to execute the DROP PROFILE command.

DROP PUBLIC DATABASE LINK

Allows you to execute the DROP PUBLIC DATABASE LINK command. As with the CREATE PUBLIC DATABASE LINK system privilege, there is no corresponding DROP ANY DATABASE LINK system privilege.

DROP PUBLIC SYNONYM

Allows you to execute the DROP PUBLIC SYNONYM command.

DROP ROLLBACK SEGMENT

Allows you to execute the DROP ROLLBACK SEGMENT command for any tablespace in the database.

DROP TABLESPACE

Allows you to execute the DROP TABLESPACE command for any tablespace in the database.

DROP USER

Allows you to execute the DROP USER command for any user in the database.

EXECUTE ANY LIBRARY (Oracle8)

Allows you to execute an external function defined in any library in any schema.

EXECUTE ANY PROCEDURE

Allows you to execute any function, procedure, or package in the database.

EXECUTE ANY TYPE (Oracle8)

Allows you to reference and execute any type or method in any schema.

FORCE ANY TRANSACTION

Allows you to execute the COMMIT FORCE command for any in-doubt transaction in the database.

FORCE TRANSACTION

Allows you to execute the COMMIT FORCE command for any in-doubt transaction you have created.

GRANT ANY PRIVILEGE

Allows you to execute the GRANT system privilege command for any role that has not been granted to you WITH ADMIN OPTION.

GRANT ANY ROLE

Allows you to execute the GRANT role command for any role that has not been granted to you WITH ADMIN OPTION. Also allows you to execute the REVOKE role command for any role that has not been granted to you WITH ADMIN OPTION. You may need to have the ALTER USER privilege to specify whether or not the role is a default role.

INSERT ANY TABLE

Allows you to execute the INSERT statement for any table in the database. In order to insert directly into data dictionary tables, you must have the INSERT_CATALOG_ROLE role.

LOCK ANY TABLE

Allows you to execute the LOCK TABLE command for all tables in the database.

MANAGE TABLESPACE

Allows you to execute the ALTER TABLESPACE command to take tablespaces offline, to take tablespaces online, or to begin or end backups.

SELECT ANY SEQUENCE

Allows you to execute the SELECT statement to retrieve the next sequence value for any sequence in the database, except those owned by SYS.

SELECT ANY TABLE

Allows you to execute the SELECT statement to query any table in the database. In order to select directly from tables in the data dictionary, you must have the SELECT_CATALOG_ROLE role.

UNLIMITED TABLESPACE

Allows you to have unlimited quotas in every tablespace in the database. This system privilege is automatically granted when the RESOURCE role is granted. The UNLIMITED TABLESPACE system privilege is the only system privilege that cannot be granted to a role.

UPDATE ANY TABLE

>   Allows you to execute the UPDATE statement for all tables and views in the
>   database. In order to update tables in the data dictionary directly, you must
>   have the UPDATE_CATALOG_ROLE role.

New System Privileges in Oracle8

Table 15-6 lists the system privileges that were introduced with Oracle8.

Table 15-6. Oracle8 System Privileges

ALTER ANY LIBRARY	ALTER ANY TYPE
CREATE ANY DIRECTORY	CREATE ANY LIBRARY
CREATE ANY TYPE	CREATE LIBRARY
CREATE TYPE	DROP ANY DIRECTORY
DROP ANY LIBRARY	DROP ANY TYPE
EXECUTE ANY LIBRARY	EXECUTE ANY TYPE

Initial Roles

After you have created a new database, up to 15 roles can be created. Six of these
initial, or default, roles are automatically created by the *sql.bsq* script during the
CREATE DATABASE command. The other nine are created by various SQL scripts
executed by the DBA during the process of configuring the database.

Automatic Roles

The roles listed below are automatically created by the CREATE DATABASE command. In fact, the SQL statements to do this are included in the *sql.bsq* file. Note,
however, that Oracle warns that the CONNECT, DBA, and RESOURCE roles may
not be automatically created in the future.

CONNECT

>   Based upon the CONNECT system privilege in Oracle V6. With this role, you
>   can connect to the database and create objects that are not segments. Interest-
>   ingly, this role also has the CREATE TABLE privilege, but you must be explic-
>   itly granted quotas in order to create the table.

>   As part of backward compatibility with Oracle V6, you can bypass the CREATE
>   USER command and simply issue a GRANT CONNECT TO *userid* IDENTIFIED
>   BY *password* statement. In this case, Oracle will first execute a CREATE USER
>   *userid* IDENTIFIED BY *password* statement, followed by the GRANT CON-
>   NECT TO *userid* statement. We strongly recommend that you not use this fea-
>   ture, since it is not guaranteed to remain valid in future releases.

DBA

Based upon the DBA system privilege in Oracle V6. This role has every system privilege except UNLIMITED TABLESPACE, which cannot be granted to a role. The DBA role has also been granted the EXP_FULL_TABLESPACE, IMP_FULL_TABLESPACE, DELETE_CATALOG_ROLE, EXECUTE_CATALOG_ROLE, and SELECT_CATALOG_ROLE roles.

DELETE_CATALOG_ROLE

Required to delete from any object owned by SYS. Granted explicitly to the DBA role and SYS schema.

EXECUTE_CATALOG_ROLE

Required to execute any object owned by SYS. Granted to the DBA, EXP_FULL_DATABASE, and IMP_FULL_DATABASE roles and to the SYS schema.

RESOURCE

Based upon the Oracle V6 RESOURCE system privilege. This role expands upon the CONNECT role, allowing you to create procedures, snapshots, triggers, and types.

As part of backward compatibility with Oracle V6, when you GRANT RESOURCE to a userid, Oracle automatically grants the UNLIMITED TABLESPACE system privilege. We recommend that you either create a different role that emulates the RESOURCE role, or automatically revoke the UNLIMITED TABLESPACE system privilege after granting RESOURCE. Otherwise, you will not be able to restrict users to specific tablespaces using quotas.

SELECT_CATALOG_ROLE

Required to select directly from any object owned by SYS. Granted explicitly to the DBA, EXP_FULL_DATABASE, and IMP_FULL_DATABASE roles and to the SYS schema.

Optional Roles

The roles described in this section are created by executing one of the SQL scripts shipped with the database. They are documented here for completeness. Table 15-7 shows which scripts create which roles.

AQ_ADMINISTRATOR_ROLE

Used by the Advanced Queueing mechanism. Allows you to create and maintain queue tables.

AQ_USER_ROLE

Used by the Advanced Queueing mechanism. Allows you to send and retrieve queued messages.

EXP_FULL_DATABASE

Allows you to perform a full export. This role is explicitly looked for by the EXP (Export) utility when you perform a full export. Having all the system privileges is not sufficient to perform a full export.

HS_ADMIN_ROLE

Allows you to manage Heterogeneous Services.

IMP_FULL_DATABASE

Allows you to perform an import from a full export. This role is explicitly looked for by the IMP (Import) utility when you import from a full export. Having all the system privileges is not sufficient to create any object.

PLUSTRACE

Provides sufficient privileges to execute the SQL*Plus SET AUTOTRACE command.

RECOVERY_CATALOG_OWNER

Defines the owner of the recovery catalog to RMAN.

SNMPAGENT

Used in support of the SNMP intelligent agent within Oracle Enterprise Manager.

TKPROFER

Provides sufficient privileges to run TKPROF.

Table 15-7. Location of Scripts to Create Initial Roles

Role	Script Location
AQ_ADMINISTRATOR_ROLE	*$ORACLE_HOME/rdbms/admin/dbmsaqad.sql*
AQ_USER_ROLE	*$ORACLE_HOME/rdbms/admin/dbmsaqad.sql*
EXP_FULL_DATABASE	*$ORACLE_HOME/rdbms/admin/catexp.sql*
HS_ADMIN_ROLE	*$ORACLE_HOME/rdbsm/admin/caths.sql*
IMP_FULL_DATABASE	*$ORACLE_HOME/rdbms/admin/catexp.sql*
PLUSTRACE	*$ORACLE_HOME/plus80/plustrce.sql*
SNMPAGENT	*$ORACLE_HOME/rdbms/admin/catsnmp.sql*
RECOVERY_CATALOG_OWNER	*$ORACLE_HOME/rdbms/admin/catalog.sql*
TKPROFER	*$ORACLE_HOME/rdbms/admin/utltkprf.sql*

Cross-Reference: Roles and System Privileges

Table 15-8 shows which Oracle system privileges are assigned to the initial roles described in the preceding sections.

Table 15-8. Cross-Reference Listing of System Privileges and Roles

System Privilege	CONNECT	DBA	EXP_FULL_DATABASE	IMP_FULL_DATABASE	RECOVERY_CATALOG_OWNER	RESOURCE	SNMPAGENT
ALTER ANY CLUSTER		✓					
ALTER ANY INDEX		✓					
ALTER ANY LIBRARY		✓					
ALTER ANY PROCEDURE		✓					
ALTER ANY ROLE		✓					
ALTER ANY SEQUENCE		✓					
ALTER ANY SNAPSHOT		✓					
ALTER ANY TABLE		✓		✓			
ALTER ANY TRIGGER		✓					
ALTER ANY TYPE		✓		✓			
ALTER DATABASE		✓					
ALTER PROFILE		✓					
ALTER RESOURCE COST		✓					
ALTER ROLLBACK SEGMENT		✓					
ALTER SESSION	✓	✓			✓		
ALTER SYSTEM		✓					
ALTER TABLESPACE		✓					
ALTER USER		✓					
ANALYZE ANY		✓					✓
AUDIT ANY		✓		✓			
AUDIT SYSTEM		✓					
BACKUP ANY TABLE		✓	✓				
BECOME USER		✓		✓			
COMMENT ANY TABLE		✓		✓			
CREATE ANY CLUSTER		✓		✓			
CREATE ANY DIRECTORY		✓		✓			
CREATE ANY INDEX		✓		✓			
CREATE ANY LIBRARY		✓		✓			
CREATE ANY PROCEDURE		✓		✓			
CREATE ANY SEQUENCE		✓		✓			
CREATE ANY SNAPSHOT		✓		✓			
CREATE ANY SYNONYM		✓		✓			
CREATE ANY TABLE		✓		✓			

Table 15-8. Cross-Reference Listing of System Privileges and Roles (continued)

System Privilege	CONNECT	DBA	EXP_FULL_DATABASE	IMP_FULL_DATABASE	RECOVERY_CATALOG_OWNER	RESOURCE	SNMPAGENT
CREATE ANY TRIGGER		✓		✓			
CREATE ANY TYPE		✓		✓			
CREATE ANY VIEW		✓		✓			
CREATE CLUSTER	✓	✓			✓	✓	
CREATE DATABASE LINK	✓	✓		✓	✓		
CREATE LIBRARY		✓					
CREATE PROCEDURE		✓			✓	✓	
CREATE PROFILE		✓		✓			
CREATE PUBLIC DATABASE LINK		✓		✓			
CREATE PUBLIC SYNONYM		✓		✓			
CREATE ROLE		✓		✓			
CREATE ROLLBACK SEGMENT		✓		✓			
CREATE SEQUENCE	✓	✓			✓	✓	
CREATE SESSION	✓	✓			✓		
CREATE SNAPSHOT		✓					
CREATE SYNONYM	✓	✓			✓		
CREATE TABLE	✓	✓			✓	✓	
CREATE TABLESPACE		✓		✓			
CREATE TRIGGER		✓			✓	✓	
CREATE TYPE		✓				✓	
CREATE USER		✓		✓			
CREATE VIEW	✓	✓			✓		
DELETE ANY TABLE		✓					
DROP ANY CLUSTER		✓		✓			
DROP ANY DIRECTORY		✓		✓			
DROP ANY INDEX		✓		✓			
DROP ANY LIBRARY		✓		✓			
DROP ANY PROCEDURE		✓		✓			
DROP ANY ROLE		✓		✓			
DROP ANY SEQUENCE		✓		✓			

Table 15-8. Cross-Reference Listing of System Privileges and Roles (continued)

System Privilege	CONNECT	DBA	EXP_FULL_ DATABASE	IMP_FULL_ DATABASE	RECOVERY_ CATALOG_ OWNER	RESOURCE	SNMPAGENT
DROP ANY SNAPSHOT		✓		✓			
DROP ANY SYNONYM		✓		✓			
DROP ANY TABLE		✓		✓			
DROP ANY TRIGGER		✓		✓			
DROP ANY TYPE		✓		✓			
DROP ANY VIEW		✓		✓			
DROP PROFILE		✓		✓			
DROP PUBLIC DATABASE LINK		✓		✓			
DROP PUBLIC SYNONYM		✓		✓			
DROP ROLLBACK SEGMENT		✓		✓			
DROP TABLESPACE		✓		✓			
DROP USER		✓		✓			
EXECUTE ANY LIBRARY		✓					
EXECUTE ANY PROCEDURE		✓	✓	✓			
EXECUTE ANY TYPE		✓					
FORCE ANY TRANSACTION		✓					
FORCE TRANSACTION		✓					
GRANT ANY PRIVILEGE		✓					
GRANT ANY ROLE		✓					
INSERT ANY TABLE		✓		✓			
LOCK ANY TABLE		✓					
MANAGE TABLESPACE		✓					
RESTRICTED SESSION		✓					
SELECT ANY SEQUENCE		✓					
SELECT ANY TABLE		✓	✓	✓			
UNLIMITED TABLESPACE							
UPDATE ANY TABLE		✓					

Initial Users

Several users are created as part of the database build process. Two of these, SYS and SYSTEM, are created by the *sql.bsq* file. The other users are created by the various initialization files, depending upon which options you choose.

Summary of Initial Users

The following lists all initial users in alphabetical order:

CTXSYS
>   Used as part of a demo.

DBSNMP
>   Used to support the Oracle Enterprise Manager SNMP intelligent agents.

MDSYS
>   Contains support for multidimensional databases.

ORDSYS
>   Contains support for Oracle image objects.

RMAN
>   The recommended name of the user that owns the recovery catalog, used by
>   the RMAN facility. Actually, this can be any user.

SCOTT
>   The ubiquitous userid used for years for Oracle demos and training classes.
>   Owns the infamous EMP and DEPT tables.

SYS
>   Owns the data dictionary and is the user to which you connect when you
>   CONNECT INTERNAL. This user is automatically granted the DBA role.

SYSTEM
>   Used to manage the database, and occasionally to hold tables and packages
>   that support additional features within the database. This user is automatically
>   granted the DBA role.

Cross-Reference: Roles Assigned to Initial Users

Table 15-9 shows the roles assigned to the initial users described in the previous
section.

Table 15-9. Cross-Reference Listing of Roles and Initial Users

	Initial User							
Role Assigned	CTXSYS	DBSNMP	MDSYS	ORDSYS	RMAN	SCOTT	SYS	SYSTEM
AQ_ADMINISTRATOR_ROLE							✓	✓
AQ_USER_ROLE							✓	
CONNECT	✓	✓	✓	✓		✓	✓	
DBA	✓						✓	✓

Table 15-9. Cross-Reference Listing of Roles and Initial Users (continued)

| | Initial User | | | | | | | |
Role Assigned	CTXSYS	DBSNMP	MDSYS	ORDSYS	RMAN	SCOTT	SYS	SYSTEM
DELETE_CATALOG_ROLE							✓	
EXECUTE_CATALOG_ROLE							✓	
EXP_FULL_DATABASE							✓	
HS_ADMIN_ROLE							✓	
IMP_FULL_DATABASE							✓	
RECOVERY_CATALOG_OWNER					✓		✓	
RESOURCE	✓	✓	✓	✓		✓	✓	
SELECT_CATALOG_ROLE							✓	
SNMPAGENT		✓					✓	

Cross-Reference: System Privileges Assigned to Initial Users

Table 15-10 shows the system privileges assigned to the initial users. Note that since the SYS and SYSTEM users are granted the DBA role by default, they actually acquire all the privileges granted through that role.

Table 15-10. Cross-Reference Listing of System Privileges and Users

| | Granted to | | | | | |
Privilege Assigned	CTXSYS	DBSNMP	MDSYS	ORDSYS	SYS	SYSTEM
ALTER ANY CLUSTER	✓		✓			
ALTER ANY INDEX	✓		✓			
ALTER ANY LIBRARY	✓		✓			
ALTER ANY PROCEDURE	✓		✓			
ALTER ANY ROLE	✓		✓			
ALTER ANY SEQUENCE	✓		✓			
ALTER ANY SNAPSHOT	✓		✓			
ALTER ANY TABLE	✓		✓			
ALTER ANY TRIGGER	✓		✓			
ALTER ANY TYPE	✓		✓			
ALTER DATABASE	✓		✓			
ALTER PROFILE	✓		✓			

Table 15-10. Cross-Reference Listing of System Privileges and Users (continued)

Privilege Assigned	Granted to					
	CTXSYS	DBSNMP	MDSYS	ORDSYS	SYS	SYSTEM
ALTER RESOURCE COST	✓		✓			
ALTER ROLLBACK SEGMENT	✓		✓			
ALTER SESSION	✓		✓			
ALTER SYSTEM	✓		✓			
ALTER TABLESPACE	✓		✓			
ALTER USER	✓		✓			
ANALYZE ANY	✓		✓			
AUDIT ANY	✓		✓			
AUDIT SYSTEM	✓		✓			
BACKUP ANY TABLE	✓		✓			
BECOME USER	✓		✓			
COMMENT ANY TABLE	✓		✓			
CREATE ANY CLUSTER	✓		✓			
CREATE ANY DIRECTORY	✓		✓			
CREATE ANY INDEX	✓		✓			
CREATE ANY LIBRARY	✓		✓			
CREATE ANY PROCEDURE	✓		✓			
CREATE ANY SEQUENCE	✓		✓			
CREATE ANY SNAPSHOT	✓		✓			
CREATE ANY SYNONYM	✓		✓			
CREATE ANY TABLE	✓		✓	✓		
CREATE ANY TRIGGER	✓		✓			
CREATE ANY TYPE	✓		✓	✓		
CREATE ANY VIEW	✓		✓			
CREATE CLUSTER	✓		✓			
CREATE DATABASE LINK	✓		✓			
CREATE LIBRARY	✓		✓	✓		
CREATE PROCEDURE	✓		✓	✓		
CREATE PROFILE	✓		✓			
CREATE PUBLIC DATABASE LINK	✓		✓			
CREATE PUBLIC SYNONYM	✓	✓	✓	✓		
CREATE ROLE	✓		✓			
CREATE ROLLBACK SEGMENT	✓		✓			

Table 15-10. Cross-Reference Listing of System Privileges and Users (continued)

Privilege Assigned	CTXSYS	DBSNMP	MDSYS	ORDSYS	SYS	SYSTEM
			Granted to			
CREATE SEQUENCE	✓		✓			
CREATE SESSION	✓		✓	✓		
CREATE SNAPSHOT	✓		✓			
CREATE SYNONYM	✓		✓			
CREATE TABLE	✓		✓			
CREATE TABLESPACE	✓		✓			
CREATE TRIGGER	✓		✓			
CREATE TYPE	✓		✓			
CREATE USER	✓		✓			
CREATE VIEW	✓		✓			
DELETE ANY TABLE	✓		✓		✓	
DROP ANY CLUSTER	✓		✓			
DROP ANY DIRECTORY	✓		✓			
DROP ANY INDEX	✓		✓			
DROP ANY LIBRARY	✓		✓			
DROP ANY PROCEDURE	✓		✓			
DROP ANY ROLE	✓		✓			
DROP ANY SEQUENCE	✓		✓			
DROP ANY SNAPSHOT	✓		✓			
DROP ANY SYNONYM	✓		✓			
DROP ANY TABLE	✓		✓			
DROP ANY TRIGGER	✓		✓			
DROP ANY TYPE	✓		✓	✓		
DROP ANY VIEW	✓		✓			
DROP PROFILE	✓		✓			
DROP PUBLIC DATABASE LINK	✓		✓			
DROP PUBLIC SYNONYM	✓		✓	✓		
DROP ROLLBACK SEGMENT	✓		✓			
DROP TABLESPACE	✓		✓			
DROP USER	✓		✓			
EXECUTE ANY LIBRARY	✓		✓			
EXECUTE ANY PROCEDURE	✓		✓		✓	
EXECUTE ANY TYPE	✓		✓		✓	

Table 15-10. Cross-Reference Listing of System Privileges and Users (continued)

Privilege Assigned	CTXSYS	DBSNMP	MDSYS	ORDSYS	SYS	SYSTEM
			Granted to			
FORCE ANY TRANSACTION	✓		✓			
FORCE TRANSACTION	✓		✓			
GRANT ANY PRIVILEGE	✓		✓			
GRANT ANY ROLE	✓		✓			
INSERT ANY TABLE	✓		✓			
LOCK ANY TABLE	✓		✓		✓	
MANAGE TABLESPACE	✓		✓			
RESTRICTED SESSION	✓		✓			
SELECT ANY SEQUENCE	✓		✓			
SELECT ANY TABLE	✓		✓		✓	
UNLIMITED TABLESPACE	✓		✓		✓	
UPDATE ANY TABLE	✓	✓	✓	✓		✓

16

Tools and Utilities

There are few things more frustrating to a DBA than to be in the middle of a crisis (DBAs do nothing but handle crises, right?), working with a familiar Oracle tool or utility, and suddenly be unable to recall a command or option syntax. All work must stop while you hunt for the appropriate manual, which usually means finding the documentation CD-ROM and loading the documentation viewer, then searching for what you need. Meanwhile, users are demanding to know when the system will be up.

This chapter summarizes the syntax and options used with the most popular Oracle tools and utilities. While it is not a comprehensive listing of each and every option, you will find the most commonly used options and commands listed in an easy reference format. Of course, for complete information, you will still need to refer to the appropriate Oracle manual.

SQL*Plus

SQL*Plus, introduced in Chapter 9, is Oracle's primary interface to the database, and allows the execution of SQL and PL/SQL as well as providing formatting and operational control. Our discussion of SQL*Plus in this book is intended only as a quick reference. For a complete discussion of this tool, see Jonathan Gennick's *Oracle SQL*Plus: The Definitive Guide* (O'Reilly & Associates, 1999).

Command-Line Syntax

The syntax for invoking SQL*Plus from a command-line prompt is:

```
sqlplus [username[/password]][@hostname] [@script] [parm1] [parm2] ...
```

username

The Oracle username for the account to be connected.

password

The password for the username. If the password is omitted, SQL*Plus prompts for the password.

hostname

The hostname assigned to the database being connected to, as contained in the *tnsnames.ora* file or Oracle Names.

script

The name of a SQL script to be executed upon successful connection to the database.

parm1, parm2 ...

Optional parameters that are passed to SQL*Plus and may be used as substitution variables within a SQL*Plus script. String parameters containing spaces or special characters must be enclosed in single quotes.

The actual name of the SQL*Plus executable may vary from platform to platform and from release to release. For example, the executable name for SQL*Plus Version 3.3 for Windows 95 (command-line version) is *PLUS33.EXE*, and the GUI version is *PLUS33W.EXE*.

SQL*Plus Editing Commands

The following commands implement SQL*Plus editing capabilities, and may be entered directly from a SQL*Plus prompt or included in a SQL*Plus script.

APPEND

```
A[PPEND] text
```

Adds (appends) *text* to the end of the current line.

CHANGE

```
C[HANGE] {/old/new | /text}
```

Changes the current line.

/old/new

Changes *old* to *new* in the current line.

/text

Deletes *text* from the current line.

CLEAR

```
CL[EAR] BUFF[ER]
```

Deletes all lines from the buffer.

DEL

```
DEL
```

Deletes the current line.

GET

```
GET filename
```

Places the contents of *filename* into the buffer, replacing the current buffer contents.

INPUT

```
I[NPUT]
```

Adds one or more lines starting after the current line.

LIST

```
L[IST] [n | * | LAST | m n]
```

When specified without arguments, LIST displays all lines in the buffer.

n
> Displays line *n*.

*
> Displays the current line.

LAST
> Displays the last line in the buffer.

m n
> Displays the range of lines starting at *m* and ending with *n*.

SAVE

```
SAVE filename [CREATE | REPLACE | APPEND]
```

Saves the contents of the buffer into *filename*. The buffer contents are preserved.

CREATE
> Creates a new file; if this option is specified, *filename* must not already exist.

REPLACE

Replaces the contents of the existing file; if *filename* does not exist, creates it.

APPEND

Adds the contents of the buffer to the end of the specified file.

START

```
START filename
```

Runs a series of commands, SQL statements, and PL/SQL statements contained in *filename*. This is equivalent to specifying @*filename* on the command line. Command files may be nested—that is, a command file may contain another START *filename* command.

Formatting SQL*Plus Output

The following commands implement the formatting capabilities of SQL*Plus, and may be entered from a SQL*Plus prompt or included in a SQL*Plus script.

BREAK

```
BRE[AK]  [ON column | expression | ROW | REPORT [action [action]]]...
```

Specifies where and how to change the formatting of a report.

column

Causes the *action* to take place whenever the value of the specified *column* changes.

expression

Causes the *action* to take place whenever the value of the *expression* changes.

ROW

Causes the *action* to take place whenever SQL*Plus returns a row.

REPORT

Causes the corresponding COMPUTE command to be executed at the end of the report.

action

Can be one or more of the following:

SKI[P] n

Skips *n* lines before printing the row where the break occurred.

SKI[P] PAGE

Skips the necessary number of lines to advance to a new page. If SET NEWPAGE 0 is specified, prints a formfeed.

NODUP[LICATES]

Causes blanks to be printed (rather than the value of the break column) when the value is the same as the value in the preceding row.

DUP[LICATES]

Causes the value of the break column to be printed for every row.

BREAK

Lists all current BREAK definitions.

BTITLE

```
BTI[TLE] [ON | OFF]  [printspec [text | variable] ...]
```

Specifies formatting for the title at the bottom of each page. If you specify BTITLE without arguments, it displays the current BTITLE definition. If you specify *text* or *variable*, BTITLE formats that title at the bottom of the page.

ON

Turns the bottom title on without affecting its definition.

OFF

Turns the bottom title off without affecting its definition.

printspec

One or more of the following clauses used to place and format *text* or *variable*:

COL n

Starts *text* or *variable* in column *n*.

S[KIP] [n]

Skips *n* lines before printing *text* or *variable* (the default is 1).

TAB n

Skips *n* print positions forward (or backward, if *n* is negative) before printing *text* or *variable*.

LE[FT]

Prints *text* or *variable* aligned with the left margin.

CE[NTER]

Prints *text* or *variable* centered on the page. The SQL*Plus line size is used to calculate page width.

RI[GHT]

Prints *text* or *variable* aligned with the right margin.

BOLD

Prints *text* or *variable* in bold print.

FORMAT charstring

> Formats *text* or *variable* according to the format model specified in *charstring*.

text

> A character string to be printed on the page. Multiple words must be enclosed in single quotes.

variable

> A user variable or a system-maintained variable.

CLEAR

```
CL[EAR] option
```

Resets or erases the current value of a SQL*Plus option.

option

> May be one of the following:
>
> *BRE[AKS]*
>
> > Removes the definitions set by the BREAK command.
>
> *BUF[FER]*
>
> > Clears all text from the buffer.
>
> *COL[UMNS]*
>
> > Resets column definitions set by the COLUMN command to the default definition.
>
> *COMP[UTES]*
>
> > Removes all definitions set by the COMPUTE command.
>
> *SCR[EEN]*
>
> > Clears the screen.
>
> *SQL*
>
> > Clears all text from the buffer.
>
> *TIMI[NG]*
>
> > Deletes all timing areas created by the TIMING command.

COLUMN

```
COL[UMN] column | expression [option ...]
```

Specifies the display characteristics for a *column* or *expression,* optionally using one or more *options.* If an option is not specified, the command displays the current display attributes for *column* or *expression.*

column

> The column name used in a SQL statement.

expression

The expression used in a SQL statement.

option

One or more of the following:

ALI[AS] alias

Assigns *alias* to the *column* or *expression*, which can then be used in BREAK, COMPUTE, or other COLUMN commands.

CLE[AR]

Resets attributes for this *column* or *expression* to defaults.

FOLD_A[FTER]

Inserts a carriage return after the heading and after each row of the *column* or *expression*.

FOLD_B[EFORE]

Inserts a carriage return before the heading and before each row of the *column* or *expression*.

FOR[MAT] format

Specifies a character string format that describes the format for display of the *column* or *expression*.

HEA[DING] string

Defines a column heading using *string*, which must be enclosed in single or double quotes if it contains blanks or punctuation, and which can contain the HEADSEP character ("|" by default), each occurrence of which will cause SQL*Plus to begin a new line of heading.

JUST[IFY] {L[EFT] | C[ENTER] | C[ENTRE] | R[IGHT]}

Aligns the heading as specified. By default, NUMBER columns default to RIGHT and other columns default to LEFT.

LIKE {expression | alias}

Copies the display attributes of another column (identified by *alias*) or *expression* defined in a prior COLUMN command, except that attributes specified in this COLUMN command are not copied.

NEWL[INE]

Starts a new line before displaying the value for the *column* or *expression*.

NEW_V[ALUE] variable

Specifies that the column value is to be held in *variable*, which can then be used in the TTITLE command.

NOPRI[NT]

Prevents the printing of the *column* or *expression*.

NUL[L] charstring

Specifies a *charstring* to be displayed when the value of the *column* or *expression* is NULL.

OFF

Disables the display attributes for the *column* or *expression* without affecting the attributes' definitions.

OLD_V[ALUE] variable

Specifies that the previous value of the *column* or *expression* is to be held in *variable*, which can then be used in the BTITLE command.

ON

Enables the display attributes for the *column* or *expression* that had been previously set to OFF.

TRU[NCATED]

Specifies that a CHAR string too long for the column is to be truncated.

WOR[D_WRAPPED]

Specifies that a CHAR string too long for the column is to be wrapped to the next line, starting with the first full word of the string that does not fit in the width of the column.

WRA[PPED]

Specifies that a CHAR string too long for the column is to be wrapped to the next line, starting with the first character of the string that does not fit in the width of the column.

COMPUTE

```
COMP[UTE] [function ... OF {expression | column | alias}...
    ON {expression | column | alias | REPORT | ROW}]
```

Calculates and displays summary lines using standard computations on selected subsets of rows.

function

One or more of the following standard mathematical functions (separated by spaces if more than one is specified):

AVG
COU[NT]
MAX[IMUM]
MIN[IMUM]
NUM[BER]
STD
SUM
VAR[IANCE]

OF {expression | column | alias}

> Specifies the *expression*(s), *column*(s), or *alias(es)* to use in the computation, which are also listed in the SQL SELECT statement.

ON {expression | column | alias | REPORT | ROW}

> Specifies the entity that, when its value changes, will trigger COMPUTE to display the computed value. ON must match a corresponding BREAK statement.

TTITLE

```
TTI[TLE] [ON | OFF] [printspec [text | variable] ...]
```

Specifies formatting for the title at the top of each page. If you specify TTITLE without arguments, it displays the current TTITLE definition. If you specify *text* or *variable*, TTITLE formats that title at the top of the page.

ON

> Turns the top title on without affecting its definition.

OFF

> Turns the top title off without affecting its definition.

printspec

> One or more of the following clauses used to place and format *text* or *variable*:

COL n

> Starts *text* or *variable* in column *n*.

S[KIP] [n]

> Skips *n* lines before printing *text* or *variable* (the default is 1).

TAB n

> Skips *n* print positions forward (or backward, if *n* is negative) before printing *text* or *variable*.

LE[FT]

> Prints *text* or *variable* aligned with the left margin.

CE[NTER]

> Prints *text* or *variable* centered on the page. LINESIZE is used to calculate page width.

RI[GHT]

> Prints *text* or *variable* aligned with the right margin.

BOLD

> Prints *text* or *variable* in bold print.

FORMAT charstring
> Formats *text* or *variable* according to the format model specified in *charstring*.

text
> A character string to be printed on the page. Multiple words must be enclosed in single quotes.

variable
> A user variable or a system-maintained variable.

Other SQL*Plus Commands

SQL*Plus provides the following additional commands, which may be entered directly from a SQL*Plus prompt or included in a SQL*Plus script.

CONNECT

```
CONN[ECT] username[/password[@hostname]]
```

Connects the specified *username* to the database.

username
> The Oracle username.

password
> The password associated with the *username* provided. If *password* is omitted, SQL*Plus will prompt for one.

@hostname
> The hostname assigned to the database being connected to, as contained in the *tnsnames.ora* file or Oracle Names.

COPY

```
COPY {[FROM username[/password]@database_spec] |
TO username[/password]@database_spec] |
[FROM username[/password]@database_spec TO username[/password]@database_spec}
{APPEND | CREATE | INSERT | REPLACE}
destination_table [(column[,column ...])]} USING query)
```

Copies data returned from a query to another table in either the local or remote database.

username
> The name of the user account (schema) from which and to which data will be copied.

password
> The password associated with the specified user account.

database_spec

The SQL*Net connect string for the database being connected to.

TO

Specifies the *username, password,* and *database_spec* for the database to which data is to be copied. If TO is omitted, the account SQL*Plus is currently logged into will be used.

FROM

Specifies the *username, password,* and *database_spec* for the database from which data is to be copied. If FROM is omitted, the account SQL*Plus is currently logged into will be used.

APPEND

Causes rows to be inserted into *destination_table* if it exists; otherwise, *destination_table* is created.

CREATE

Creates *destination_table* before inserting rows. If *destination_table* already exists, an error results.

INSERT

Causes rows to be inserted into *destination_table*. If *destination_table* does not exist, an error results.

REPLACE

Replaces the *destination_table* with the results of the query. If *destination_table* does not exist, it will be created.

destination_table

The name of the table to be created or the table to which rows are being added.

column

The name of a column in *destination_table* in which data will be inserted. If columns are specified, the number of columns must match those being returned by the query.

query

Any valid SQL SELECT statement that returns the rows and columns that COPY will copy.

DESCRIBE

Oracle8:

```
DESC[RIBE] {[username.]object[@database_spec ].[column] |
   [username.]object[.subobject]}
```

Oracle7:

```
DESC[RIBE] {[username.]object[@database_spec ] |
   [username.]object[.subobject]}
```

Lists the column definitions for the specified database object.

column
> The name of a column to be described (Oracle8 only).

database_spec
> The SQL*Net connect string for the database being connected to.

object
> The name of the object being described, which can be a table, view, synonym, function, procedure, or package.

subobject
> The name of a function or procedure in a package to be described.

username
> The name of the user account (schema) that owns the *object*.

DISCONNECT

```
DISC[ONNECT]
```

Commits any pending transactions and disconnects the current user from the database without exiting SQL*Plus.

EDIT

```
EDIT [filename[.extension]
```

Invokes the system editor as specified by the value of the user variable _EDITOR. If the editor is invoked without a *filename,* the current contents of the buffer are passed to the editor and returned to the buffer when editing is complete.

filename
> The filename of a file to be opened by the editor. If *filename* does not exist, it will be created.

extension
> The extension portion of *filename* for those systems that support extensions.

EXECUTE

```
EXE[CUTE] statement
```

Executes a single PL/SQL *statement*; commonly used to reference a stored procedure.

EXIT

```
EXIT [SUCCESS | FAILURE | WARNING | n | variable [COMMIT | ROLLBACK]
```

Commits all pending transactions (unless AUTOCOMMIT is set to OFF), passes a return code to the operating system, and exits SQL*Plus.

SUCCESS
> Exits normally with a return code indicating success. This is the default.

FAILURE
> Exits with a return code indicating failure.

WARNING
> Exits with a return code indicating a warning.

n   Exits with a specific numeric return code.

variable
> Exits with a user-defined or system *variable* whose value will be used as the return code.

COMMIT
> Commits pending changes to the database before exiting.

ROLLBACK
> Rolls back pending changes before exiting.

HELP

```
HELP [topic]
```

Invokes the SQL*Plus Help System and displays help information on *topic* if specified; otherwise, displays a list of all topics.

topic
> A topic from the list of SQL*Plus topics.

HOST

```
HO[ST] [command]
```

Executes an operating system command without leaving SQL*Plus. If *command* is not specified, displays a system prompt and remains in operating system mode until EXIT is entered.

command
> Any valid operating system command.

PAUSE

```
PAU[SE] [text]
```

Displays an empty line followed by a line containing *text* (if specified), then waits for the user to press the return key.

text

A text string (quotes are not necessary) to appear on the output device.

REMARK

```
REM[ARK]
```

Indicates that all characters following on the same line are to be treated as a comment and ignored by SQL*Plus.

SET

```
SET system_variable value
```

Sets a SQL*Plus *system variable* to the specified *value*.

system_variable

The name of a valid SQL*Plus system variable (see the "SQL*Plus System Variables" section, later in this chapter).

value

A valid value for the system variable.

SHOW

```
SHO[W] variable
```

Lists the current value of one of the following SQL*Plus system variables. In addition, note that any value that can be SET may also be used as a *variable*.

```
ALL
APPI[NFO]
BTI[TLE]
ERR[ORS] [{FUNCTION | PROCEDURE | PACKAGE | PACKAGE BODY | TRIGGER | VIEW |
    TYPE | TYPE BODY} [schema.] name]
LABEL
LNO
PNO
REL[EASE]
REPF[OOTER]
REPH[EADER]
SPOO[L]
SQLCODE
TTI[TLE]
USER
```

SPOOL

```
SPOOL
```

Displays the current spooling status.

```
SPO[OL] [filename[.extension]] [OFF | OUT]
```

Spools all following SQL*Plus output to a file or printer until SPOOL OFF is encountered.

filename[.extension]

> The filename and optional extension for the file in which the output will be stored. If an *extension* is not supplied, *.LIS* or *.LST* (depending on the platform) will be used as an extension.

OFF

> Stops spooling.

OUT

> Stops spooling and sends the output file to the default printer.

STORE

```
STORE {SET} filename[.extension] [CRE[ATE] | REP[LACE] | APP[END]]
```

Saves attributes of the current SQL*Plus environment in *filename* with the optional *.extension*. The resulting file is a list of SET commands (Oracle8 only).

CREATE

> Creates a new file; *filename* must not already exist if this option is specified.

REPLACE

> Replaces the contents of the existing file; if the filename does not exist, creates it.

APPEND

> Adds the contents of the buffer to the end of the specified file.

TIMING

```
TIMING
```

Lists the number of active timers.

```
TIMI[NG] [START text | SHOW | STOP]
```

Starts, stops, or lists elapsed timers.

START text

> Sets up a timer and gives it the name *text*.

SHOW

Lists the current timer's name and timing data.

STOP

Lists the current timer's name and timing data, then deletes the timer.

WHENEVER OSERROR

```
WHENEVER OSERROR
{ {EXIT [SUCCESS | FAILURE | n | variable | :BindVariable]
    [COMMIT | ROLLBACK]} |
{CONTINUE [COMMIT | ROLLBACK | NONE]}
```

Specifies action to be taken by SQL*Plus if an operating system error occurs.

EXIT

Directs SQL*Plus to exit as soon as an operating system error is detected.

SUCCESS

Exits normally with a return code indicating success. This is the default.

FAILURE

Exits with a return code indicating failure.

n

A specific numeric return code to be returned.

variable

A user-defined or system variable whose value will be used as the return code.

BindVariable

A variable created in SQL*Plus with the VARIABLE command, then referenced in PL/SQL.

CONTINUE

Turns off the EXIT option.

COMMIT

Directs SQL*Plus to execute a COMMIT before exiting or continuing after an operating system error.

ROLLBACK

Directs SQL*Plus to execute a ROLLBACK before exiting or continuing after an operating system error.

NONE

Directs SQL*Plus to take no action after an operating system error.

WHENEVER SQLERROR

```
WHENEVER SQLERROR
{ {EXIT [SUCCESS | FAILURE | n | variable | :BindVariable]
    [COMMIT | ROLLBACK]} |
{CONTINUE [COMMIT | ROLLBACK | NONE]}
```

Specifies action to be taken by SQL*Plus if an error is generated by SQL or a PL/SQL block.

EXIT

Directs SQL*Plus to exit as soon as a SQL or PL/SQL error is detected.

SUCCESS

Exits normally with a return code indicating success. This is the default.

FAILURE

Exits with a return code indicating failure.

n

A specific numeric return code to be returned.

variable

A user-defined or system variable whose value will be used as the return code.

BindVariable

A variable created in SQL*Plus with the VARIABLE command and then referenced in PL/SQL.

CONTINUE

Turns off the EXIT option.

COMMIT

Directs SQL*Plus to execute a COMMIT before exiting or continuing after a SQL or PL/SQL error.

ROLLBACK

Directs SQL*Plus to execute a ROLLBACK before exiting or continuing after a SQL or PL/SQL error.

NONE

Directs SQL*Plus to take no action after a SQL or PL/SQL error.

SQL Variables and Related Commands

SQL*Plus provides a mechanism for the creation and use of user variables. The following commands are used to manipulate SQL*Plus user variables, and may be entered directly from a SQL*Plus prompt or included in a SQL*Plus script.

&

```
&n
```

Replaces each occurrence of &*n* with the corresponding parameter from the command line. For example, &1 would be replaced with the value of the first parameter specified on the command line.

```
&var
```

Creates a SQL*Plus variable *var* and prompts for a value each time *&var* is encountered.

```
&&var
```

Creates a SQL*Plus variable *var* and prompts for a value the first time *&&var* is encountered. Retains this value and uses it each time *&&var* is encountered subsequently until *var* is undefined.

ACCEPT

```
ACC[EPT] var [type] [PROMPT text | NOPROMPT] [HIDE]
```

Reads a line of input and stores it in the variable *var*.

type
> Restricts the type of input allowed; may be either NUMBER or CHAR.

PROMPT
> If specified, displays *text* on the screen before accepting input.

NOPROMPT
> If specified, does not display *text* on the screen before accepting input.

HIDE
> Prevents input from being displayed on the screen.

DEFINE

```
DEF[INE] var | var = text
```

Creates a variable *var* and assigns the CHAR variable *text* to it.

```
DEFINE [var]
```

Lists the current value of variable *var* or of all user variables if *var* is not specified.

PRINT

```
PRI[NT] var
```

Displays the current value of the bind variable *var* that was created with the VARI-ABLE command.

UNDEFINE

```
UNDEF[INE] var
```

Deletes the variable *var*.

VARIABLE

```
VAR[IABLE]
```

Displays a list of all bind variables declared.

```
VAR[IABLE] var [NUMBER | CHAR |
```

Declares a bind variable *var* that can be referenced in PL/SQL.

*SQL*Plus System Variables*

The following SQL*Plus system-level variables may be referenced in the SQL*Plus SET and SHOW commands.

APPINFO

```
APPI[NFO]{ON | OFF | text}
```

Sets automatic registering of command files through the DBMS_APPLICATION_ INFO package. This enables the performance and resource usage of each command file to be monitored by the DBA.

OFF
> Turns off automatic registering.

ON
> Turns on automatic registering.

text
> Text to be displayed by DBMS_APPLICATION_INFO.

ARRAYSIZE

```
ARRAY[SIZE] n
```

Sets the number of rows (*n*) that SQL*Plus will fetch from the database at one time. Valid values are 1 to 5000.

AUTOCOMMIT

```
AUTO[COMMIT] {OFF | ON | IMM[EDIATE] | n}
```

Controls when Oracle commits pending changes to the database.

OFF

Suppresses automatic committing, forcing you to commit changes manually.

ON

Commits pending changes to the database after Oracle executes each successful SQL command or PL/SQL block.

IMMEDIATE

Functions the same way as ON.

n   Commits after performing *n* successful SQL commands or PL/SQL blocks.

AUTOPRINT

AUTOP[RINT] {OFF | ON}

Sets the automatic PRINTing of bind variables ON or OFF after each PL/SQL block or SQL statement in which they are referenced.

AUTOTRACE

AUTOT[RACE] { OFF | ON | TRACE[ONLY]} [EXP[LAIN]] [STAT[ISTICS]]

Displays a report on the execution of successful SQL DML statements; can include execution statistics and the query execution path.

OFF

Does not display a trace report.

ON

Displays a trace report.

TRACEONLY

Displays a trace report, but does not print query data, if any.

EXPLAIN

Shows the query execution path by performing an EXPLAIN PLAN.

STATISTICS

Displays SQL statement statistics.

BLOCKTERMINATOR

BLO[CKTERMINATOR] c

Sets the non-alphanumeric character used to end PL/SQL blocks to *c*. To execute the block, you must issue a RUN or "/" (slash) command. The default is the "." character.

CMDSEP

```
CMDS[EP] {c | OFF | ON}
```

Sets the non-alphanumeric character used to separate multiple SQL*Plus commands entered on one line to *c*.

OFF

Turns off the ability to enter multiple commands on a line.

ON

Automatically sets the command separator character to the default value of semicolon (;).

COLSEP

```
COLSEP text
```

Sets the text to be printed between SELECTed columns. The default is the space character (" ").

COMPATIBILITY

```
COM[PATIBILITY] {V7 | V8 | NATIVE}
```

Specifies the version of Oracle to which you are currently connected.

V7 Specifies Oracle7.

V8 Specifies Oracle8.

NATIVE

Specifies that you wish the database to determine the setting. For example, if you are connected to Oracle8, compatibility will default to V8.

CONCAT

```
CON[CAT] {OFF | ON}
```

Sets the character you can use to terminate a substitution variable reference; you issue this command to tell SQL*Plus that the character immediately following the variable should not be interpreted as a part of the substitution variable name. The default is the "." character.

OFF

Specifies that no CONCAT character is to be set.

ON

Resets the value of CONCAT to a period.

COPYCOMMIT

```
COPYC[OMMIT] n
```

Controls the number of batches after which the COPY command commits changes to the database. Since the size of a batch is controlled by ARRAYSIZE, the number of rows copied before each commit will be ARRAYSIZE × *n*. If you set COPY-COMMIT to zero, COPY performs a commit only at the end of a copy operation. The default is 0.

COPYTYPECHECK

```
COPYTYPECHECK {OFF | ON}
```

Sets the suppression of the comparison of datatypes performed while inserting or appending to tables with the COPY command.

DEFINE

```
DEF[INE] {c | OFF | ON}
```

Sets the character used to prefix substitution variables to *c*.

OFF

Specifies that SQL*Plus will not scan commands for substitution variables and replace them with their values. The setting of DEFINE to OFF overrides the setting of the SCAN variable.

ON

Changes the value of *c* back to the default "&", not to the most recently used character.

ECHO

```
ECHO { OFF | ON}
```

Controls whether the START command lists each command in a command file as the command is executed.

OFF

Suppresses the listing of commands.

ON

Lists the commands.

EDITFILE

```
EDITF[ILE] filename[.ext]
```

Sets the default filename for the EDIT command. For more information about the EDIT command, see "EDIT," earlier in this chapter.

EMBEDDED

```
EMB[EDDED] {OFF | ON}
```

Controls where on a page each report begins. In addition, if EMB[EDDED] is set to ON, page numbering will continue from one report to another. If it is set to OFF, page numbering will begin with 1 for each report.

OFF

Forces each report to start at the top of a new page.

ON

Allows a report to begin anywhere on a page.

ESCAPE

```
ESC[APE] {c | OFF | ON}
```

Defines the character you enter as the escape character. The escape character is used to indicate that SQL*Plus should treat the substitution character as an ordinary character rather than as a request for a variable substitution.

OFF

Undefines the escape character.

ON

Enables the escape character, and changes the value of *c* back to the default "\".

FEEDBACK

```
FEED[BACK] {n | OFF | ON}
```

Displays the number of records returned by a query when a query selects at least *n* records. The default for *n* is 6.

OFF

Turns the feedback display off.

ON

Enables the feedback display and sets *n* to 1.

FLAGGER

```
FLAGGER {OFF | ENTRY | INTERMED[IATE] | FULL}
```

Checks to make sure that SQL statements conform to the ANSI/ISO SQL92 standard. You may execute SET FLAGGER even if you are not connected to a database. Standard flagging will remain in effect across SQL*Plus sessions until a SET FLAGGER OFF (or ALTER SESSION SET FLAGGER = OFF) command is successful or you exit SQL*Plus. When standard flagging is enabled, SQL*Plus displays a warning for the CONNECT, DISCONNECT, and ALTER SESSION SET FLAGGER commands, even if they are successful.

FLUSH

```
FLU[SH] {OFF | ON}
```

Controls when output is sent to the user's display device.

OFF

Allows the host operating system to buffer output.

ON

Disables buffering by the host operating system.

HEADING

```
HEA[DING] {OFF | ON}
```

Controls printing of column headings in reports.

OFF

Suppresses column headings.

ON

Prints column headings in reports.

HEADSEP

```
HEADS[EP] {c | OFF | ON}
```

Defines the character you enter as the heading separator character.

OFF

Specifies that SQL*Plus print a heading separator character like any other character.

ON

Changes the value of *c* back to the default, " | ".

Note that headings are interpreted when they are defined, so subsequent changes to HEADSEP won't affect existing heading definitions.

LINESIZE

```
LIN[ESIZE] {80 | n}
```

Sets the total number of characters that SQL*Plus displays on one line before beginning a new line.

LOBOFFSET

```
LOBOF[FSET] {n | 1}
```

Sets the starting position from which CLOB and NCLOB data is retrieved and displayed.

LONG

```
LONG {80 | n}
```

Sets the maximum width, in bytes, for displaying LONG, CLOB, and NCLOB values and for copying LONG values.

LONGCHUNKSIZE

```
LONGC[HUNKSIZE] {80 | n}
```

Sets the size, in bytes, of the increments in which SQL*Plus retrieves a LONG, CLOB, or NCLOB value.

NEWPAGE

```
NEWP[AGE] {1|n|NONE}
```

Sets the number of blank lines to be printed from the top of each page to the top title.

NONE

Specifies that SQL*Plus will not print a blank line or formfeed between the report pages.

A value of zero places a formfeed at the beginning of each page, including the first page, and clears the screen on most terminals.

NULL

```
NULL text
```

Sets the *text* that represents a null value in the result of a SQL SELECT command.

NUMFORMAT

```
NUMF[ORMAT] format
```

Sets the default format for displaying numbers. For number format descriptions, see the FORMAT clause of the COLUMN command in this chapter.

NUMWIDTH

    NUM[WIDTH] *n*

Sets the default width for displaying numbers. The default for *n* is 10.

 NUMFORMAT overrides NUMWIDTH, so SETNUMWIDTH 5 and SET
NUMFORMAT 999,999.99 results in a 10-character wide column.

PAGESIZE

    PAGES[IZE] *n*

Sets the number of lines in each page. You can set PAGESIZE to zero to suppress
all headings, page breaks, titles, the initial blank line, and other formatting information. The default for *n* is 24.

RECSEP

    RECSEP {WR[APPED] | EA[CH] | OFF}

Displays or prints record separators.

WRAPPED
    Specifies that SQL*Plus will print a record separator only after wrapped lines.

EACH
    Specifies that SQL*Plus will print a record separator after each row.

OFF
    Specifies that SQL*Plus will not print a record separator.

A record separator consists of a single line of the RECSEPCHAR (record-separating
character) repeated LINESIZE times.

RECSEPCHAR

    RECSEPCHAR *c*

Defines the record-separating character (*c*). The default is a space (" ") character.

SERVEROUTPUT

Oracle7:

    SERVEROUT[PUT] {OFF | ON} [SIZE *n*]

Oracle8:.

```
SERVEROUT[PUT] {OFF | ON} [SIZE n]
[FOR[MAT]  {WRA[PPED] | WOR[D_WRAPPED] | TRU[NCATED]}]
```

Controls whether to display the output (generated by the DBMS_OUTPUT.PUT_
LINE procedure) of stored procedures or PL/SQL blocks in SQL*Plus.

OFF

Suppresses the output of DBMS_OUTPUT.PUT_LINE.

ON

Displays the output.

SIZE

Sets the number of bytes of the output that can be buffered within the server.
The default for *n* is 2000, and *n* must be between 2000 and 1,000,000.

FOR[MAT] WRA[PPED[

Specifies that SQL*Plus will wrap output; line breaks will occur in the middle
of words, if necessary.

FOR[MAT] WOR[D_WRAPPED]

Specifies that SQL*Plus will word-wrap output; line breaks will only occur at
line boundaries.

FOR[MAT] TRU[NCATED]

Specifies that SQL*Plus will not wrap output, but will truncate it at the end of
the line.

SHIFTINOUT

```
SHIFT[INOUT] {VIS[IBLE]|INV[ISIBLE]}
```

Allows correct alignment for terminals that display shift characters. The SET SHIFT-
INOUT command is useful for terminals that display shift characters together with
data (for example, IBM 3270 terminals).

VIS[IBLE]

Displays shift characters.

INV[ISIBLE]

Does not display shift characters.

SHOWMODE

```
SHOW[MODE] { OFF | ON }
```

Controls whether SQL*Plus lists the old and new settings of a SQL*Plus system
variable when you change the setting with SET.

OFF

Suppresses the listing of old and new settings.

ON

Lists the settings (has the same behavior as the obsolete SHOWMODE BOTH).

SQLCASE

```
SQLC[ASE] {MIX[ED] | LO[WER] | UP[PER]}
```

Converts the case of SQL commands and PL/SQL blocks, including any quoted text literals, just prior to execution.

MIX[ED]

Specifies that case will not be changed.

LO[WER]

Specifies that all characters will be converted to lowercase.

UP[PER]

Specifies that all characters will be converted to uppercase.

SQLCONTINUE

```
SQLCO[NTINUE] text
```

Sets the character sequence SQL*Plus displays as a prompt after you continue a SQL*Plus command on an additional line. The default is ">".

SQLNUMBER

```
SQLN[UMBER] { OFF | ON}
```

Sets the prompt for the second and subsequent lines of a SQL command or PL/SQL block.

OFF

Sets the value of the prompt to be the same as SQLPROMPT.

ON

Sets the prompt to the line number.

SQLPREFIX

```
SQLPRE[FIX] c
```

Sets the SQL*Plus prefix character. While you are entering a SQL command or PL/SQL block, you can enter a SQL*Plus command on a separate line, prefixed by the SQL*Plus prefix character, which must be a non-alphanumeric character. The default is "#".

SQLPROMPT

    SQLP[ROMPT] text

Sets the SQL*Plus command prompt. The default is "SQL>".

SQLTERMINATOR

    SQLT[ERMINATOR] {c | OFF | ON}

Sets the character used to end and execute SQL commands to *c*.

OFF

Means that SQL*Plus recognizes no command terminator; a SQL command is terminated by entering an empty line.

ON

Resets the terminator to the default semicolon (;).

SUFFIX

    SUF[FIX] text

Sets the default file extension that SQL*Plus uses in commands that refer to command files. SUFFIX does not control extensions for spool files. The default is "SQL".

TAB

    TAB {OFF | ON}

Determines how SQL*Plus formats whitespace in terminal output.

OFF

Specifies that SQL*Plus use spaces to format whitespace in the output.

ON

Specifies that SQL*Plus use the TAB character to format whitespace.

TERMOUT

    TERM[OUT] {ON | OFF}

Controls the display of output generated by commands executed from a command file.

OFF

Specifies that output not be displayed.

ON

Specifies that SQL*Plus display output generated by commands on the terminal screen.

TIME

```
TI[ME] {OFF | ON}
```

Controls whether or not the time is displayed as part of the current prompt.

TIMING

```
TIMI[NG] {OFF | ON}
```

Controls the display of timing statistics.

TRIMOUT

```
TRIM[OUT] {OFF | ON}
```

Determines whether SQL*Plus allows trailing blanks at the end of each line displayed on the terminal.

OFF

Specifies that SQL*Plus will display trailing blanks.

ON

Specifies that SQL*Plus will remove blanks at the end of each line, which improves performance, especially when accessing SQL*Plus from a slow communications device.

TRIMSPOOL

```
TRIMS[POOL] {OFF | ON}
```

Determines whether SQL*Plus allows trailing blanks at the end of each spooled line.

OFF

Specifies that SQL*Plus will include trailing blanks.

ON

Specifies that SQL*Plus will remove blanks at the end of each line.

UNDERLINE

```
UND[ERLINE] {c | OFF | ON}
```

Sets the character used to underline column headings in SQL*Plus reports to *c*.

OFF

Turns underlining off.

ON

Turns underlining on and changes the value of *c* back to the default "-".

VERIFY

```
VER[IFY] {OFF | ON}
```

Controls whether or not SQL*Plus lists the text of a SQL statement or PL/SQL command before and after SQL*Plus replaces substitution variables with values.

WRAP

```
WRA[P] {OFF | ON}
```

Controls whether or not SQL*Plus truncates the display of a SELECTed row if it is too long for the current line width.

Export

Export (exp) is an Oracle-supplied utility that copies the contents of the database to a proprietary-format file that may be used by Oracle's Import utility to restore some or all of the database objects contained in the file. This section provides the detailed syntax for the Export utility; see Chapter 4, *Preventing Data Loss*, for an introduction to the use of Export in performing backups.

Command-Line Syntax

Export may be invoked from a host system command line or batch script using the following syntax:

```
exp [username[/password]][@hostname] [parameters]
```

username

The Oracle username for the account to run Export.

password

The password for the username. If the password is omitted, SQL*Plus will prompt for the password.

hostname

The hostname assigned to the database being connected to, as contained in the *tnsnames.ora* file or Oracle Names.

parameters

A list of Export parameters separated by commas or spaces.

Parameter File Syntax

Export may be invoked from a host system command line or batch script using the following syntax, which references detailed instructions stored in a parameter file:

```
exp [username[/password]][@hostname] parfile=filename
```

username

The Oracle username for the account to run Export.

password

The password for the username. If the password is omitted, SQL*Plus will prompt for the password.

hostname

The hostname assigned to the database being connected to, as contained in the *tnsnames.ora* file or Oracle Names.

filename

The name of an operating system file containing a list of Export parameters; see the description in "Export Parameters" for details. Specify one parameter per record, using one of the following syntax options:

```
parameter=value
parameter=(value)
parameter=(value1, value2, ...)
```

Interactive Mode Syntax

Export may be invoked in an interactive mode from a host system command prompt, using the following syntax:

```
exp [username[/password]][@hostname]
```

username

The Oracle username for the account to run Export.

password

The password for the username. If the password is omitted, SQL*Plus will prompt for the password.

hostname

The hostname assigned to the database being connected to, as contained in the *tnsnames.ora* file or Oracle Names.

When running in interactive mode, Export will prompt for some, but not all, parameters as follows. Defaults appear at the end of each line:

```
Username: SYSTEM
Password:
Enter array fetch buffer size: 4096 >Export file: expdat.dmp >
(1)E(ntire database), (2)U(sers), or (3)T(ables): (2)U >
Export grants (yes/no): yes >
Export table data (yes/no): yes >
Compress extents (yes/no): yes >
```

The option to export the E(ntire) database is only presented if the username specified has the EXPORT_FULL_DATABASE privilege (see Chapter 15, *System Privileges and Initial Roles*).

The actual name of the Export executable may vary from platform to platform, and from release to release. For example, the executable name for Export for Windows 95 is *exp73.exe* (for Version 7.3) or *exp80* (for Version 8.0), and is therefore entered on the command line as **exp**73 or **exp**80.

Export Parameters

The following is a description of the Export parameters that may be specified, either on a command line or in a parameter file:

BUFFER=buffersize

Specifies the size, in bytes, of the buffer used to fetch rows. This parameter determines the maximum number of rows in an array fetched by Export as:

rows = buffer / maximum_row_size

If you specify zero, Export fetches one row at a time. Tables with LONG, LOB, BFILE, REF, ROWID, or type columns are always fetched one row at a time. BUFFER applies only to conventional path export, and has no effect on a direct path export. The default is operating system dependent.

COMPRESS={Y | N}

Specifies how Export manages the initial extent for table data. The default, COMPRESS=Y, causes Export to write a CREATE object statement for use in a subsequent import that will cause the object to be created with a single initial extent. If COMPRESS=N is specified, Export uses the current storage parameters, including the values of the INITIAL extent size and the NEXT extent size.

CONSISTENT={Y | N}

Specifies whether Export uses the SET TRANSACTION READ ONLY statement to ensure that the data seen by Export is consistent to a single point in time and does not change during the execution of the EXP command. You should specify CONSISTENT=Y when you anticipate that other applications will update the database after an export has started. The default is CONSISTENT=N.

CONSTRAINTS={Y | N}

Specifies whether the Export utility exports table constraints. The default is CONSTRAINTS=Y.

DIRECT={Y | N}

Specifies direct path or conventional path export. DIRECT=Y causes Export to extract data by reading the data directly, bypassing the SQL processing layer, which can be much faster than a conventional path export. The default is DIRECT=N. Note that direct path export cannot be used to export tables containing any of the following column types: REF, LOB, BFILE, or object type columns, which include VARRAYs and nested tables.

FEEDBACK=n

When set greater than zero, specifies that Export should display a progress meter in the form of a dot for each *n* number of rows exported. The default is FEEDBACK=0.

FILE=filename[.extension]

Specifies the name of the Export file. The default filename is *expdat.dmp*. The default extension is *.dmp*, but you can specify any extension.

FULL={Y | N}

When set to FULL=Y, causes Export to perform a full database export, which exports all objects from the entire database. The default is FULL=N. The EXP_FULL_DATABASE role is required to export in this mode.

GRANTS={Y | N}

Specifies whether the Export utility exports grants. The grants that are exported depend on whether you export in full database or user mode. In full database mode, all grants on a table are exported; in user mode, only those granted by the owner of the table are exported. The default is GRANTS=Y.

HELP={Y | N}

Determines whether a help message with descriptions of the Export parameters is displayed. The default is HELP=N.

INCTYPE={INCREMENTAL | CUMULATIVE | COMPLETE}

If used, specifies that one of the following types of incremental export is to be run:

INCREMENTAL

Exports all database objects that have changed since the last incremental, cumulative, or complete export, as tracked by the table SYS.INCEXP, then updates the table with a new ITIME and EXPID.

CUMULATIVE

Exports all database objects that have changed since the last cumulative or complete export, as tracked by the table SYS.INCEXP, then updates the table with a new CTIME, ITIME, and EXPID.

COMPLETE

> Exports all objects, then updates the tables SYS.INCEXP and SYS.INCVID. (A FULL=Y export does not update these tables unless you specify the INCTYPE parameter.)

INDEXES={Y | N]

> Specifies whether Export will export all indexes. The default is INDEXES=Y. INDEXES=N specifies that indexes are not to be exported. Note that even though indexes are exported, index creation may be suppressed during import using the INDEXES=N parameter of the Import utility.

LOG=logfile[.extension]

> Specifies the name of an operating system file to receive informational and error messages. There is no default, and if LOG is not specified, messages will not be sent to a file.

OWNER=(username[,username...])

> If used, indicates that the export is a user-mode export and lists the users whose objects will be exported. There is no default.

PARFILE=filename[.extension]

> If used, specifies the name of an operating system file that contains a list of Export parameters. There is no default, and this parameter is used only when running export in command-line mode.

POINT_IN_TIME_RECOVER={Y | N]

> Determines if the Export utility will export one or more tablespaces in an Oracle database so that when running Import you can recover the tablespace to a prior point in time without affecting the rest of the database. The default is N.

RECORD={Y | N]

> Determines if Export will create a record of an incremental or cumulative export in the system tables SYS.INCEXP, SYS.INCFIL, and SYS.INCVID. The default is RECORD=Y.

RECORDLENGTH=length

> Specifies the length (in bytes) of the records written to the export output file. The default is operating system specific, and the maximum is 64K.

RECOVERY_TABLESPACES=(tablespace_name[,tablespace_name...])

> Specifies the tablespaces to be exported for recovery using point-in-time recovery. There is no default.

ROWS={Y | N]

> Specifies whether the rows of data in tables are written to the Export file. The default is ROWS=Y. ROWS=N can be specified to export the structure of all exported objects without their contents.

STATISTICS={ESTIMATE | COMPUTE | NONE}

Specifies the type of database optimizer statistics to generate when the exported data is restored using the Import utility. The default is STATIS-TICS=ESTIMATE, and other options are COMPUTE and NONE.

TABLES=(tablename[,tablename...])

Specifies that Export is to be run in table mode, and lists the table and partition names to export. There is no default. Tables or partitions (Oracle8 only) may be specified as *schema.table:partition_name*, where:

schema

Specifies the name of the user's schema from which to export the table or partition. If omitted, the schema specified by USERID is used, except when FULL=Y is specified.

table

Indicates the name of a table to be exported. If a table in the list is partitioned and you do not specify a partition name, all its partitions are exported.

partition_name

Indicates that the export is a partition-level export. Partition-level export lets you export one or more specified partitions within a table. If this value is omitted for a partitioned table, all partitions will be exported.

Multiple tables may be listed, as shown here:

```
TABLES = (scott.emp, scott.dept, harry.sales:a)
```

USERID=username/password@hoststring

Specifies the *username/password@hoststring* of the user initiating the export if it is not specified on the command line. There is no default.

Import

Import (imp) is an Oracle-supplied utility that reads the proprietary format file created by Export and can restore some or all of the database objects contained in the file to an Oracle database. This section provides the detailed syntax for the Import utility; see Chapter 9, *Oracle Tools*, for a discussion of Import's capabilities.

Command-Line Syntax

Import may be invoked from a host system command line or batch script using the following syntax:

```
imp [username[/password]][@hostname] [parameters]
```

username

The Oracle username for the account to run Import.

password

The password for the username.

hostname

The hostname assigned to the database being connected to, as contained in the *tnsnames.ora* file or Oracle Names.

parameters

A list of Import parameters separated by commas. See the description of the parameters in a later section.

Parameter File Syntax

Import may be invoked from a host system command line or batch script using the following syntax, which references detailed instructions stored in a parameter file:

```
imp [username[/password]][@hostname] parfile=filename
```

username

The Oracle username for the account to run Import.

password

The password for the username.

hostname

The hostname assigned to the database being connected to, as contained in the *tnsnames.ora* file or Oracle Names.

filename

The name of an operating system file containing a list of Import parameters. See the section "Import Parameters," later in this chapter, for details on parameter files and their values. Specify one parameter per record, using one of the following syntax options:

```
parameter=value
parameter=(value)
parameter=(value1, value2, ...)
```

Interactive Mode Syntax

Import may be invoked in an interactive mode from a host system command prompt, using the following syntax:

```
imp [username[/password]][@hostname]
```

username

The Oracle username for the account to run Import.

password

The password for the username.

hostname

The hostname assigned to the database being connected to, as contained in the *tnsnames.ora* file or Oracle Names.

When running in interactive mode, Import will prompt for some, but not all, parameters as follows. Defaults appear at the end of each line.

```
Username: SYSTEM
Password:
Import file: expdat.dmp >
Enter insert buffer size (minimum is 4096) 30720>
List contents of import file only (yes/no): no >
Ignore create error due to object existence (yes/no): no >
Import grants (yes/no): yes >
Import table data (yes/no): yes >
Import entire export file (yes/no): no >
Username: SCOTT
Enter table names. Null list means all tables for user
Enter table name or . if done:
```

Note that if the you answer "Y" to the prompt "Import entire export file (yes/no): no >" no further prompts are issued and all data is imported. If you answer "N", usernames and tables to be imported are prompted for, as shown.

The actual name of the Import executable may vary from platform to platform, and from release to release. For example, the executable name for Import for Windows 95 is *imp73.exe* (for Version 7.3) or *imp80* (for Version 8.0), and is therefore entered on the command line as `imp73` or `imp80`.

Import Parameters

The following is a description of the parameters that may be specified to Import, either on a command line or in a parameter file:

ANALYZE={Y | N}

Specifies whether the Import utility executes SQL ANALYZE statements found in the export file. See STATISTICS in the section "Export Parameters." The default is ANALYZE=Y.

BUFFER=buffersize

Specifies the size, in bytes, of the buffer used to load rows. This parameter determines the maximum number of rows in an array loaded by Import as:

rows = buffer / maximum_row_size

If you specify zero, Import loads one row at a time. Tables with LONG, LOB, BFILE, REF, ROWID, or type columns are always loaded one row at a time. The default is operating system dependent.

CHARSET=charsetname

Applies to Oracle Version 6 export files only, and specifies the actual character set used at the time of export. The Import utility will verify whether the specified character set is ASCII or EBCDIC based on the character set in the Export file. If that file was created with Oracle7 or Oracle8, the character set is specified within the Export file, and conversion to the current database's character set is automatic. There is no default.

COMMIT={Y | N}

Specifies whether Import should commit after each array insert. The default is COMMIT=N, which causes Import to commit after loading each table. If COMMIT=N and a table is partitioned, each partition in the Export file is imported in a separate transaction. Specifying COMMIT=Y prevents rollback segments from growing too large, and is advisable if the table has a uniqueness constraint, since if the import is restarted, any rows that have already been imported are rejected with a non-fatal error. If a table does not have a uniqueness constraint and COMMIT=Y is specified, Import could produce duplicate rows when the data is reimported.

DESTROY={Y | N}

Specifies whether existing datafiles making up the database should be reused if tablespaces are being recreated by Import. The default is DESTROY=N.

 If datafiles are stored on a raw device, DESTROY=N does not prevent files from being overwritten.

FEEDBACK=n

When set greater than zero, specifies that Import should display a progress meter in the form of a dot for each *n* number of rows imported. The default is FEEDBACK=0.

FILE=filename[.extension]

Specifies the name of the file created by the Export utility to be used as input to import. The default filename is *expdat.dmp*.

FROMUSER=(username[,username...])

Specifies a list of schemas containing objects to import. The default for users without the IMP_FULL_DATABASE role is a user-mode import, where objects for the current user are imported. If the specified user does not exist in the database, the objects will be imported into the schema of the current user unless TOUSER is also specified.

FULL={Y | N}

Specifies whether or not to import the entire Export file. The default is FULL=N.

GRANTS={Y | N}

Specifies whether to import grants that were exported. If the export was a user-mode export, the Export file contains only the grants granted by the owner. If the export was a full database mode export, the Export file contains all grants. The default is GRANTS=Y.

HELP={Y | N}

Determines whether a help message with descriptions of the Import parameters is displayed. The default is HELP=N.

IGNORE={Y | N}

Specifies how object creation errors are handled. If IGNORE=Y is specified, Import ignores creation errors when it attempts to create database objects. The default is IGNORE=N, which causes Import to log and/or display the object creation error before continuing.

INCTYPE={SYSTEM | RESTORE}

Specifies that one of the following types of incremental import is to be run. The default is RESTORE.

SYSTEM

Imports the most recent version of system objects, including foreign function libraries and object type definitions, but does not import user data or objects.

RESTORE

Imports all user database objects and data contained in the Export file.

INDEXES={Y | N}

Specifies whether indexes are to be recreated or updated after table data is imported. Use of INDEXES=Y assumes that INDEXES=Y was specified for the Export utility when the file was created. The default is INDEXES=Y. System-generated indexes such as LOB indexes, OID indexes, or unique constraint indexes are re-created by Import regardless of the setting of this parameter.

INDEXFILE=filename[.extension]

Specifies a file to receive table, index, and cluster creation commands. Table and cluster commands are included as remarks, but can be edited. There is no default for this parameter, and it can only be used with the FULL=Y, FROMUSER, TOUSER, or TABLES parameters.

Since Release 7.1, the commented CREATE TABLE statement in the INDEXFILE has not included PRIMARY/UNIQUE KEY clauses.

LOG=filename[.extension]

Specifies the name of an operating system file to receive informational and error messages. There is no default, and if LOG is not specified, messages will not be sent to a file.

PARFILE=filename[.extension]

Specifies the name of an operating system file that contains a list of Import parameters. There is no default, and this parameter is used only when running Import in command-line mode.

POINT_IN_TIME_RECOVER={Y | N}

Determines if Import will recover one or more tablespaces in an Oracle database to a prior point in time without affecting the rest of the database. The Export file must have been created with POINT_IN_TIME_RECOVER=Y. The default is POINT_IN_TIME_RECOVER=N.

RECORDLENGTH=length

Specifies the length, in bytes, of records in the Export file being imported. This parameter is required if the Export file was created on an operating system that uses a different default value. The default is operating system specific.

ROWS={Y | N}

Specifies whether to import the rows of table data. The default is ROWS=Y. If ROWS=N is specified, tables will be created but no data rows will be inserted.

SHOW={Y | N}

If SHOW=Y is specified, the SQL statements contained in the Export file are listed to the display only, and objects are not imported. SHOW=Y can be used only with the FULL=Y, FROMUSER, TOUSER, or TABLES parameters. The default is SHOW=N.

SKIP_UNUSABLE_INDEXES={Y | N}

Specifies whether Import skips building indexes set to the Index Unusable state. Without this parameter, row insertions that attempt to update unusable indexes fail. The default is SKIP_UNUSABLE_INDEXES=N.

TABLES=(tablename[,tablename...])

Specifies a list of table names to import. Table names may not be qualified by a schema name. There is no default for this parameter.

TOUSER=(username[,username])

> Specifies a list of usernames whose schemas will be the target of the import. If multiple schemas are specified, the schema names must be paired with schema names in a corresponding FROMUSER parameter. For example:
>
> ```
> FROMUSER=(scott,harry) TOUSER=(dave,brian)
> ```

USERID=username/password@hoststring

> Specifies the *username/password@hoststring* of the user performing the import if it is not specified on the command line. There is no default.

SQL*Loader

SQL*Loader is an Oracle-supplied utility that is used to read data from operating system files in a variety of formats and to load rows of data into an Oracle database. For a discussion of the capabilities of SQL*Loader, see Chapter 9, *Oracle Tools*.

Command-Line Syntax

SQL*Loader may be invoked from a host system command-line prompt or from a batch script, using the following syntax:

```
sqlload [USERID=username/password[@hostname]]
[,BAD=badfile] [,BINDSIZE=bindsize]
[,CONTROL=controlfile] [,DATA=datafile]
[,DIRECT={TRUE|FALSE}] [,DISCARD=discard_count]
[,DISCARDMAX=max_discard_count] [,ERRORS=max_error_count] [,FILE=filename]
[,LOAD=max_record_count] [,LOG=logfile]
[,PARFILE=parfile] [,PARALLEL=[TRUE | FALSE}] [,ROWS=rows_per_commit]
[,SILENT=({[[HEADER][,FEEDBACK][,ERRORS][,DISCARDS]
[,PARTITIONS]] | ALL)}] [SKIP=skip_count]
[,SKIP_UNUSABLE_INDEXES={TRUE | FALSE}]
[,SKIP_INDEX_MAINTENANCE={TRUE | FALSE}]
```

Note that the actual name of the SQL*Loader executable may vary from platform to platform, and from release to release. For example, the executable name for SQL*Loader for Windows 95 is *sqlldr73.exe*, and is therefore entered on the command line as **sqlldr73**.

BAD

> Specifies the name of a file to store records that cause errors during insert or are improperly formatted. If a *badfile* is not specified, the name of the control file is used by default, along with the *.bad* extension. This file has the same format as the input datafile, so it can be loaded by the same control file after corrections are made.

BINDSIZE

Specifies the maximum size in bytes of the bind array. The default size is operating system dependent.

CONTROL

Specifies the name of the file that describes how to load data. If the file extension or file type is not specified, it defaults to *.ctl*. If a *controlfile* is not specified, you will be prompted for one. See the "Control File Syntax" section, later in this chapter, for more information on the contents and syntax of the control file.

DATA

Specifies the name of the file containing the data to be loaded. If a *datafile* is not specified, the data will be expected in the control file. If the file extension is not specified, it defaults to *.dat*.

DIRECT

Specifies the load method to use. TRUE specifies the direct path load, and FALSE (the default) specifies the conventional path load.

DISCARD

Specifies a file to store records that are neither inserted into a table nor rejected. This file has the same format as the input datafile, so it can be loaded by the same control file after appropriate corrections are made.

DISCARDMAX

Specifies the number of records that may be discarded before the load is terminated. If the parameter is omitted, all discards are allowed.

ERRORS

Specifies the number of insert errors that will be allowed before the load is terminated. The default is 50. When SQL*Loader is performing a single-table load, any data inserted prior to load termination due to errors will be committed. SQL*Loader maintains the consistency of records across all tables, so multitable loads do not terminate immediately if errors exceed the error limit. Before terminating a load, SQL*Loader completely processes the current bind array to filter out the bad rows contained in the bind array.

FILE

Specifies the database file from which to allocate extents. It is used only for parallel loads to allow data to be loaded with minimal disk contention.

LOAD

Specifies the maximum number of logical records to load. The default is to load all records.

LOG

Specifies the file that will store logging information about the SQL*Loader process. If a *logfile* is not specified, the name of the control file is used with the extension *.log*.

PARFILE

Specifies the file that contains command-line parameters. Parameters can appear either on the command line or in *parfile*. If a parameter appears in both, the value specified on the command line will override that specified in the *parfile*. The PARFILE is especially useful when the length of a command line would otherwise exceed the system command-line length limitation.

PARALLEL

Specifies whether direct loads can operate in multiple concurrent sessions to load data into the same table.

ROWS

For conventional path loads, specifies the number of rows in the bind array. The default is 64. For direct path loads, ROWS specifies the number of data-file rows to be read before a data save. The default is to read all rows before a save. Since direct load uses buffers that are the same size as the system's I/O blocks, only full buffers are written to the database, so the value of ROWS is approximate.

SILENT

Specifies types of SQL*Loader messages to be suppressed. The following keywords may be specified:

HEADER

Suppresses the SQL*Loader header messages.

FEEDBACK

Suppresses the "commit point reached" feedback messages.

ERRORS

Suppresses the data error messages that occur when a record generates an Oracle error that causes it to be written to the bad file.

DISCARDS

Suppresses the messages for each record written to the discard file.

PARTITIONS (Oracle8)

Suppresses writing the per-partition statistics for direct load of a partitioned table.

ALL

Implements all of the keywords.

SKIP

Specifies the number of logical records from the beginning of the file that should not be loaded. By default, no records are skipped. This is useful when continuing loads that have been interrupted for some reason. It cannot be used for multiple-table direct loads when a different number of records were loaded into each table.

SKIP_UNUSABLE_INDEXES (Oracle8)

Allows SQL*Loader to load a table with indexes that are in Index Unusable (IU) state prior to the beginning of the load. Indexes that are not in IU state at load time will be maintained by SQL*Loader. Indexes that are in IU state at load time will not be maintained, but will remain in IU state at load completion. Indexes that are UNIQUE and marked IU are not allowed to skip index maintenance.

SKIP_INDEX_MAINTENANCE (Oracle8)

Prevents index maintenance for direct path loads, and causes the index partitions that would have had index keys added to them to be marked Index Unusable because the index segment is inconsistent with respect to the data it indexes. Index segments that are not affected by the load retain the state they had prior to the load.

USERID

Used to provide your Oracle *username/password@hostname*. If USERID is omitted, you are prompted for it. If only a slash is used, USERID defaults to your operating system logon. A *hostname* can be specified for a conventional path load into a remote database.

Control File Syntax

Detailed instructions to SQL*Loader are contained in a control file, which may contain entries with the following syntax:

```
[OPTIONS
  [SKIP=n[,]]
  [LOAD=n[,]]
  [ERRORS=n[,]]
  [ROWS=n[,]]
  [BINDSIZE=n[,]]
  [SILENT={FEEDBACK | ERRORS | DISCARDS | ALL},]]
  [DIRECT={TRUE | FALSE}[,]] [PARALLEL={TRUE | FALSE}])]
[{UNRECOVERABLE | RECOVERABLE}]
{LOAD [DATA] | CONTINUE_LOAD [DATA]}
  [{INFILE | INDDN} {filename | *} [CHARACTERSET charsetname]
[os_options] [READBUFFERS n]
    [{INSERT | APPEND | REPLACE | TRUNCATE}]
    [{BADFILE | BADDN} filename]
    [{DISCARDFILE | DISCARDDN} filename]
```

```
      [{DISCARD | DISCARDMAX} n]
      [{CONCATENATE n | CONTINUEIF {[THIS | NEXT]
   [(start [:end]) | LAST} operator {'string' | X'hexstring'}}]
      [PRESERVE BLANKS]
   INTO TABLE [schema.]tablename [INSERT | APPEND | REPLACE | TRUNCATE]
      [SORTED [INDEXES] (indexname[, ...])] [SINGLEROW]
      [WHEN condition [AND condition ...] [FIELDS delimiter_spec]
      [TRAILING [NULLCOLS]]
      [SKIP n]
      [REENABLE [DISABLED_CONSTRAINTS] [EXCEPTIONS tablename]
   (column_name {RECNUM | SYSDATE | CONSTANT value | SEQUENCE
   [( {n | MAX | COUNT} [,incr) ) | column_spec}
   [POSITION ({start | * [+n]} [{: | -}end]})] [datatype_spec] [PIECED]
      [NULLIF ({fieldname | {start | * [+n]}
   [{: | -}end]}) operator {'string' | X'hexstring' | BLANKS]]
      [DEFAULTIF ({fieldname | {start | * [+n]}
   [{: | -}end]}) operator {'string' | X'hexstring' | BLANKS]]
      [, ...] )
```

OPTIONS

Allows you to specify runtime parameters in the control file, rather than on the command line. Values specified on the command line override values specified in the OPTIONS statement of the control file. If specified, the OPTIONS statement must precede the LOAD keyword. See the earlier "Command-Line Syntax" section for information on the OPTIONS parameters.

UNRECOVERABLE

Loaded data is not logged, which improves load performance. (Other changes to the database are logged.) This option can be specified for a direct path load only; it cannot be specified for a conventional load.

RECOVERABLE

Loaded data is logged in the redo log. This option is the default for direct path loads, and all conventional loads are recoverable.

LOAD

Used with the optional keyword DATA to specify the characteristics of the input data to be loaded by SQL*Loader.

CONTINUE_LOAD

Used to continue an interrupted load when using direct table load. When using CONTINUE_LOAD, you must specify the SKIP value for each table. Note that SKIP cannot be specified on the command line or using the OPTIONS keyword if CONTINUE_LOAD is specified.

INFILE

Specifies the name of a file that contains input data. If an asterisk (*) is used in place of the filename, the data to be loaded will be in the control file, immediately following the BEGINDATA keyword. Multiple INFILE parameters may be specified. *filename* may be any filename valid for your operating system.

INDDN

Has the same meaning as INFILE, and may be used interchangeably.

CHARACTERSET

Specifies the name of the character set used for this datafile. SQL*Loader will automatically convert CHAR, DATE, and EXTERNAL fields as they are loaded. Multiple character sets may be used, but only one character set may be specified for each datafile.

os_options

An operating system–dependent, file processing options string may be specified for each input file. See your Oracle operating system specific documentation for more information.

READBUFFERS

Used for direct loads only; specifies the number of buffers (*n*) to be used to read logical records. The default is 4, and this value should not be changed unless an ORA-02374 (no more slots for read buffer queue) error is encountered.

INSERT

This keyword, which may be used with the LOAD/CONTINUE_LOAD or INTO TABLE keywords, specifies that the table to be loaded must be empty. If the table is not empty, an error results and SQL*Loader terminates. INSERT is the default. When this keyword is specified before any INTO TABLE clause, it will control the loading of all tables, but it may be overridden by a table-loading keyword in an INTO TABLE clause.

APPEND

This keyword, which may be used with the LOAD/CONTINUE_LOAD or INTO TABLE keywords, specifies that the table is to be extended by adding new rows. When this keyword is specified before any INTO TABLE clause, it will control the loading of all tables, but it may be overridden by a table-loading keyword in an INTO TABLE clause.

REPLACE

This keyword, which may be used with the LOAD/CONTINUE_LOAD or INTO TABLE keywords, specifies that all existing rows in the table are to be deleted, and then new rows inserted. The user running SQL*Loader must have the DELETE privilege on the table. When this keyword is specified before any INTO TABLE clause, it will control the loading of all tables, but it may be overridden by a table-loading keyword in an INTO TABLE clause.

TRUNCATE

This keyword, which may be used with the LOAD/CONTINUE_LOAD or INTO TABLE keywords, specifies that the table is to be truncated and new rows are to be inserted. The user running SQL*Loader must have the DELETE privilege on the table. When this keyword is specified before any INTO TABLE clause, it will control the loading of all tables, but it may be overridden by a table-loading keyword in an INTO TABLE clause.

BADFILE

Specifies the name of a file *(filename)* to contain records rejected by SQL*Loader. The file is only created if one or more records are rejected, and the name may be overridden by a BAD parameter on the command line.

BADDN

This parameter has the same meaning as BAD, and may be used interchangeably.

DISCARDFILE

Specifies the name of a file *(filename)* to contain records that are discarded by SQL*Loader because they do not meet any of the loading criteria. The file is only created if one or more records are discarded, and the name may be overridden by a DISCARDFILE parameter on the command line.

DISCARDDN

Has the same meaning as DISCARDFILE, and may be used interchangeably.

DISCARD

Limits the number of records discarded for this datafile to *n*. When *n* records have been discarded, processing of this datafile is terminated, and processing continues with the next datafile, if one exists. A different number of discards may be specified for each datafile.

DISCARDMAX

The same as DISCARD, and may be used interchangeably.

CONCATENATE

Used to create one logical record from multiple physical records. SQL*Loader will add *n* number of physical records to form one logical record. If the number of physical records to be continued varies, CONTINUEIF must be used.

CONTINUEIF

Used to create one logical record from multiple physical records. The keyword CONTINUEIF is followed by a condition that is evaluated for each physical record as it is read.

THIS

Used with CONTINUEIF, and specifies that if the condition is true in this record (as determined by the starting and ending columns optionally specified by *start:end*), the next physical record is read and concatenated to the current physical record, continuing until the condition is false. If the condition is false in the current record, the current physical record is the last physical record of the current logical record. THIS is the default.

NEXT

Used with CONTINUEIF, and specifies that if the condition is true in the next record (as determined by the starting and ending columns optionally specified by *start:end*), the next physical record is concatenated to the current record, continuing until the condition is false. If the condition is false in the next record, the current physical record is the last physical record of the current logical record.

start:end

Used with CONTINUEIF THIS or CONTINUEIF NEXT, specifies the starting and ending column numbers in the physical record. If you omit *end*, the length of the continuation field is the length of the byte string or character string. If you use *end*, and the length of the resulting continuation field is not the same as that of the byte string or character string, the shorter one is padded. Character strings are padded with blanks, hexadecimal strings with zeros.

The positions in the CONTINUEIF clause refer to positions in each physical record. This is the only time you refer to character positions in physical records. All other references are to logical records.

LAST

This test is similar to THIS, but the test is always against the last non-blank character. If the last non-blank character in this physical record meets the test, the next physical record is read and concatenated to the current physical record, continuing until the condition is false. If the condition is false in the current record, the current physical record is the last physical record of the current logical record. CONTINUEIF LAST differs from CONTINUEIF THIS and CONTINUEIF NEXT. With CONTINUEIF LAST, the continuation character is not removed from the physical record. Instead, this character is included when the logical record is assembled.

operator

The supported operators used with the CONTINUEIF keyword are equal and not equal, which may be expressed as: = != ¬= <>

For the equal operator, the field and comparison string must match exactly for the condition to be true. For the not-equal operator, they may differ in any character.

string

A string of characters to be compared to the continuation field defined by *start* and *end*, according to the operator. The string must be enclosed in double or single quotation marks. The comparison is made character by character, blank padding on the right if necessary.

X'hex_string'

A string of bytes in hexadecimal format, used in the same way as the character string above. X'1FB033' would represent the three bytes with values 1F, B0, and 33 (hex).

PRESERVE BLANKS

Retains leading whitespace when optional enclosure delimiters are not present. It also leaves trailing whitespace intact when fields are specified with a predetermined size. This keyword preserves tabs and blanks.

INTO TABLE

Used to specify the table (*tablename*) into which data is to be loaded. To load multiple tables, include one INTO TABLE clause for each table to be loaded. The table name may optionally be preceded by a *schema*. If *schema* is not specified, the schema of the account running SQL*Loader will be assumed. Note that the meanings of INSERT, APPEND, REPLACE, and TRUNCATE are the same as those described for LOAD and CONTINUE_LOAD.

SORTED INDEXES

This keyword, which applies only to direct path loads, specifies that the data to be loaded is already sorted in the sequence specified by the index *index-name*, which must already exist prior to the load.

SINGLEROW

This keyword, which is used only with direct path loads with APPEND, specifies that each index entry should be inserted directly into the index, one row at a time. Normally, when loading with APPEND, index entries are accumulated in a temporary storage area and merged into the existing index at the end of the load.

WHEN

Used to choose rows of data to insert into a table by specifying a *condition*. SQL*Loader determines values for all fields in a record, then determines whether the row should be inserted by evaluating the WHEN clause. The *condition* may be specified using either a column name (e.g., `WHEN DEPTNO='20'`) or using a column position number (e.g., `WHEN (2) = '10'`). Multiple comparisons may be combined using the AND keyword.

FIELDS

Specifies the default *delimiter_spec* clause. This default may be overridden for any particular column by specifying a different *delimiter_spec* after that column name.

TRAILING NULLCOLS

Specifies that if the control file definition specifies more fields for a record than the record actually contains (i.e., the record is too short), any relatively positioned columns that are not present should be treated as NULL.

SKIP n

When used following a *table_name* with CONTINUE_LOAD, specifies the number of records to skip for this table before resuming the load. SKIP is used only with direct path load.

REENABLE [DISABLED_CONSTRAINTS] [EXCEPTIONS]

When used with direct path load, specifies that disabled check constraints or referential (foreign key) constraints should be reenabled when the load is completed. The EXCEPTIONS keyword specifies the name of an existing table (*filename*) that contains the ROWID of each row that has violated a constraint, along with the name of the violated constraint. The keyword DISABLED_CONSTRAINTS is optional and is used for readability only.

RECNUM

When used following a *column_name*, specifies that the number of the logical record from which this row is loaded should be used as the value for the specified column. In other words, the column is set to the logical record number.

SYSDATE

When used following a *column_name*, specifies that the column be set to the value of SYSDATE, the system date.

CONSTANT value

When used following a *column_name*, specifies that the column should be assigned *value*, which will be converted automatically to match the column type. Note that the CONSTANT keyword should not be used to assign a value of NULL.

SEQUENCE

When used following a *column_name*, specifies that a unique value will be assigned to *column_name* for each row loaded. Start may be specified as *n*, a specific starting value; COUNT, which specifies that the sequence start with the number of rows already in the table, plus *increment*; or MAX, which specifies that the sequence start with the current maximum value for the column, plus *incr* (increment). *incr* may be specified as a positive number, and has a default of 1 if omitted.

POSITION

Specifies a field's position and length in the logical input record. The field position may be specified either explicitly as *start* or relative to the previous field as *+n*, where *n* indicates the offset, or number of characters to be skipped, from the previous field. If *+n* is used, *end* is derived from the datatype; otherwise, the end of the field is specified by :*end*.

PIECED

This keyword, used only with direct path loads, is used to notify SQL*Loader that the last field of the logical record may be processed in pieces, reusing a single buffer.

NULLIF condition

This keyword, when used following a *column_name*, specifies that if *condition* is true, the column should be assigned a value of NULL.

Note that the same result can be achieved through the use of the SQL NVL function applied to the column. If you want the value of the column to be NULL for all rows inserted, simply omit the column specification altogether.

DEFAULTIF

When used following a *column_name*, specifies that when a condition is true, the column will be assigned a value of zero if it is defined as NUMBER. The column will be assigned a value of NULL if it is defined as CHAR, DATE, or numeric EXTERNAL.

delimiter_spec

When *delimiter_spec* is included in a control file entry, it may use the following syntax:

```
{TERMINATED [BY] {WHITESPACE | 'string' | X'hexstring'}
   | ENCLOSED [BY] {WHITESPACE | 'string' | X'hexstring'}
   | TERMINATED [BY] {WHITESPACE | 'string' | X'hexstring'} [OPTIONALLY]
[ENCLOSED [BY]   {WHITESPACE | 'string' | X'hexstring'}]}
```

The *Oracle Server Utility User's Guide* contains a full syntax description.

datatype_spec

When *datatype_spec* is used in a control file entry, it may use the following syntax:

```
INTEGER [EXTERNAL [(length)] [delimiter_spec]]
FLOAT [EXTERNAL [(length)] [delimiter_spec]
ZONED {(precision[,scale]) | EXTERNAL [(length)] [delimiter_spec]}
DECIMAL {(precision[,scale]) | EXTERNAL [(length)] [delimiter_spec]}
DOUBLE
SMALLINT
BYEINT
RAW [(length)]
GRAPHIC [EXTERNAL] [(length)]
VARGRAPHIC [(maximum_length)]
VARCHAR [(maximum_length)]
CHAR [(length)] [delimiter_spec]
DATE [(length)] ["mask"] [delimiter_spec]
```

The *Oracle Server Utility User's Guide* contains a full syntax description.

Appendix:
Resources for the DBA

In this appendix, we've pulled together a variety of resources—both online and offline—that we use frequently in our own work as Oracle database administrators. We think you'll find them helpful.

Books

A number of books on the market today address the needs of the DBA. We list here those titles we find the most helpful and accurate:

Aronoff, Eyal, Kevin Loney, and Noorali Sonawalla. *Advanced Oracle Tuning and Administration* (Osborne McGraw-Hill, 1997). The most comprehensive discussion and explanation of the EXPLAIN PLAN facility available anywhere. No DBA should be without it.

Feuerstein, Steven. *Oracle PL/SQL Programming*, Second Edition (O'Reilly & Associates, 1997). Hands down, the definitive guide to PL/SQL. If you need information about PL/SQL, it's in this book.

Feuerstein, Steven, Charles Dye, and John Beresniewicz. *Oracle Built-in Packages* (O'Reilly & Associates, 1998). The follow-up volume to *Oracle PL/SQL Programming*. Presents detailed information about the vast array of packages built into the Oracle database.

Gurry, Mark, and Peter Corrigan. *Oracle Performance Tuning*, Second Edition, (O'Reilly & Associates, 1996). A comprehensive and in-depth treatment of the entire range of topics related to Oracle tuning.

Lomasky, Brian, and David Kreines. *Oracle Scripts* (O'Reilly & Associates, 1998). A complete toolkit of scripts to automate many DBA tasks. Every DBA will find a virtual goldmine on the included CD-ROM.

Loney, Kevin. *Oracle8 DBA Handbook* (Osborne McGraw-Hill, 1997). This latest edition of Kevin's standard text for DBAs presents a lot of background material and explanation, and is well-suited for DBAs at any level.

Niemiec, Richard, and Bradley Brown. *Oracle DBA Tips and Techniques* (Osborne McGraw-Hill, 1999). A wealth of tips, techniques, and workarounds from two experienced DBAs.

————. *Oracle Performance Tuning Tips and Techniques* (Osborne McGraw-Hill, 1997). Rich Niemiec and Brad Brown are tuning experts, and they provide a great deal of information about Oracle tuning.

Theriault, Marlene, and William Heney. *Oracle Security* (O'Reilly & Associates, 1998). The definitive source of information on security and its implementation in the Oracle environment.

Velpuri, Rama. *Oracle Backup and Recovery Handbook* (Osborne McGraw-Hill, 1997). A complete treatment of the Oracle backup and recovery process, by one of Oracle's internal experts.

Velpuri, Rama, and Anand Adkoli. *Oracle Troubleshooting* (Osborne McGraw-Hill, 1997). When you run into a really serious Oracle problem, this is one of the first books you will want to refer to.

Other Publications

Select

This publication, produced as a membership benefit by the International Oracle Users Group–Americas (IOUG-A), contains a variety of articles and columns on DBA issues, as well as DBA-related tips, techniques, and practices.

Oracle Magazine

This magazine, which is published by Oracle Corporation, is primarily a marketing tool, but also carries articles (often by Oracle technical staff) on current DBA issues.

In addition, many Oracle user groups and special interest groups publish newsletters that contain useful information for Oracle DBAs.

Organizations

International Oracle Users Group–Americas (IOUG-A)
401 North Michigan Avenue
Chicago, IL 60611
Voice: +1.312.245.1579
Fax: +1.312.527.6785

European Oracle Users Group (EOUG)
Brigittenauer Lände 50-54
A-1203 Vienna, Austria
Voice: +43 1 33777 870
Fax: +43 1 33777 873
Email: *eoug@at.oracle.com*

Asia-Pacific Oracle Users Group
PO Box 3046
The Pines, Doncaster East
VIC 3109, Australia
Voice: +61 3 9842 3246
Fax: +61 3 9842 3050

Web Sites

www.oracle.com
> The web site of Oracle Corporation. Contains a wide variety of pages of interest to DBAs, as well as links to other DBA resources, including Oracle Support.

www.ioug.org
> Operated by the IOUG-A. Contains technical articles from *Select* magazine, papers from IOUG-Alive conferences, a technical discussion forum, and other areas of interest to DBAs.

www.eoug.org
> The web site of the EOUG. Contains information of general interest to Oracle DBAs, information about EOUG conferences and educational events, and information about European, Middle Eastern, and African user groups.

apoug.oracle.com.sg
> The web site of the Asia Pacific Oracle Users Group. Contains information of interest to Oracle users in the Asia and Pacific Rim regions, as well as useful links to other Oracle resources.

www.oug.com
> Operated by a consortium of Oracle user groups and special interest groups. Contains a number of useful Oracle-related links.

Discussion Groups

comp.databases.oracle.server
> This discussion group features a wide variety of information relating to Oracle server technology. It should be of interest to both new and experienced DBAs.

www.ioug.org

This web site includes a discussion area where items of interest to DBAs are posted and discussed.

List Servers

Oracle-L

Telport's DBA discussion list. Subscribe by including "SUBSCRIBE ORACLE-L" in the body of a message to *majordomo@teleport.com*.

oracledba

A generic DBA discussion list. Subscribe by including "SUBSCRIBE ORACLE-L" in the body of a message to *oracledbarequest@MailingList.net*.

ODTUG-Warehouse-Ldata

Oracle Development Tools' Data Warehouse discussion list. Subscribe by including "SUBSCRIBE ODTUG-Warehouse-L *<your name>*" in the body of a message to *listserv@fatcity.com*.

Index

About the Authors

David C. Kreines is the Manager of Database Services for Rhodia, Inc., a subsidiary of Rhone-Poulenc S.A., and the coauthor of *Oracle Scripts* (O'Reilly & Associates, 1998). Dave has worked with Oracle as a developer and database administrator since 1985, on a wide variety of platforms from PCs to mainframes. He is an Oracle Certified Professional, certified as a DBA, and has been a frequent contributor to Oracle conferences, user groups, and publications, both in the United States and in Europe. Dave served two terms as president of the International Oracle Users Group–Americas, and spent ten years on the board of directors.

Brian Laskey is a Senior Database Administrator for Management Information Consulting (MIC), a Virginia-based consulting firm that specializes in assisting Fortune 1000 companies in ERP systems integration and e-commerce. Brian has been an Oracle database administrator for eleven years, working with Oracle on MVS, VMS, Unix, NT, DOS, and Windows. He is an Oracle Certified Professional, certified as a DBA for both Oracle 7.3 and Oracle 8.0. He has presented papers at the IOUW and IOUG-A Live! conferences, as well as at regional conferences. He is currently serving his second term as vice president of finance of the International Oracle Users Group–Americas, and has been a member of the board of directors of the IOUG-A for the past two years. He has just been reelected to the IOUG-A board for a term to expire in 2001.

Colophon

Our look is the result of reader comments, our own experimentation, and feedback from distribution channels. Distinctive covers complement our distinctive approach to technical topics, breathing personality and life into potentially dry subjects.

The animals on the cover of *Oracle Database Administration: The Essential Reference* are ladybug beetles (family *Coccinellidae*), also known as lady beetles or ladybird beetles. Due to an attractive appearance and a diet of plant-eating aphids (some females consume up to 75 a day), these small, red or orange black-spotted beetles rank high in global opinion polls, and are even associated in some cultures with Christian symbols. In German, ladybugs are called "Marienkafer," or Mary's beetle; in French, one name for them is "les vaches de la vierge" or Cows of the Virgin.

Ladybugs are effective in reducing garden pests and can be ordered from garden catalogs by the pound; they also frequently spend the winter inside people's homes, which in Canada and the U.S. is said to bring good luck. Elsewhere, the beetles are thought to signify good weather, good harvest, or other good fortune.

There are thousands of ladybug species worldwide, and a few are plant eaters and pests themselves. Their colorful wing covers are more than just a pretty picture: predators generally avoid red or orange-and-black insects, as they tend to taste terrible. Other defensive maneuvers include playing dead, the production of a foul odor, and fierce-looking larvae.

Madeleine Newell was the production editor and copyeditor for *Oracle Database Administration: The Essential Reference*. Sheryl Avruch was the production manager; Ellie Fountain Maden, Nancy Kotary, and Nicole Arigo provided quality control. Robert Romano created the illustrations using Adobe Photoshop 4 and Macromedia FreeHand 7. Mike Sierra provided FrameMaker technical support. Seth Maislin wrote the index. Maureen Dempsey, Bette Hugh, and Michael Blanding provided production assistance.

Edie Freedman designed the cover of this book, using a 19th-century engraving from the Dover Pictorial Archive. The cover layout was produced by Kathleen Wilson with QuarkXPress 3.32 using the ITC Garamond font. Whenever possible, our books use RepKover™, a durable and flexible lay-flat binding. If the page count exceeds RepKover's limit, perfect binding is used.

The inside layout was designed by Nancy Priest and implemented in FrameMaker 5.5.6 by Mike Sierra. The text and heading fonts are ITC Garamond Light and Garamond Book. The description of ladybug beetles was written by Nancy Kotary.

More Titles from O'Reilly

Oracle

Advanced Oracle PL/SQL *Programming with Packages*

By Steven Feuerstein
1st Edition October 1996
690 pages, Includes diskette
ISBN 1-56592-238-7

This book explains the best way to construct packages, a powerful part of Oracle's PL/SQL procedural language that can dramatically improve your programming productivity and code quality, while preparing you for object-oriented development in Oracle technology. It comes with PL/Vision software, a library of PL/SQL packages developed by the author, and takes you behind the scenes as it examines how and why the PL/Vision packages were implemented the way they were.

Oracle Built-in Packages

By Steven Feuerstein,
Charles Dye & John Beresniewicz
1st Edition April 1998
956 pages, Includes diskette
ISBN 1-56592-375-8

Oracle's built-in packages dramatically extend the power of the PL/SQL language, but few developers know how to use them effectively. This book is a complete reference to all of the built-ins, including those new to Oracle8. The enclosed diskette includes an online tool that provides easy access to the many files of source code and documentation developed by the authors.

Oracle PL/SQL Programming: Guide to Oracle8i Features

By Steven Feuerstein
1st Edition October 1999
272 pages, Includes diskette
ISBN 1-56592-675-7

This concise and engaging guide will give you a jump start on the new PL/SQL features of Oracle8i (Oracle's revolutionary "Internet database"). It covers autonomous transactions, invoker rights, native dynamic SQL, bulk binds and collects, system-level database triggers, new built-in packages, and much more. Includes a diskette containing 100 files of reusable source code and examples.

Oracle Web Applications: PL/SQL Developer's Introduction

By Andrew Odewahn
1st Edition September 1999
256 pages, ISBN 1-56592-687-0

This book is an easy-to-understand guide to building Oracle8i (Oracle's "Internet database") Web applications using a variety of tools – PL/SQL, HTML, XML, WebDB, and Oracle Application Server (OAS). It also covers the packages in the PL/SQL toolkit and demonstrates several fully realized Web applications. This book provides the jump-start you need to extend relational concepts to Web content and to make the transition from traditional programming to the development of useful Web applications for Oracle8i. Also covers Web development for Oracle8 and Oracle7.

Oracle PL/SQL Programming, 2nd Edition

By Steven Feuerstein with Bill Pribyl
2nd Edition September 1997
1028 pages, Includes diskette
ISBN 1-56592-335-9

The first edition of *Oracle PL/SQL Programming* quickly became an indispensable reference for PL/SQL developers. The second edition focuses on Oracle8, covering Oracle8 object types, object views, collections, and external procedures, and more. The diskette contains an online Windows-based tool with access to more than 100 files of source code.

Oracle PL/SQL Language Pocket Reference

By Steven Feuerstein, Bill Pribyl & Chip Dawes
1st Edition April 1999
104 pages, ISBN 1-56592-457-6

This pocket reference boils down the most vital information from Oracle PL/SQL Programming into an accessible quick reference that summarizes the basics of PL/SQL: block structure, fundamental language elements, data structures (including Oracle8 objects), control statements, and use of procedures, functions, and packages. It includes coverage of PL/SQL features in the newest version of Oracle, Oracle8i.

O'REILLY®

TO ORDER: **800-998-9938** • **order@oreilly.com** • **http://www.oreilly.com/**
OUR PRODUCTS ARE AVAILABLE AT A BOOKSTORE OR SOFTWARE STORE NEAR YOU.
FOR INFORMATION: **800-998-9938** • **707-829-0515** • **info@oreilly.com**

Oracle

Oracle PL/SQL Built-ins Pocket Reference

By Steven Feuerstein,
John Beresniewicz & Chip Dawes
1st Edition October 1998
78 pages, ISBN 1-56592-456-8

This companion quick reference to
Steven Feuerstein's bestselling *Oracle PL/SQL
Programming* and *Oracle Built-in Packages*
will help you use Oracle's extensive set of
built-in functions and packages, including
those new to Oracle8. You'll learn how to
call numeric, character, date, conversion,
large object (LOB), and miscellaneous functions, as well as
packages like DBMS_SQL and DBMS_OUTPUT.

Oracle PL/SQL Developer's Workbook

By Steven Feuerstein with Andrew Odewahn
1st Edition May 2000
592 pages, ISBN 1-56592-674-9

A companion to Feuerstein's other
bestselling Oracle PL/SQL books, this
workbook contains a carefully constructed
set of problems and solutions that will test
your language skills and help you become
a better developer. Exercises are provided
at three levels: beginner, intermediate, and expert. It covers the
full set of language features: variables, loops, exception handling,
data structures, object technology, cursors, built-in functions
and packages, PL/SQL tuning, and the new Oracle8i features
(including Java and the Web).

O'REILLY®

TO ORDER: **800-998-9938** • *order@oreilly.com* • *http://www.oreilly.com/*
OUR PRODUCTS ARE AVAILABLE AT A BOOKSTORE OR SOFTWARE STORE NEAR YOU.
FOR INFORMATION: **800-998-9938** • **707-829-0515** • *info@oreilly.com*

How to stay in touch with O'Reilly

1. Visit Our Award-Winning Web Site

http://www.oreilly.com/

★ "Top 100 Sites on the Web" —*PC Magazine*
★ "Top 5% Web sites" —*Point Communications*
★ "3-Star site" —*The McKinley Group*

Our web site contains a library of comprehensive product information (including book excerpts and tables of contents), downloadable software, background articles, interviews with technology leaders, links to relevant sites, book cover art, and more. File us in your Bookmarks or Hotlist!

2. Join Our Email Mailing Lists

New Product Releases

To receive automatic email with brief descriptions of all new O'Reilly products as they are released, send email to:
ora-news-subscribe@lists.oreilly.com
Put the following information in the first line of your message (*not* in the Subject field):
subscribe ora-news

O'Reilly Events

If you'd also like us to send information about trade show events, special promotions, and other O'Reilly events, send email to:
ora-news-subscribe@lists.oreilly.com
Put the following information in the first line of your message (*not* in the Subject field):
subscribe ora-events

3. Get Examples from Our Books via FTP

There are two ways to access an archive of example files from our books:

Regular FTP

- ftp to:
  ftp.oreilly.com
  (login: anonymous
  password: your email address)
- Point your web browser to:
  ftp://ftp.oreilly.com/

FTPMAIL

- Send an email message to:
  ftpmail@online.oreilly.com
  (Write "help" in the message body)

4. Contact Us via Email

order@oreilly.com
To place a book or software order online. Good for North American and international customers.

subscriptions@oreilly.com
To place an order for any of our newsletters or periodicals.

books@oreilly.com
General questions about any of our books.

software@oreilly.com
For general questions and product information about our software. Check out O'Reilly Software Online at **http://software.oreilly.com/** for software and technical support information. Registered O'Reilly software users send your questions to: **website-support@oreilly.com**

cs@oreilly.com
For answers to problems regarding your order or our products.

booktech@oreilly.com
For book content technical questions or corrections.

proposals@oreilly.com
To submit new book or software proposals to our editors and product managers.

international@oreilly.com
For information about our international distributors or translation queries. For a list of our distributors outside of North America check out:
http://www.oreilly.com/distributors.html

5. Work with Us

Check out our website for current employment opportunites:
http://jobs.oreilly.com/

O'Reilly & Associates, Inc.
101 Morris Street, Sebastopol, CA 95472 USA
TEL   707-829-0515 or 800-998-9938
      (6am to 5pm PST)
FAX   707-829-0104

O'REILLY®

International Distributors

http://international.oreilly.com/distributors.html

UK, EUROPE, MIDDLE EAST AND AFRICA (EXCEPT FRANCE, GERMANY, AUSTRIA, SWITZERLAND, LUXEMBOURG, AND LIECHTENSTEIN)

INQUIRIES
O'Reilly UK Limited
4 Castle Street
Farnham
Surrey, GU9 7HS
United Kingdom
Telephone: 44-1252-711776
Fax: 44-1252-734211
Email: information@oreilly.co.uk

ORDERS
Wiley Distribution Services Ltd.
1 Oldlands Way
Bognor Regis
West Sussex PO22 9SA
United Kingdom
Telephone: 44-1243-843294
UK Freephone: 0800-243207
Fax: 44-1243-843302 (Europe/EU orders)
or 44-1243-843274 (Middle East/Africa)
Email: cs-books@wiley.co.uk

FRANCE

INQUIRIES & ORDERS
Éditions O'Reilly
18 rue Séguier
75006 Paris, France
Tel: 33-1-40-51-52-30
Fax: 33-1-40-51-52-31
Email: france@oreilly.fr

GERMANY, SWITZERLAND, AUSTRIA, LUXEMBOURG, AND LIECHTENSTEIN

INQUIRIES & ORDERS
O'Reilly Verlag
Balthasarstr. 81
D-50670 Köln, Germany
Telephone: 49-221-973160-91
Fax: 49-221-973160-8
Email: anfragen@oreilly.de (inquiries)
Email: order@oreilly.de (orders)

CANADA (FRENCH LANGUAGE BOOKS)

Les Éditions Flammarion ltée
375, Avenue Laurier Ouest
Montréal (Québec) H2V 2K3
Tel: 00-1-514-277-8807
Fax: 00-1-514-278-2085
Email: info@flammarion.qc.ca

HONG KONG

City Discount Subscription Service, Ltd.
Unit A, 6th Floor, Yan's Tower
27 Wong Chuk Hang Road
Aberdeen, Hong Kong
Tel: 852-2580-3539
Fax: 852-2580-6463
Email: citydis@ppn.com.hk

KOREA

Hanbit Media, Inc.
Chungmu Bldg. 210
Yonnam-dong 568-33
Mapo-gu
Seoul, Korea
Tel: 822-325-0397
Fax: 822-325-9697
Email: hant93@chollian.dacom.co.kr

PHILIPPINES

Global Publishing
G/F Benavides Garden
1186 Benavides Street
Manila, Philippines
Tel: 632-254-8949/632-252-2582
Fax: 632-734-5060/632-252-2733
Email: globalp@pacific.net.ph

TAIWAN

O'Reilly Taiwan
1st Floor, No. 21, Lane 295
Section 1, Fu-Shing South Road
Taipei, 106 Taiwan
Tel: 886-2-27099669
Fax: 886-2-27038802
Email: mori@oreilly.com

INDIA

Shroff Publishers & Distributors Pvt. Ltd.
12, "Roseland", 2nd Floor
180, Waterfield Road, Bandra (West)
Mumbai 400 050
Tel: 91-22-641-1800/643-9910
Fax: 91-22-643-2422
Email: spd@vsnl.com

CHINA

O'Reilly Beijing
SIGMA Building, Suite B809
No. 49 Zhichun Road
Haidian District
Beijing, China PR 100080
Tel: 86-10-8809-7475
Fax: 86-10-8809-7463
Email: beijing@oreilly.com

JAPAN

O'Reilly Japan, Inc.
Yotsuya Y's Building
7 Banch 6, Honshio-cho
Shinjuku-ku
Tokyo 160-0003 Japan
Tel: 81-3-3356-5227
Fax: 81-3-3356-5261
Email: japan@oreilly.com

THAILAND

TransQuest Publishers (Thailand)
535/49 Kasemsuk Yaek 5
Soi Pracharat-Bampen 15
Huay Kwang, Bangkok
Thailand 10310
Tel: 662-6910421 or 6910638
Fax: 662-6902235
Email: puripat@.inet.co.th

ALL OTHER ASIAN COUNTRIES

O'Reilly & Associates, Inc.
101 Morris Street
Sebastopol, CA 95472 USA
Tel: 707-829-0515
Fax: 707-829-0104
Email: order@oreilly.com

AUSTRALIA

Woodslane Pty., Ltd.
7/5 Vuko Place
Warriewood NSW 2102
Australia
Tel: 61-2-9970-5111
Fax: 61-2-9970-5002
Email: info@woodslane.com.au

NEW ZEALAND

Woodslane New Zealand, Ltd.
21 Cooks Street (P.O. Box 575)
Waganui, New Zealand
Tel: 64-6-347-6543
Fax: 64-6-345-4840
Email: info@woodslane.com.au

ARGENTINA

Distribuidora Cuspide
Suipacha 764
1008 Buenos Aires
Argentina
Phone: 5411-4322-8868
Fax: 5411-4322-3456
Email: libros@cuspide.com

O'REILLY®

TO ORDER: **800-998-9938** • **order@oreilly.com** • **http://www.oreilly.com/**
OUR PRODUCTS ARE AVAILABLE AT A BOOKSTORE OR SOFTWARE STORE NEAR YOU.
FOR INFORMATION: **800-998-9938** • **707-829-0515** • **info@oreilly.com**